W9-BSO-207

Please remember that this is a library book,
and that it belongs only temporarily to each
person who uses it. Be considerate. Do
not write in this, or any, library book.

The Curriculum

SUNY Series,
FRONTIERS IN EDUCATION
Philip G. Altbach, Editor

The Frontiers in Education Series draws upon a range of disciplines and approaches in the analysis of contemporary educational issues and concerns. Books in the series help to reinterpret established fields of scholarship in education by encouraging the latest synthesis and research. A special focus highlights educational policy issues from a multidisciplinary perspective. The series is published in cooperation with the School of Education, Boston College. A complete listing of books in the series can be found at the end of this volume.

The Curriculum

Problems,
Politics,
and Possibilities

Second Edition

EDITED BY

Landon E. Beyer
Michael W. Apple

State University of New York Press

Published by
State University of New York Press, Albany

© 1998 State University of New York

For information, address State University of New York Press,
State University Plaza, Albany, N.Y., 12246

Production by Marilyn P. Semerad
Marketing by Dana E. Yanulavich

Library of Congress Cataloging-in-Publication Data

The curriculum : problems, politics, and possibilities / edited by
    Landon E. Beyer, Michael W. Apple. — 2nd ed.
        p.   cm. — (SUNY series, frontiers in education)
    Includes bibliographical references and index.
    ISBN 0–7914–3809–0 (alk. paper). — ISBN 0–7914–3810–4 (pbk. :
alk. paper)
        1. Curriculum planning—United States.   2. Education—United
States—Curricula.   3. Educational sociology—United States.
4. Education—Aims and objectives—United States.   I. Beyer, Landon
E., 1949–   .   II. Apple, Michael W.   III. Series.
LB2806.15.C87   1998
375´.001´0973—dc21   97–49330
                                                            CIP

10 9 8 7 6 5 4 3 2 1

Landon E. Beyer dedicates this book to his parents, Harold W. Beyer and Helen A. (Meier) Beyer, with love and gratitude, and with thanks for their unfailing encouragement to pursue his dreams.

Michael W. Apple dedicates this book to all of the many educators who have devoted their lives to struggling to make educational institutions more responsive, caring, and socially just.

CONTENTS

Introduction   **1**

1. Values and Politics in the Curriculum   3
   Landon E. Beyer and *Michael W. Apple*

I. Curriculum: Its Past and Present

2. The Effort to Reconstruct the Modern American Curriculum   21
   Herbert M. Kliebard

3. Contestation and Curriculum: The Efforts of American Socialists, 1900–1920   34
   Kenneth N. Teitelbaum

4. What Goes on in Classrooms? Is This the Way We Want It?   58
   Kenneth A. Sirotnik

II. Curriculum and Planning

5. Models of Curriculum Planning   79
   George J. Posner

6. Multicultural Curricula: "Whose Knowledge?" and Beyond   101
   Susan E. Noffke

7. What We've Learned from "Living in the Future"   117
   Barbara Brodhagen, Gary Weilbacher, and *James A. Beane*

III. Curriculum and Knowledge Selection

8. Curriculum Platforms and Moral Stories   137
   Thomas E. Barone and *Donald S. Blumenfeld-Jones*

9. The Culture and Commerce of the Textbook   157
   Michael W. Apple

10. Democracy and the Curriculum   177
    George H. Wood

IV. Curriculum and the Work of Teachers

11. Toward a Theory of Culturally Relevant Pedagogy   201
    Gloria Ladson-Billings

12. Teaching, Gender, and Curriculum   230
    Sara E. Freedman

13. Schooling for Democracy: What Kind?   245
    Landon E. Beyer

V. Curriculum and Technology

14. The Regime of Technology in Education   267
    Douglas D. Noble

15. A Critical Analysis of Three Approaches to the Use of Computers in Education   284
    Michael J. Streibel

16. Teaching and Technology: The Hidden Effects of Computers on Teachers and Students   314
    Michael W. Apple

VI. Curriculum and Evaluation

17. The Human Problems and Possibilities of Curriculum Evaluation   339
    George Willis

CONTENTS

18. Developing Curriculum through School Self-Evaluation 358
   Helen Simons

19. Democratic Evaluation: Aesthetic, Ethical Stories in Schools 380
   Landon E. Beyer and *Jo Anne Pagano*

Contributors 397

Index 405

Introduction

ONE

Values and Politics in the Curriculum

Landon E. Beyer and *Michael W. Apple*

O ver the past few decades, educators have witnessed a slowly growing but significant change in the way they approach their work. This change is only visible over the long haul, yet few things have had such an important impact. We are referring here to the transformation of curriculum theory and practice from a concern with *what* should be taught and *why* we should teach it to problems associated with *how to* organize, build, and above all now, evaluate curriculum and teaching. The difficult ethical and political questions of content, of what knowledge and which forms of experience are of most worth, have been pushed to the background in our attempts to define technically oriented methods that will "solve" our problems once and for all. Professional curriculum debate now tends to be over procedures, not over what counts as legitimate knowledge. This shift is occurring not only in education. As a number of commentators have documented, in many areas of our cultural and political lives, technique is winning out over substance.[1]

The concern with technique is not inconsequential, of course. "How to's" play a valued role in curriculum design and teaching. However, in the process, the field itself and the people who make decisions about what happens inside schools have become increasingly subject to the dynamics of what is best

3

called *deskilling*. The sensibilities and skills that were and are so very critical for justifying our educational programs, for understanding why we should be doing *x* rather than *y*, and for building a more democratic set of educational institutions, atrophy and hence are ultimately lost.[2]

This is especially serious today because, as we will note later, public education is under a concerted attack from right-wing forces that wish to substitute an ethic of private gain and an accountant's profit-and-loss sheet for the public good. What education is for is shifting.[3] In the face of such a well-financed and well-organized attack, many committed and hard-working educators often no longer have the resources (neither monetary nor conceptual) to argue back effectively. In this way, schools become more like miniature factories dominated by concerns for input and output, efficiency, and cost savings. The more democratic visions of education and the multitude of creative strategies educators have developed over the years to put them into practice wither. We are now in danger of having them eliminated from our collective memory.

The *Curriculum: Problems, Politics, and Possibilities* wants to preserve that collective memory and wants to build on that memory to provide a set of resources so that those educators who are deeply concerned with what is happening to curricula, teachers, and students in schools can better act on the questions of what, why, and how to. It aims at reintegrating the ethical, personal, and political into curriculum discourse and decision making. In order to do this, the volume must be both critical of some existing and long-lasting tendencies (for there is currently a good deal of negative pressure on education and no small amount of less-than-exciting school practices) and at the same time be supportive of the more thoughtful and democratic tendencies that exist or are currently emerging.

One of our major goals in this volume is to stimulate thoughtful practice and more politically sensitive curriculum inquiry. Many people in the field with a good deal of experience will undoubtedly agree with this, for the literature abounds with material on the "reflective practitioner," and some of it is very good. However, we wish to go further. Our objective is perhaps best embodied in the concept of *praxis*. This involves not only the justifiable concern for reflective action, but thought and action combined and enlivened by a sense of power and politics. It involves both conscious understanding of and action in schools on solving our daily problems. These problems will not go away by themselves, after all. But it also requires critically reflective practices that alter the material and ideological conditions that cause the problems we are facing as educators in the first place.

As we have argued elsewhere to do this we need to think about education relationally.[4] We need to see it as being integrally connected to the cultural, political, and economic institutions of the larger society, institutions that may be strikingly unequal by race, gender, and class.[5] Schools embody and reproduce many of these inequalities. They may alleviate some of them, in part due to the committed labor of so many teachers, administrators, community activists, and others. However, as the literature on the hidden curriculum and on "cultural reproduction" has demonstrated, schools unfortunately may recreate others.[6] Because of this, part of our concern in curriculum must be with these connections between our educational institutions and differential cultural, political, and economic power.

Even though stressing the political nature of curriculum and teaching is essential, not all of our curriculum dilemmas can be totally understood this way. The problems associated with selecting from that vast universe of possible knowledge, of designing environments to make it accessible, of making it meaningful to students, all of these *are* political in fundamental ways. But an array of other crucial and complementary ways of thinking about the dilemmas we confront needs to be fully integrated into our relational and political sensitivity if we are not to lose our way.

In thinking about curriculum, a number of general issues confront us if we take the importance of thoughtful practice seriously. While no list can ever do justice to the complexity of curriculum deliberations, the following gives some flavor of the complex questions about which we have to make decisions.

1. *Epistemological.* What should count as knowledge? As knowing? Should we take a behavioral position and one that divides knowledge and knowing into cognitive, affective, and psycho-motor areas, or do we need a less reductive and more integrated picture of knowledge and the mind, one that stresses knowledge as process?

2. *Political.* Who shall control the selection and distribution of knowledge? Through what institutions?

3. *Economic.* How is the control of knowledge linked to the existing and unequal distribution of power, goods, and services in society?

4. *Ideological.* What knowledge is of most worth? Whose knowledge is it?

5. *Technical.* How shall curricular knowledge be made accessible to students?

6. *Aesthetic.* How do we link the curriculum knowledge to the biography and personal meanings of the student? How do we act "artfully" as curriculum designers and teachers in doing this?

7. *Ethical.* How shall we treat others responsibly and justly in education? What ideas of moral conduct and community serve as the underpinnings of the ways students and teachers are treated?

8. *Historical.* What traditions in the field already exist to help us answer these questions? What other resources do we need to go further?

The last set of historical questions is something to which the two of us have given considerable thought. We are very conscious of the work that has made it possible for the current generation of critically minded curriculum people to become more sophisticated in raising the issues on the preceding list. Many past and continuing efforts have been made to bring these issues to our attention by a number of significant figures in the field. Among the most important of these individuals have been Dwayne Huebner, James Macdonald, Maxine Greene, Elliot Eisner, and Joseph Schwab. Be it Schwab's emphasis on the ultimately deliberative nature of curriculum, Huebner's eloquent insistence that we focus on language, environment, and politics, Macdonald's struggles to put the person first, Eisner's attempts to provide an aesthetic approach to curriculum, or Greene's impassioned advocacy of a curriculum theory based on literature and the poetics and politics of personal knowing—all have provided a foundation and resources for the quest for a more adequate, and more humane, grounding for curriculum theory and practice that so many people concerned with curriculum are now undertaking.[7] All recognize the inherent complexity of education and reject the comforting illusion that we can ever find the one right set of techniques that will guarantee certainty of outcome. Finally, all of them take education seriously, as worthy of our very best thought. Education is a process that must embody the finest elements of what makes us human, that frees us in the process of teaching us what is of value. For all of them, it is not something that is reducible to techniques of standardized testing, systems management, behaviorism, and competency-based instruction, to being a mirror of economic and industrial needs defined by the few, and so forth.

Our attempt to integrate contemporary thought in the curriculum field within the larger social whole has a democratic as well as historical context that needs to be respected, even cherished. The hallmark of too much curriculum reform work has been its insistence on a hierarchical, top-down model of conceptualization, development, and implementation that we find intellectually and politically dishonest. In most cases, "new curricula" and standardized techniques of teaching, management, and accountability have been developed by academics in higher education, research and development agencies, and state and federal departments of education that are then superimposed on the work of teachers so as to "improve" classroom practice and curriculum deliberation.[8] As opposed to such a stratified model, this volume argues that meaningful curriculum reform must occur within those institutions, and by those people, most intimately connected to the lives of students: teachers, administrators, students, and community members whose work in schools aids the process of genuinely transforming educational practice.[9]

One of the connecting threads of this volume is the extent to which the authors included here are involved not just in the production of critically oriented theory and research—although surely this is not to be taken lightly or undervalued—but in the concrete, daily political and educational struggles in teaching, curriculum development and design, the preparation of future teachers and administrators, and the like. As educators and political actors, the authors included in this volume are keenly aware of the responsibilities they bear in helping effect substantial changes in the lives of teachers and students and of those most oppressed by current social inequalities—especially as they occur on the basis of race, gender, ethnicity, age, social class, sexual orientation, and cultural affinity. The chapters included in this volume are eloquent witness to the position that scholarship, aesthetic awareness, ethical obligation, and political involvement can be separated only at the expense of a more just, humane, and decent school environment and social order.

By asking all of us to see education relationally, to recognize its intimate connections to the inequalities in the larger society, we are self-consciously aligning ourselves with a program aimed at what Marcus Raskin has called "the common good." This program of criticism and renewal asserts the political and ethical principle that "no inhuman act should be used as a short cut to a better day," and, especially, that at each step of the way any social program—be it in the economy, in education, or elsewhere—"will be judged against the likelihood that it will result in linking equity, sharing, personal dignity, security, freedom, and caring."[10] This means that those pursuing such a program "must . . . assure themselves that the course they follow, inquire into, [and] analyze . . . will dignify human life, recognize the playful and creative aspects of people," and see others not as objects but as "coresponsible" subjects involved in the process of democratically deliberating over the ends and means of all of their institutions.[11]

Compare this language—the language of equity, sharing, personal dignity, security, freedom, and caring—with the dominant educational discourse today. The language of efficiency, standards, competency, assessment, cost effectiveness, and so on impoverishes our imagination and limits our educational and political vision. It also, and very importantly, distances us from the more personal and situational language of teachers who must make informed, flexible, and humane decisions in very uncertain and trying circumstances. One should inquire, in fact, into the possibility that such attempts at bureaucratizing and rationalizing the work of curriculum and teaching is part of a much longer history in which the paid labor that has been defined as largely women's work (we should remember that 87 percent of elementary school

7

teachers and 67 percent of teachers overall are women) has been constantly subject to pressures to bring it under external bureaucratic control and to eliminate the elements of connectedness and caring that such work has often embodied.[12]

And, finally, the dominance of the language of efficiency cuts us off from a significant part of our own past in curriculum work. One cannot read Dewey, Rugg, and other men and women who helped form a more socially sensitive tradition in curriculum without recognizing the utter import that the impulse toward the common good, toward a democratized polity and a democratizing culture, played in their own educational theories and proposals.[13] While a number of the authors in this volume rightly wish to go beyond some of the political limitations of the positions advocated by these earlier educators, there can be no doubt that the same impulse provides the impetus for their own efforts. Without such a critical and democratic impulse, one becomes a trainer not an educator.

The substantiation of alternative ideas, forms of language, and images of possibility are central components of the personal and political issues that form the core of this volume. Thus, while celebrating and building on the ideas and struggles of those who preceded us, we also share a commitment to what Raymond Williams has called "the practice of possibility" as this may be realized in democratically organized practices in schools.[14]

What sets this volume apart from others is something else as well, however. An interest in the historical antecedents of the curriculum field and the development of alternatives that are at once politically informed and educationally appropriate has also prevented this volume from unilaterally dismissing those areas of curriculum scholarship that some critics might regard as traditional, conventional, or in the mainstream. Much of this scholarship is, to be sure, in need of critical interrogation, political analysis, and conceptual clarification. Yet we do not wish to follow totally a disturbing tendency toward rejecting the whole of the mainstream literature in the field—perhaps especially by some of those who have correctly sought to develop alternative theories and practices. This rejection, although partly correct and certainly understandable, is questionable on at least two grounds. First, such rejectionism uniformly dismisses all previous work when this is clearly not justified. Even though portions of it need to be challenged and superseded, we still have much to learn from those writing in this mode, as this volume amply attests. Second, this tendency to reject what has come before is itself symptomatic of the ahistoricism that tends to characterize our field. Although we may reject the aims and values of a good deal of conventional work in curriculum, we discount and overlook it at our own peril.

If curriculum design, and all educational decisionmaking, is to be a democratically based deliberative practice that is both critical of existing inequalities and powerful in envisioning alternative possibilities, then it should be open to the best of conventional work. Simply because a good deal of current educational research may have an interest in technical control and certainty,[15] this does not mean that we cannot learn something from it, for we are dealing with very complex institutions, and good empirical work (conceived of in its very broadest sense) can be essential. As Schwab insightfully states, the work of curriculum design and implementation is complicated. Sounding quite Deweyan, he states, "It treats both ends and means and must treat them as mutually determining one another." For him, then, deliberation

> must try to identify with respect to both [ends and means] what facts may be relevant. It must try to ascertain the relevant facts in the concrete case. It must try to identify the desiderata in the case. It must generate alternative solutions. . . . It must then weigh alternatives and their costs and consequences against one another, and choose, not the right alternatives for there *is* no such thing, but the best one.[16]

Now Schwab may see the process of curriculum debate as more "rational" than it really can and should be. He may also underplay the growing recognition that "facts" are not there simply to be found. They are constructed by the educational and ideological agendas of the people who ask the questions that generate such data. Yet his points about being open to as much, often contradictory, information as possible and weighing this in regard to *both* ends and means are not to be dismissed. Not all past and current "conventional" curriculum work is wrong and some of it may be very helpful in our attempt to "generate alternative solutions" and "weigh alternatives and their costs and consequences against each other." What is crucial here, of course, is that this "weighing" is done with regard to the values we noted before, the values of equity, sharing, personal dignity, security, freedom, and caring. And this can only be done if we look honestly and openly at the kind of society in which we now live, the patterns of differential power and benefits that now exist inside and outside of education, and the ways some of our current perspectives make it increasingly difficult for us to face this reality.

Perhaps this point can be made clearer if we reflect on the ways slogan systems tend to dominate our work in education. We have seen, for example, in the last several years, the phrases "back to basics," "effective teaching," "authentic assessment," and so on, paraded as the definitive cure for whatever educational ailments allegedly plague us at the moment. Currently, the main slogan vying for popular approval seems to be a commitment to "excellence," and the provision of programs and materials committed to its realization.

Such slogans are used in an attempt to garner support for the particular points of view or interests embodied by the group promoting them. In the current conservative climate, "excellence" has often served as an excuse to cut budgets, tighten centralized controls, and attempt to redefine the goals of the schools as primarily those needed by business and industry. It does contain progressive possibilities. After all, none of us would object to schools doing "excellent" teaching. However, in the social struggle over the means and ends of "excellence," over its very definition, the voice of women, people of color, labor, and others seems to have been muted. The voice of "efficient management" has been heightened.[17]

The chapters in this volume provide the sort of analytic sophistication necessary to think through the issues, ideas, and values that attend the development of such slogans, so that we might see more clearly what these overused, often amorphous language forms actually mean. At the same time, the authors included herein are concerned with uncovering the personal, political, social, and ideological roots of such slogans, so that educators and others may make more informed and reflective judgments about the political interests that guide educational policies and practices.[18]

For those looking for a "how to" book that sets out the universal aims, processes, and orientations that should guide curricular deliberation and classroom practice, this volume may not be entirely satisfying. We have not attempted to set out such a complete and directive work for several reasons. First, such an attempt would belie the very commitment to democratic participation and organization that lies at the heart of this book's political sensibility. While the authors whose work appears here do offer suggestions for ways of thinking about curriculum design and development, the restructuring of classrooms, enlivening teaching practices, and so on, they cannot go much further than providing such suggestions. The actual work involved in redesigning curriculum and teaching practices, the details of how and where this is to be done, must be worked out *collaboratively* with those teachers, administrators, community members, and students with whom most of us interact every day. Second, "how to" questions—for logical and political reasons—can only be dealt with after the sort of "why" questions explored here are addressed and at least tentatively resolved. How we go about the concrete activities involved in curriculum and teaching will be affected by our answers to the critical questions raised in this volume. Because, as we noted, all too often educators have assumed that "how to" questions can supplant more normatively oriented investigations and inquiries, this volume seeks to redress this mistaken notion by highlighting the importance of the "prior questions" raised in the ensuing chapters.

This is not, of course, to suggest that the kinds of issues represented here are more important, or more valuable, than the more concrete, physical, and intellectual work engaged in by teachers and others. Indeed, the political nature of our commitments demands that we actively collaborate with others in the exploration of alternative practices. Only through such collaboration can the principle of the integration of theory and practice, of educational praxis, be actually implemented.

Because the curriculum field is one of those areas that contains representative, perennial questions and areas of inquiry, *The Curriculum: Problems, Politics, and Possibilities* is organized around these major thematic issues that tend to characterize the field, issues that themselves respond to the list of questions and concerns we introduced earlier. This volume suggests ways in which the progressive and critical perspective that has informed a good deal of recent curriculum thought can be harnessed in formulating alternative responses to the characteristic problems of our field. Within each of the six major divisions comprising this collection, we show how this more critical perspective can provide ways of thinking about a central issue that not only offer real choices, but that make clear the valuative, political, and ethical dimensions of those choices. In providing a more contextual and progressive analysis of the defining issues of curriculum studies, this book will extend the range and viability of that body of inquiry in a way that broadens the parameters of the curriculum field generally. And by including a diversity of views within the divisions of this work, we acknowledge the important questions and perspectives raised by such a diverse body of writing.

These perennial issues include: (1) the nature of curriculum as a field of study, both historically and within the current social and political context; (2) the problems posed in thinking about how to plan and organize curricula for schools; (3) the criteria with which to include specific content areas within the formal curriculum; (4) the constraints on curriculum development and theory imposed by the workplace of teaching; (5) the influence of technology on curriculum work; and (6) the problems involved in curriculum evaluation. These issues are largely constitutive of curriculum inquiry today and form the major divisions of this collection.

The Organization of This Book

Part I: Curriculum: Its Past and Present

In chapter 2 of this volume, Herbert M. Kliebard outlines the general history of the curriculum field, indicating those interest groups, values, and assumptions that have historically struggled for control of the school curriculum. This chapter serves as a reminder of the historical legacy of our field and situates the more particular debates that follow.

11

Yet, the history of the field is not only represented in these major "professional" interest groups. There were other, lesser known and even more politically active, segments of the community who attempted to build alternatives to the dominant models of education. Among the most important of these was the Socialist Sunday School Movement, a group of teachers and parents who believed that only by creating different institutions could more democratic visions be taught to their children. In chapter 3, Kenneth N. Teitelbaum explores the more particular political history of this lesser known part of curriculum, indicating the ways in which nonmainstream groups have sought to frame curriculum form and content in ways that further their own commitments. The general aim of this chapter is to provide a historical example of what has been done by committed groups of people who have recognized the inherently political nature of curriculum and teaching.

Only parts of this past have lasted and made an impact on schools today. What *are* schools like today? Summarizing recent investigations of the typical classroom in the United States, Kenneth A. Sirotnik indicates the current situations in classrooms in chapter 4. He gives us an empirical picture of some of the realities of curriculum and teaching. This reality provides some of the basis for the criticism and prospects for renewal that follow.

Part II: Curriculum and Planning

Chapter 5 outlines the central models and theories of curriculum planning. In it, George J. Posner provides an analytic discussion of the major ways of thinking about curriculum planning we have inherited and their implications for teaching. Beyond this, Posner provides a basis for the exploration of alternative theories and models that may be necessary for future, more progressive, curriculum work.

Beyond the conceptual boundaries of curriculum planning, we must become more sensitive to the politics of organizing and planning and to the history of curriculum making especially for marginalized students. Chapter 6, by Susan E. Noffke, focuses on issues related to multicultural issues in curriculum and the contexts of teaching. She brings to the fore the vital question of children's relationship to knowledge and how that relationship affects the role of teachers and their efforts to create novel curriculum projects.

The possibilities for an integrated approach to curriculum, and its relationship to democratic classrooms, is explored in chapter 7. Barbra Brodhagen, Gary Weilbacher, and James A. Beane make clear that the quality of the interactions among teachers and students is vitally related to the kinds of issues and questions that can be considered in the classroom. Such interactions change the nature of classroom experiences for both teachers and students.

Part III: Curriculum and Knowledge Selection

While curriculum and teaching are political matters, they are at the same time intensely personal and theoretical ones. Our notion of self in this context is fluid, effected through the experiences we have that constitute our environment. As Thomas E. Barone and Donald S. Blumenfeld-Jones suggest in chapter 8, the emergence of personal narratives forms a central part of our notion of self. The narrative of teaching as always becoming links the teacher with past and present, and to an ethical conception of teaching and living.

Much curriculum continues to be designed and marketed by textbook publishing houses with their own internal "narrative," as it were. If we are to fully understand the meaning of the curriculum in use in our schools, we must understand the political economy of culture and how it effects the dynamics of the textbook publishing industry. These dynamics have important implications for the kinds of knowledge that are sanctioned in school curricula and the effects they have on students. These and related issues are explored in chapter 9 by Michael W. Apple.

Once we raise the issue of the importance of personal meaning, of increasing our responsiveness to other forms of knowing, we need to ask why it is that the forms of knowledge that curriculum designers employ and that we teach to students as most important *are* so limited. This is a question about power. Because of this, chapter 10 explores the politics of content selection in curriculum. While the previous two chapters in this section outline important conceptual and humanistic concerns regarding the formal curriculum, here George H. Wood discusses the linkages between knowledge and larger patterns of influence, status, and power. It provides one of the important boundaries within which curriculum as knowledge selection must be articulated.

Part IV: Curriculum and the Work of Teachers

Gloria Ladson Billings's interest in what culturally relevant pedagogy might mean leads her to consider various explanations for student performance, and to outline some of her own research activities. In chapter 11 she critically analyzes the deficit paradigms that have prevailed in the literature on African American students, and also provides examples of committed teaching for those students. Her work, like those of others included in this volume, involves a shift toward looking in the classrooms of those teachers through their own experiences.

Chapter 12 documents the ways in which teachers' work is caught in larger transformations that are changing the nature of the workplace. It is written by Sara E. Freedman, a leader of the Boston Women's Teachers' Group. These changes have important social class and gender connections

13

and are related to the deskilling, depowering, and depersonalizing of teaching. This has special relevance for this book, because changes in the teacher's workplace are part of a larger social and cultural dynamic that is affecting all levels of education.

The final chapter in this section, by Landon E. Beyer, looks at the contours of teaching and curriculum through the various ways in which education for democracy has been conceptualized. He analyses the meaning of democracy and related ideas and values that have been put forward by the new right. After critiquing that conception of democratic life, he offers a progressive alternative for reconstructing the school and rebuilding the school curriculum.

Part V: Curriculum and Technology

Curriculum, as Huebner reminds us, is about the accessibility of knowledge, about making traditions available to students.[19] How is knowledge often made accessible to students? This is usually done through texts, teacher talk, and increasingly through technology. The first chapter in this section outlines some of the problems associated with the technicization of curriculum work. Douglas D. Noble provides a detailed history of the growth of certain aspects of educational technology, especially the computer. Here again we see the importance of understanding where we have come from, of knowing why certain things are made available, if we are to know the limits and possibilities of our actions in education.

Of equal import are the ways in which a variety of forms of technology may be reasonably and productively employed in schools. This is the task of Michael J. Streibel. While the previous chapter raises a number of important questions about the history and legitimacy of technology in education, such questions do not imply that technology is always and uniformly determined by this past. Although he is critical of some of the uses to which computers are put in schools, Streibel looks specifically at some of the more educationally productive and humane ways in which technological forms have been and could be incorporated into school practice.

Even with what Streibel tells us, however, we still confront differential power and social pressures to use technology in specific ways in school. The computerization of schooling needs to be seen in its current economic and political context if we are to be realistic about who will benefit from its use in classrooms. In chapter 16, Michael W. Apple addresses some of these economic and political dynamics. Linking growing technicism in curriculum with what is happening to people's jobs in the larger society and to teachers themselves, Apple broadens the sort of debate that must go on in thinking about how computers should be employed.

Part VI: Curriculum and Evaluation

Chapter 16, by George Willis, outlines some of the more humanistic problems involved in programs of evaluation. Particular perspectives on evaluation embody presuppositions about those who are the subjects in evaluative studies. The use of statistical analysis, for example, promotes a view of the participants that is decidedly different from that prompted by case study or ethnographic methodologies. Questions explored by Willis include the picture of humanness that is embedded in evaluative activities, the role of value orientations in deciding evaluative possibilities, and the relevance of the information that evaluations provide.

The possibilities of evaluation are further explored by Helen Simons as she considers the relationship between curriculum and evaluation in schools. The development of effective curriculum, Simons reminds us, should empower students and teachers to evaluate their own efforts, in the process providing feedback that can be instrumental in creating local curriculum development activities. Such emphases would serve to resist the tendencies toward national norms and standards for curriculum and evaluation that are removed from the day-to-day activities and lives of teachers and students.

In the final chapter in this book, Landon E. Beyer and Jo Anne Pagano return to the question of how values—in this case, aesthetic and ethical ones—are central to the process of evaluation. Through the use of aesthetic experience, narrative, and a sensitivity to the politics of schooling, teachers can further the pursuit of democracy by creating new forms of educative evaluation.

Notes

1. For further discussion of this, see Michael W. Apple, *Ideology and Curriculum*, 2d ed. (New York: Routledge, 1990).

2. The concept of deskilling is elaborated in greater detail in Michael W. Apple, *Education and Power*, 2d ed. (New York: Routledge, 1995), especially chapter 5, and Michael W. Apple, *Official Knowledge* (New York: Routledge, 1993).

3. See Michael W. Apple, *Teachers and Texts: A Political Economy of Class and Gender Relations in Education* (New York: Routledge and Kegan Paul, 1986); and Landon E. Beyer and Daniel P. Liston, *Curriculum in Conflict: Social Visions, Educational Agendas, and Progressive School Reform* (New York: Teachers College Press, 1996).

4. Apple, *Ideology and Curriculum*, 2d ed., op. cit.; and Landon E. Beyer, "The Relevance of Philosophy of Education," *Curriculum Inquiry*, 27 (Spring 1997): 81–94.

5. For empirical information on these inequities, see Michael W. Apple, *Cultural Politics and Education* (New York: Teachers College Press, 1996), chapter 4.

6. See Michael W. Apple and Lois Weis, eds., *Ideology and Practice in Schooling* (Philadelphia: Temple University Press, 1983); for some of the complex debates about this issue, see Apple, *Education and Power*, op. cit.; Michael W. Apple, ed., *Cultural and Economic Reproduction in Education* (Boston: Routledge and Kegan Paul, 1982); and Henry Giroux, *Theory and Resistance in Education* (South Hadley, Mass.: Bergin and Garvey, 1983).

7. A representative sampling of these works can be found in the essays of Huebner, Macdonald, and Greene collected in William F. Pinar, ed., *Curriculum Theorizing: The Reconceptualists* (Berkeley, Calif.: McCutchan, 1975). See also Joseph Schwab, "The Practical: A Language for Curriculum" in Arno Bellack and Herbert M. Kliebard, eds., *Curriculum and Evaluation* (Berkeley, Calif.: McCutchan, 1977); and Elliot Eisner, *The Educational Imagination* (New York: Macmillan, 1985).

8. Arthur Wise, *Legislated Learning* (Berkeley, Calif.: University of California Press, 1979).

9. Some of the best routes toward such a transformative practice are outlined in Michael W. Apple and James A. Beane, eds., *Democratic Schools* (Washington, D.C.: Association for Supervision and Curriculum Development, 1995); and Landon E. Beyer, ed., *Creating Democratic Classrooms: The Struggle to Integrate Theory and Practice* (New York: Teachers College Press, 1996).

10. Marcus Raskin, *The Common Good* (New York: Routledge and Kegan Paul, 1986), p. 8.

11. Ibid.

12. See Apple, *Teachers and Texts*, op. cit.; Madeleine Grumet, *Bitter Milk* (Amherst: University of Massachusetts Press, 1988); Nel Noddings, *Caring: A Feminine Approach to Ethics and Moral Education* (Berkeley: University of California Press, 1984); and Jo Anne Pagano, *Exiles and Communities: Teaching in the Patriarchal Wilderness* (Albany: State University of New York Press, 1990).

13. The best single source for some of this history is Herbert M. Kliebard, *The Struggle for the American Curriculum*, 2d ed. (New York: Routledge and Kegan Paul, 1995).

14. Raymond Williams, *The Long Revolution* (London: Chatto and Windus, 1961). Compare this to the nicely articulated distinction between the "language of critique" and the "language of possibility" made in Stanley Aronowitz and Henry Giroux, *Education Under Siege* (South Hadley, Mass.: Bergin and Garvey, 1985), pp. 6–7.

15. Apple, *Ideology and Curriculum*, op. cit.; and Landon E. Beyer, *Critical Reflection and the Culture of Schooling: Empowering Teachers* (Victoria: Deakin University Press, 1989).

16. Schwab, "The Practical: A Language for Curriculum," op. cit.

17. See Ira Shor, *Culture Wars* (New York: Routledge and Kegan Paul, 1986); and Beyer and Liston, op. cit.

18. See, for example, Apple and Weis, ed., *Ideology and Practice in Schooling*, op. cit.; and Landon E. Beyer, "'Uncontrolled Students Eventually Become Unmanage-

able': The Politics of Classroom Discipline," in Ronald E. Butchart and Barbara McEwan, eds., *Classroom Discipline in American Schools: Problems and Possibilities for Democratic Education* (Albany: State University of New York Press, 1998); and "Teachers' Reflections on the Struggle for Democratic Classrooms," *Teaching Education* 8, 1 (1995).

19. Dwayne Huebner, "Curriculum as the Accessibility of Knowledge," paper presented at the Curriculum Theory Study Croup, Minneapolis, Minn., March 2, 1970.

I
Curriculum: Its Past and Present

TWO

The Effort to Reconstruct
the Modern American Curriculum

Herbert M. Kliebard

I n any time and place, what we call *the* American curriculum is actually an assemblage of competing doctrines and practices. Even in ancient Athens, Aristotle noted that a wide disagreement existed as to what was an appropriate course of study:

> At present opinion is divided about the subjects of education. All do not take the same view about what should be learned by the young, either with a view to plain goodness or with a view to the best life possible; nor is opinion clear whether education should be directed mainly to the understanding, or mainly to moral character. If we look at actual practice, the result is sadly confusing; it throws no light on the problem whether the proper studies to be followed are those which are useful in life, or those which make for goodness, or those which advance the bounds of knowledge. Each sort of study receives some votes in its favor.[1]

Many of the same differences regarding the purposes of education and what studies are most conducive to achieving those purposes have extended from Aristotle's time to the present.

21

It has become almost trite to say that these differences become more acute in periods of significant social change. It is in these periods that the sharpest conflicts develop between what are regarded as the tried-and-true studies and those that represent or symbolize new social forces and directions. Analysis of these trends and conflicts becomes more difficult when we realize, first of all, that a lag may occur between a significant social change and its recognition on a widespread scale. For example, industrialization is widely regarded as having one of the most far-reaching effects on the fabric of American social life. It was accompanied by the dislocation of many people from farm and rural communities to large urban centers, a consequent redefinition of family life, and a transformation of what we mean by *community*. But, for many American citizens, life went on very much as before. It was not until such related events as the tremendous growth in mass journalism in the 1880s, which brought news to small towns and hamlets of such things as urban blight and vice and corruption in the cities, that most Americans sensed the coming of a new kind of society. Likewise, enormous growth in rail transportation in the same period made it possible to break down the isolation that had been largely the case in the towns and villages where most Americans lived.

Second, the response to change, even when widely recognized, is anything but uniform. In many cases, new roles are advocated for social institutions that are perceived as decaying or at least no longer functioning in the way they once did. In the modern era at least, many of the social functions that were once performed by other social agencies such as the family or by religious institutions are seen as the province of the schools, so that even among those who see a need for a radical transformation of social institutions, there may be wide differences as to what directions that transformation should take. To speak, then, of a curricular response to social change as simply a conflict between conservatives on one hand, who envision schools that are consistent with earlier social values, and reformers, on the other, who see a new role for the schools, is really an oversimplification. Reformers as well as conservatives come in various stripes, and the directions they advocate in terms of a curricular response to social change tend to differ as much from one another as from the status quo that they seek to replace.

The Social and Educational Impact of Evolutionary Theory

In the nineteenth century, the status quo in curricular matters, at least in most western societies, tended to be associated with a form of the liberal arts which was dominated by classical languages, masterpieces of literature, and elegance of linguistic expression. In England, to take one example, the standard form of education was associated with building character, a sense of duty, and, especially as expressed by someone like Thomas Arnold of Rugby, with a spirit of service to the empire. Nevertheless, that standard built around classical languages and literary and other humanistic studies came under intense criticism by educational reformers such as Herbert Spencer and Thomas Henry Huxley just after the nineteenth century was half over. Both had been strongly influenced by the rise of science in general and by Darwin's theory of evolution in particular. Spencer tried to carry forward evolutionary theory into the social realm arguing basically that the laws that Darwin had enunciated in terms of the descent of the species could be applied to ethics, economics, sociology, and education. His 1859 essay, "What Knowledge Is of Most Worth?" is widely regarded as a classic of educational reform and contains within it significant indications of certain directions that curriculum reform did in fact take in the late nineteenth and twentieth centuries. For one thing, Spencer sought to replace humanistic studies in the curriculum with scientific ones. His answer to the question he posed in his title was unambiguous:

What knowledge is of most worth?—the uniform reply is—Science. This is the verdict on all the counts. For direct self-preservation, or the maintenance of life and health, the all-important knowledge is—Science. For that indirect self-preservation which we call gaining a livelihood, the knowledge of greatest value is—Science. For the due discharge of parental functions, the proper guidance is to be found only in—Science. For that interpretation of national life, past and present, without which the citizen cannot rightly regulate his conduct, the indispensible key is—Science. Alike for the most pefect production and highest enjoyment of art in all its forms, the needful preparation is still—Science. And for the purposes of discipline—intellectual, moral, religious—the most efficient study is, once more—Science.[2]

Spencer thus sought to assert the primacy of scientific studies over the more traditional humanistic ones.

In making this claim, Spencer was appealing to a criterion that he tried to establish in judging the worth of school subjects. To him, the supreme criterion by which a program of studies was to be judged was its contribution to self-preservation. Just as survival was the key to evolution, so it became the supreme criterion by which the value of school subjects would be judged. Poetry, although its study could conceivably contribute to the development of taste, was not nearly as valuable a subject as science, which could contribute to such vital areas as health, successful childrearing, and even proper social relations. In making such claims, Spencer was appealing, consciously or unconsciously, to a rising middle class that saw the traditional curriculum not only

23

as exclusionary but as remote from practical affairs and the interests of a modern industrial society.

Spencer's program for reform of the curriculum was also revolutionary in another sense. He saw the curriculum not merely as including a large measure of science but curriculum development as itself scientific. He appealed to the idea that curriculum development involved not simply making considered judgments about what should or should not be included in the course of study, but that scientific laws, when discovered, could dictate the correct content for the curriculum. In particular, Spencer was an exponent of the proposition (widely held in the nineteenth century) that, "The genesis of knowledge in the individual must follow the same course as the genesis of knowledge in the race."[3] In other words, Spencer was appealing to a universal law, which asserted that the course of human history was somehow recapitulated in individual development, and thus the curriculum could be determined through a scientific study of the interrelationship between these two factors. In asserting that a truly scientific curriculum was possible, Spencer was proposing what amounted to the most revolutionary of his reforms.

While there are obvious differences in terms of both social and educational traditions as between England and the United States, a parallel movement for curricular reform developed in America during the late nineteenth century. Actually, Spencer himself enjoyed even greater popularity in America than in England, with such social Darwinists as William Graham Sumner of Yale University spreading and popularizing his message. In general, Sumner preached a doctrine of economic and social laissez faire under the assumption that the best social policy was to give natural forces free rein just as they do in the biological sphere. Sumner maintained, for example, "that it is at the present time a matter of patriotism and civic duty to resist the extension of State interference. It is one of the proudest results of political growth that we have reached the point where individualism is possible."[4] The question for Sumner and other social Darwinists was essentially, "Which may we better trust, the play of free social forces or legislative and administrative interference?[5] By implication at least, education was merely an impediment to the doctrine of the survival of the fittest because it represented an obstacle to the free flow of natural laws. (Spencer, for example, actively opposed compulsory state education.)

The major alternative to the social Darwinist view on education was represented by the work of another American sociologist, Lester Frank Ward. Ward, like Spencer and Sumner, was strongly influenced by Darwinian theory, but his interpretation of that theory led him to take almost the opposite social policy direction. Rather than advocating a policy of permitting natural social forces to have free play, Ward in practically all his sociological works emphasized psychic control of the evolutionary process and state intervention in social and economic affairs. He believed that human beings, unlike the lower animals, have evolved the means to master the forces of nature. They had the power to intervene in the forces of nature and redirect those forces in the interest of human welfare. As the human species evolved the power of intelligence, redirecting the evolutionary process became possible. In fact, intelligent intervention itself became part of the evolutionary process. Like Huxley, Ward believed that survival of the fittest was no iron law in the arena of civic, economic, and social relations. The job of advanced societies was to eliminate insofar as possible the mere struggle for survival. Modern medicine, for example, represented a massive intervention into blind evolutionary forces. It should not be surprising, therefore, that Ward saw education as a vital weapon in the arsenal of society. Through a carefully designed and universal system of education, knowledge could be distributed more widely and thus increase the influence of intelligence in human affairs. In emphasizing the power of intelligence and its potential for social melioration, Ward anticipated, if not influenced, the work of John Dewey. The competing interpretations of the implications of evolution for an industrial society by Spencer and Sumner on one hand and Ward and Dewey on the other indicate that significant social change may give rise not to a single but to multiple interpretations of social and educational policy.

The Social and Educational Climate in the 1890s

Competing interpretations of how the twentieth-century curriculum should be reformed emerged immediately out of a period of unrest in the 1890s. The combination of a heightened perception of a transformation in certain social institutions, such as the family and the church, and the psychological force of the pending end to a millennium led social leaders and lay public alike to reexamine the kind of world in which they were living. Crises such as the 1893 economic panic lent further credence to the already widespread idea that a new world was in the making. To some extent, this reexamination amounted to a feeling of alarm in the sense that, with old institutions decaying, society itself seemed in danger of collapsing. With news of crime and corruption in cities reaching large audiences through the popular press and with face-to-face communities giving way to an increasingly depersonalized urban society, it should not be surprising that a new role should be sought for the schools with a revitalized curriculum at the core.

Perhaps the most modest of these efforts followed the lines of Huxley's attempt to create a more equitable balance between the sciences and the humanities in what passed for a liberal education. But, the influence of the new science, particularly as enunciated by Darwin, did not simply raise questions

25

about the reigning theology of the day; more important, as Dewey once pointed out, it transformed our way of thinking about science itself in areas such as society, morals, and education.[6] Harvard University's powerful president, Charles W. Eliot, for example, sought to establish the doctrine of the equivalence of school subjects, putting science and modern foreign languages on an equal footing with the classical subjects of Latin, Greek, and mathematics.[7] Eliot's reforms were largely contained within the general context of the liberal arts, attempting to modify some of its standard conventions but retaining the ideal of a curriculum whose main function was to liberate the human spirit, inspire an appreciation of beauty, and give one the intellectual mastery that was needed to make independent and sound judgments under a variety of circumstances.

Under the press of the perception that a new world was in the making, however, moderate reformers of the sort that Eliot represented began to seem quite tame, and, in the context of what became a massive drive to reconstruct the American curriculum even came to be regarded as a kind of old guard seeking to forestall the massive changes in the program of studies that was demanded by a modern world. Like Eliot, William Torrey Harris, for example, the influential Commissioner of Education at the time, did not see in the social transformation the necessity to institute a reform of the curriculum that went beyond a selection of the great resources of Western civilization. His opposition to such late nineteenth curricular innovations as manual training earned him the reputation of the "the greater conservator." But as the turn of the century approached, center stage in the educational world was turned over to reformers with a much more radical agenda. Three streams of curricular reform emerged around the turn of the century, each challenging in quite different ways the time-honored ideals represented by the liberal arts, even in the modified forms expressed by leaders such as Eliot and Harris.

Social Efficiency as a Response to Social Change

The two major ingredients that made up social efficiency both as a response to social change and a particular way to reform the American curriculum were, first, an effort to inject into the curriculum a stronger element of direct social control than had ever existed before;[8] and, second, an extraordinarily dedicated effort to trim waste in the curriculum by excising studies that had not demonstrated usefulness. In most cases, those subjects were the traditional subjects deemed to be of no practical value. The appeal of an orderly society more self-consciously regulated by social control along with the promise of reform effected not by massive social change but by cutting waste proved to be a potent combination. One of the early manifestations of the appeal of efficiency lay in the scientific management movement led by Frederick Winslow Taylor, who sought to reduce complex processes of manufacture to their most elemental steps and then train workers in the efficient performance of those simple steps. Thus, waste would be reduced sharply by setting precise standards for each unit of work and holding workers to that standard. The appeal to science in this sense lay primarily in an appeal to a kind of objective standard, precision in measuring outcomes, and predictability as to how things will turn out.

It was not long before the budding curriculum field adopted in large measure this version of science and tried to apply it to the job of creating a curriculum. *Scientific curriculum making*, as it was most frequently called, represents a very direct parallel to scientific management in almost all of its main dimensions. Major national figures in the curriculum world, such as Franklin Bobbitt and W. W. Charters, articulated a position in which minute particulars of the curriculum would be identified through a scientific process of activity analysis. This involved categorizing adult activities into several major categories such as leisure, citizenship, and family living, and then setting detailed objectives in each of the categories. These were direct parallels to the scientific standards that Taylor had prescribed for the process of manufacture. Achieving these objectives was governed by the simple criterion of efficiency. Whatever accomplished those objectives with the least amount of waste was the route to take in developing a curriculum.

But the elimination of waste also had a social dimension. It was also wasteful to teach anything to those who would have no use for it. Why, for example, should we teach algebra or foreign languages to those who, in their adult lives, have no use for mathematics beyond simple calculation or for expressing themselves in other than their native tongues? Therefore, an important concomitant of scientific curriculum-making became curriculum differentiation in which different curricula were prescribed for different groups depending on certain characteristics. These criteria included some measure of native intelligence, probable destination (particularly whether one was destined to go to college or not), and even social class. In this way, the curriculum could be geared directly to the activities one needed to perform in one's adult life. Future engineers would get one kind of education and future truck drivers another. Needless to say, although the practice undoubtedly has a certain utilitarian appeal, it raises in very vivid terms the whole issue of education as social predestination. Although the motivations of the scientific curriculum-makers were most likely humanitarian (e.g., adapting the curriculum to meet the real needs of the school clientele), the question remains as to whether education under these circumstances advanced or stunted social mobility.

Child Study and the Curriculum

At the same time that leaders of the scientific curriculum movement were making their voices heard in the educational world, a different reform movement, based on quite different premises, was rising to prominence. The direct utility of social efficiency may have been especially inviting to the curriculum-makers in the early decades of the twentieth century, but its influence was not supreme. At the same time that hard efficiency promised a new era in curriculum reform, the appeal of a natural order of development in the child found strong supporters as well. In a sense, the idea of a child-centered curriculum as well as social efficiency drew on the new status that science enjoyed in the modern world. In the case of child study, science was represented by the idea that the vital question of what should be taught need not remain merely the subject of speculation and vague philosophical argument, but could be derived from natural laws in the same way that Darwin had discovered the laws of natural selection. In particular, the study of the child's own instincts, thought processes, and interests would become the source of the curriculum. Once data on the child's and the adolescent's stages of development could be processed, a scientifically attuned curriculum could be derived.

Leading the way in this direction was one of America's most eminent psychologists, G. Stanley Hall. As leader of the child-study movement in the late nineteenth century, Hall most clearly represented the position that the issue of what should be taught could be derived from careful collection of data on the child's natural interests as well as the modes of thought most characteristic of children and adolescents at various stages in their development. Like Spencer, Hall felt (along with his allies in the American Herbartian movement) that the stages through which a child passed were parallel to the stages of human history. Thus, if there was a historical epoch which might be called savagery, then there would be a stage in the development of children that corresponded to that epoch and in which certain characteristics of the savage were evident. In a curriculum sense, this meant that the materials appropriate for study during that period should reflect that scientifically determined parallel. Thus, it was common in Herbartian schools to teach Longfellow's "Hiawatha" around the second grade because of its special appeal to children going through their savage state of development.

Culture-epochs theory as a specific curriculum theory was rather short-lived, but the idea persisted far into the twentieth century that somehow the child, himself or herself, was the real key to the curriculum riddle. One of the most successful efforts in that direction was launched by William Heard Kilpatrick through his fervent advocacy of the project method.[9] As the basic idea developed, it became clear that the curriculum that was being advocated under that name and later under such labels as the "activity curriculum" and "the experience curriculum" really sought to reverse the standard approach to curriculum making. For most people, creating a curriculum means deciding what you want to teach and then finding a way to interest students in that subject matter. Kilpatrick and his followers proposed starting with student interests and then bringing in subject matter instrumentally as it bore on pursuing those interests. Therefore, in a typical project, students would decide among themselves what they wanted to do (e.g., staging a play, discovering more about their community) and then the traditional subjects of reading, arithmetic, social studies, and so on would be studied in the context of accomplishing that purpose. For Kilpatrick, "purposing," the expression of the child's own interest in pursuing some activity, remained the essential first step in the curriculum-making process.

According to this approach, the actual learning of subject matter was distinctly secondary to the process of learning (although leaders of the movement like Kilpatrick would also claim that subject matter actually was better mastered under these circumstances than under the traditional ones). The idea of "learning how to learn" with its emphasis on student initiative and active involvement in decision making remained a controlling purpose. To some extent, this emphasis depended on the notion of a problem-solving method which bore some resemblance to what is frequently thought of even today as the scientific method. Advocates of this form of curriculum continued to claim that when children have the opportunity to engage in real (not artificial) problem solving within the school setting, they would form habits of thought that would stand them in good stead in their later lives: They would learn to deal systematically with problems as yet unforseen. However, although some practical benefit would derive from a curriculum organized according to these principles, it would not be nearly as directly functional or as adult oriented as in the case of scientific curriculum making. The principal focus was on the immediate lives of the students rather than on their future adult roles.

It was natural, therefore, that an antagonism should develop between these contemporaneous movements. Social efficiency oriented educators charged that the activity curriculum did not ensure that children and adolescents would really learn what they need to know because the curriculum was dictated by the sometimes fleeting and sometimes trivial interests of children. In this sense, child-centered curricula acquired an association with "soft" education in which the knowledge and skills that one really needed in the modern world were not really addressed. Although social efficiency education contained within it a strong antiacademic bias, it was serious business. It prepared one directly and efficiently for what life held in store. By contrast, child-centered education seemed to a great many hard-headed school people to be largely frivolous.

The Era of Social Reconstructionism

As already indicated, early portents of a desire to use the schools as an instrument of social change can be found in the late-nineteenth-century writing of Lester Frank Ward, whose sociological studies led him to believe that the equitable distribution of the world's store of knowledge could reduce invidious class distinctions as well as differences in the status and condition of men and women. For about the first three decades of this century, that impulse to use the curriculum as a force for social change remained something of a subterranean force erupting occasionally in the work of social theorists such as Albion Small.[10] Social reconstructionism's most enduring appeal was to a small coterie of left-wing intellectuals who, beneath the glitter of the "roaring twenties," saw a need to reconstruct social conditions on a major scale. By instilling a critical intelligence in the youth of America as well as an understanding of the dark side of industrialization and its impact on social institutions, a new generation could bring about the needed social change.

Once the stock market crashed in October 1929 and worldwide economic depression was beginning to become visible, the current of social reconstructionism began to flow with vastly increased force. Social reconstructionism's new visibility was probably most dramatically epitomized by the speech that George S. Counts delivered at the 1932 annual meeting of the Progressive Education Association (PEA).[11] The PEA had been formed in 1919 under the leadership of such child-oriented educators as Marietta Johnson and Stanwood Cobb. During the 1920s, the organization grew from a relative handful of members, largely associated with private schools, to a major platform for expressing experimental ideas about education. Over the course of that development, however, the character of the organization also began to change. In particular, professors in major colleges of education (notably Teachers College, Columbia University) such as Harold Rugg and Counts began to assume positions of leadership in the PEA, and the direction of the organization began to change as well. Even Dewey, upon accepting the position of Honorary President, was gently critical of the overwhelmingly child-oriented stand that the organization had followed.[12]

This change in the organization's membership and direction as well as the impact of the Great Depression set the stage for Counts's dramatic challenge to the organization at its 1932 meeting. Accusing the organization of following a program of "anarchy or extreme individualism,"[13] he called for a program much more directly attuned to social welfare and to ameliorating the social conditions of the poor and racial minorities. He alluded to the deficiencies of capitalism that had been responsible for these conditions and called on the schools to confront the social issues of the day directly. Once more, the antagonism between rival reform movements became the subject of open debate and controversy. From the point of view of the social reconstructionist, a child-centered curriculum was too romantic, too much concerned with the child as an individual and lacking in the social concern that would lead to a curriculum directly tied to the social, political, and economic conditions that the country faced. Counts advised the PEA membership not to be unduly cautious in their policies and to put forward a program of social reform through the curriculum not even stopping short of what he called "the bogeys of *imposition* and *indoctrination*" in order to advance it.[14] Although social reconstructionism excited much attention in the curriculum world of the 1930s, there is little evidence as to the success of the movement in terms of actual practice. There is some reason to believe that curriculum reforms tied to a critical appraisal of American society were not well received in schools across the country. To a large extent, for example, those reforms were perceived as being promulgated by a small group of eastern intellectuals.

The most notable exception to the relative lack of success of social reconstructionism in terms of school practice was the series of social studies textbooks written by Counts's colleague at Teachers College, Harold Rugg. Based on generalizations culled from the works of what he called "frontier thinkers," Rugg sought to infuse in his series what he considered to be advanced social ideas. He touched on the issues of changing gender roles, discrepancies of wealth and power in the United States, and militaristic tendencies. In his treatment of World War I, for example, he minimized discussion of battles and individual events and included discussion of secret alliances and economic factors leading to the outbreak of war such as competition for trade. At one point, he even suggested that "the American people, accustomed to peace, were educated to support war."[15] In terms of sales and readership, the Rugg series was a huge success, but as World War II approached, the demand that school boards abandon the series mounted, and, by 1941, its sales began to decline sharply. Criticism of the American social system lost most of whatever popularity it enjoyed in the context of imminent American participation in a great world conflict. The decade of popularity that the Rugg series enjoyed as well as its rather precipitous decline are actually interesting examples of how ideas on curriculum interact with general social, political, and economic conditions.

The Impact of Curriculum Reform in the Twentieth Century

In any society, whether Aristotle's or ours, there can be no unanimity of opinion at any given time on what is most worthwhile in the culture. Therefore, that each of the main currents of curriculum reform that found its way into the twentieth century attracted powerful adherents should not be surprising. The curriculum, after all, is a selection of elements from the culture and reflects to some extent the diversity that exists within the culture. Great value is accorded at one and the same time to intellectual mastery, safe driving, and occupational proficiency as components in the curriculum. Moreover, social conditions, such as the Great Depression and the Cold War, created climates that were at least temporarily conducive to different positions at different times. What emerges as a dominant strain in the curriculum is not a function of the force of a particular proposal alone but the due interaction of curriculum ideas and sympathetic or antagonistic social conditions. Therefore, over the course of time, one would expect that first one current then another should assume prominence and that, to some extent, they should all exist side by side.

The three currents of curriculum reform must also be seen against the backdrop of a traditional humanist curriculum that consisted of conventional subjects such as English, history, and mathematics. That curriculum proved more resilient than many reformers expected. The substitution of the project for the subject as the basic building block of the curriculum, as the followers of Kilpatrick advocated, was too fundamental a change for most to accept, as was the substitution of "areas of living" as the social efficiency educators proposed. Even John Dewey, the quintessential American educational reformer, was, more often than not, interested in reconstructing the existing subjects than in replacing them with something else.

Finally, in periods when curriculum reform had charged the atmosphere, it was probably more important for school systems simply to change than to change in a particular ideological direction. While there have always been particular trends favoring one approach to curriculum rather than another, the major currents of curriculum reform actually tend to exist side by side. At the same time that some proponents of curriculum reform were proclaiming that the curriculum should be derived from the spontaneous interests of children, others were proposing that the curriculum should be a direct and specific preparation for adulthood. Still others saw an urgent need to infuse into the curriculum a strong element of social criticism. Each doctrine had an appeal and a constituency. And, rather than make a particular ideological choice among apparently contradictory curriculum directions, it was perhaps more politically expedient on the part of practical school administrators to make a potpourri of all of them. This, in fact, is what the American curriculum has become.

Notes

1. Aristotle, *Politics* (New York: Oxford University Press, 1945), p. 244.

2. Herbert Spencer, *Education: Intellectual Moral and Physical* (New York: Appleton, 1860), pp. 84–85.

3. Ibid., p. 117.

4. William Graham Sumner, "State Interference," in *Social Darwinism*, Stow Parsons, ed. (Englewood Cliffs, N.J.: Prentice-Hall, 1963), p. 108.

5. Ibid., p. 109.

6. John Dewey, "Darwin's Influence upon Philosophy," *Popular Science Monthly* 75 (July 1909):90–98.

7. National Education Association, *Report of the Committee on Secondary School Studies* (Washington, D.C.: Government Printing Office, 1893).

8. See, for example, Barry Franklin, *Building the American Community: The School Curriculum and the Search for Social Control* (London: Falmer, 1986).

9. William Heard Kilpatrick, "The Project Method," *Teachers College Record* 19 (September 1918):319–35.

10. See, for example, Albion Small, "Demands of Sociology upon Pedagogy," *Journal of Proceedings and Addresses of the Thirty-fifth Annual Meeting of the National Education Association*:174–84.

11. George S. Counts, "Dare Progressive Education be Progressive?" *Progressive Education* 9:257–63.

12. John Dewey, "Progressive Education and the Science of Education," *Progressive Education* 5 (July–August–September 1928):197–204.

13. Counts, op. cit., p. 258.

14. Ibid., p. 259.

15. Harold O. Rugg, *A History of American Government and Culture* (New York: Ginn, 1931):559.

THREE

Contestation and Curriculum: The Efforts of American Socialists, 1900–1920

Kenneth N. Teitelbaum

A merican public schooling is marked by a dual tension that emanates from its being enmeshed in a capitalist democratic state. At the same time that it strives to serve industrial needs, it is also expected to promote democratic purposes.[1] While the former has dominated throughout this century, at various historical moments one or the other imperative may hold sway. In the 1960s, for example, social movements that promoted egalitarian principles and policies seemed to make headway over the forces that sought more direct linkages between schools and the needs of capital production and accumulation. The more recent period has witnessed the ascendency of conservative, business-oriented interests in educational debates about organization, policy, and the curriculum.

During the past century, this tension has resulted in public schooling in effect functioning as a "contested terrain." Conflicts over goals and practices have taken place not just within the corridors, meeting rooms, and classrooms of schools but outside of them as well. The history of educational debates in the United States has included the direct involvement not only of federal and state education officials, community school board members, teacher educators, school administrators, teachers, and parents, but also political and business leaders, conservative and liberal social reformers, and working-class, gender, racial, and ethnic interest groups.[2] In varying ways, to differing extents, and with unequal results, all have sought to influence educational goals, school organization, and everyday teaching and curriculum.

The focus of this historical essay is between 1900 and 1920, a period when American society experienced a marked intensification of industrialization, immigration, urbanization, and bureaucratization. Widespread and rapid changes occurred in material conditions, ideologies, and culture. These were particularly critical years in the evolution of American education, a time when public schooling greatly expanded and commanded heightened attention from many segments of society. While elite groups sought to link the public school system more closely to an ideology based on social control and efficiency, others viewed it primarily as a viable and, in fact, crucial vehicle for social and economic reform. With the closing of the frontier and the growth of corporate business, schooling seemed to play an increasingly key role in American life, with regard not only to individual success but also to what American society was going to look like in the years ahead.[3]

The social ferment of the period in general also created the impetus and the opportunities for radical agitation. Socialist activists were generally optimistic that they could play a decisive role in the reconstruction of American life. As one former Socialist Party member later recollected, in 1912 "we all thought that socialism was around the corner."[4] Evidence at the time supported a somewhat optimistic perspective, as hundreds of radical activists won election to political office, thousands of skilled and unskilled laborers were recruited to allied political parties, unions and fraternal groups, and public questioning of traditional political and economic relations was widespread.[5]

Socialist contestation of dominant social relations took many forms during this time. Not only were there efforts to oppose existent practice but also attempts to construct an emergent culture that stressed new meanings and values.[6] Particularly noteworthy were the publication of several hundred radical newspapers and periodicals, in English and more than a dozen other languages, and the sponsorship of numerous debating, literary and dramatic clubs, choruses, libraries, street corner speeches, rallies, and parades. American Socialists also developed their own formal educational activities for adults, such as correspondence courses, lyceum lectures, local study classes, and schools such as the Rand School of Social Science in New York City and the Finnish Working People's College in Smithville, Minnesota. These educational ventures provided instruction in the nature of industrial capitalism, the class struggle, radical economics and philosophy, and subjects of more practical or cultural interest to workers (e.g., union organizing, public speaking, bookkeeping, shorthand, composition, English literature, and popular music.)[7]

In an attempt to promote significant changes from within the democratic capitalist state, radicals also sought to become public school board members and school administrators and teachers. Between 1909 and 1911, for instance, more than one hundred Socialist school officials were elected in small towns such as Muscatine, Iowa and Basin, Montana; in small cities such as Flint, Michigan and Berkeley, California; and in large cities such as Cincinnati, Ohio and Milwaukee, Wisconsin. At the same time, the party established its own Socialist Teachers Bureau to help match radical teachers with sympathetic school administrators.[8] And in numerous articles, pamphlets, books, and speeches, Socialists and other radicals directly challenged the content and processes of the formal education provided by the state, which they increasingly viewed as in large part functioning to advance the interests of dominant (i.e., nonworking-class) groups in society. Finally, grass-roots radicals also organized their own educational and recreational activities for the children of working-class families, such as clubs, choruses, camps, picnics, parades, and the like. In the more formal and structured of these endeavors, Sunday Schools, they created a body of curricula that opposed the dominant messages being transmitted in the public schools and by other social institutions.

This chapter focuses on two kinds of attempts by American Socialists during 1900 and 1920 to contest overtly mainstream school curriculum: their oral and written critiques of public schooling and, in more detail, their creation of alternative Sunday Schools for children. This discussion is intended to address two general points. First, while school curriculum selection tends to be viewed as neutral and consensual, a close examination of our past reveals that serious challenges have been levied not only against the perspective of curriculum work but also against the particular arrangement of materials, values, and ideas that have dominated our public school practice. Second, a consideration of a specific body of knowledge that by and large has *not* found its way into mainstream curriculum making might be helpful to those today who attempt to develop an emancipatory vision in the curriculum field, or what others have referred to as a "language of possibility."[9]

Socialist Critiques of Public School Curriculum

While support for the institution of public schooling remained strong among American Socialists at the turn of the century, a more critical perspective of the internal dynamics of public school classrooms also began to emerge. Many radical educational critics were clearly influenced by the critiques of schooling by proponents of progressive education. However, unlike child-centered advocates, Socialists linked the public schools more directly to their capitalistic character and maintained a primary focus on what they thought would be of most benefit to the country's millions of skilled and unskilled laborers. Moreover, classrooms were portrayed as not just teaching academic and social skills to individual children but preparing (or not preparing) groups of children for their role in the struggle to eliminate economic inequities and to establish a more democratic form of citizenship. Socialist critics thus outlined ways in which the public school curriculum was fostering not just passivity and uncritical thinking in general, but also a hierarchial division of mental and manual labor, a glorification of the profit motive, and the acceptance of such social conditions as poverty, unemployment, and union busting. In essence, schools were viewed not just in relation to the wider society but more specifically to the revolutionized society Socialists sought to bring about.[10]

Radical educational critics of the time were becoming more aware that working-class viewpoints were being systematically eliminated from public schools when they stood in opposition to dominant capitalist interests. The political slant of school curriculum was hardly sympathetic to the forces of reform, let alone radical change, in American society.[11] This was especially the case in the emerging social studies field. For example, Socialist garment unions, such as the International Ladies' Garment Workers' Union (ILGWU) and the Amalgamated Clothing Workers of America (ACWA), complained that the public schools had "serious gaps," in particular with regard to an ignorance of the economic foundations of American life and of the existence and historical importance of such figures as Nat Turner, Mother Jones, and Eugene Debs. The valuable contributions of organized labor were ignored; schools seemed to be generally hostile to labor, often using it as a scapegoat for social problems. Terms such as *free enterprise* went unchallenged and unanalyzed despite the realities of the corporate structure.[12]

Socialist activists interested in educational issues urged fellow radicals to become more concerned about the school's role in educating future wage workers in "a habit of slavish obedience to the capitalist rule and of prejudice against the working-class movement." They argued that, "Socialists have need to watch schools where the minds of their children are in danger of being perverted to capitalist purposes."[13] Specific examples of public school teaching and administration drew the ire of local radical activists in many areas of the country. In 1902, the inculcation of militarism in public schools was condemned by the Social Democratic Party in Yonkers, New York. They protested the procurement of $1,100 by the local board of education to buy guns for the high school cadet corps, suggesting that the measure was a ploy to train students in the military spirit, in particular so that later they would be able and willing to help the state militia when called on to suppress strikes.[14] Similarly, a 1919 pageant at North Division High School in Milwaukee, Wisconsin, entitled "The Land of Opportunity," was severely criticized by local

Socialists as "a vicious slam at organized labor . . . [that] holds up to the approval of the children the ideal of militarism." One father commented in amazement that "they would dare to attempt such a thing in a district of the city populated by the very working class they are seeking to insult."[15] Elizabeth Thomas, a Socialist school board member in Milwaukee, called for an official inquiry of the incident.[16] The Socialist-dominated Federated Trades Council (FTC) conducted its own investigation and found that the pageant represented "a disgraceful attempt to blacken the local labor movement in the eyes of the school children, many of them from working-class homes."[17] At issue in particular was the last of six scenes of the pageant. The previous five scenes depicted why people from other countries had emigrated to the United States; for example, because of religious persecution, military oppression, and heavy taxation. The FTC described the action of the sixth scene as follows:

> The last episode was devoted to the United States, but instead of presenting a land of opportunity, it was devoted to the labor question. As a prelude, several girls, dressed in black, called Frenzies and meant to represent discontent, came upon the stage and danced about, led by another figure dressed entirely in red, who was called License. Then Peace, all dressed in white and bearing an American flag, appeared and drove the Frenzies and License away. At this point labor came on the scene, labor being represented by a crowd of ill-dressed and hungry-looking workmen in the land of opportunity. A labor speaker stood upon a box and urged the men to commit violence, and another, called a loyal workman, answered him. The workmen became riotous, one of them shot another, and down the aisle from the front of the hall came a company of regulars, carrying guns. They rushed the stage, charged the workingmen at the point of bayonets, and the workmen crouched down at the back of the stage. A judge-like individual, who was called Law and Order, appeared and made a long speech over the body of the dead workmen, telling the workmen to be good and "not to bite the hand that feeds them." This ended the pageant.[18]

The public protests of Thomas, the FTC, and other local Socialists apparently "fell on deaf ears."[19]

Another dispute in Milwaukee centered around the schools' use of the *Current Events* newspaper. Socialist activists in New York City had earlier criticized the paper's "propagandistic" depiction of Bolshevik rule in Russia.[20] Editors of the socialist *Milwaukee Leader* complained that it was nothing more than "a staunch defender of the capitalist system [that] is systematically poisoning the minds of our children."[21] In the spring of 1920, the Rules Committee of the Milwaukee School Board, with two socialist members, voted 3 to 1 to ban *Current Events* from the local public schools, asserting that its articles were too partisan and antagonistic toward labor.[22] However, at a stormy monthly meeting of the entire school board, the committee's minority report, which claimed that the newspaper's perspective was simply "patriotic," was accepted by a 10-to-4 vote. Elizabeth Thomas commented: "It is quite amusing to talk of a free press when *Current Events*, with only one side of the story, is allowed to circulate in the schools. If the papers which give the other side were allowed in the schools, we could begin to talk of free speech."[23]

While radicals were clearly not hesitant to criticize individual teachers and administrators for activities with which they had serious disagreement, in general they did not portray individual school participants as primarily to blame. Just as it was not the fault of the individual worker when he or she failed to embrace the socialist cause, here too it was somehow "the system" that was to blame, that worked against the individual teacher (or worker) seeing the folly or evil of his or her ways. This reliance on "the system" and the "false consciousness" of individual participants to explain nonprogressive actions was summed up rather hyperbolically by Bruce Calvert:

Most of them [teachers] know no better. They are themselves the ripe products of the system. They but do as they have been taught. They have never been asked or permitted to think. They have just blindly accepted what was fed to them and asked no questions for God's sake. Some, a very few, do know better. But they are about as potent as a grasshopper in the maw of an elephant to make any changes. They have to teach what they are told, at the cost of their jobs if they refuse. . . . All is cut and dried for them. They get their orders from the man higher up.[24]

Along with their criticisms of public schools, radical critics also suggested ways in which education might look different in a Socialist America. Scott Nearing, for instance, stressed the need to inculcate more of a sense of social morality along with individual morality, of social responsibility and cooperation rather than intense individualism and competition. William English Walling argued for a curriculum informed by the need for fundamental social change.[25] Similarly, a 1917 editorial in the socialist *Milwaukee Leader* stressed the need

to educate the child to make him a useful member of society. It is their [the Socialists'] purpose that the schools shall equip the children to cope with their environment and to bring out the best that is in them—not by grinding them through an educational mill as sausages are ground from a machine, but by giving the individual opportunity to develop to his fullest capacity in the direction that his talents are most promising. But in giving the individual opportunity, at the same time they recognize the need for cultivating the social consciousness and community spirit.[26]

Charles P. Steinmetz of Schenectady, New York, perhaps cut to the core of the socialist difference when he suggested that "under capitalism our children are taught that their main mission in life is to make a living," while "under Socialism they will be taught that the only thing worth working for or worth living for is to make this a better world to live in."[27] All children were capable of benefitting from an education guided by such a perspective. Thus, with implications for the emerging support for curriculum differentiation in the public schools, Nearing emphasized that although "the people cannot all be scholars," there was no necessity for that to be the case, since "they can all be intelligent upon the great issues of life."[28] Another *Milwaukee Leader* editorial criticized the public school curriculum for being "dominated by the forces of standpattism and reaction[,] . . . by men and women who have the stocks-and-bonds outlook upon life." In contrast, "Socialists do not want to teach the children Socialism. They only want to teach them to think for themselves— to lead their minds out, which is the true meaning of education—and protect them from the deadening effects of prejudice and falsehood."[29]

This dilemma, perhaps a common one in radical educational theory, of teaching children to think for themselves while at the same time guarding against their learning of "prejudice and falsehood," was commonly left unexplored and sometimes even unrecognized. Moreover, Socialist educational critics appear to have embraced a rather mechanistic view of the relationship between capitalist economic relations and public educational practice. At the same time, however, they did adopt a less myopic and more democratic perspective of the social and political character of school curriculum than was the case for most other contemporary observers.

A Socialist Alternative: Sunday Schools for Working-Class Children

Although relatively few in number, some grass-roots radical activists sought to go beyond critiques of public schooling and general suggestions of what a socialist education might look like. With very little or no financial remuneration and with little tangible support from the national and state leaderships of the Socialist Party of America, they organized alternative educational experiences for working-class children. The most formal of these were two-hour weekend schools, most commonly referred to as Socialist Sunday Schools.[30] In these settings, children from radical working-class families, ages six to fourteen, were offered a curriculum intended to counter the overly competitive, individualistic, antiworking-class, nationalistic, and militaristic themes that seemed to prevail in contemporary public schools and other social institutions. These Sunday Schools represent another component of socialist contestation of mainstream American culture and curriculum.

Between 1900 and 1920, local Socialist activists established at least one hundred English-speaking[31] Sunday Schools for children in sixty-four cities and towns in twenty states. The schools most prominently mentioned in newspaper and personal accounts were located in Boston, Haverhill, Brockton, Providence, Hartford, New York City, Newark, Rochester, Buffalo, Philadelphia, Pittsburgh, the District of Columbia, Cleveland, Chicago, Milwaukee, and Los Angeles. New York City had at least fourteen different schools in operation during this twenty-year period, Chicago had ten, and Milwaukee, Boston, Cleveland, Pittsburgh, and Providence each had at least three different schools.[32] Like the political movement from which they sprang, the Socialist Sunday Schools lacked uniformity, especially with regard to the facilities and materials they enjoyed. School enrollments also varied a great deal, no doubt reflecting differences in the size of communities, the strength of local radical movements, and the commitment of local socialists to educational as opposed to strictly political and economic ventures. Some "schools" really consisted of one or two classes, with fewer than ten children in each class. Such was the case initially for the school in Newport, Kentucky, which was organized in March 1909 with only five children but had thirty-five students and two teachers by the summer.[33] On the other end of the scale were schools in the Brownsville section of Brooklyn, with more than six hundred children attending in 1917–18, and in Rochester, New York, with about four hundred students in 1913–14.[34] The majority of schools had an enrollment of about seventy to one hundred students. While some schools lasted for only one school year, most others lasted for several years. A few schools, particularly ones in New York City, remained in operation for a decade or more.

While such differences did exist, certain general patterns within the movement did emerge. Of course, all of the schools shared a profound sense of the ills of the capitalist system and of the need for Socialist transformation of American society, as well as the belief that such a perspective needed to be transmitted to youngsters in a formal educational setting. The schools were usually organized by members of the Socialist Party, both men and women (though predominantly the latter). They were secular in nature, meeting on Sundays because it was the only day off for many American workers at the time. (This made it more likely that parents could take young children to school and remain for adult classes, socialize, and participate in Sunday School activities). They also generally eschewed any ethnic identification,

41

adopting the Socialist Party's approach in downplaying such differences for the sake of class solidarity.[35]

Participants cited three rationales in particular for the establishment of the Sunday Schools. One was that the schools, albeit meeting only two hours each week, could play a key role in helping to counteract the growing influence of capitalist social institutions on working-class youth. Virtually all aspects of dominant culture were included in such arguments. For instance, Kendrick Shedd of the Rochester and Milwaukee schools lamented the extent to which "the young are being systematically 'doped' into a condition of insensibility toward the vital things in life. They are being baseballized and funnypaperized and tangoized and pleasurized and motion-picturized until they have no thought of anything worth while [sic] in life."[36] Frances Gill of New York City referred to the public schools when she argued that, "It is inconceivable that the children of the workingmen should receive their only education and preparation for life from schools whose every interest is bound up in the maintenance and perpetuation of the instruments of their own oppression." It followed, then, that because "the educational system of the elementary schools is not adapted to the needs of the workingman's child, it should be supplemented by an organized effort to correct its faults of omission and commission."[37] Similarly, Helen Lowy of Chicago, Illinois, recounted how a principal spoke to night school students on the benefits of the Republican Party and, according to Lowy, closed with the hope that "you will all pray that Theodore Roosevelt will be elected." She concluded, "Thus it is that they teach our children in our public schools, and this influence we must counteract in our Socialist Sunday Schools."[38] The argument of another advocate illustrated the dialectical relationship between hegemonic culture and the forces of counterhegemony: she suggested that, "if the Public School system were what it should be there would be no need for Socialist [Sunday] Schools."[39]

A second, related rationale involved the role that the schools could play in helping to establish a sense of community and continuity within the radical movement at a time when generational differences in life experiences appeared to be growing. In the face of a multitude of influences geared to the contrary, the Sunday Schools could help to socialize the children of radical working-class families to form a lifelong commitment to Socialist principles and culture. While many informal ways existed to encourage an attachment to the radical community, for instance familial influences, party local affairs, parades, clubs, and the like, proponents stressed the more systematic role that a formal weekend education for children could provide. The staff of the West Hoboken, New Jersey school, for example, expressed the concern that "a large percentage of children of Socialists and sympathizers are lost to the movement every year. The parents, either through inability to render the subject interesting or from some other cause, allow the children to go astray as a result of the patriotic teachings of the public schools or the influence of the capitalist press."[40] The Socialist Sunday Schools could be a first step in help-ing to prevent this kind of loss to the radical community. In turn, as Kendrick Shedd suggested, working in the Socialist school also had a salutary effect on the older comrades. He wrote: "They [the adults] grow in the process. They themselves become innoculated. They grow enthusiastic. They grow in spirit and in purpose. They renew their youth and light anew the slumbering fire. . . . They grow less crusty. Their heart beats a little faster. They are help-ing."[41] In dual ways, then, for the present and for the future, for adults and for children, the schools could help to foster a stronger Socialist community.

The third rationale was that the schools could help the children of radi-cal, working-class families to attain a more intelligent understanding and ap-preciation of specific Socialist tenets and Socialist Party positions. Exactly what would constitute an appropriate education was not always made clear nor agreed upon. But the children would at least be exposed to a body of knowledge and a way of thinking that they would not receive formally else-where. As one observer put it, the children could at least be given "some ele-mentary understanding of what the working class was fighting for."[42] The staff of the Los Angeles, California school announced their intention to pro-vide the children with "a correct knowledge of history and economics."[43] And Esther F. Sussman of Hartford, Connecticut, reported that the children there were being taught "the fundamentals of scientific Socialism so that when they grow up they may be able to face and overcome the social problems of the day with intelligence and broadmindedness."[44]

Of course, the schools were never expected to offer a *complete* socialist ed-ucation for youth, only a more formal and systematic one than could be pro-vided at home and at other party-sponsored activities. Yet despite the limitations of time, funding, and staffing inherent in this alternative schooling movement, it did put together a perhaps surprisingly extensive body of cur-riculum materials. While considerable disagreement was evident among par-ticipants about the specific form that radical teaching should take and different methods did predominate in different schools, the curriculum as a whole consisted of lecture outlines; discussion questions; readers and maga-zines; poems, essays, and sayings for recitations; games and role-playing activ-ities; field trips and nature hikes; guest speakers; flag drills; songs; and plays and pageants. The more successful schools made use of lesson topics, ques-tions, recitations, song cards, and dramatic scripts that were locally developed and professionally printed. Other schools depended more heavily on other socialist and nonsocialist sources, such as the *Young Socialists' Magazine* and the anthropological books of Katherine Dopp, or had to adapt lessons from more adult-oriented materials, such as Walter Thomas Mills's *The Struggle for*

Existence.[45] But in all schools, it was hoped that the children could receive a systematic education guided by a social vision that seemed to be sorely missing from the public schools.

Alternative Curriculum Themes from the Socialist Perspective

• These schools were closely allied with a political movement that in large part defined issues affecting the quality of life and the possibilities of change in terms of the processes and structures of the social system. It is hardly surprising, then, that much of the curriculum of the Socialist Sunday Schools was what would be thought of today as "social studies." As Kendrick Shedd stressed, "Anything that concerns the conditions under which human beings live is of interest to us."[46] In a general sense, the schools focused on the development of "social awareness" and, as William F. Kruse of the party's Young People's Office noted, on the will and desire of students to "work as well as talk for their ideal."[47] More specific themes were also present and provide a more concrete indication of the contested messages of these Socialist schools. While some were emphasized more and taught more directly than others, they each represented a significant element of Socialist teaching. Although not easily separated from each other, twelve major themes can be highlighted.

The first curricular theme involved the concept of "the abstract individual." Michael Apple described this individualism as related to the fact that "our sense of community is withered at its roots. We find ways of making the concrete individual into an abstraction and, at the same time, we divorce the individual from larger social movements which might give meaning to 'individual' wants, needs, and visions of justice."[48] Socialist curriculum materials were infused with a perspective emphasizing the place of the individual in the social world, and the interdependence of the individual with countless others, especially workers. Such was the case, for instance, when teachers and students from the Omaha, Nebraska school took trips to local manufacturing plants in 1904. Bertha Mailly, then a teacher at the school (and who later helped initiate schools in Boston, Massachusetts and New York City), discussed with the children how one guide at a shoe factory told the children proudly about the work of the machines without any reference to the laborers in the plant. Mailly made a point of stressing the children's debt to such unknown workers for the shoes that they wore.[49]

A second theme integrated into the Socialist Sunday School curriculum involved an emphasis on the students being conscious and proud of being a part of the working-class community. The dignity of labor (if not all laborers) was often stressed and virtually every social problem was viewed primarily from the perspective of its effect on workers. Moreover, class struggle, rather than class compromise, was suggested as the effective strategy for workers to follow. This theme was imparted, for instance, in a series of lessons developed by Bertha Fraser of Brooklyn.[50] Her course of study included three lessons devoted "to a comparison between the working class and the idle class: first, in connection with food; second, clothing; and last the homes." A follow-up lesson focused on "the cause of the contrast—the unequal distribution of the products due to the exploitation of labor, and the consequent suffering of the working class." The last two lessons dealt "with the remedy and how it is to be applied."

Cooperative and collectivist rather than competitive and privatized economic relations was a third theme of this curriculum. Lesson materials focused on the nature and advantages of public ownership and management of industry at a time when public ownership of utilities was considered a radical demand. This sense of cooperation and collectivism was in fact broadly applied, so that "working together" in a variety of ways was viewed not only as a key to working-class success in contesting the capitalist system but also to more equitable and congenial social relations. Thus, an entire year's curriculum for a Milwaukee school was guided by the general theme of "cooperation in everyday life."[51] Thirty-one lessons comprised this course of study, including the following lesson topics: Playing Together; Keeping Well Together; Learning Together; Owning Together; Being World Citizens Together; Governing Together; Judging Together; Investing Together; Owning Books Together; Rejoicing Together; Running a Newspaper Together; Building Together; and Running Industry Together. Role-playing activities (although they were not referred to as such), accompanied by discussion questions, played a prominent part in the lessons. Plans for the initial lesson on "Singing Together," for example, looked like this:

1. Let a number of children try to sing different songs at the same time. Then the same song starting at different times. Then the same song starting together but at different pitches. Then end with utter confusion and shouting and disorder.
2. Dismiss children to go to the classes. Class hints: What was the trouble? Shall we stop singing altogether? Why not? How shall we have good singing? What is needed to sing together? Why not have each sing alone?
3. School reassembles. Superintendent reminds school of disorder at beginning of lesson. Any suggestions for better way of doing things? Children will volunteer results of class period. A number of children will then try to sing together in orderly manner. More are added. Finally the whole school together gives everyone a chance to take part,

45

each helping the other, and results in harmony and good feeling. Singing separately in competition gives only one or two a chance, while the majority must remain silent, or results in disorder and confusion and noise. Let us sing together.[52]

The fourth theme was internationalism, the sense of viewing oneself as inextricably linked to the interests of others (i.e., workers) in other nations. Correspondence with schools and youth clubs in other countries was carried out not just to gather information but also to encourage a linkage with radical political movements abroad. International songs and flags were a part of the lessons at most schools. In 1913, for example, a flag drill at the Rochester Socialist Sunday School included the following recitation by a group of students: "To the Cause of the World-Workers, and of International Solidarity and Brotherhood, Symbolized by this Crimson Banner, We Hereby Dedicate Our Strength, Our Hopes, and Our Lives!" A "parade of nations" followed, with Socialist vote tallies from different nations written on the front of cards that the children carried.[53] Rather than discouraging this emphasis, World War I intensified the schools' focus on the international character of a successful Socialist movement. Future workers in the United States needed to realize that workers in other countries shared a common enemy, the capitalist system, and a common aim, its overthrow.

The related fifth theme was antimilitarism, especially during the middle years of the second decade when the European conflict started and the United States massed troops along the Mexican border. This was associated with what David S. Greenberg of New York City referred to as "anti-sham patriotism."[54] Militarist adventures were viewed as primarily hurting the lives of workers (who had to fight in such endeavors), breaking down a feeling of internationalism, and taking attention and funds away from domestic needs. Illustrating this perspective are the first and last verses of a song written by Kendrick Shedd and used in Rochester and Milwaukee schools and no doubt in others as well. It is entitled "War What For?":

In this here song we sing of war, war, war, war,
We know too well what it is for, for, for, for
In war the working men kill, kill, kill, kill
So that the rich their coffers fill, fill, fill, fill.

I never would a soldier be, be, be, be
Unless it were to make men free, free, free, free
If they will call me a traitor, if I won't be shot,
I'd rather be a traitor than a patriot![55]

The sixth theme involved a revisionist interpretation of history, economics, and sociology. Socialist Sunday School children were exposed to lessons that transformed traditional social studies content so that the laboring class was perceived as an instrumental motor for social progress. Heroes and heroines whose birthdays were celebrated in the pages of the *Young Socialists' Magazine* included William Lloyd Garrison, Susan B. Anthony, William Morris, Karl Marx, Mother Jones, Eugene Debs, and other national and international social critics and activists. Socialist agitators were portrayed not as a lunatic fringe of bombthrowers but rather as the only hope for workers to significantly improve their lot. The plight of the poor was viewed not as the result of defective skills or character on the part of the individual but rather primarily caused by capitalist economics. This latter aspect was expressed in an essay entitled "Why Men Are As They Are," written by Abraham Jacobson, an eleven-year-old student at a New York City school:

> In the capitalist system it cannot be different, because most children, instead of educating themselves, go to work and work all their lives from early morning till late at night. When they are married and have children they hardly have time to see their children, because they go to work while their children sleep, and when they come home it is the same. Some men work seven days out of a week to make some kind of a poor living. When these men meet by some chance, with their friend, they are afraid to tell him the truth about their work, because their friend might go up to the boss and work for cheaper wages than his friend did. In this way people cannot be kind, true, or honest.[56]

The seventh theme involved the study of anthropology and in particular the evolution of the human race, with an emphasis on the progress of people from the Stone Age to the Iron Age to feudalism to capitalism, with the logical next step in "the struggle for existence" being socialism. It was an optimistic message, and one that embraced a liberal notion of progress, but it subverted conventional teaching by positing the necessity and inevitability of a next, socialist stage of human civilization. Anthropological accounts were further guided not so much by a sense of how "primitive" early people were but by the cooperative and collective spirit that had stood them well, a spirit that was portrayed as "natural" to humankind but suppressed by capitalist social relations. According to one school participant, the goals of such lessons were also "to show the child that change and adaptation are ever universal," and to foster "the general principle to go from old to new, from simple to complex, from concrete to abstract, to appeal to the imagination."[57]

Social equity was the eighth theme of the Socialist Sunday School curriculum. The materials generally adopted the political vision of most Socialist

Party members that class struggle was preeminent, that is, that racial and gender inequities could not be fully addressed until the capitalist organization of society was eradicated. Economic interests were viewed as decisive throughout history and "wage slavery" was the condition that in particular needed to be the focus. True equality of opportunity meant that workers had to have the same advantages in life as managers and owners, that, in essence, wage slavery had to be eliminated. Adequate levels of food, clothing, and shelter were viewed as the most basic concerns of human life, from the beginning of civilization to the present, with only a socialistic society being able to guarantee that all individuals would not suffer from the want of them.

The ninth theme focused on specific social problems. In fact, many of the lesson outlines represent a kind of social problems approach more than they do the direct teaching of socialist principles. What differentiated the social problems approach of these socialist teachers from other educators was their consistent emphasis on poverty, unemployment, unhealthy and unsafe work conditions, child labor, alcoholism, poor housing and sanitary facilities, the despoliation of nature, disease, and the like being endemic to industrial capitalism. Social problems were not viewed as isolated phenomena that could be individually attacked and resolved by well-meaning reformers but rather as integral features of capitalist America. For instance, in the "Slums, Sweatshops, Sickness and Disease" lesson from the "Home Destroyers" series that was used by the Rochester school, students learned that there could be "no true homes for workers while Capitalism robs them of health, time, comforts, life." In another lesson that focused on "Divorce," attention was placed on the economic pressures that made it difficult for spouses to stay together (e.g., "What drives people to divorce? If homes were 'sweet' would there be so many divorces? Is divorce a matter of religion or economics?").[58] Aiming "to develop the children into useful citizens" at the Third Assembly District Socialist Sunday School in the Bronx thus did not refer merely to voting and participating in uncontroversial social service activities. It meant helping to bring about the eradication of serious social problems in the only way that could be effective, by agitating for the end of capitalism.[59]

The tenth theme of the socialist curriculum also placed considerable emphasis on the everyday conditions of workers' lives and sought to expand the children's awareness and appreciation for the need for good hygiene, healthy diets, proper exercise, safety, nature outings, and so forth. The emphasis here was on public health: concern for these aspects of everyday life was not just for the benefit of the individual but also for the community. After all, sickness can spread to others, nature can be enjoyed by others, and it is the responsibility of everyone not just for themselves but for others to learn to take care of these matters. Such aspects would frequently be linked to other, more political concerns. This can be seen in a recitation performed by students in Rochester and Buffalo (and probably elsewhere as well), entitled "We Want":

We want more of sunshine and air;
We want less of worry and care.
We want every joy for each girl and boy,
And we want for each mortal his share.

We want all the best of the Earth;
We want more of pleasure and mirth.
We want all the best and we want the rest,
And we want all the value we're worth.

We want to be well and to know,
We want for good health and a fair show,
We want to be bright and we long for light,
And we all want to live and to grow.

We want of the world full control,
We'll have nothing less than the whole,
All value we make the whole we'll take,
And the time to develop the soul.

The eleventh theme involved the presentation of the Cooperative Commonwealth as potentially embracing the ideal conditions of human life. Such a socialist society would feature public ownership and management of industry and social property, economic equality, the elimination of prejudice, and more healthy and equitable living conditions and personal relations. Associated with this focus was the notion that Socialism should in fact be identified with "happiness." This was used as an argument for augmenting the curriculum, so that in many schools lectures and recitations were accompanied by games, trips, concerts, pageants, picnics, and the like. If the children had fun, they would think of being part of a socialist community as an enjoyable experience. Of course, even children's games could be instilled with a radical message. For instance, a former student of the Los Angeles school remembers that games such as "Tag" and "Tug of War" were given "worker versus boss" interpretations.[61]

Finally, the Socialist Sunday School curriculum sought to instill a generally critical approach to everyday life, dominated as it was by capitalist social

49

institutions. Public schools, for example, were not portrayed as politically neutral and the children were taught not to accept at face value what was being taught in them. While no one recommended that the children out-rightly reject the messages and practices of the public schools while they were there, the entire content of this alternative curriculum was intended to reveal that if "truths" existed, and they certainly did for these Socialists, they would not necessarily be found in mainstream social institutions.

It was not just a matter of focusing on different heroes and different in-terpretations of important events. In some lessons, alternative notions of everyday concepts were also considered. At the Rochester school, discussion questions about "justice," for example, were developed by Kendrick Shedd and comprised part of the 1912–13 curriculum:

> Is competition just?
> Do the workers get justice?
> Have we political justice?
> Name some instances of political injustice.
> Are these things just:
>> Child wage workers?
>> Mothers employed outside of their homes?
>> Use of militia to settle strikes?
>> War? Capitalist courts? Capitalist press?
>> Suppression of Free Speech and Assemblage?
> What is justice?[62]

Shedd's lessons were thus intended to begin with a discussion that related the general topic to contemporary social conditions and to then conclude with a definitional question. Children were encouraged to view commonsensical everyday notions critically and then, in the light of the unsatisfactory nature of prevailing views, to adopt alternative perspectives of them. What might be considered abstract philosophical constructs were linked to the unequal rela-tions of social life, in particular as they are experienced by the working class.

While this has not been an exhaustive discussion of Socialist children's schools, it should serve to highlight their major organizational features and their specific curricular themes. Of course, this oppositional educational movement never really had much of an opportunity to develop its principles and practices beyond a limited amount of time and a limited school setting. The momentum for organizing Sunday Schools essentially disappeared dur-ing the split in the radical movement and repressive political climate from 1918 to 1921. Still, the character of this educational movement was notewor-thy for its overt challenge to the values and ideas that predominated in the public schools. Perhaps the central difference of this Socialist curriculum was summarized in 1910 by Sadie Lindenberg, a student at a Socialist Sunday School in Brooklyn. She described what she was learning in this way:

> Not alone has it broadened my outlook on all questions connected with life in general, but it has also caused me to view with kindred feeling the sufferings of all less fortunate than myself.
>
> The Social [*sic*] school has taught me to distinguish more clearly the difference between government as it is and as it should be. It has taught me to be useful to all people, to be a useful member of the community, taking an absorbing interest in all things that concern the welfare of all its members. Thus you see that the Social school has taken me from the drift, as it were, and educated me to feel the impulses of affectionate interest in all things pertaining to the welfare and good of all people.[63]

Conclusion

The primary intent of this historical essay has been to illuminate the very existence of past contestation, not so much the reasons why the groups and individuals discussed are among the "losers" in the struggle for the American curriculum. That Socialist Sunday School advocates were not the victors can be explained in large part with reference to the demise of the political movement with which they strongly attached themselves. But maybe we should not be too certain of their defeat. While we cannot reasonably posit some future triumph of their educational ideas and practices, perhaps things might have looked quite different if their efforts had never taken place.

The question naturally arises of whether this examination of past contestation matters at all for current curriculum theory and practice. Clearly, the Socialists developed a critical perspective and a body of lesson materials and activities that should not be adopted directly as a critical pedagogy today. It would be somewhat ridiculous to expect otherwise, considering that this work took place more than sixty-five years ago, when public ownership of utilities and unemployment insurance were considered radical demands and when progressive educational ideas were first being widely discussed. Moreover, the character of the Socialist curriculum itself is perhaps deficient. For example, there is a serious devaluing of other social categories of domination besides class, most notably gender and race; although the social vision embedded in the materials stresses critique, cooperation, and collectivism, the activities planned for the children are lacking in opportunities for creative self-expression, self-criticism, and collaboration; and while to be congratulated for emphasizing the significance of material relations in our everyday lives, the focus is overly economistic. Moreover, it perhaps represents more of a curriculum for Socialist children than a Socialist curriculum for children. That is, while the children did not all come from Socialist families, their backgrounds were predominantly working class and politically radical. There was never the necessity to develop a full-blown educational theory that was fully cognizant of the nature of childhood learning and that could accommodate the diversity and lack of progressive politics that mark the general community of school children.

But there are two related claims to consider here. First, Socialist contestation of mainstream curriculum, as represented in their critiques of public schooling and their Sunday School curriculum, perhaps do offer hints of "really [or critically] useful knowledge" for children from which to draw upon. This idea of "really useful knowledge" has a long history in radical circles, dating back to the efforts of radical working-class educational associations in early-nineteenth-century England. Drawing on the work of Richard Johnson, the American Socialist Sunday School curriculum can be viewed as having addressed three aspects of this conception of educational knowledge.[64] First, it encouraged the children to have pride in their working-class backgrounds and to view their subordinate status as shared and systematic, thus creating a sense of solidarity with others from the same social class. Second, it utilized the everyday concerns of workers' lives to elaborate on the social problems that many people face and the relationship between these problems and the character of contemporary society. Third, it focused on the need for fundamental social change and, more specifically, comprehensive strategies to overcome effectively the hardships and sense of powerlessness that oppressed groups experience.

While the Socialist Sunday School curriculum is seriously outdated and even wrongheaded in some ways, even for those sympathetic to its central focuses on equality and justice, it did attempt to include these three features of really (or critically) useful knowledge. Perhaps a modified version of this curriculum can help to guide current attempts to construct lesson ideas and activities that emphasize more equitable social and economic relations. The Socialist alternative certainly provides new meaning to the commonplace overall goal of social studies instruction, that is, the promotion of "good citizenship."

More generally, a serious consideration of past contestation can perhaps help to clarify the political nature of school curriculum development. The fundamentally political character of curriculum refers not only to the fact that some involved in the curriculum selection process have more power to decide matters than others; but also to the realization that school knowledge is tied to issues of cultural and economic reproduction. Indeed, if the messages of the Socialists seem overly propagandistic or political in tone, it may only be because they are not the usual ones we have come to expect in schools. For instance, learning in a public school to invest in the stock market is as much an act of advocacy as learning in a Socialist school to pool one's resources in cooperative ventures. And while our public schools do not sing about "The Red Flag" or portray corporate capitalists as inhuman individuals motivated primarily by greed, they do have ultra-patriotic essay contests sponsored by the Daughters of the American Revolution (DAR), the singing of the militarist "Star Spangled Banner," the staging of playlets about the first Thanksgiving that offer little mention of how the colonists treated Native Americans, and many other instances of lessons that are steeped in "propagandistic" overtones. Recently, there has also emerged an "Adopt-A-School" program that encourages local businesses (e.g., banks, real estate firms, energy companies) to supply supplementary materials and support for local public schools. While it is clear that the current fiscal crisis in school funding is the immediate impetus for such a program, what may be less clear to school participants are the ideological nature and possible pedagogical ramifications of such a venture. To what extent, for example, might product advertising be taught as nutrition education, the benefits of nuclear energy as energy education, industry public relations as environmental education, and corporate promotion as economics education?[65] And whose interests would be primarily served by such instruction?

The Socialists discussed in this chapter were not the elite theorists and organizers of the Socialist Party. But they knew full well, more than sixty years ago, that schooling is in part a decidedly political enterprise, that school reform is not just an educational process but a political one as well. In essence, the question in teaching is not whether to advocate or not, but the nature and extent of one's advocacy. The question is not whether to encourage a particular social vision in the classroom but what kind of social vision it will be. The efforts of American Socialists during the Progressive Era help to underscore the political nature of schooling, reminding people then and now that what is taught is not necessarily reality but a *particular* version of it.

Herbert Kliebard observed almost two decades ago that to many curriculum developers and researchers there seems to be "something anomalous and perhaps even subversive about attempting to see the field of curriculum in some kind of historical perspective."[66] In a way, perhaps a reason for this is because in the historical perspective, alternatives to current practice become known and clarified. This can only muddy the waters of fortifying the present arrangements of economic and cultural power. An awareness of past contestation of American curriculum work can thus reveal not only the inherently political nature of dominant educational practice but also concrete alternatives to it. It may further help us to better understand the possibilities of transformation and, perhaps most importantly, the possibilities within people.[67] In an age wrought with pessimism and cynicism, this may indeed be a considerable achievement for which to strive.

Notes

1. Martin Carnoy and Henry M. Levin, *Schooling and Work in the Democratic State* (Stanford, Calif.: Stanford University Press, 1985).

2. See, for example, William J. Reese, *Power and the Promise of School Reform: Grass-Roots Movements During the Progressive Era* (Boston: Routledge and Kegan Paul, 1986).

3. See, for example, Howard Zinn, *A People's History of the United States* (New York: Harper and Row, 1980); David F. Noble, *America by Design* (New York: Alfred A. Knopf, 1977); Richard L. Ehrlich, ed., *Immigrants in Industrial America, 1850–1920* (Charlottesville: University Press of Virginia, 1977); David B. Tyack, *The One Best System* (Cambridge, Mass.: Harvard University Press, 1976); Joel H. Spring, *Education and the Corporate State* (Boston: Beacon, 1972); James Weinstein, *The Corporate Ideal in the Liberal State, 1900–1918* (Boston: Beacon, 1968); and Robert Wiebe, *The Search for Order, 1877–1920* (New York: Hill and Wang, 1967).

4. Quoted in Betty Yorburg, *Utopia and Reality: A Collective Portrait of American Socialists* (New York: Columbia University Press, 1969), p. 11.

5. See, for example, Mari Jo Buhle, *Women and American Socialism, 1870–1920* (Urbana: University of Illinois Press, 1981); James R. Green, *Grass-Roots Socialism: Radical Movements in the Southwest, 1895–1943* (Baton Rouge: Louisiana State University Press, 1978); Bruce M. Stave, ed., *Socialism and the Cities* (Port Washington, N.Y.: Kenikat, 1975); James Weinstein, *The Decline of Socialism in America, 1912–1925* (New York: Vintage, 1969); David A. Shannon, *The Socialist Party of America* (Chicago: Quadrangle, 1955); and Lillian Symes and Travers Clement, *Rebel America* (New York: Harper and Bros., 1934).

6. The notion of "emergent culture" is discussed in Raymond Williams, *Marxism and Literature* (Oxford: Oxford University Press, 1977).

7. Socialist educational activities for adults are discussed in Kenneth Teitelbaum, *Schooling for 'Good Rebels': Socialist Education for Children in the United States, 1900–1920* (Philadelphia: Temple University Press, 1993). A paperback edition of this book is available from Teachers College Press.

8. "Socialist Elective Officials—United States," in the *Socialist Party of America Papers*, microfilm edition (Glen Rock, N.J.: Microfilming Corporation of America, 1975), reel 6; and miscellaneous reports, in ibid., reel 76.

9. Stanley Aronowitz and Henry A. Giroux, *Education Under Siege: The Conservative, Liberal, and Radical Debate over Schooling* (South Hadley, Mass.: Bergin and Garvey, 1985).

10. See, for example, Joseleyne Slade Tien, "The Educational Theories of American Socialists, 1900–1920" (unpublished Ph.D. dissertation, Michigan State University, 1972), p. 92.

11. For documentation of antireform sentiments in nineteenth-century school textbooks, see Ruth M. Elson, *Guardians of Tradition: American Schoolbooks in the Nineteenth Century* (Lincoln: University of Nebraska Press, 1964).

12. Robert Joseph Schaefer, "Educational Activities of the Garment Unions, 1890–1948" (unpublished Ph.D. dissertation, Columbia University, 1951), pp. 5–9.

13. *The Worker*, October 6, 1901.

14. *The Worker*, January 12, 1902.

15. *Milwaukee Leader*, November 19, 1919.

16. *Milwaukee Leader*, December 27, 1919.

17. *Milwaukee Leader*, January 23, 1920.

18. Ibid.

19. Ibid.

20. *New York Call*, October 28, 1919.

21. *Milwaukee Leader*, March 7, 1921.

22. *Milwaukee Leader*, May 27, 1920.

23. *Milwaukee Leader*, June 2, 1920.

24. *New York Call*, August 19, 1917. For a critical (and, I think, somewhat distorted) interpretation of the Socialists' tendency to take a condescending view of workers, see Aileen S. Kraditor, *The Radical Persuasion: Aspects of the Intellectual History and the Historiography of Three American Radical Organizations* (Baton Rouge: Louisiana State University Press, 1981).

25. Joselyne Slade Tien, op. cit., pp. 131–32.

26. *Milwaukee Leader*, March 5, 1917.

27. *Appeal to Reason*, August 8, 1914.

28. Scott Nearing, *A Nation Divided (or Plutocracy Versus Democracy)* (Chicago: Socialist Party of the United States, 1920).

29. *Milwaukee Leader*, March 19, 1923.

30. Although most of the schools were called "Sunday Schools," several of them were actually known by other names, such as the Children's Socialist Lyceum in Los Angeles and the Arm and Torch League in Cincinnati. No doubt local factors at particular times encouraged the adoption of different names. But all the schools referred to as "Socialist Sunday Schools" in this chapter were basically considered as such at the time.

31. There were at least as many non-English-speaking radical (usually socialist) weekend children's schools established by radical groups from the German, Jewish, Finnish, and other ethnic communities. Schools which used a language other than English are not included in this analysis. Their characters (e.g., curriculum) were slightly different with regard to their ethnic identification. For more on these other schools, see Kenneth Teitelbaum, op. cit., pp. 41–45. For a detailed discussion of anarchist schools for children in the United States, see Paul Avrich, *The Modern School Movement: Anarchism and Education in the United States* (Princeton, N.J.: Princeton University Press, 1980).

32. For a listing of the locations of most of the Socialist Sunday Schools, see Kenneth Teitelbaum and William J. Reese, "American Socialist Pedagogy and Experimentation in the Progressive Era: The Socialist Sunday School" *History of Education Quarterly* 23 (Winter 1983):439. For a discussion of many of the individual schools, see Teitelbaum, op. cit., especially pp. 45–89.

33. *Socialist Woman* 2 (September 1909):9; and *Progressive Woman* 3 (October 1909):14.

34. *New York Call*, November 17, 1917 and March 7, 1918; and "Rochester Socialist Sunday School Scrapbooks, Vols. II and III," in the *Kendrick Philander Shedd Papers*, located at the University of Rochester, Rush Rhees Library, Rochester, N.Y. (Henceforth, this collection will be referred to as *Shedd Papers*.)

35. The nature of the Socialist Sunday Schools is discussed at greater length in Teitelbaum, op. cit.

36. *Milwaukee Leader*, January 19, 1915.

37. *The Worker*, January 26, 1907.

38. Helen Lowy, "The Importance of Socialist Sunday Schools," *Progressive Woman* 4 (December 1910):15.

39. *New York Call*, April 7, 1912.

40. *New York Call*, October 2, 1910. Socialist youth activists rarely considered the possibility that some children, especially those who were able to attain a more middle-class lifestyle as they grew older, "went astray" simply because they found the socialist message presented to them to be unpersuasive.

41. *New York Call*, July 25, 1915.

42. Oakley C. Johnson, *The Day Is Coming: Life and Work of Charles E. Ruthenberg* (New York: International Publishers, 1957), p. 47.

43. *Progressive Woman* 3 (December 1909):14.

44. *Young Socialists' Magazine* 4 (September 1911):15.

45. For a discussion of Dopp (who had been a student of John Dewey's at the University of Chicago) and her books (which were published by Rand McNally and Company), see Teitelbaum, op cit., especially pp. 149–50. See also Walter Thomas Mills, *The Struggle for Existence* (Chicago: International School of Social Economy, 1904).

46. *New York Call*, June 20, 1915.

47. William F. Kruse, "Socialist Education for Children," *Young Socialists' Magazine* 11 (March 1917):9–10.

48. Michael W. Apple, *Ideology and Curriculum* (London: Routledge & Kegan Paul, 1979), p. 9.

49. *The Worker*, January 24, 1904.

50. Bertha Matthews Fraser, *Outlines of Lessons for Socialist Schools for Children* (New York: Children's Socialist Schools Committee of Local Kings County, Socialist Party, 1910).

51. Lesson outlines for this course of study were published throughout the 1917–18 school year in the *Milwaukee Leader*.

52. *Milwaukee Leader*, September 29, 1917.

53. "Rochester Socialist Sunday School Scrapbooks, Vol. IV," *Shedd Papers*.

54. David S. Greenberg, *Socialist Sunday School Curriculum* (New York: Socialist Schools Publishing Association, 1913).

55. *New York Call*, May 13, 1913.

56. *The Worker*, July 20, 1907.

57. *New York Call*, March 21, 1913. See also Bertha H. Mailly, "Socialist Schools," *Unity of Labor* 1 (April 1911?):10–11. Katherine Dopp's books were used for just such purposes.

58. "Rochester Socialist Sunday School Scrapbooks, Vol. II," *Shedd Papers*.

59. *New York Call*, December 6, 1918.

60. "Rochester Socialist Sunday School Scrapbooks, Vol. II," *Shedd Papers*.

61. Peggy Dennis, "The Twenties," *Cultural Correspondence* 6–7 (Spring 1978):84.

62. "Rochester Socialist Sunday School Scrapbooks, Vol. II," *Shedd Papers*.

63. *New York Call*, May 8, 1910.

64. Richard Johnson, "'Really useful knowledge': Radical education and working-class culture, 1790–1848," in John Clarke, Chas Critcher, and Richard Johnson, eds., *Working Class Culture: Studies in History and Theory* (London: Hutchinson, 1979), pp. 75–102. Also see Stanley Aronowitz and Henry A. Giroux, op. cit., pp. 157–58.

65. Sheila Harty, *Hucksters in the Classroom: A Review of Industry Propaganda in Schools* (Washington, D.C.: Center for Study of Responsive Law, 1979).

66. Herbert M. Kliebard, "The Curriculum Field in Retrospect," in Paul W. F. Witt, ed., *Technology and the Curriculum* (New York: Teachers College Press, 1968), pp. 69–70.

67. See interview with E. P. Thompson, in Henry Abelove, Betsy Blackmar, Peter Dimock, and Jonathan Schneer, eds., *Visions of History* (New York: Pantheon, 1984), p. 16.

FOUR

What Goes on in Classrooms?
Is This the Way We Want It?

Kenneth A. Sirotnik

Considerable time and energy have been expended on developing the formal curriculum of American schooling as though this curriculum would have some impact on or connection with what goes on in public school classrooms. Reams of paper and countless hours of staff time at state and district levels, for example, go into the development and dissemination of curriculum frameworks and guides that set forth educational philosophy statements and general goals and, to varying degrees, the specific objectives, learning activities, teaching strategies, and assessment procedures, which, taken as a whole, comprise a general definition of *curriculum*.[1]

Periodically, chunks of time are also spent by national commissions reviewing the current state of education and developing similar agendas of expectations for schools. Other segments of the community (business groups, social agencies, parents, etc.) also contribute, directly or indirectly, to the formal curriculum through school boards, task forces, surveys, and so forth. It is hard to imagine any greater sum of energy and effort than that being spent in this last decade of the millennium by the nearly countless task forces at federal, state, and local levels busying themselves with the "standards movement" and trying to specify curricular expectations for content, teaching, learning, performance, and the conditions necessary within which to do it all.

Much in the way of human, fiscal, and material resources, then, underlie the architecture of curriculum and, therefore, underlie what I refer to as *curricular expectations*. For example, the goal statement, "To develop students' capacities to be critical and creative thinkers," establishes several curricular expectations for the ways in which teachers might interact with students, students might interact with each other, content and activities might be organized, student learning might be evaluated, and so forth. The goal statement, "To develop students' mental capabilities to store and retrieve information and follow instructions" establishes several curricular expectations that probably overlap very little with those for the previous goal statement. This chapter focuses on the juxtaposition of our expectations for schooling with what, in fact, appears to be happening in classrooms across the United States.

Authors in this volume have made it clear that curriculum proposals have not been entirely uniform over the history of public schooling. Indeed, perhaps the only uniform trend in these expectations has been the swinging back and forth of the curriculum pendulum between the "hard" and "soft," between "back-to-the-basics education" and "progressive education," between "meritocratic" and "democratic" notions of educational "excellence" and "equity." Notwithstanding the more specific, substantive concerns of these competing curricular visions, the pendulum appears to be driven largely by political/ideological constellations of values, beliefs, and human interests.[2] On the one hand are those who see schools as benign agents of socialization, as places where the Mannian and Jeffersonian notions of preparing all the nation's youth both to serve and reap the benefits of their society are played out. On the other hand are those who see schools as malevolent agents of social control, as convenient places where society can reproduce racist and sexist attitudes and socioeconomic stratifications. To be sure, characterizing schooling (and the implied curriculum) in such polarized terms tends to overlook other important sources of disagreement. Kliebard, for example, notes at least three "currents of curriculum reform" counter to the liberal arts/humanist tradition of curriculum in the nineteenth century: the social efficiency emphasis on training students for their future; the child study emphasis on development and growth; and the social reconstructionist emphasis on building a new and better social order.[3]

My point here, however, is not to develop a definitive taxonomy of curricular tensions, but simply to emphasize their existence both historically and currently. Again, this can be no better illustrated than by the ideological fallout from the current "standards movement" and controversies over who controls the public schools, what they are for, and what and how they should teach. These tensions, however categorized, comprise what Goodlad, Klein, and Tye have called the *ideological* domain of curriculum.[4] But, as these authors point

59

out, additional domains must be described and interpreted if one wishes to engage in a thorough curriculum inquiry.[5] For example, what curriculum does one see upon inspecting the written curriculum guides at state and district levels referred to above? What one sees in this *formal* curriculum is not surprising considering the history of crosscurrents in the ideological curriculum. As Boyer and Goodlad both noted in their reports on schooling, "we want it all—the academic/intellectual, career/vocational, social, and personal functions of schooling.[6]

Consider the way these functions have been manifested in general goal statements for schooling. In *A Study of Schooling*, for example, we found that teachers, parents, and students from elementary through secondary levels rated all four goal areas above an average 3.5 rating on a 4-point scale of importance.[7] Even when these respondents were forced to choose between the four goal areas, consensus was not obtained on any one of them. In Table 4.1, we can see that although "intellectual development" is usually the most-emphasized apparent (what seems to go on) or ideal (what ought to go on) function, a substantial number of persons viewed other functions to be of primary importance. Note, for example, the shift in primary importance from intellectual development to the other functions as the respondents shift from the apparent to the ideal perspectives. These data—part of the *perceived* curriculum domain—anticipate a major thematic question of this chapter: Do people actually want a considerably broader curriculum than what really goes on (and what is perceived to go on or be experienced) in schools and classrooms?

TABLE 4.1

Teacher, Parent and Student Views of the Single Most Emphasized Apparent and Ideal Functions of Schooling[a]

		Function							
		Intellectual		Social		Personal		Vocational	
Level & Data Source		Apparent	Ideal	Apparent	Ideal	Apparent	Ideal	Apparent	Ideal
Elementary	N[b]								
Teachers	278	78.5	48.9	12.2	14.0	6.1	33.5	3.2	3.5
Parents	1653	68.9	57.6	13.6	9.3	11.4	24.5	6.0	8.6
Students	1565	61.4	47.1	11.1	13.8	11.9	17.3	15.5	21.8
Junior High									
Teachers	392	64.4	46.7	16.3	13.9	8.7	29.3	10.7	10.1
Parents	5099	56.3	51.1	19.5	9.5	11.2	21.1	13.0	18.2
Students	4655	64.1	38.0	11.7	13.4	11.2	18.3	13.1	30.3
Senior High									
Teachers	653	52.2	45.6	18.0	9.9	6.8	29.7	23.0	14.8
Parents	3961	43.1	46.5	19.0	8.7	10.2	19.3	27.8	25.5
Students	6727	61.6	27.3	10.2	15.9	13.2	25.6	14.9	31.1

[a]Table entries are percentages.
[b]Average number of respondents.

These curricular expectations are manifest in one form or another in virtually all formal curriculum documents at the state level. In analyzing the content of these documents, Goodlad and his associates synthesized a short but impressive array of the most commonly appearing goals for schooling in the United States.[8] (See the Appendix to this chapter.) The list as specified is not to be found in any one formal curriculum document, yet essential features of the list are found in all of them.[9] As Goodlad summarized, "We are not without goals for schooling. But we are lacking an articulation of them and commitment to them."[10] (Will this be the epitaph for Goals 2000 and the current standards movement?)

I emphasize the diverse array of curricular expectations for schooling held by significant constituencies and the often conflicting ideological commitments running through them because they serve in striking contrast to what appears to happen in American classrooms.[11] They serve to illuminate what I must infer to be a chronic case of educational doublespeak—what we say we want and what, in effect, we promote in the name of public school education.

What Goes on in Classrooms?

In reviewing the information upon which much of what follows is based, I realize that these data are nearly two decades old.[12] This poses a considerable problem as to what tense to use in recounting the results. I recall a conversation that I had during the design phase of *A Study of Schooling* with some public school teachers as I explained to them what we planned to do—go in and observe in excess of one thousand elementary and secondary classrooms on three different occasions, looking for the kinds of teacher-student interactions and classroom configurations that appear to characterize the process of teaching and learning. Their response was similar to this: "Typical educational researchers . . . they go and spend a lot of money to find out what we already know—teachers spend most of their time talking to the class or monitoring students as they work on written assignments; students, of course, spend most of their time presumably listening to the teacher or doing in-class assignments."

I then recalled a conversation several years later with some educational researchers as I explained some of our study's observational findings: teachers spend most of their time talking to the class or monitoring students as they work on written assignments; students, thus, spend most of their time presumably listening to the teacher or doing in-class assignments. Their response was, "So, what else is new?"

No one ever said being an empiricist was going to be easy. I have decided to use the present tense and leave it to interested researchers to demonstrate that things have suddenly changed in contrast to nearly a century of previous classroom life. Consider, for example, Cuban's analysis of "constancy and change" in American classrooms from 1890 to 1980.[13] What he found was a lot of constancy and little change. In describing and interpreting nearly 7,000 quantitative, qualitative, and even pictorial accounts of classroom life—including the observational data collected on the 1,016 classes in *A Study of Schooling*—Cuban concludes that "the data show striking convergence in outlining a stable core of teacher-centered instructional activities in the elementary school and, in high school classrooms, a remarkably pure and durable version of the same set of activities."[14]

This is not to say that Cuban did not find any evidence of change over ninety years. He notes, for example, several historians (e.g., Cremin and Spring) who claim that fundamental changes occurred in American classrooms in the 1920s and 1930s under the influence of the progressive education movement. He goes on, however, to note some fairly convincing counterarguments by others (e.g., Bowles and Gintis; Katz; Tyack; and Zilversmit).[15] Cuban then quotes Dewey himself who, around 1950, notes that the progressive movement "is largely atmospheric; it hasn't yet really penetrated and permeated the foundations of the educational institution."[16] We see similar accounts of troubled efforts more recently to fundamentally alter classroom practices in accord with new curriculum standards and more constructivist ways of teaching and learning. A case in point would be California's attempt to reform mathematics education and the disappointing (but not surprising) results of case studies reported in the Fall 1990 issue of *Educational Evaluation and Policy Analysis*.

Regardless of the historical verdict, it seems fair to speculate that classrooms have, to some extent, become a bit more open, loosely structured, less formal places, probably due to child-centered reforms, particularly at the elementary levels of schooling. Nonetheless, descriptions of classrooms based on the earliest observational studies at the turn of the century are remarkably consistent with those based on subsequent and substantial observational studies on up through the late 1970s.[17] In 1912, for example, Stevens interpreted her observational data thus: "The fact that one history teacher attempts to realize his educational aims through the process of 'hearing' the textbook, day after day, is unfortunate, but pardonable; that history, science, mathematics, foreign language, and English teachers, collectively are following in the same groove, is a matter for theorists and practitioners to reckon with."[18] Let us see what the data in *A Study of Schooling* portrayed some seventy years later.[19]

Focusing on average teacher-student interactions at both elementary and secondary levels, about 75 percent of class time is instructional, 20 percent is spent on routines (roll taking, preparation, cleanup, etc.), and the remaining 5 percent is almost evenly divided between discipline/behavioral control and miscellaneous social, noninstructional interactions. Nearly 70 percent of the total class time involves verbal interaction or "talk," mostly in the instructional context. Teachers talk about one-half of the total time in class while students talk less than one-fifth of the time; in effect, teachers out-talk students by a ratio of nearly 3 to 1. The rest of the teachers' time is approximately divided into 10 percent chunks devoted to working alone (usually at their desks), monitoring/observing students, and moving around the classroom.

The modal teacher-initiated, instructional activity—ranging from 18 percent of the time in elementary classes to 28 percent in high school classes—is instructing or explaining, usually to the total class. Only 6 percent of the instructional time is spent asking questions; 5 percent of this time involves direct questioning calling mainly for factual recall and comprehension, while 1 percent is devoted to higher cognitive and affective learning. Providing corrective feedback is rarely noticed (less than 3 percent at elementary and secondary levels); providing guidance, encouragement, or praise is also rare, totaling barely in excess of 3 percent at the elementary level and less than 2 percent at the secondary levels.

Student-initiated interactions with teachers, of any type in any context, occupy one-third of the time in elementary classes and only one-fifth of the time in secondary classes. Much of this time is spent in the instructional context, responding to the teacher (about 15 and 10 percent, respectively, at elementary and secondary levels). Interestingly, only 5 percent of the teachers' time is spent responding to student-initiated interactions. All interactions appear to take place in a relatively neutral affective environment; less than 3 percent of classroom time can be characterized as really positive or negative in tone.

The observation instrument also permitted shifting away from specific teacher-student interactions and focusing on more general classroom configurations of people and activities. These results simply reinforced the above findings. The modal categories of activities involving the most students at any point in time at either elementary or secondary levels are explaining/lecturing by the teacher or working on written assignments. Among the rarest categories of activities involving the fewest numbers of students are demonstration, discussion, reading, role play, and simulation. Whatever the activities in progress, more than a 50 percent likelihood exists that students will be directed by the teacher (usually as a total class group); nearly a 40 percent likelihood of working independently (usually on a class assignment); and less than a 10 percent likelihood of working together in smaller groups on some common task.

Finally, although some differences between classes due to subject matter did occur, these did not mitigate against the general patterns noted already.

The elementary data, however, afforded us the opportunity to estimate the amount of time allocated to the various subject areas commonly taught at this level.[20] These estimates are as follows: English/reading/language arts, 64.0 percent; mathematics, 17.5 percent; science, 8.7 percent; the arts, 5.0 percent; and social studies, 4.9 percent. It is hard to imagine getting much closer to "the basics" than this.

More recently, my colleagues and I went in search of the school curriculum using selected subject areas (mathematics, science, language arts, and social studies) as points of entry into the available literature rather than focusing on instructional practices and classroom interactions as in the *Study of Schooling*.[21] What we found, however, was similar, insofar as little evidence was uncovered that either the planned or enacted curriculum in these content areas has changed in most schools and classrooms in any fundamental way. We also found that there was no content area where even subject-matter scholars were agreed that what was apparently being taught should be taught.

In sum, although there are heroic and exemplary practices in curriculum and instruction in some schools and classrooms across the nation, most of the nation's children and youth are likely exposed to the kind of content, teaching, and learning practices described above.

Is This the Way We Want it?

For whatever reasons, it seems clear that many curricular expectations established by typical arrays of common goals for American public schools enjoy little in the way of empirical support based on what goes on in classrooms. In fact, if these expectations were aligned with typical classroom life, goal statements in the formal curriculum would read more like this: to develop in students the abilities to think linearly, depend on authority, speak when spoken to, work alone, become socially apathetic, learn passively and nonexperientially, recall information, follow instructions, compartmentalize knowledge, and so on.

Is this the way we want it? Obviously, this question is rhetorical and meant to engender critical deliberation on the disjuncture between curricular expectations set in motion by espoused goals and the curricular realities of most classrooms. "Yes," "No," and "Maybe" are all possible answers to the question, depending on high inference arguments rooted in interpretive critiques of the political, symbolic, and periodic nature of educational reform rhetoric. For example, the answer may be a qualified "Yes" if the perennial call to get back to the basics is really a widely shared view of public schooling.[22] There may be some question as to whether "the basics" are being taught well; but, in light of the above summary, getting back to them should be easy.

Many examples could be offered to help illustrate the gap between curricular rhetoric and classroom reality. I will note briefly only two. First, consider the often-stated goal area of critical thinking. Then examine critically the "critical thinking" curriculum that one finds in many classrooms. I believe that much of this curriculum, although certainly a cut above ordinary classroom fare, mostly equates "critical thinking" with Bloom's Taxonomy and/or problem solving of the deductive and inductive variety. Rarely does the curriculum treat critical thinking as a dialectical process of reflective thought and communication, of competent discourse between people having both common and conflicting values, needs, and human interests.[23]

The typical classroom interactions, activities, and climates observed in *A Study of Schooling* were, of course, anything but "critical"—students speaking less than 20 percent of the time in class (and this is usually in response); students rarely conversing with one another or engaging in discussion, role play, simulations, or demonstrations; questions being addressed to students that are preponderantly those demanding only basic recall and comprehension skills; and little affect being generated other than what can be described as "neutral."

A second example, and one intimately related to the acritical nature of classroom life, is the ubiquitous way in which we evaluate the outcomes of teaching and learning. We see how well students can pick the "most correct" answer out of four or five possible answers to relatively artificial, well-structured, mini-problems. Then we standardize all this so that we can compare students to one another more than to what we tried to teach them. We assess student achievement in this fashion in an ambiguous world where most questions are complex, interdependent, and ill structured, and where there are likely to be more "solutions" floating about in search of problems rather than the other way around.[24] To be sure, the recent and relatively sustained reform efforts to move toward more complex performance assessments that reflect higher levels of cognition, curriculum, and instruction are noteworthy; it is too soon to tell, however, whether these efforts will be just one more cycle through the politics of educational reform and the revolving door of reform talk.[25]

In light of the above arguments and data from previous studies, I find the continual displays of lists of lofty educational goals a curious phenomenon. What is the purpose of such lists? What roles are these goals—and the formal curriculum surrounding them—really intended to play? What interests are being served by curriculum documents that essentially gather dust in state and district offices?[26] Do the goals serve to remind us of what we wish we could do and what we ought to be doing in schools, if only we could? Are they beacons of hope in increasingly difficult educational conditions and circumstances? Or perhaps, as some sociologists and organizational theorists might suggest, the formal curriculum is merely a symbolic device whereby, through ceremony and ritual, the revered, multiple functions of schooling are confirmed and, a priori, believed to actually occur.[27] More insidious, perhaps, is the smoke screen provided by this mythology of lofty purpose relative to the supplies and demands—met rather well by schools—of a socially, economically, and politically stratified society.[28]

I leave it to others more situated in curriculum theory and practice than I to question more thoroughly the function of educational rhetoric vis-à-vis educational practice. It seems clear to me, however, that the issues raised herein, problematic as they are specifically for schools, are more fundamentally problems of a political society—a society that uses schools as basic skills training sites for youth, child-care facilities for the community, workplaces for adults, and political footballs for local, state, and federal governments. How, for example, can schools behave constructively and proactively in a society governed by those who would, on the one hand, issue commission reports (like *A Nation at Risk*) suggesting that we are caught in a web of educational mediocrity while, on the other, decrease funded support for public school improvement and advocate subsidies for private schooling?

Not particularly sanguine about the likelihood of profound societal changes, however, I have written this chapter in the effort to promote a kind of "truth in advertising" for those committed to the ideals of equity and excellence in public schooling. It is done with the hope that a more honest alignment of the formal and observed curriculum may provide a more authentic point of departure for a critical dialogue on what schooling ought to be about.

Critical Inquiry in Schools

I am, indeed, hopeful. This hope resides mostly in the vast and latent reservoirs of power and caring represented in the millions of teachers, administrators, district staff members, and college- and university-based educators who can be empowered to engage in school improvement practices through *critical inquiry*.

In other work, my colleagues and I have attempted to explore the potential of critical inquiry and outline the process.[29] Essentially, critical inquiry is a rigorous, time-consuming, collaborative, informed, school-based dialectic around generic questions such as: What is going on in the name of X? (X is a place-holder for things like educational goals and schooling functions; instructional practices like the use of time, tracking students, and achievement testing; organizational practices like leadership, decision making, and communication; etc.). How did it come to be that way? Whose interests are being (and are not being) served by the way things are? What information and knowledge do we have—and need to get—that bear upon the issues? (Get it and continue the dialogue.) Is this the way we want it? What are we going to *do* about all this? (Get on with it.)

These six questions are not just another Organizational Development-type exercise in "needs assessment," "prioritizing," and the like. They are not capable of being "boxed and arrowed" in a linear flowchart. All of these questions can be relevant (and usually are) at any time during critical inquiry. The questions must be thought of as heuristics—much like probes are used in interviews—designed to keep the inquiry alive and productive. The first two questions are intended to remind participants that problems have a present and historical context, and that they must be situated in these contexts in order to be understood. The third question demands of participants that they confront (constructively) the political reality of significant educational issues; that they recognize and contend with embedded values and human interests. The fourth question demands of participants that the inquiry be informed—that knowledge of all types be brought to bear upon the issues. Finally, the last two questions are intended to remind participants that all is not talk; that, notwithstanding the omnipresent ambiguity in educational organizations, action can and must be taken, reviewed, revised, retaken, and so forth.

At the heart of critical inquiry, therefore, is the willingness and ability of people to engage in competent discourse and communication.[30] This is no mean undertaking, especially within and between places called schools and school districts, and potential collaborators in colleges and universities. Strong leadership that empowers rather than disenfranchises participants is required, as is leadership that can effectively facilitate group processes. Much work has been done in the area of group facilitation, and it will not be reviewed here. But I emphasize again that we are not talking about OD-type games that can be packaged and played out by organizational consultants. We are talking about rigorous and sustained discourse wherein people have a good chance of being understood and trust one another as being sincere in their intentions, and the discussion is infused with knowledge of all types, and values and human interests are legitimate issues in the dialogue. To come close to this kind of conversation, people must have real opportunities to enter into the discourse and challenge constructively what others have to say and the basis on which they say it; say how they feel and what their own beliefs, values, and interests are; and participate equally in controlling the discussion.

Clearly, the methodology being advocated consists of informed discourse, a language of empowerment, and experimental action, with the full recognition that education and schooling is a political activity. The human interests being served through the euphemisms of educational rhetoric, therefore, must be called into question continually as part of the inquiry process. As Orwell noted keenly almost half a century ago, "The great enemy of clear language is insincerity. When there is a gap between one's real and one's declared aims, one turns as it were instinctively to long words and exhausted idioms, like cuttlefish squirting out ink. In our age, there is no such thing as "keeping out of politics."[31]

As educators, we need to be critically (and perhaps painfully) aware of what we say we do, what we actually do, and the political and ethical contexts in which we do it. Public education is fundamentally a *normative* enterprise out of which flow major implications for what schools are for, how curriculum is conceptualized and practiced, what constitutes a profession of teaching, how the preparation of educators is conceptualized and practiced, and so on.[32] It is my view, for example, that the answer to the question, "Is this the way we want it?" *should be* "No!" And to the extent that we continue to make impossible—by action or inaction—the conditions and circumstances for critical inquiry in schools, we will never get beyond descriptive questions of "what is" and to the more crucial imperative, "This is the way it *ought* to be!"

With no intent to develop the argument further, I will suggest that an appropriate normative position must begin with our nation's commitment to a democratic conception of the common public school and the guarantee of an excellent and equitable education for all children and youth. Fairly clear moral imperatives can be argued for the practice of public education that flow directly from conceptions of human caring, social justice, and our political democracy—not only in terms of individual and social responsibilities, but in terms of what it means to be human *across* (as well as within) our various cultures and what it means to generate, understand, and act upon knowledge. Kerr, for example, argues that:

> While various kinds of training . . . and specific content emphases . . . might be defensible for particular purposes, by themselves they cannot and should not be expected to substitute for the central task of schooling: education as an initiation into the ways of understanding and inquiring. Education so conceived cannot be improved by courses in critical thinking, for it is itself an initiation into the disciplines of critical thinking. It cannot be passed over in favor of "basic education," for there is no education that is more basic.[33]

I believe that as educators committed to public schooling, we can do no less than realize such curricular expectations in future observations of classroom life.

Notes

1. In John I. Goodlad, M. Frances Klein, and Kenneth A Tye, "The Domains of Curriculum and Their Study," in *Curriculum Inquiry: The Study of Curriculum Practice,* John I. Goodlad and Associates, eds. (New York: McGraw Hill, 1979), the following commonplaces broadly define curriculum: goals and objectives, materials, content, learning activities, teaching strategies, evaluation, grouping practices, and use of time and space.

2. Alex Molnar, "Schools and Their Curriculum: A Continuing Controversy," in *Current Thought on Curriculum*, Alex Molnar, ed. (Alexandria, Va.: Association for Supervision and Curriculum Development, 1985). See also the review by William F. Pinar and C. A. Bowers, "Politics of Curriculum: Origins, Controversies, and Significance of Critical Perspectives," in *Review of Research in Education 18*, Gerald Grant, ed. (Washington, D.C.: American Educational Research Association, 1992).

3. Herbert M. Kliebard, "Three Currents in American Curriculum Thought," in Molnar, *Current Thought on Curriculum,* op. cit., and chapter 2 herein.

4. John I. Goodlad, M. Frances Klein, and Kenneth A. Tye, "The Domains of Curriculum and Their Study," in *Curriculum Inquiry: The Study of Curriculum Practice*, John I. Goodlad and Associates, eds. (New York: McGraw Hill, 1979).

5. Briefly, these are the formal, perceived, operational, and experiential domains— what is written down in state and local curriculum documents, what is thought to be the curriculum by interested persons (particularly teachers), what is observed to happen in classrooms, and what is experienced by students, respectively. The perceived and experiential domains are probably the hardest to deal with empirically, and I treat them only in passing in this chapter. For more extensive treatments, see Barbara Benham Tye, *Multiple Realities: A Study of Thirteen American High Schools* (Lanham, Md.: University Press of America, 1985); John I. Goodlad, *A Place Called School: Prospects for the Future* (New York: McGraw Hill, 1984); Jeannie Oakes, *Keeping Track: How Schools Structure Inequality* (New Haven, Conn.: Yale University Press, 1985); and Kenneth A. Tye, *The Junior High: School in Search of a Mission* (Lanham, Md.: University Press of America, 1985).

6. Ernest L. Boyer, *High School: A Report on Secondary Education in America* (New York: Harper and Row, 1983); Goodlad, *A Place Called School.*

7. The only exceptions were parent and teacher ratings of the importance of the career/vocation function for *elementary* schools; yet these were still above 3.0 on the average. See Betty C. Overman, *Functions of Schooling: Perceptions and Preferences of Teachers, Parents and Students* (A Study of Schooling Technical Report No. 10, 1980, ERIC No. ED 214 880).

8. Goodlad, *A Place Called School*, op. cit., pp. 51–56. See also, Patricia A. Bauch, *States' Goals for Schooling* (A Study of Schooling Technical Report No. 35, 1982); and M. Frances Klein, *State and District Curriculum Guides: One Aspect of the Formal Curriculum* (A Study of Schooling Technical Report No. 9, 1980, ERIC No. ED 214 879).

9. Similar findings were noted by Theodore R. Sizer, *Horace's Compromise: The Dilemma of the American High School* (Boston: Houghton Mifflin, 1984), p. 77.

10. Goodlad, *A Place Called School*, op. cit., p. 56.

11. Take as an illustration the cluster of "vocational goals" and the "enculturation goals" (particularly III.C.4 in the Appendix). One can easily infer the impending ideological conflicts between those seeing schools as benevolent agents for socializing future citizens and those advocating radical social reconstruction as the only viable means for countering the hegemonic agency of schooling. (See Stanley Aronowitz and Henry A. Giroux, *Education Under Siege: The Conservative, Liberal, and Radical Debate Over Schooling* (South Hadley, Mass.: Bergin and Garvey, 1985.) For example, if I were constructing "vocational/career" goals, I would probably end up using language suggesting the emancipation and empowerment of young people through a curriculum of reflection and critique of historical and current social, economic, and political conditions and circumstances. In any case, the array of goals in the Appendix is *not* being suggested as *the* list of "oughts" for American schooling; rather, the list is a convenient means for highlighting discrepancies between the existing and operational curriculum and, it is hoped, provoking a more critical inquiry into both.

12. Data collection took place in the spring and fall of 1977. I first reported the observation summary analyses in "A Study of Schooling Technical Report No. 29," 1981, ERIC No. 214 897; subsequently, they were reported in Kenneth A. Sirotnik, "What You See Is What You Get: Consistency, Persistency, and Mediocrity in Classrooms," *Harvard Educational Review* 53 (1983):16–31.

13. Larry Cuban, *How Teachers Taught: Constancy and Change in American Classrooms 1890–1980* (New York: Longman, 1984).

14. Ibid., p. 238.

15. Ibid., pp. 104–106. See Samuel Bowles and Herbert Gintis, *Schooling in Capitalist America* (New York: Basic, 1976); Lawrence Cremin, *Transformation of the Schools* (New York: Vintage, 1961); Michael Katz, *Class, Bureaucracy and School* (New York: Praeger, 1971); Joel Spring, *Education and the Rise of the Corporate State* (Boston: Beacon, 1972); David Tyack, *The One Best System* (Cambridge, Mass.: Harvard University Press, 1974); and Arthur Zilversmit, "The Failure of Progressive Education, 1920–1940," in *Schooling in Society*, ed. Lawrence Stone (Baltimore, Md.: Johns Hopkins Press, 1976).

16. Cuban, *How Teachers Taught*, op. cit., p. 113; quote is from *Dewey on Education*, Martin Dworkin, ed. (New York: Teachers College Press, 1959), pp. 129–30.

17. Compare, for example Romiett Stevens, *The Question as a Measure of Efficiency in Instruction: A Critical Study of Classroom Practice* (New York: Teachers College Press, Contributions to Education No. 48, 1912) to reports such as E. J. Amidon and J. B. Hough, eds., *Interaction Analysis: Theory, Research and Application* (Reading, Mass.: Addison-Wesley, 1967); Michael Dunkin and Bruce J. Biddle, *The Study of Teaching* (New York: Holt, Rinehart & Winston, 1974); John I. Goodlad, M. Frances Klein, and Associates, *Behind the Classroom Door* (Worthington, Ohio: Jones, 1970); James Hoetker and William P. Ahlbrand, "The Persistence of the Recitation," *American Educational Research Journal* 6 (1969):145–67; and Philip W. Jackson, *Life in Classrooms* (New York: Holt, Rinehart & Winston, 1968).

18. Stevens, "The Question as a Measure of Efficiency," p. 16.

19. Observational data on 129 elementary and 887 secondary classes were collected from a purposive sample of schools from across the nation which varied considerably in terms of school size, economic status of the community, race/ethnicity of the student body, and regional location and characteristics. Each class was observed over a two-week period on three different occasions (full days at the elementary level and full periods at the secondary level). Primary data were collected through the "five-minute interaction" and "classroom snapshot" portions of the observational system. The former feature provided a fairly continuous accounting of how time was spent in the classroom, focusing on the teacher and the interactive process between teacher and students. The latter feature provided an accounting of all people in the classroom in terms of activities in progress and grouping configurations. More details of the observational system can be found in Sirotnik, "What You See Is What You Get."

20. Each elementary class was observed for approximately four hours on each of three days. The four hours were chosen so as to maximize the opportunity to observe instructional activity.

21. Nathalie J. Gehrke, Michael S. Knapp, and Kenneth A. Sirotnik, "In Search of the School Curriculum," in *Review of Research in Education* 18, Gerald Grant, ed. (Washington, D.C.: American Educational Research Association, 1992).

22. And the call is usually loud and clear; a recent example can be found in the report *First Things First: What Americans Expect from Their Public Schools* (New York: Public Agenda Foundation, 1994).

23. See, for example, the critiques by Richard W. Paul, "Critical Thinking: Fundamental to Education for a Free Society," *Educational Leadership* 42 (September 1984):4–14; and "Bloom's Taxonomy and Critical Thinking Instruction," *Educational Leadership* 42 (May 1985):36–39. For an analysis of what critical teaching and learning can be about in a specific subject area, see Walter C. Parker, Michele Mueller, and Laura Wendling, "Critical Reasoning on Civic Issues," *Theory and Research in Social Education* 17 (Winter 1989):7–32.

24. See Norman Frederiksen, "The Real Test Bias: Influences of Testing on Teaching and Learning," *American Psychologist* 39 (1984):193–202; and James G. March, "Model Bias in Social Action," *Review of Educational Research* 42 (1972):413–29.

25. See Larry Cuban, "Reforming Again, Again, and Again," *Educational Researcher* 19 (January–February 1990):3–13.

26. In *A Study of Schooling*, teachers were asked how much influence each of eleven different sources had on what they taught in various subjects. Although some variation was obtained across subjects, percentages of teachers responding "a lot" (versus "some," "little," or "none") to the influence of state and district curriculum guides were in the neighborhoods of 10 percent and 20 percent, respectively. These were in contrast to "a lot" responses generally in the 70 percent to 90 percent range for the source "your own background, interests, and experiences." See M. Frances Klein, *Teacher Perceived Sources of Influence on What Is Taught in Subject Areas* (A Study of Schooling Technical Report No. 15, 1980, ERIC No. ED 214 885).

27. John W. Meyer and Brian Rowan, "Institutionalized Organizations: Formal Structure as Myth and Ceremony," *American Journal of Sociology* 83 (1977):340–63.

28. See, for example, the arguments in Oakes, *Keeping Track*, op. cit.; Clarence Karier, *Shaping the American Educational State, 1900 to Present* (New York: Free Press, 1975); Arthur G. Powell, Eleanor Farrar, and David K. Cohen, *The Shopping Mall High School: Winners and Losers in the Educational Marketplace* (Boston: Houghton Mifflin, 1985); and Joel Spring, *The Sorting Machine: National Education Policy Since 1945* (New York: McKay, 1976).

29. Much of this work can be found in Kenneth A. Sirotnik and Jeannie Oakes, "Critical Inquiry for School Renewal: Liberating Theory and Practice," in *Critical Perspectives on the Organization and Improvement of Schooling*, Kenneth A. Sirotnik and Jeannie Oakes, eds. (Boston: Kluwer-Nijhoff, 1986); Kenneth A. Sirotnik, "Evaluation in the Ecology of Schooling: The Process of School Renewal," in the 1987 Yearbook, Part I, of the National Society for the Study of Education, *The Ecology of School Improvement*, John I. Goodlad, ed. (Chicago: University of Chicago Press, 1987); Kenneth A. Sirotnik, "The School as the Center of Change," in *Schooling for Tomorrow: Directing Reforms to Issues That Count*, Thomas J. Sergiovanni and John H. Moore, eds. (Boston: Allyn & Bacon, 1989); and Kenneth A. Sirotnik, "Critical Inquiry: A Paradigm for Praxis," in *Forms of Curriculum Inquiry*, Edmund C. Short, ed. (New York: State University of New York Press, 1991).

30. The conceptual and practical work of philosophers and activists such as Jürgen Habermas and Paulo Freire is particularly relevant here as it might be applied to the work settings of educators. See Jürgen Habermas, *Communication and the Evolution of Society* (Boston: Beacon, 1979) and Paulo Freire, *Education for Critical Consciousness* (New York: Continuum, 1973). See also, Sirotnik and Oakes, "Critical Inquiry for School Renewal," op cit.

31. George Orwell, "Politics and the English Language," *The Collected Essays, Journalism, and Letters of George Orwell*, vol. 4 in *In Front of Your Nose 1945–1950* (p. 137), Sonia Orwell and Ian Angus, eds. (New York: Harcourt Brace Jovanovich, 1968). Thanks to my colleague Roger Soder for bringing Orwell's essay to my attention.

32. See John I. Goodlad, Roger Soder, and Kenneth A. Sirotnik (eds.), *The Moral Dimensions of Teaching* (San Francisco: Jossey-Bass, 1990).

33. Donna H. Kerr, "Authority and Responsibility," in *The Ecology of School Renewal*, 86th Yearbook of the National Society for the Study of Education, Part I, John I. Goodlad, ed. (Chicago: University of Chicago Press, 1987).

Appendix

A Summary of Typical Educational Goals Espoused for Public Schooling in America

I. *Academic Goals*

A. Mastery of Basic Skills and Fundamental Processes

1. Learn to read, write, and handle basic arithmetical operations.
2. Learn to acquire ideas through reading and listening.
3. Learn to communicate ideas through writing and speaking.
4. Learn to utilize mathematical concepts.
5. Develop the ability to utilize available sources of information.

B. Intellectual Development

1. Develop the ability to think rationally, including problem-solving skills, application of principles of logic, and skill in using different modes of inquiry.
2. Develop the ability to use and evaluate knowledge, i.e., critical and independent thinking that enables one to make judgments and decisions in a wide variety of life roles—citizen, consumer, worker, etc.—as well as in intellectual activities.
3. Accumulate a general fund of knowledge, including information and concepts in mathematics, literature, natural science, and social science.
4. Develop positive attitudes toward intellectual activity, including curiosity and a desire for further learning.
5. Develop an understanding of change in society.

II. *Vocational Goals*

A. Career and Education—Vocational Education

1. Learn how to select an occupation that will be personally satisfying and suitable to one's skills and interests.

2. Learn to make decisions based on an awareness and knowledge of career options.
3. Develop salable skills and specialized knowledge that will prepare one to become economically independent.
4. Develop habits and attitudes, such as pride in good workmanship, that will make one a productive participant in economic life.
5. Develop positive attitudes toward work, including acceptance of the necessity of making a living and an appreciation of the social value and dignity of work.

III. Social, Civic, and Cultural Goals

A. Interpersonal Understandings

1. Develop a knowledge of opposing value systems and their influence on the individual and society.
2. Develop an understanding of how members of a family function under different family patterns as well as within one's own family.
3. Develop skill in communicating effectively in groups.
4. Develop the ability to identify with and advance the goals and concerns of others.
5. Learn to form productive and satisfying relations with others based on respect, trust, cooperation, consideration, and caring.
6. Develop a concern for humanity and an understanding of international relations.
7. Develop an understanding and appreciation of cultures different from one's own.

B. Citizenship Participation

1. Develop a historical perspective.
2. Develop knowledge of the basic workings of the government.
3. Develop a willingness to participate in the political life of the nation and the community.
4. Develop a commitment to the values of liberty, government by consent of the governed, representational government, and one's responsibility for the welfare of all.
5. Develop an understanding of the interrelationships among complex organizations and agencies in a modern society, and learn to act in accordance with it.
6. Exercise the democratic right to dissent in accordance with personal conscience.

7. Develop economic and consumer skills necessary for making informed choices that enhance one's quality of life.
8. Develop an understanding of the basic interdependence of the biological and physical resources of the environment.
9. Develop the ability to act in light of this understanding of the interdependence.

C. *Enculturation*

1. Develop insight into the values and characteristics, including language, of the civilization of which one is a member.
2. Develop an awareness and understanding of one's cultural heritage and become familiar with the achievements of the past that have inspired and influenced humanity.
3. Develop understanding of the manner in which traditions from the past are operative today and influence the direction and values of society.
4. Understand and adopt the norms, values, and traditions of the groups of which one is a member.
5. Learn how to apply the basic principles and concepts of the fine arts and humanities to the appreciation of the aesthetic contributions of other cultures.

D. *Moral and Ethical Character*

1. Develop the judgment to evaluate events and phenomena as good or evil.
2. Develop a commitment to truth and values.
3. Learn to utilize values in making choices.
4. Develop moral integrity.
5. Develop an understanding of the necessity for moral conduct.

IV. *Personal Goals*

A. *Emotional and Physical Well-Being*

1. Develop the willingness to receive emotional impressions and to expand one's affective sensitivity.
2. Develop the competence and skills for continuous adjustment and emotional stability, including coping with social change.
3. Develop a knowledge of one's own body and adopt health practices that support and sustain it, including avoiding the consumption of harmful or addictive substances.

4. Learn to use leisure time effectively.
5. Develop physical fitness and recreational skills.
6. Develop the ability to engage in constructive self-criticism.

B. *Creativity and Aesthetic Expression*

1. Develop the ability to deal with problems in original ways.
2. Develop the ability to be tolerant of new ideas.
3. Develop the ability to be flexible and to consider different points of view.
4. Develop the ability to experience and enjoy different forms of creative expression.
5. Develop the ability to evaluate various forms of aesthetic expression.
6. Develop the willingness and ability to communicate through creative work in an active way.
7. Seek to contribute to cultural and social life through one's artistic, vocational, and avocational interests.

C. *Self-Realization*

1. Learn to search for meaning in one's activities, and develop a philosophy of life.
2. Develop the self-confidence necessary for knowing and confronting one's self.
3. Learn to assess realistically and live with one's limitations and strengths.
4. Recognize that one's self-concept is developed in interaction with other people.
5. Develop skill in making decisions with purpose.
6. Learn to plan and organize the environment in order to realize one's goals.
7. Develop willingness to accept responsibility for one's own decisions and their consequences.
8. Develop skill in selecting some personal, lifelong learning goals and the means to attain them.

II
Curriculum and Planning

FIVE

Models of Curriculum Planning

George J. Posner

How does one plan a curriculum? For many students of curriculum, the answer to this question constitutes a major goal of their studies. In this chapter, we will attempt to determine the ways educators have addressed this question.

Many students find answers to this question in the curriculum literature to be somewhat confusing. The so-called Tyler Rationale prescribes four "questions" that any curriculum planner must address;[1] Taba provides seven "steps" to follow;[2] Walker's "naturalistic model" describes three "elements" of curriculum planning;[3] Johnson's "model" represents the curriculum as an "output of one system and an input of another";[4] and Goodlad's "conceptual system" describes three different "levels of curriculum decision making.[5]" What accounts for this wide array of answers to the question of curriculum planning? Or, alternatively, are they answers to different questions?

In this chapter, I argue that this wide variety of approaches to curriculum planning can be partially understood as a set of responses to different curriculum planning questions. We will examine answers to three different questions related to curriculum planning:

1. The procedural question: What steps should one follow in planning a curriculum?
2. The descriptive question: How do people actually plan curricula; i.e., what do they do?
3. The conceptual question: What are the elements of curriculum planning and how do they relate to one another conceptually?

In order to understand curriculum planning more fully, we must examine not only different curriculum planning questions, but also different curriculum planning perspectives. I maintain[6] that one perspective on curriculum planning has dominated curriculum thought and, thus, influenced not only the answers to the three questions outlined above, but even the formulation of these questions. I then examine briefly another perspective that not only answers the three questions in radically different ways but also argues for the priority of other questions and, in particular, underlying ideological questions.

The Technical Production Perspective

The dominant perspective is best represented in Ralph Tyler's work. Tyler's rationale for curriculum planning has been a major influence on curriculum thought since its publication in 1949.[7] It has been interpreted by most educators as a procedure to follow when planning a curriculum; that is, as an answer to the *procedural* question, what steps does one follow in planning a curriculum?[8] Because of its importance, I examine its features.

Tyler suggests that when planning a curriculum, four questions must be answered. First, planners must decide what educational purposes the school should seek to attain. These "objectives" should be derived from systematic studies of the *learners*, from studies of contemporary life in *society*, and from analyses of the *subject matter* by specialists. These three sources of objectives are then screened through the school's *philosophy* and through knowledge available about the *psychology of learning*. The objectives derived in this way should be specified as precisely and unambiguously as possible, so that evaluation efforts can be undertaken to determine the extent to which the objectives have been attained.

Second, planners must determine what educational experiences can be provided that are most likely to attain these purposes. Possible experiences are checked for consistency with objectives and for economy.

Third, the planner must find ways that these educational experiences can be organized effectively. The planner attempts to provide experiences that have a cumulative effect on students. Tyler recommends that experiences build on one another and enable learners to understand the relation among their learning activities in various fields. In so doing, attention should be given to the *sequence* of experiences within each field (e.g., mathematics) and to *integration* of knowledge across fields. Certain concepts, skills, and values are sufficiently complex to require repeated study in increasing degrees of sophistication and breadth of application, and sufficiently pervasive to help the student relate one field to another. The planner uses these *organizing elements* to provide the sequence and integration the curriculum requires.

Finally, the planner must determine whether the educational purposes are being attained. Objective evaluation instruments (e.g., tests, work samples, questionnaires, and records) are developed to check the curriculum's effectiveness. The criterion for success is behavioral evidence that the objectives of the curriculum have been attained.

The Tyler Rationale and, in particular, his four questions regarding the selection of educational purposes, the determination of experiences, the organization of experiences, and the provision for evaluation, have dominated thought on curriculum planning for nearly fifty years. Moreover, the publication of Tyler's syllabus represents not the beginning of its influence but, instead, a distillation of ideas derived from the founders of the curriculum field in the first quarter of this century.[9] In fact, Bobbitt's seminal books on curriculum[10] and, in particular, their focus on the development of specific objectives based on scientific methods, established the basic approach to curriculum planning continued by Tyler in his syllabus.

Since its publication in 1949, educators representing a wide range of orientations have turned to the Tyler Rationale for an analysis of the procedural questions of curriculum. Test-oriented behaviorists such as James Popham use it explicitly for the selection of objectives.[11] Course planning guides, such as those by Posner and Rudnitsky[12] and by Barnes,[13] use elaborations of the Tyler Rationale as the basis for their handbooks. Even humanistic educators such as Elliott Eisner, who have spent considerable effort criticizing Tyleresque objectives and evaluation approaches, when it comes time to discuss procedure, revert (perhaps unknowingly) to a step-by-step approach that differs only slightly from the Tyler Rationale.[14]

Perhaps the major reason for the domination of curriculum planning by the Tyler Rationale is its congruence with our assumptions about both schooling and curriculum planning. Unquestioned acceptance of these assumptions even makes conceiving of an alternative to this basic approach impossible.

Schooling is assumed to be a process whose main purpose is to promote or produce learning. Students are termed *learners*; objectives are conceived in terms of desirable learning; evaluation of the school's success is targeted almost exclusively on achievement test scores; "educational" goals are distinguished from "noneducational" goals by determining if they can be attributed to learning;[15] "curriculum" is defined (not by Tyler but by his followers, such as Goodlad) in terms of "intended learning outcomes."[16] Thus, schooling is conceived as a *production system,* in which individual learning outcomes are the primary product. After all, if learning is not what schooling is for, then what could be its purpose?

Further, curriculum planning is assumed to be an enterprise in which the planner objectively and, if possible, scientifically develops the means necessary to produce the desired learning outcomes. There is no place for personal biases and values in selecting the means; effectiveness and efficiency in accomplishing the ends are primary. This *means-end reasoning* process serves as the logic underlying all rational decision making. Educational experiences are justified by the objectives that they serve.

This means-ends rationality is taken a step further when ends not only serve as the primary justification for means but also as the starting point in planning. After all, as this perspective rhetorically asks, How can one decide on educational means except by referring to educational ends? The use of a travel metaphor convinces planners that they must determine the destination before deciding on the route they should take and thus assume a *linear* view of means and ends.

This means-ends rationality leads to the assumption that it is a *technical* matter to decide such issues as instructional method and content, a matter best reserved for people with technical expertise about the methods and content optimally suited for particular objectives. As technical experts, they have the responsibility of disallowing their own values from clouding the objectivity of their work; that is, they try to keep their work value free. Even decisions about purpose are conceived as a technical matter based on specialized knowledge which experts develop, either from studies of learners and contemporary society or by virtue of their subject matter expertise. After all, who is better equipped to make these decisions than the people with the most knowledge relevant to the decisions?

I refer to views on curriculum planning that uncritically accept these assumptions as based on a *technical production* perspective. They are *technical* if they consider educational decisions to be made objectively, primarily by experts with specialized knowledge; they are *production oriented* if they view schooling as a process whose main purpose is to produce learning, in which the logic of educational decison making is based on means-ends reasoning. Furthermore, they are *linear* technical production models if they require the determination of ends before deciding on means.

The technical production perspective has served as a basis for a variety of models intended to guide curriculum thought (particularly when complemented with the assumption of linearity). I examine some major analyses of curriculum planning that accept the central assumptions of this perspective but differ in important ways. They can be interpreted as answers to the basic procedural, descriptive, and conceptual questions of curriculum planning.

The Procedural Question

As a basic approach to curriculum development, the Tyler Rationale was used as a point of departure by many writers sympathetic to its general orientation. Some of these writers, most notably Hilda Taba, attempted to refine it by adding steps and by further subdividing each of Tyler's four planning steps.[17]

Taba

Taba's work represents the most detailed elaboration of the Tyler Rationale. Like Tyler, she explicitly accepts the assumption that curriculum planning is a technical (or "scientific") rather than a political matter.

> *Scientific* curriculum development needs to draw upon analysis of society and culture, studies of the learner and the learning process, and analyses of the nature of knowledge in order to determine the purposes of the school and the nature of its curriculum.[18] (Emphasis added.)

She argues for a "systematic," "objective," "scientific," and "research-oriented" approach to curriculum development, requiring "objectivity."[19] She laments that

> the tradition of rigorous scientific thinking about curricula is not as yet well established. . . . Curriculum designs are espoused on the basis of their concurrence with a set of beliefs and feelings, rather than by their verifiable consequence on learning or their contribution to educational objectives.[20]

Her view of curriculum development "requires expertness of many varieties,"[21] including

> technical skills in curriculum making, mastery of intellectual discipline, the knowledge of social and educational values which underlie educational decisions, and the understanding of the processes of educational decisions and human engineering.[22]

Like Tyler, Taba also accepts the assumption that learning is the ultimate purpose of schooling. Her focus on the selection and organization of "learning experiences," her preoccupation with learning outcomes and learning objectives in her evaluation approach, her emphasis on learning theory in the selection of objectives, and the centrality of learning objectives in her curriculum development model all imply a learning-oriented view of schooling. As Taba succinctly states: "curricula are designed so that students may learn."[23]

Her approach is more prescriptive than Tyler's regarding the procedure of curriculum planning. Whereas Tyler offers four questions that must be addressed, Taba forcefully argues for the *order* of her seven steps.

> If one conceives of curriculum development as a task requiring orderly thinking, one needs to examine both the order in which decisions are made and the way in which they are made to make sure that all relevant considerations are brought to bear on these decisions. This book is based on an assumption that there is such an order and that pursuing it will result in a more thoughtfully planned and a more dynamically conceived curriculum. This order might be as follows:
>
> Step 1: Diagnosis of needs;
> Step 2: Formulation of objectives;
> Step 3: Selection of content;
> Step 4: Organization of content;
> Step 5: Selection of learning experiences;
> Step 6: Organization of learning experiences; and
> Step 7: Determination of what to evaluate and of ways and means of doing it.[24]

Thus, Taba's model is not only a technical-production model but also linear.

Schwab

Joseph Schwab takes issue with several of Tyler's and Taba's views, including the focus on objectives, the clear separation of ends and means, and the insistence on an orderly planning procedure.[25] In order to characterize planning more appropriately, he offers curriculum planners the concept of "deliberation."

> Deliberation is complex and arduous. It treats both ends and means and must treat them as mutually determining one another. It must try to identify, with respect to both, what facts may be relevant. It must try to ascertain the relevant facts in the concrete case. It must try to identify the desiderata in the case. It must generate alternative solutions. It must make every effort to trace the branching pathways of consequences which may flow from each alternative and affect desiderata. It must then weigh alternatives and their costs and consequences against one another, and choose, not the *right* alternative, for there is no such thing, but the *best* one.[26]

Schwab's concept of deliberation is the centerpiece of this "practical" language for developing curricula. For Schwab, this practical language is preferable to the single-theory approaches that have dominated curriculum development. Single-theory curricula, such as a science curriculum based on Piagetian theory, a course on the novel as a source of vicarious experience, or a math curriculum based on set theory, are fundamentally flawed, according to Schwab. They are flawed in three ways in their reliance on a single principle or theory for curriculum planning.

1. *The Failure of Scope* . . . One curriculum effort is grounded in concern only for the individual, another in concern only for groups, others in concern only for cultures, or communities, or societies, or minds, or the extant bodies of knowledge. . . . No curriculum, grounded in but one of these subjects, can possibly be adequate or defensible.[27]

2. *The Vice of Abstraction* . . . All theories, even the best of them . . . , necessarily neglect some aspects and facets of the facts of the case. A theory (and the principle derived from it) covers and formulates the *regularities* among the things and events it subsumes. It abstracts a general or ideal case. It leaves behind the nonuniformities, the particularities, which characterize each concrete instance of the facts subsumed. . . . Yet curriculum is brought to bear, not on ideal or abstract representations, but on the real thing, on the concrete case, in all its completeness and with all its differences from all other concrete cases on a large body of facts concerning which the theoretic abstraction is silent.[28]

3. *Radical Plurality* . . . Nearly all theories in all the behavioral sciences are marked by the coexistence of competing theories. . . . All the social and behavioral sciences are marked by the "schools," each distinguished by a different choice of principle of enquiry, each of which selects from the intimidating complexities of the subject matter the small fraction of the whole with which it can deal. . . . The theories which arise from enquiries so directed are, then, radically incomplete, each of them incomplete to the extent that competing theories take hold of different aspects of the subject of enquiry and treat it in a different way. . . . In short, there is every reason to suppose that any one of the extant theories of behavior is a pale and incomplete representation of actual behavior. . . . It follows that such theories are not, and will not be, adequate by themselves to tell us what to do with actual human beings or how to do it. What they variously suggest and the contrary guidances they afford to choice and action must be mediated and combined by eclectic arts and must be massively supplemented, as well as mediated, by knowledge of some other kind derived from another

source. . . . It is this recourse to accumulated lore, to experience of actions and their consequences, to action and reaction at the level of the concrete case, which constitutes the heart of the practical. It is high time that curriculum do likewise.[29]

Curriculum planning can be no more based on single theory than can other complex decisions such as choosing a spouse, buying a car, or selecting a president.

In order to repair these deficiencies of theory as a basis for curriculum planning, Schwab offers the "eclectic" as an approach to curriculum planning. Theory brings certain features of a phenomenon into focus, helping the curriculum planner to understand better that aspect of the situation. For example, Piagetian theory helps the planner understand the student's cognitive development. Curriculum planners trained in the "eclectic arts" not only can use theory to view phenomena, they also know which aspects of the phenomenon each theory obscures or blurs. For example, Piagetian theory obscures the social psychology and sociology of classrooms. Finally, the eclectic arts allow the curriculum planner to use various theories in combination "without paying the full price of their incompleteness and partiality."[30]

In order to avoid the "tunnel vision" associated with any theory, Schwab recommends not only a deliberative method for curriculum planning but also suggests the participants in this process. According to Schwab, at least one representative of each of the four "commonplaces" of education must be included, i.e., the learner, the teacher, the subject matter, and the milieu. (Note the similarity with Tyler's three "sources.") In addition to representation of each of these four commonplaces, a fifth perspective, that of the curriculum specialist (trained in the practical and eclectic arts), must be present.[31]

Schwab's approach to curriculum planning accepts some assumptions of the Tyler Rationale and rejects others. Curriculum planning for both Schwab and for Tyler is a technical matter requiring expert knowledge. The representatives of each of the four commonplaces are to be experts in each commonplace. For example, the representative of "the learner" is to be a psychologist, not a student. Furthermore, the curriculum specialist is to be a trained expert in the arts of the practical and of the eclectic (as Schwab defines them).

Furthermore, Schwab's indictment of theory-driven curriculum development would lead to a general condemnation of any predetermined framework to be used as a starting point. Because theories and ideologies are both belief systems that reduce the educational planner's ability to discern the complexities of a particular situation and to consider alternatives, they must be avoided. Thus, Schwab, too, requires a nonideological posture for curriculum development.

Although technical in its reliance on experts, Schwab's approach rejects the constraints inherent in the clear separation of means and ends, insisting instead on a more flexible, varied, and iterative planning process. Deliberation is not characterized by specified procedural steps carried out in prescribed order.

The Descriptive Question

The problem with the Tyler Rationale, according to some writers, is that it does not describe what curriculum developers actually do when they plan a curriculum. Of course, none of the procedural models were intended to describe the actual work of practitioners. Nevertheless, the difficulties in implementing the Tyler Rationale suggest possible inherent weaknesses in its basic approach. Perhaps a more useable approach to curriculum planning can derive from an empirical investigation of curriculum development projects, particularly studies of notably successful ones.

Walker

Decker Walker's naturalistic model is based on this premise.[32] This model consists of three elements: "the curriculum's *platform*, its *design*, and the *deliberation* associated with it."[33]

The *platform* is "the system of beliefs and values that the curriculum developer brings to his task and . . . guides the development of the curriculum. . . . The word *platform* is meant to suggest both a political platform and something to stand on."[34]

Platforms consist of "conceptions," "theories," and "aims." Beliefs about what is learnable and teachable (such as "creativity can be taught") and, more generally, about what is possible, are conceptions. Beliefs about what is true are theories; for example, a belief that "motivation to learn is primarily based on the individual's history of successes and failures." Beliefs about "what is educationally desirable" are "aims"; for example, "we should teach children to learn how to learn." In addition to these three carefully conceptualized and explicit types of planks in a curriculum's platform, two others are significant. "Images" of good teaching, of good examples, and of good procedures to follow, though not explicit, often are influential in curriculum decisions. For example, exemplary literary works, physics problems, and teaching techniques often underlie curricular choices.[35]

In contrast with Tyler and Taba, Walker, like Schwab, prefers to view a curriculum not as an object or as materials but as the events made possible by the use of materials. It follows, then, that a curriculum's design can be specified by "the series of *decisions* that produce it . . . [that is] by the choices that enter into its creation."[36]

87

The process by which design decisions are made is "deliberation," a concept borrowed directly from Schwab. Deliberation, for Walker, consists of *"formulating decision points, devising alternative choices* at these decision points, *considering arguments* for and against suggested decision points and . . . alternatives, and finally, *choosing* the most defensible alternative. . . ."[37] Alternatives are compared in terms of their consistency with the curriculum's platform, and, when necessary, additional sources of information (or "data") are sought.

When planners resolve difficult decisions stemming from contradictions in the platform, they may preserve and accumulate these "precedents" for later situations, much as the courts use prior decisions as a basis for present decisions by simply citing precedent. Walker refers to "the body of precedents evolved from the platform" as "policy."[38] He thus distinguishes the principles accepted from the start (i.e., the platform) from those that evolve from the application of the platform to design decisions.

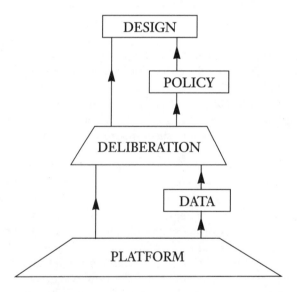

Figure 5.1. A schematic diagram of the main components of the naturalistic model.[39]

Walker's model, like Schwab's, is less linear than Tyler's or Taba's and relegates objectives to a less central position in the curriculum development process. Objectives constitute only one type of one component (i.e., aims) of Walker's platform. There is, thus, no clear separation of ends and means. Walker's platform includes beliefs about both. Although he does not specifically mention ideological beliefs as possible planks in a platform, he does not preclude them. But, like Schwab, Walker's model leaves unquestioned the assumption regarding the primary role of experts. Surprisingly, Walker never raises the issue of the discrepancy between the platforms of the project director, on the one hand, and of the teachers or students who ultimately must negotiate the meaning of the curriculum, on the other hand.

As Walker himself points out:

> While Schwab's view of curriculum making [and Walker's model which is based on it] is less linear and comprehensive and more flexible and dialectical than the Tyler rationale, the same kinds of questions that Tyler asks need to be addressed at some point in deliberation. We still need to ask what our purposes are and how we might achieve them; we still need to find out if we have done so in our particular setting. Schwab himself recognizes this, and so the dominance of the Tyler Rationale in thinking about curriculum making seems to be unshaken.[40]

The Conceptual Question

Tyler begins his book by denying that his Rationale is "a manual for curriculum construction"; it does not describe "the steps to be taken . . . to build a curriculum."[41] Instead, he regards his Rationale as one "conception of the elements and relationships involved in an effective curriculum."[42] In fact, he concludes his book with an often overlooked statement:

> The purpose of the rationale is to give a view of the elements that are involved in a program of instruction and their necessary interrelations. The program may be improved by attacks beginning at any point, providing the resulting modifications are followed through the related elements until eventually all aspects of the curriculum have been studied and revised.[43]

Therefore, although often regarded as a linear procedural model, the Tyler Rationale is most appropriately viewed as a conceptual model. Just as Taba elaborated the Tyler Rationale into a detailed procedural model, Goodlad and Johnson have used Tyler's work as a point of departure for their own conceptual models.

Goodlad

John Goodlad, one of Tyler's students in a course using the Rationale as a syllabus, adopts virtually every aspect of Tyler's model in his own conceptual model.[44] He shares Tyler's concern with providing an account of rationality in curriculum planning, attributing "human frailty" to any departures from the strict means-ends logic.

However, Goodlad's major contribution to curriculum models is his elaboration of the Tyler Rationale, describing three levels of curriculum planning. The *instructional level* is closest to the learner. Curriculum planning at this level involves selecting the "organizing centers for learning"[45] (the stimuli to which the student responds), and deriving the precise educational objectives from the institution's educational aims.

The level above the instructional level Goodlad terms *institutional*. Curriculum planning here involves formulating general educational objectives and selecting illustrative learning opportunities.

The highest level Goodlad terms *societal*. Curriculum planning at this level is done by the "institution's sanctioning body,"[46] such as a school board. This body is responsible for formulating educational aims in order to attain a set of selected values.

Since Goodlad first proposed the three levels, his model has been substantially elaborated by extending them to include the state and federal levels.[47] The notion of levels contributes significantly to curriculum planning models by providing a technical production perspective on the question: Who should decide what in curriculum planning? This seemingly political and ethical question is thus answered as a technical question, that is, Who has access to the appropriate "data sources"?[48]

Johnson

Mauritz Johnson's conceptual model evolved over a ten-year period from 1967 to 1977. His early (and most often cited) version in 1967 stipulated a definition of curriculum as "a structured series of intended learning outcomes," and carefully distinguished between often confused concepts, including curriculum development and instructional systems, platforms and theories, sources of curriculum and criteria for curriculum selection, curricular and instrumental content, curriculum evaluation and instructional evaluation, and education and training.[49] But he recognized that his 1967 model was incomplete: It did not provide for goal setting, instructional planning, evaluation, situational (or frame) factors, or managerial aspects. Johnson's 1977 P-I-E model (i.e., planning, implementation, and evaluation) provided this needed elaboration.[50] Although highly complex, it can be reduced to the basic claim that rational planning involves a planning, an implementation, and an evaluation aspect (the "linear technical" dimension), each of which can, in turn, be planned, implemented, and evaluated (the managerial dimension). Thus, one can plan, implement, and evaluate a given planning process, a given approach to implementation, and a given evaluation strategy. Furthermore, all of these activities are governed by a set of natural, temporal, physical, economic, cultural, organizational, and personal "frame factors" that act as resources and restrictions on both curriculum and instruction.[51]

The basic P-I-E model, when applied to curriculum and instruction, results in five elements: goal setting, curriculum selection, curriculum structuring, instructional planning, and technical evaluation. The comparability of Johnson, Goodlad, Tyler, and Taba is clear.

TABLE 5.1

Johnson's model compared with two other analyses of curriculum and curriculum development.[52]

Elements Johnson (1977)	Questions Tyler (1950)	Steps Taba (1962)
Goal setting	What educational purposes?	Diagnosing needs
Curriculum selection		Formulating specific objectives Selecting content
Curriculum structuring		Organizing content Checking balance and sequence
Instructional planning	What educational experience? How to organize educational experiences?	Selecting learning experiences Organizing learning experiences
Technical evaluation	How to determine whether purposes are attained?	Determining what and how to evaluate

Not only do Johnson's concepts correlate closely with Tyler's questions, Goodlad's data sources, and Taba's steps, but at a deeper level Johnson shares all the major assumptions of the technical production models. Johnson argues that the theoretical (i.e., understanding) and the ideological (i.e., advocacy) "exist in . . . conceptually distinct worlds."[53] Further, he claims that technology may be influenced by theory and research, but not by ideology. Like Tyler, Johnson disavows Taba's linear planning approach, but assumes a means-end logic underlying rational planning. Furthermore, like Goodlad, Johnson's concept of curriculum as "intended learning outcomes" makes clear his assumption of learning as the primary purpose of schooling.

A Critical Perspective

The works of Tyler, Taba, Walker, Schwab, Johnson, and Goodlad represent the dominant thinking in the curriculum field regarding curriculum planning. Although dissent is found among these works regarding specific aspects of the technical production perspective, I have argued that they share many assumptions. The same point regarding family resemblances and family squabbles might be made for another perspective that has emerged as a response to the dominant viewpoint. As might be expected, this perspective, termed *critical*, takes issue with each of the basic assumptions of the dominant view. This perspective is best understood by examining how it responds to each of the three questions posed by the dominant viewpoint. For this analysis, I focus on Paulo Freire's work.

Freire

Paulo Freire's criticism of schooling practices is captured by his analysis of the banking metaphor.

> Education . . . becomes an art of depositing, in which the students are the depositories and the teacher is the depositor. Instead of communicating, the teacher issues communiques and makes deposits which the students patiently receive, memorize, and repeat. This is the "banking" concept of education, in which the scope of action allowed to the students extends only as far as receiving, filing, and storing the deposits.[54]

The view of curriculum planning that follows from the banking concept of schooling is "that the educator's role is to regulate the way the world 'enters into' the students."[55] The curriculum planner's task is "to organize a process . . . to 'fill' the students by making deposits of information which *he* considers to constitute true knowledge."[56] (Emphasis added.) Thus, Freire is drawing attention to the dominant perspectives's assumption that those with special knowledge make decisions for and about those without that knowledge. This criticism echoes the view of Tyler's critics who claim that his Rationale embodies a "factory" metaphor in which the student is merely the raw material to be fashioned by the "school-factory" into a "product drawn to the specifications of social convention."[57] The critical perspective then, asks us to question the authority of experts in curriculum planning and urges a more democratic relationship between teacher and student.

As an alternative to the curriculum-planning models associated with the technical-production perspective, Freire describes the "emancipatory" approach. Briefly stated, the approach emphasizes "critical reflection" on one's own "concrete situation."[58] In contrast with the banking method, Freire's "problem-posing"[59] method requires "dialogue"[60] in which teacher and student are "critical coinvestigators."[61] They both

> develop their power to perceive critically the way they exist in the world with which and in which they find themselves; they come to see the world not as a static reality, but as a reality in process, in transformation.[62]

This "critical consciousness"[63] is developed in a series of steps. First, a team of educators helps the people in a particular place to develop "generative themes"[64] (e.g., culture, underdevelopment, alcoholism) that represent their view of reality. From this set of themes, a group of professional educators and nonprofessional local volunteers, through "dialogue," cooperatively identify themes to be used for the curriculum and develop instructional materials for each of them. Then the materials are used in "culture circles"[65] as the focus of discussions. The materials, including readings, tape-recorded interviews, photographs, and role plays, are designed to reflect characteristics of people's lives and, thus, to stimulate critical reflection about their lives. Ultimately this process leads to "praxis," action based on "critical reflection,"[66] the goal of Freire's pedagogy.

Although Freire's approach does, in fact, answer the procedural question with a step-by-step approach to curriculum planning, it conflicts with most of the basic assumptions of the technical production model. This approach takes issue with the authority of "experts" in curriculum planning decisions. "Dialogue" requires "critical reflection" by both teacher and student as "coinvestigators."[67] The problem-posing approach also requires dialogue with the "students" for the formulation of the generative themes to be used in the curriculum; "[t]his view of education starts with the conviction that it cannot present its own program but must search for this program dialogically with the people."[68]

The "ideological pretense of the value-free curriculum decision"[69] is abandoned. Abandoning this pretense also undermines the assumption that curriculum development involves purely technical decisions. Thus, curriculum planning is not viewed as a technical matter, but instead as a political and ideological matter. The purpose of the process is for the people "to come to feel like masters of their thinking by discussing the thinking and views of the world explicitly and implicitly manifest in their own suggestions and those of their comrades."[70] Similarly, the end product is not a learning outcome but critical reflection and action upon reality. Of course, learning outcomes, such as ability to reflect critically, are desirable. But political action by the oppressed aimed at their own liberation is the ultimate purpose. To reduce this approach to a set of intended learning outcomes would be to miss its point of political activism.

It is important to note that Freire is at once providing (1) a *descriptive* account of the way teaching and, by implication, curriculum planning is conducted, through the use of the banking metaphor; (2) a *procedural* model by which curriculum should be planned, that is, through the use of generative themes; and (3) a *conceptual* analysis of the fundamental elements of education and their relationships, through an analysis of key concepts including oppression, liberation, critical reflection, dialogue, problem-posing, praxis, humanization, the theme, codification, object/subject, among others.

Many other scholars approach curriculum planning from a critical perspective. They ask descriptive and conceptual questions which implicitly attempt to undermine the assumptions on which the technical production perspective rests:

1. What knowledge does the curriculum count as legitimate, and what does it not count?[71]
2. To what extent does the curriculum organization presuppose and serve to "legitimate a rigid hierarchy between teacher and taught?"[72]
3. How does the curriculum enable the school to achieve its primary purposes of social reproduction and hegemony?[73]
4. Who has the greatest access to high-status and high-prestige knowledge?
5. Who defines what counts as legitimate knowledge?[74]
6. Whose interests does this definition serve?[75]
7. How do the dominant forms of evaluation serve to legitimize curriculum knowledge?[76]
8. To what extent is the schools' sorting function more significant than its educative function?
9. What are the features of the schools' hidden or implicit curriculum, and to what extent does this aspect of schooling mediate teaching the official curriculum?

Underlying these questions is a view that "power, knowledge, ideology, and schooling are linked in ever-changing patterns of complexity."[77] These questions implicitly criticize the view that schools and their curricula can, should, or do provide students with experiences objectively derived from or even primarily justified by a set of learning objectives and that the primary purpose of schooling is to facilitate learning in individuals. For those critical theorists concerned primarily with the hidden curriculum, the official curriculum is largely trivial in its significance when compared with implicit messages in the schools' rules and norms of behavior. To other critical theorists, the official curriculum is significant not because of its explicit learning objectives, but because of the knowledge it legitimizes and delegitimizes, the effects of this process, and the manner in which it distributes this knowledge differently to different classes of students.

Thus, a critical perspective, although it attempts to provide answers to the procedural, descriptive, and conceptual questions, focuses on another question, a quesiton that takes issue with a fundamental assumption of the technical production perspective: If all curriculum decisions are inherently ideological and political, and therefore an objectively based means-end rationality is itself an ideological pretense, then what is the mode of curriculum rationality?

Ideological Questions

Writers taking the strict technical production perspective attempt to produce ideologically neutral models. Johnson, for example, using ideas from Scheffler, draws a sharp distinction between definitions of curriculum (together with the models on which they are based) which are "programmatic (doctrinal)" and those which are "analytic" or explanatory.[78] He is clearly impatient with confusions of this sort that have plagued the curriculum field. Unfortunately, according to Johnson, various curriculum writers use their curriculum planning models as ideological "platforms" rather than as descriptions or explanations.[79] These platforms have exhorted educators to offer experiences "having a maximum of lifelikeness for the learner,"[80] "to develop individuals along lines consonant with our ideal of the authentic human being,"[81] and to discipline "children and youth in group ways of thinking and acting,"[82] to mention just three notable examples.

These ideological positions are to be avoided and even condemned, according to writers from the technical production perspective. They claim that it is up to the school, not curriculum theorists, to decide what purposes the school curriculum should adopt. Recall that Tyler's first question is followed by a set of technical procedures that any school can use to decide on its purposes. Thus, the rationality of curriculum planning from the technical production perspective is not based on a particular purpose, ideology, or doctrine, but on deciding that purpose objectively and systematically and then by using effective and efficient means for accomplishing it. Therefore, this perspective considers ideological questions to be a procedural step in curriculum planning, not questions to be answered definitively for all curriculum planning.

Critical theorists, however, disagree. Freire regards the development of a critical consciousness to be the only defensible pedagogical purpose. Giroux agrees with Herbert Marcuse that curriculum planning must be committed to "the emancipation of sensibility, reason and imagination, in all spheres of subjectivity and objectivity."[83] Each critical theorist has his or her own ideology. Each agrees that the dominant perspective's pretense of neutrality serves to divert criticism of the dominant ideology.

Conclusion

The problem with studying a topic by answering a series of questions should now be apparent. The questions one asks and what one accepts as a legitimate answer channel the investigation. We have seen how this happens in curriculum models. Different models can be seen as answers to different questions or as different notions of legitimate answers.

Each of the two perspectives examined has made a contribution. The technical production perspective has provided a view of rationality in curriculum planing and has outlined what techniques a curriculum planner needs to master. The critical perspective raises our consciousness regarding the assumptions underlying our work in curriculum. By giving us ground to stand on outside the dominant approach, it has enabled us to examine critically the technical production perspective, to identify its blind spots, and to understand its political and social implications.

Study of curriculum models thus provides two necessary and complementary elements: curriculum development technique and a curriculum conscience. Knowing how to develop a curriculum is what I term *technique*. Being able to identify the assumptions underlying curriculum discussion, that is, understanding what is being taken for granted, is what I term a *curriculum conscience*. A curriculum planner without the former is incompetent ("but what can you do?") and without the latter is ungrounded ("merely a technician"). A "complete" curriculum planning model is not what the field needs. The field needs curriculum planners not only able to use various models but also aware of the implications of their use.

Notes

1. Ralph W. Tyler, *Basic Principles of Curriculum and Instruction* (Chicago: University of Chicago Press, 1949).

2. Hilda Taba, *Curriculum Development: Theory and Practice* (New York: Harcourt, Brace & World, 1962).

3. Decker Walker, "A Naturalistic Model for Curriculum Development," *School Review* (November 1971):51–65.

4. Mauritz Johnson, "Definitions and Models in Curriculum Theory," *Educational Theory* 17, 1 (April 1967):127–40. Also reprinted in Bellack and Kliebard, 3–19.

5. John I. Goodlad and Maurice N. Richter, Jr., "Decisions and Levels of Decision Making: Process and Data-Sources," in Arno A. Bellack and Herbert M. Kliebard, eds., *Curriculum and Evaluation* (Berkeley, Calif.: McCutchan, 1977), 506–16.

6. See similar arguments by Daniel Tanner and Laurel N. Tanner, *Curriculum Development: Theory into Practice*, 2d ed. (New York: Macmillan, 1980); William H. Schubert, *Curriculum: Perspective, Perdigm, and Possibility* (New York: Macmillan, 1986); and Decker F. Walker and Jonas F. Soltis, *Curriculum and Aims* (New York: Teachers College Press, 1986).

7. Tyler, op. cit.

8. Note, however, that Tyler himself disagrees with this interpretation. I discuss this matter further in a subsequent section.

9. See Kliebard's chapter 2 herein for a thorough treatment of recent curriculum history.

10. Franklin Bobbitt, *The Curriculum* (Boston: Houghton Mifflin, 1918); and Franklin Bobbitt, *How to Make a Curriculum* (Boston: Houghton Mifflin, 1924).

11. W. James Popham and Eva L. Baker, *Systematic Instructing* (Englewood Cliffs, N.J.: Prentice-Hall, 1970).

12. George J. Posner and Alan N. Rudnizsky, *Course Design: A Guide to Curriculum Development for Teachers*, 3d ed. (New York: Longmen, 1987).

13. Douglas Barnes, *Practical Curriculum Study* (London: Routledge & Kegan Paul, 1982).

14. Elliot W. Eisner, *The Educational Imagination* (New York: Macmillan, 1985).

15. This distinction is attributable to Mauritz Johnson, not Tyler, who avoided definitions in his book. See Mauritz Johnson, *Intentionality in Education: A Conceptual Model of Curricular and Instructional Planning and Evaluation* (Albany, N.Y.: Center for Curriculum Research and Services, 1977), pp. 47–48.

16. Goodlad, op. cit.

17. Taba, op cit.

18. Ibid., p. 10.

19. Ibid,. pp. 462–66.

20. Ibid., p. 463.

21. Ibid., p. 479.

22. Ibid., p. 480.

23. Ibid., p. 12.

24. Ibid., pp. 11–12.

25. Joseph J. Schwab, *The Practical: A Language for Curriculum* (Washington, D.C.: Naitonal Education Association, 1970). A shorter version was published in *School Review* 78 (November 1969):1–24, and reprinted in several anthologies, including Bellack and Kliebard, op. cit., pp. 26–44.

26. Ibid., p. 36.

27. Ibid., pp. 21–23.

28. Ibid., pp. 25–26.

29. Ibid., p. 28.

30. Ibid., p. 12. Joseph J. Schwab, "The Practical 3: Translation into Curriculum," *School Review* 79 (1973):501–22.

31. Ibid.

32. Walker, op. cit.

33. Ibid., p. 22.

34. Ibid., p. 52.

35. Ibid.

36. Ibid., p. 53.

37. Ibid., p. 54.

38. Ibid., pp. 57–58.

39. Ibid., p. 58.

40. Walker and Soltis, op. cit., p. 51.

41. Tyler, op. cit., p. 1.

42. Ibid., p. 1.

43. Ibid., p. 128.

44. Goodlad and Richter, op. cit.

45. Ibid., p. 510.

46. Ibid., p. 510.

47. See, for example, Michael W. Kirst and Decker F. Walker, "An Analysis of Curriculum Policy Making," *Review of Educational Research*, 41, 5 (1971):479–509. Also reprinted in Bellack and Kliebard, op. cit., pp. 538–68.

48. Goodlad and Richter, op. cit., p. 506.

49. Johnson, 1967, op. cit.

50. Johnson, 1977, op. cit.

51. Ibid.

52. Ibid., p. 34.

53. Ibid., p. 9. Paulo Freire, *Pedagogy of the Oppressed* (New York: Seabury Press, 1970).

54. Ibid., p. 58.

55. Ibid., p. 62.

56. Ibid., pp. 62–63.

57. Herbert M. Kliebard, "Bureaucracy and Curriculum Theory," in Bellack and Kliebard, op. cit., p. 613.

58. Freire, op. cit., p. 52.

59. Ibid., p. 66.

60. Ibid., p. 76.

61. Ibid., p. 97.

62. Ibid., p. 7.

63. Ibid., p. 54.

64. Ibid., p. 86.

65. Ibid., p. 113.

66. Ibid., pp. 52–53.

67. Ibid., p. 68.

68. Ibid., p. 118.

69. Henry A. Giroux, "Toward a New Sociology of Curriculum," in Henry A. Giroux, Anthony N. Penna, and William F. Pinar, eds., *Curriculum and Instruction* (Berkeley, Calif.: McCutchan, 1981), p. 106.

70. Freire, op. cit., p. 118.

71. Michael F. D. Young, "An Approach to the Study of Curricula as Socially Organized Knowledge," in Michael F. D. Young, ed., *Knowledge and Control* (London: Collier-Macmillan, 1971). Also in Bellack and Kliebard, op. cit., pp. 254–85; Giroux, op. cit., p. 104.

72. Young, op. cit., p. 36.

73. Ibid.; Giroux, op. cit.

74. Young, op. cit.

75. Giroux, op. cit.

76. Ibid.

77. Ibid., p. 194.

78. Johnson, 1967, op. cit., pp. 4–5.

79. Ibid., p. 5.

80. Harold O. Rugg, ed., *The Foundations of Curriculum-Making*, 26th Yearbook of the National Society for the Study of Education (Part II) (Bloomington, Ind.: Public School Publishing Co., 1972), p. 18.

81. Robert S. Zais, *Curriculum: Principles and Foundations* (New York: Harper and Row, 1976), p. 239.

82. B. Othanel Smith, William O. Stanley, and J. Harlan Shores, *Fundamentals of Curriculum Development*, rev. ed. (Yonkers-on-Hudson, N.Y.: World Book Co., 1957), p. 3.

83. Giroux, op. cit., p. 106.

SIX

Multicultural Curricula:
"Whose Knowledge?" and Beyond

Susan E. Noffke

A t the 1991 meeting of the American Educational Research Association, a paper presentation by Violet Harris on, "Helen Whiting and the Education of Colored Children 1930–1960: Emancipatory Pedagogy in Action" included a rich description of an important educator, interesting in several ways.[1] First, there was a clear use of African and African American culture in the works that Helen Whiting developed. Having read about current efforts at an African and African American Infusion Project[2] and about Afrocentrism,[3] I was struck by the similarity, at least at the level of addressing the current controversy, over whose knowledge ought to be in the curriculum. I had earlier come across work from the 1930s[4] which seemed to be focused on developing curricula from a Native American perspective. I wondered how widespread such "multicultural" efforts were.

Two other aspects to Helen Whiting's work were also salient. Perhaps because of the gross inequities in funding for schools for African American children during the 1930s, or perhaps as a result of the influence of such progressive era educational work as the project method, unit teaching, or the idea of building curriculum from the world of the child, the work Harris described seemed to differ from some current curricula in two distinctive ways. First, the relationship of the learner to knowledge in the earlier era appeared to be more than that of "recipient" of a "given" content. Second, Whiting seemed to be working toward a particular definition of the role of teachers that would make them more guides of inquiry than dispensers of information. I had earlier read an autobiographical work by Septima Clark[5] that describes not only the use of African words and African-influenced dialects in teaching; it also projects an image of teaching that emphasizes the creativity and resourcefulness of the teacher, rather than the availability of resources. I wondered to what extent such conceptions of the learner and the teacher were common to multicultural curriculum efforts. My ongoing look at attempts to create curriculum materials in this area did not lead me to be too optimistic.

This chapter analyzes several examples of multicultural projects from two earlier periods, the 1930s and the 1940s, and offers a look at recent curriculum developments in light of them. The term *multicultural* is here used in a very broad sense, recognizing the many differences in meanings for the term.[6] I have chosen these eras in order to highlight an important reality. While many scholars trace current multicultural efforts to the turmoil of the 1960s, there has been a long tradition of making the curriculum more responsive to the fact that we are a diverse nation, and one in which the patterns of racism, sexism, class bias, and other forms of oppression have played important roles. These early descriptions are then compared to examples from current efforts in this area. These efforts are examined in relation to three central questions: (1) In addition to the inclusion of different content knowledge, what, if any, are the distinguishing characteristics of the organization of the curriculum or the nature of knowledge? (2) What is the implied or explicitly stated relationship between the learner and knowledge? and (3) What is the role of the teacher evident in the curriculum?

Considering the span of time involved in this study, I have varied the kinds of documents used for analysis. They include works from the 1930s located through extensive searches of educational journals of the time, and documents from the 1940s produced by the National Council for the Social Studies and the National Education Association. The latter documents report efforts and ideas about intergroup or intercultural education. Current documents analyzed here include curriculum guides and teaching materials. The difference in source material is to a certain extent necessary, but it also provides a range of ways of looking at curriculum. It is important to note, too, that I am not suggesting that the selected works are typical of general school activity for the time, nor that they are models. Rather, they are examples that may help us see patterns in historical and contemporary efforts in this area.

Such patterns, it is argued, may have implications for current efforts in multicultural curriculum development.

In the Center during Depression and Progressivism

When looking through the major educational journals of the pre–World War II progressive era, the reader could pretend for long periods of time that diversity was not an issue in the United States. The progressive education movement's leaders were relatively silent on the issue of diversity.[7] While the problem of the version of apartheid present in the United States, segregation, does emerge, especially in relation to schools (but rarely in relation to the violent ways in which the separation of race, class, and gender were maintained), the overall impression is that diversity, especially racial diversity, was not an issue. It is within this context that the works described below were authored.

An article by Horace Mann Bond in a 1935 issue of the *Journal of Negro Education* highlights and evaluates many of the ongoing efforts to reform school curricula for African American children in the south.[8] The work of Carter G. Woodson and the Association for the Study of Negro Life and History in "a long and arduous campaign to introduce materials dealing with Negro life into the schools" is noted. So are the efforts of the Commission of Interracial Cooperation in "efforts designed to reform attitudes and policies of white schools."[9] The third kind of curriculum reform described is the process of statewide curriculum revision, then gaining momentum in the South. Following what were called the "conventional steps in curriculum revision," states were involved in "pupil activities, teachers' committees, 'specialist' service furnished by the state colleges and department of education, worked into the program of experiment, trial and adoption over a period of years."[10] While the first two types of curriculum reform receive a good measure of critique, it is the third, the process of "scientific curriculum making" through "activity analysis" that receives the greatest attention. Bond notes that

the method of "activity analysis" in the construction of a curriculum presupposes an elastic, democratic social order in which there are no artificial barriers set against the social mobility of the individual. . . . Beginning with such a theory . . . any activities peculiar to Negro children, and so susceptible to inclusion in a "Negro" curriculum, concede the falsity of the initial premise. . . . The conflict is in the application of a procedure, theoretically founded on equalitarianism, to a practical situation which is shot through with inequality.[11]

It is not only the curriculum efforts of the "social efficiency"[12] progressives that are rejected. Bond's critique reaches deeply into the fundamental functions of educational systems, perhaps responding to the challenge of the social reconstructionists to build "the new social order"[13]:

> Let us confess that the schools have never built a new social order, but have always in all times and in all lands been the instruments through which social forces were perpetuated. If our new curriculum revision is to do better, it must undertake an acceptance of the profound social and economic changes which are now taking place in the world.[14]

Instead of building curriculum from the world as it is, Bond advocates rational choices over social and economic issues of the time, seeming to imply a focus on the *processes* which ought to be part of the curriculum for children: "An honest and rational course of study will give children an opportunity to make the sane choices, and the inclusion of such matter in curricula may be quite as important to the next generation as instruction in 'the beauty of the birds and bees.'"[15]

Bond's comments are reflective to a large extent of the intense debate during this period over the directions education ought to take, both within the African American communities and within the society as a whole. His positions on both the process of curriculum decision making and on the relationship of the schools to issues of social and economic justice seem relevant to work in multicultural curriculum development today.

It is important here to note that although connections to ideas and works developing within the dominant curriculum orientations can be made, African American educational efforts must not be subsumed under the progressive label. Horace Mann Bond is but one of several African American scholars and activists who worked at developing ideas about curriculum directly related to the needs of African American communities. Such curriculum theorizing, as Watkins points out, "is inextricably tied to the history of the Black experience in the United States. Black social, political, and intellectual development in all cases evolved under socially oppressive and politically repressive circumstances involving physical and intellectual duress and tyranny."[16] While journals such as W. E. B. DuBois's *The Crisis*, offer commentaries on progressive educational innovations—for example, on the Montessori Method[17]—such reports are alongside those dealing with social and political struggle, including continuing attention to the predominance of lynching as a means of repression.[18]

In addition to a rich tradition of writings about curriculum and education in general, many reports of actual practices with children can be found. *The*

Negro History Bulletin, begun in 1937 with Carter G. Woodson as managing editor, is filled with information on African American history. But it is also clearly focused on providing concrete examples of work in schools and resources for children, teachers, and parents. Articles contain visions of teaching and learning not unlike those common in writers such as Dewey:

> Education should develop the child on all sides and teach him to live democratically within a social group. The ultimate goal should be the ability of the whole group as individuals to live in a spirit of understanding, permitting each group to make a worthy contribution to the "Good Life."
>
> Children must be inspired, they must be stimulated, they must be lifted to the best that is in them. Teachers can do this by guiding them to straight thinking as a logical approach to the solution of their problems, giving them a true history to base their aspirations upon, teaching them not to sidetrack facts, but to study them intelligently, and instructing them to think, learn, feel and work to the fullest and best that is in them.[19]

Projects described in the pages of this journal emphasize building from children's questions, cooperative plan making, cooperative group work, and involved research by children and the integration of the arts, ideas not uncommon during the time. Yet their base is not in the study of the development of the child, but in the critique of the existing social system, including the lack of inclusion of "Negro contributions" in the school curriculum.[20]

An article describing a curriculum project in Atlanta appeared in the March 1935 issue of *Progressive Education*, one of the few issues of that journal which directly incorporated issues related to the diversity of U.S. society. Among the many articles dealing with efforts both to address the needs of "minority" groups within the United States and to understand other cultures, are several that describe what could be seen as curriculum reform projects. In one such report, Helen Whiting (the Assistant State Supervisor of Elementary Schools of Georgia, and a member of the editorial board of the *Negro History Bulletin*) recounts her work in social studies with fourth and fifth graders at an Atlanta University summer session in 1934.[21]

In some ways the work in that summer institute was not different from many other reports of progressive education projects of the time. Children were involved in pursuing topics emanating from their own interest, stimulated by the teacher. They sought information, with the help of the teacher, and drew on community resources. They integrated the arts with other subject areas, preparing concrete objects and presentations which were shared with their peers and with members of the community. All through the process, the children were the decision makers, with the teacher's primary role being one of resource gatherer and guide. Students were directly connected to their work; they were active seekers of knowledge, growing in academic areas, but also in their sense of self-direction.

Many of these characteristics of curriculum and teaching can be seen in similar writings from this era, especially those that describe work resonating with William Heard Kilpatrick's "project method"[22] or similar to work in the Dewey School.[23] One marked difference is in the content of the children's study. Both the fourth and fifth graders began their work with discussion of the local African American community and its resources. The fourth grade went on to study aspects of the geography and history of Africa, while the fifth grade focused their attention on what would now be called African American history. In summing up the program's activities, Whiting offered comments which seem to bear a great deal of similarity to some of the current debates over the justification for multicultural education. After noting that the children did make "appreciable growth in language arts and the content subject," she emphasizes their development in aesthetics and the effect it had:

> If from these units has been instilled in these Negro boys and girls respect for their cultural heritage, and something of the idea that joy and the true art of living are of far more enduring worth and hold less uncertainty than material gain, their summer will mean more to America than mere academic gain.[24]

In Whiting's work there is a different content from that to which the majority of children of the era were exposed. Knowledge was not only integrated across subject areas and directly related to the needs established through consideration of the children's interests; it was directly related to their experiences as African Americans. While the progressive education movement generally seemed to emphasize building from the experiences of the child, it is a child as child—not as one whose particular cultural identity influences the selection and organization of knowledge. The relationship of the child to knowledge is, as in "progressive" notions of the curriculum, a close one, with the children assuming much responsibility for their learning. It is also one mediated and directed by their own identities and the communities in which they live.

Perhaps because Whiting was writing about her own efforts, it is sometimes difficult to see what her role as teacher of the children was. The article's primary attention was on the children's work. Yet there is a sense in which she does outline the teacher's work. In the initial stages of the project, the teacher, through discussion, is clearly the stimulator of interest. She also is responsible for helping the children gain access to information, sometimes typing out copies of entries in reference books in short supply for the students to read and discuss. Taken overall, the impression is one of teacher as facilitator of the children's own efforts.

While there is comparatively little reference to similar efforts in the dominant journals of the time, there is enough there and in such journals as *The Negro History Bulletin* and *The Crisis* to indicate that attempts to create school experiences reflective of the diverse groups in our country have a long history. Efforts such as those of Violet Harris,[25] Joan D. Ratteray,[26] and Ronald E. Butchart[27] in uncovering both emancipatory practices and materials deserve further attention. While the presence of alternative versions to answering the "whose knowledge" question may be evident, it is also important to note that there are also alternative conceptions of the relationship of the learner to knowledge and of the role of the teacher. The presence or absence of such conceptions in contemporary work might signify more than just changing styles of educational discourse.

In Wartime, Peacetime, and Times of Change: Between Cultures

The 1940s was a time when considerable attention was paid to the issue of increasing intolerance in U. S. society. This was also the era in which multiculturalist interests took the form of intergroup or intercultural education. Cook, in summarizing efforts taken under this label, identifies a common core: "all are interested in democratic human relations, in full citizen rights for all minority peoples, and in indoctrinating youth along these lines."[28] He also notes that many of the studies of such projects took the form of action research. Indeed, many of the authors associated with intercultural education can also be found in the early action research literature.[29] According to Oleneck, one striking characteristic of the intercultural education work was in the construction of the meaning and implications of "difference." While there was a recognition of the existence and value of subcultures within society, there was a primary focus on "promoting respect for and appreciation of individuals *in spite of* or *regardless of* differences, rather than the priority of differences as such."[30] The focus on the individual rather than the group may have been a reflection of general trends in the social sciences affecting education at the time—away from social psychological and sociological orientations and more toward an individualistic humanism and later cognitive science. However, this shift in focus may have played a significant role in the development of curriculum, producing an emphasis not on the political, economic, and social histories of oppressed groups, but rather on promoting understanding among individuals.

An important document in the intercultural education movement was the yearbook of the National Council for the Social Studies, *Democratic Human Relations*.[31] Self-descriptions of current practice as well as observational studies form the basis of the book, and there is considerable emphasis on the process of curriculum development in intercultural education. Using an overall framework for curriculum that progresses in phases (orientation, selection and organization of content, planning learning activities, and evaluation), the editors provide both a rich description of practice and an understanding of how those practices came to be.

In some of the reports of practice, there is a sense that the autonomy of the teacher was an integral part of the ability to respond to the needs of the children: one child's tears over ethnic slurs influences the curricular focus for the next year. Yet this change in the topic of study was not the sum total of the responsibility of the teacher. The authors note: "fortunately this teacher's concept of study went beyond imparting knowledge." In describing further the classroom teacher's work, the authors emphasize: "knowledge alone does not affect either our feeling or thinking as effectively as we assume."[32] They conclude: "Perhaps it is this tendency to rely upon the mastery of knowledge alone and the failure to provide directly for learnings other than informational that are responsible for the contemporary doubts about the power of teaching."[33] Perhaps it was these thoughts that led the authors to conclude:

> Current practices usually devote much time to verbal allegiance to democracy and friendship. But such general protestation must be supplemented by concrete understanding of what democracy means in a variety of social relations and by practice in democratic living in school. If democracy is to be lived, not just given lip service, more pupil participation and more attention to habits, emotional reactions, and ways of thinking will be necessary in the American classroom.[34]

Many of the ideas presented in *Democratic Human Relations* seem to be drawn from an earlier volume, *Americans All*, sponsored by the National Education Association along with the National Council of Teachers of English and the Society for Curriculum Study.[35] This book, full of rich descriptions of many projects in intercultural education, is framed in terms an overall conception of the teacher:

> The American teacher who cares about his work and not just about his paycheck is dedicated to preparing his students according to their abilities for responsible and adequate activity in their worlds. This activity, he hopes, will be both mental and physical, both emotional and objectively analytic, both political and economic. . . . His job is to provide educational opportunities which his pupils can make use of according to their abilities. He stands ready with information, with guidance, with the example of his own conduct to supply his students' needs and to make them aware of further needs.[36]

In *Democratic Human Relations*, the authors lay out a basic framework for curriculum development in intercultural education.[37] However, in the earlier collection of actual projects, *Americans All*, we can see evidence of projects that emanate not so much from the direction and materials provided by central planners, but from the work of individual teachers with groups of children. Looking at one project, "Rediscovering Folkways,"[38] is a way to get a closer look at the knowledge, the relationship of the learner to that knowledge, and the conception of the teacher's role embedded in these practices. In this article, we see a basic question about literary and folk epics and their origins evolve into a class study, extending over several weeks, involving high school students in a search through their own and others' folk tales. As in the previous section, the role of the teacher seems at times invisible; students' own search for knowledge, connected to their own experiences, is primary. The teacher-author describes the outcomes of this project:

> New understanding of their own folk came to a number of students and pride in a hitherto shamefacedly acknowledged heritage. The desire to conform to the accepted pattern and the eager attempt to measure up in every way to the American concept of scholastic values causes many a student from foreign-born parents to silence the very life blood in his veins lest he become an object of ridicule.[39]

In addition to comments about the learnings for the students and suggestions as to how the original project was modified over time, there is a summary of implications for teachers and for intercultural education in general. As Appy puts it:

> The chief weakness of our work was that we were content to produce without taking a long view. . . . Yet the responsibility for securing for the student some meaningful value in the future for that which he creates usefully today lies with the teacher. Lacking that surety, there is often no greatly valuable creation in the present. Until hundreds of projects such as ours can become more than interesting exercises in the recording and reliving of a long dead past, and until their utilization forges a strong link with the future, they are as meaningless for us as a calico pony to the Chinook Indian hurtling his Packard along the pine-shadowed road toward the reservation.[40]

The author's comments speak to the need for efforts in multicultural education to be future oriented, a call echoing the previously cited words of Bond,[41] and focused on their meanings for children. There were, no doubt, "hundreds of projects" such as those reported here. Whether they, taken together,

109

represent a distinct framing of questions of knowledge, pedagogy, and the teacher's role in the construction of meaning for students remains to be seen. The future is still in the making.

Decentering and Recentering the Curriculum

In recent years, there has been a lengthy and at times acrimonious debate over the notion of "centering" curriculum in ways that place Euro-American culture less in the limelight. If one relied solely on the kind of materials surveyed for the previous sections, for example, the reports of work in multicultural education in a recent edition of *Educational Leadership*,[42] or some of the prominent writers on multicultural education,[43] one could find efforts which seem very similar to the documents analyzed here. However, the current context has one thing that previous eras did not have: the wide availability of curriculum materials. Recent curriculum projects have been directed at developing classroom materials which offer a wide range of responses to the question of "whose knowledge."[44]

Works in these areas seem to come from two distinct sources: private agencies, sometimes concerned with one particular group,[45] and local school district, primarily urban, attempts to deal with multiculturalism.[46] In the earlier works, it is clear that for the teacher and students, curriculum development involved an interrelatedness of questions of *what* to study with *how* such study should take place. The existence of published materials need not impose a split between curriculum and pedagogy—a reduction of questions of "how to" to technical steps taken *after* the "what" question has been addressed. While the realm of multiculturalism in contemporary materials has expanded to women's issues and to a whole range of human "differences," the dominant mode or vision of the nature of curriculum development has narrowed.

The Portland Public Schools materials, for example, present an interesting collection of approaches, not just to multicultural education, but to the issue of the relationship of the student to knowledge and to the role of the teacher. Created primarily to assist teachers, "in their acknowledgment of Hispanic Heritage Month," the lessons are interdisciplinary and are part of a larger project to create materials designed "to increase students' understanding and appreciation of the history, culture and contributions to society of different ethnic groups."[47] Much of the content and organization of knowledge cannot be said to be different from other curricula that do not specifically deal with multicultural issues. Objectives are listed as, "the students will . . ." and lessons follow a standard format of listing the amount of time to be devoted, the materials, introductory background knowledge for the lesson, detailed procedures for the teacher to follow (also given in imperatives: "Teacher will . . .," "Give children simple oral directions . . ."), evaluation strategies, and follow-up suggestions. The content of the lessons, especially those for the early grades, seems to emphasize the accumulation by students of facts about the geography, language, history, and culture of Hispanic peoples, disseminated, albeit through interesting activities, by the teacher and by a series of worksheets.

While this can easily be seen to be in direct contrast to the kinds of activities from earlier periods, a closer look at contemporary curriculum reveals interesting patterns. There is a sixth-grade unit plan that models closely a classic "inquiry," involving students in theory building and data collection. There are thought-provoking units in the section for grades 9–12 that involve the students in dialogue and writing activities over important political questions. The authors of this section emphasize that "though there are no easy answers or quick fixes to the issues raised . . . we hope that students will be more aware of the questions, concerns and possible solutions to the dilemmas presented."[48] These lessons offer opportunities for both teacher and students to share and analyze their own positions on issues. The teacher is not, in one series of lessons, an impartial "chair" for the debate, but an example of how one argues through issues.

While some aspects of the curriculum are parallel to earlier efforts in that they stress the analysis of issues and the development of critical thinking, the overall pattern is one of prespecified procedures and outcomes. For example, in grades 3–5, children are to write letters to gather information about specific countries. The procedures say, "teacher may decide to which country a student will write" and "designate beforehand the information you want students to share and the format in which you want the information shared."[49]

Similar patterns may be found in the project Respecting Ethnic and Cultural Heritage (REACH) materials, an approach to multiculturalism developed under ESEA Title IV funding.[50] The secondary school materials, which are designed to be accompanied by inservice training, follow an interesting pattern of progression from human relations skills development through cultural self-awareness studies (leading to a cultural fair), and include extensive study of several nonwhite ethnic groups. The activities suggested allow students to explore a wide variety of instructional activities and engage in discussion and small-group projects. Lesson formats are again standard, with objectives, background information, and directions for the teacher—including study questions with suggested answers. In one section, pretests and posttests are provided, which include some essay writing, though short-answer, "matching" questions dominate.

Beyond "Whose Knowledge?"

Over the past twenty years a vast literature on multicultural education has been developed, covering a host of aspects of the topic. Substantial contributions have been made in the areas of theory development, policy analysis, textbook studies, bibliographic works, curriculum development, and implementation strategies. Alongside that has been much work in the areas of "critical," "emancipatory," or "empowering" pedagogy.[51] Yet there has been little attempt to systematically pursue questions about the nature of knowledge presented in curricula developed to address concerns about multicultural education, the intended relationship of the learner to such curricula, or the role of the teacher in multicultural curriculum.

The analysis presented here is only a beginning point in pursuing vital work in multicultural curriculum. Many multiculturalists emphasize pedagogy and outline alternative conceptions of curriculum development.[52] Yet one of the major obstacles to realizing their goals may be that there is such a predominance of a model of curriculum development and use that reduces knowledge to behavioral objectives, curriculum planning to rigid steps isolating aims from means, and teachers' work to the implementation of the plans of outsiders.[53] Especially within a context of state policy emphasizing standards and testing, the broad goals of multicultural education for greater social justice may be subverted at the level of practice. While current reform efforts have resulted in substantive changes in whose knowledge is represented in the curriculum, that knowledge is often "packaged" within conventional ways of thinking about curriculum and curriculum making. While some efforts, such as those of the creators of the 9–12 section of the Portland materials, do present a view of knowledge as problematic and socially constructed, there is also a great deal of emphasis in current multicultural curricula on knowledge that is merely an exchange of one set of "givens" for another. It does not emanate, necessarily, from the interests of the students; it is "out there" to be learned, although sometimes connected to the learners' and teachers' lives. The teacher's role, while again mixed, is primarily that of skillful dispenser of externally determined knowledge.

Multicultural efforts are inherently linked to the current context of teaching. Subsuming multiculturalism under practices that take major decisions about "whose knowledge" further away from the hands of teachers and parents and yet leave resources and responsibility clearly in local laps makes the importation of prepacked curricula look attractive.[54] This look back at earlier efforts to respond to issues of diversity is not intended to hold up a supposed universal of a social reconstructionist version of progressive education as a model for contemporary multicultural curriculum development. Rather, it is meant to raise questions about the ways in which multicultural curricula are to be formed. This is not only a question of "whose knowledge?"—although clearly this struggle is important. It is also a question of the children's relationship to knowledge and one of the nature of the teacher's role. Teachers and others who provide multicultural curricula need examples, yes. But they also need alternative ways of thinking through issues in curriculum planning, ones which go beyond those of scientific curriculum making. Curriculum making is an inherently political activity. In seeking to reform current curriculum, it may be wise to seek new ways of configuring the process of change. Without such efforts, even the best of innovations can be reduced to a purely technical conception of teaching and learning. In multicultural curriculum making it may be wise to keep in mind the words of Audre Lorde: "The master's tools will never dismantle the master's house."[55] Let us continue the search for new tools.[56]

Notes

1. Violet J. Harris, *Helen Whiting and the Education of Colored Children 1930–1960: Emancipatory Pedagogy in Action*. Paper presented at the Annual Meeting of the American Educational Research Association, Chicago, 1991.

2. Mwalimu j. Shujaa, *Teachers' Responses to Planned Change: The Implications of Normative Framing and Perception*. Paper presented at the Annual Meeting of the American Educational Research Association, Boston, 1990.

3. See Molefi K. Asante, *Afrocentricity* (Trenton, N.J.: Africa World Press, 1988), and "The Afrocentric Idea in Education," *Journal of Negro Education* 60, 2 (1991).

4. *Progressive Education* 9, 2 (1932).

5. Septima Clark, *Ready from Within* (Trenton, N.J.: Africa World Press, 1986/1990).

6. See Christine E. Sleeter and Carl A. Grant, "An analysis of Multicultural Education in the United States," *Harvard Educational Review* 57, 4:421–443; and Susan E. Noffke, "Curriculum for Multicultural Education," in *International Encyclopedia of Education*, 2d ed., Torsten Husen and T. Neville Postlethwaite, eds. (Oxford: Pergammon, 1994).

7. Ronald K. Goodenow, "The Progressive Educator, Race and Ethnicity in the Depression Years: An Overview," *History of Education Quarterly* 15, 4 (Winter 1975).

8. Horace Mann Bond, "The Curriculum and the Negro Child," *Journal of Negro Education* 4, 2 (April 1935).

9. Ibid., p. 161.

10. Ibid., p. 161.

11. Ibid., pp, 167–68.

12. Herbert M. Kliebard, *The Struggle for the American Curriculum, 1893–1958*, 2d ed. (New York: Routledge, 1995).

13. George S. Counts, *Dare the Schools Build a New Social Order?* (New York: John Day, 1932).

14. Bond, op. cit., p. 168.

15. Ibid., p. 168.

16. William H. Watkins, "Black Curriculum Orientations: A Preliminary Inquiry," *Harvard Educational Review* 63, 3 (Fall 1993).

17. Jessie Fauset, "The Montessori Method," *The Crisis: A Record of the Darker Races* 4, 3 (July 1912).

18. The section, "Along the Color Line" was a regular department of *The Crisis*. It reported events across a broad range of issues.

19. Elise P. Derricote, "The Negro Teacher at Work," *Negro History Bulletin* 2, 1 (October 1938).

20. Lillian A. Duckett, "A Method for Studying Negro Contributions to Progress," *Negro History Bulletin* 2, 1 (October 1938).

21. Helen Adele Whiting, "Negro Children Study Race Culture," *Progressive Education* 12, 3 (March 1935).

22. William Heard Kilpatrick, *The Project Method* (New York: Teachers College, Columbia University, 1918).

23. John Dewey and Evelyn Dewey, *Schools of Tomorrow*, (New York: E. P. Dutton, 1915).

24. Whiting, op. cit., p. 181.

25. Violet J. Harris, "Historic Readers for African American Children, 1968–1944: Uncovering and Reclaiming a Tradition of Opposition," in *Too Much Schooling, Too Little Education: A Paradox in African American Life*, Mwalimu Shujaa, ed. (Trenton, N.J.: Africa World Press, 1994).

26. Joan Davis Ratteray, "The Search for Access and Content in the Education of African Americans," in Shujaa, ibid.

27. Ronald E. Butchart, "Outthinking and Outflanking the Owners of the World: A Historiography of the African American Struggle for Education," in Shujaa, ibid.

28. Lloyd A. Cook, "Intergroup Education," *Review of Educational Research* 17 (1947):266.

29. Susan E. Noffke, *The Social Context of Action Research*. Paper presented at the Annual Meeting of the American Educational Research Association, San Francisco, 1989.

30. Michael R. Oleneck, "The Recurring Dream: Symbolism and Ideology in Intercultural and Multicultural Education," *American Journal of Education* 98 (February 1990):149.

31. Hilda Taba and William Van Til, *Democratic Human Relations: Promising Practices in Intergroup and Intercultural Education in the Social Studies* (Washington, D.C.: National Council for the Social Studies, 1945).

32. Ibid., p. 66.

33. Ibid., p. 67.

34. Ibid., p. 343.

35. National Education Association, *Americans All: Studies in Intercultural Education* (Washington, D.C.: National Education Association, 1942).

36. Ibid., p. 14; I use the gender-specific language here as contained in the original.

37. Taba and Van Til, op. cit.

38. Nellie Appy, "Rediscovering Folkways," in National Education Association, op. cit., pp. 185–93.

39. Ibid., p. 191.

40. Ibid., p. 193.

41. Bond, op. cit.

42. Multicultural Education issue, *Educational Leadership* 49, 4 (December/January 1991–1992).

43. See James A. Banks, *An Introduction to Multicultural Education* (Boston: Allyn & Bacon, 1994); Christine I. Bennett, *Comprehensive Multicultural Education* (Boston: Allyn & Bacon, 1995); Etta Hollins, Joyce E. King, and Warren C. Hayman, *Teaching Diverse Populations* (Albany: State University of New York Press, 1994); Christine E. Sleeter and Carl A. Grant, *Making Choices for Multicultural Education* (New York: Merrill, 1994).

44. The use of the phrase "whose knowledge" is as an invocation of a stream of curriculum thought, best represented in Michael W. Apple, *Ideology and Curriculum* (New York: Routledge, 1979).

45. See, for examples, the works of The National Women's History Project (7738 Bell Road, Windsor, Calif.); Educators against Racism and Apartheid (625 Linden Avenue, Teaneck, N.J.); and The Network of Educators on the Americas (P.O. Box 73038, Washington, D.C.).

46. See, for examples, Ellen Swartz, *Multicultural Curriculum Development: A Practical Approach to Curriculum Development at the School Level* (Rochester, N.Y.: Rochester City School District, 1989); Portland Public Schools, *Hispanic Heritage Lesson Plans* (Portland, OR: Portland Public Schools, Multicultural/Multiethnic Education, 1989); and Project R.E.A.C.H., *Respecting Ethnic and Cultural Heritage* (Arlington, WA: REACH Center, 1987).

47. Portland Public Schools, op. cit., preface, unpaginated.

48. Ibid., section 9–12, introduction, unpaginated.

49. Ibid., section 3–5, p. 2.

50. Project REACH, op. cit.

51. See bell hooks, *Teaching to Transgress: Education as the Practice of Freedom* (New York: Routledge, 1994); and Christine E. Sleeter, *Empowerment Through Multicultural Education* (Albany: State University of New York Press, 1991).

52. Gloria Ladson-Billings, *The Dreamkeepers: Successful Teachers of African American Children* (San Francisco: Jossey-Bass, 1994); Duane E. Campbell, *Choosing Democracy: A Practical Guide to Multicultural Education* (Englewood Cliffs, N.J.: Prentice Hall, 1996); and Carl A. Grant and Mary Louise Gomez, *Making Schooling Multicultural* (Englewood Cliffs, N.J.: Prentice Hall, 1996).

53. Critiques of behavioral objectives and the model of curriculum planning which often surrounds them can be found in Lawrence Stenhouse, *An Introduction to Curriculum Research and Development* (London: Heinemann, 1975); and Herbert M. Kliebard, "The Tyler Rationale" in *Curriculum and Evaluation*, Arno Bellack and Herbert M. Kliebard, eds. (Berkeley: McCutchan, 1977).

54. State Education Department, *A New Compact for Learning* (Albany: State University of New York Press, 1991).

55. Audre Lorde, *Sister Outsider* (Freedom, Calif.: Crossing, 1984), pp. 110–13.

56. I wish to acknowledge the helpful comments of Catherine Cornbleth and Violet Harris on this chapter.

SEVEN

What We've Learned from "Living in the Future"

Barbara Brodhagen, Gary Weilbacher, and James A. Beane

In the past few years, the term *curriculum integration* has surfaced among the many buzzwords in curriculum reform talk. That term should sound encouraging to those who remember the historical association of curriculum integration with serious progressive currents, including such reconstruction projects as the problem-centered "core" movement. Could it be that a comeback is in the offing? Indeed, some advocates of curriculum integration are using the term in that sense. But we must be careful since it is also being used as a generic name to cover any design beyond the strict separate-subject approach, including multidisciplinary approaches that do little more than imitate the mild correlations of the Herbartians or the least experimental of the Eight-Year Study schools.

The project with which this chapter is associated is an attempt to approach curriculum integration as something more than simply an instructional method. Rather we see it as a possibility for creating democratic classrooms in terms of both collaborative processes and uses of knowledge. In this chapter we will describe one example of a unit that illustrates our approach to curriculum integration. This was, in fact, the first unit we developed using the particular planning framework it involves. Following that description we will speak to some of the important lessons we have learned about doing this kind of curriculum work. These lessons are drawn not only from our own teaching experience since that first unit, but also from the stories of other teachers who have tried this approach.

Living in the Future: An Experiment with an Integrative Curriculum

In December, 1990, three teachers decided to undertake a curriculum experiment in cooperation with a university professor.[1] The young people involved were a heterogeneous group of twenty-six eighth graders.[2] The experimental program was to follow as closely as possible the middle school curriculum design theory proposed by Beane in 1990.[3] Briefly, that design suggested that the curriculum be organized around themes found at the intersection of self/personal concerns of young people and issues affecting the "common good" in the larger world. Furthermore, the curriculum was to involve the organic integration of personal, technical, and social skills as well as deliberate emphasis on democractic practice, respect for dignity, and prizing of diversity. In short, this meant that a unit was to be planned and carried out based on questions and concerns of the young people and without regard for subject area lines.

Marquette Middle School (now Georgia O'Keefe Middle School) is a culturally diverse school that draws students from a mostly lower socioeconomic area in Madison, Wisconsin. In all, about six hundred young people attend the sixth- through eighth-grade school. In the past several years, the school has had a consistently higher number of referrals and suspensions than any of the other middle schools in Madison. The professional staff has been willing to participate in several innovative programs such as the integration of special education students and teachers into regular classrooms, and the school still uses the block-time, single-teacher language arts/social studies program that was a hallmark of many progressive junior high schools years ago.

Planning the Unit

If the curriculum is to support a genuine search for self and social meaning, then it ought to be drawn from concerns young people have about themselves and their world. Moreover, those young people must fully participate in the identification of such concerns and the themes they suggest for the curriculum.

This line of reasoning poses the need for a process by which a thematic unit might be cooperatively planned. Such a process is not new in education but follows from the long history of what has often been called "teacher-pupil plannning." Here, young people and teachers come together to decide what they are going to do and how they will do it. The student and teacher roles become blended as both plan and learn together. While primary emphasis is placed on questions and concerns raised by young people, the teacher plays a crucial role in helping to pose and clarify questions as well as bringing to light related concerns—of which some young people may not be aware—in the larger world.

At the same time, the teacher must be careful not to cross the line between this kind of authentic planning and that of illusory participation in which there is "engineered consent" toward acceptance of preconceived teacher ideas. Instead, the intent is to play a facilitative role with regard to concerns of young people, to help them see connections between their concerns and the larger world, and thus to bring the most powerful kind of meaning to the curriculum.

We began our unit by eliciting questions the young people had about themselves and their world. Since the first of these requires initial thinking about themselves, the opening request was this:

We would like you to begin by thinking about yourself. Who are you? What are you like? What are your interests, problems, needs? *Make a list of words or phrases you would use if asked to tell about yourself.*[4]

After all individuals had done this, we moved to the two major questions as follows:

Still thinking about yourself and looking at the list you have made, now list questions and concerns you have about yourself. *What questions or concerns do you have about yourself?* (See table 7.1)

Then:

You have listed quesitons and concerns you have about yourself; that is, you have looked at yourself. Now we would like you to look outside yourself at the world you live in. That world has many different parts. Some are close to you—your family, your friends, your culture, your community, and so on. Others are more distant—your state, your nation, all the way to the global world. We want you to think about that world—both near and far—and list questions or concerns you have about that world. *What questions or concerns do you have about the world you live in?* (See table 7.2)

119

TABLE 7.1
Sample Questions and Concerns "About Myself"

"When will I die?"	"Will I be scared when I finally have sex?"
"Will I make it in life (education, work, marriage, etc.)?"	"Will I ever be in a life-or-death situation?"
	"Would I be scared if I had to go to war?"
"How will may kids turn out (school, drugs, etc.)?"	"What mistakes will I make?" "How will I correct them?"
"Will I be healthy?"	"Will I make it to college?"
"Will I achieve my goals?"	"Will I make enough money to support myself?"
"Will I end up doing the same things my parents are doing?"	
"Will I be smarter than my parents?"	"Am I really like what other people say I am?"
"What will I look like when I am old?"	"Will I have a child who is retarded?"
	"What is my future going to be like?"

TABLE 7.2
Sample Questions and Concerns about "the World"

"What will happen to the world (greenhouse effect, ozone, air pollution, rain forests, etc.)?"	"Why are some people gay?"
"Why are earthquakes and tornados so big?"	"Why are famous people famous and we are not famous?"
"How much is the world going to change?"	"Why are people under so much stress that they kill themselves?"
"Will there ever be world peace?"	
"Is there ever going to be an end to the world?" "Will we kill ourselves?"	"Why are there gangs?" "Why can't people get along?"
"Will we run out of resources?" "Can we stop that from happening?"	"Why do people hate blacks?" "Will prejudice ever end?"
"Why are there rich and poor people?" "Why do we use money for wars and not for poor people?"	"Why do we use money?"
	"Why did we overpopulate the world?" "Will starvation ever end?"
"How come you can cross-breed animals and not humans?"	"Why do people have to be mean to others to feel good about themselves?"
"Why do insane people have rights?"	"Why do we need a president?"

The next step in our planning involved a search for common or shared questions and concerns in both the self and world dimensions. The young people formed themselves into groups of five or six and used newsprint to share questions and concerns. No one was required to share anything from their personal lists unless they chose to. The small goups worked in turn through three guiding questions:

1. Are there questions and concerns that were expressed by several or all members of the group? If so, what are they?
2. Are there any cases where the questions raised about self are personal versions of questions or concerns about the larger world? (For example, concerns about peer-group relations might be a personal version of larger world concerns about interdependence among peoples, cultures, nations, etc.)
3. Does the discussion of common concerns—or self and world connections—suggest any broad themes that might become the topics for units? (Each group would hopefully come up with at least two or three of these.)

At this point, the whole group came together and each small group reported on its deliberations, including shared questions and concerns, and possible themes for units. All themes (table 7.3) were listed on the chalkboard (some were common across groups) and the whole group voted on which theme they wanted to pursue for the actual unit we would carry out. Having selected one, the small groups reconvened and identified questions and concerns from each group that seemed to fit under the theme. The directions for the small groups were as follows:

TABLE 7.3
Suggested Themes for Our Questions

Jobs, Money, Careers
Death and Dying
Living in the Future
Environment and Health
Conflict
Sex, Life, Genetics

What are specific questions and concerns we would want to answer within this theme? These questions may relate to personal concerns within the theme or larger world aspects of it. Groups should follow the rules of "brainstorming" where all questions are accepted and none are challenged. This will become important later since individuals or small groups may take on questions apart from those addressed by the whole group. However, the group recorder should note whether each question was of concern to everyone in the small group, a couple of people, or just one.

Next, the whole group was divided in two. Half looked at the self questions from the small groups and half looked at the world questions. Each was asked to brainstorm activities the group might do to answer various questions.

Then the groups switched so that everyone had a chance to suggest activities for both kinds of questions. After this brainstorming was completed, the whole group convened and reviewed all of the suggested activities (table 7.4). A show of hands for each possible activity revealed which were of sufficient interest for whole-group involvement and which were of interest to small groups or individuals.

TABLE 7.4
Suggested Activities

1. Make our own predictions, survey others for theirs (12)
2. Make a time capsule with predictions for self and world (9)
3. Research family histories (genetics, stress factors, lifespan averages, reasons for deaths, etc.) (18)
4. Design a model future community for Madison.
5. Research options to prevent or delay aging (4)
6. Survey others about life risks they have taken (9)
7. Talk to elders about their views of the past and future (5)
8. Do personal past histories and extend into the future (0)
9. Go to work with parents or other adults to find out what they do, what skills are needed, etc. (19)
10. Gather, analyze, and extrapolate statistics on accidents, gang violence, diseases, etc. (6)
11. Find out when and how popular technologies (VCRs cars, etc.) were invented and whether predictions for them came true (1)
12. Find past predictions for the years 1990–2000 and see if they were right (16)
13. Think of inventions for the furture (12)
14. Do scenarios for the future with and without what we want (19)
15. Hold a debate on the pros and cons of new technologies (17)
16. Interview people about how they handle change (3)
17. Plan a reunion of our group for 2015 (where, what to bring, etc.) (14)
18. Investigate future education/work requirements (11)
19. Talk to counselors about how to make plans/decisions (5)
20. Interview teachers about how their curriculum has changed (5)
21. Investigate different kinds of intelligence (8)

The last question we raised with the group was, What knowledge or skills will we need to carry out our activities so that we might answer our questions? (See table 7.5.) Responses to this question were particularly important for several reasons. First, they began to suggest what resources we might want to use. Second, they reminded all of us that we were not abandoning the teaching and learning of knowledge and skill, but rather applying them to answer our questions. Third, they gave an indication of what knowledge and skill the young people had previously been exposed to. Finally, and perhaps most revealing, the responses were of such a range and variety that many in the group were immediately able to see the idea of dissolving subject lines that was part of the general curriculum theory we were working with.

TABLE 7.5
Knowledge and Skill Needed for Our Unit (according to the students)

statistics on population growth			photography	listening
health	history		vocabulary	anatomy
computer skills	map reading		estimating	graphing
evaluation	technology	ratios		sex education
writing	art skills	patience		cultures
current events	using transportation schedules			
problem solving	question asking			measurement
comparing/contrasting		critical thinking		indexing
self-assurance	note taking			memory skills
phone skills	communication			predicting
library research skills				
	All classes—everything we do in school			

This planning process took four days or nearly seven hours. While some might see this as an inordinate amount of time, we believed that the planning was part of the unit and that it was a valuable experience in itself in terms of participation, problem posing, and empowerment. In addition, since the group had identified six possible unit themes, we would have been prepared to move on into the others once this unit had been completed. In other words, the planning we had done in seven hours probably would have set us up for a whole year.

During the planning the teachers played a secondary role to the young people. This meant posing questions, clarifying ideas, and encouraging reflection. Conversely, it also meant refraining from suggesting questions or activities before exhausting ideas of the students, or otherwise leading the group in particular directions.

As the following description of activities will suggest, these young people seemed to be quite capable of defining a significant plan for their work. However, as the unit unfolded, the teachers played a more active and visible role in helping to find resources, facilitating group work, and coordinating the schedule. On some occasions the teachers also took time to introduce or explain ideas related to the theme. These occasions were limited, however, and certainly far less than the usual teacher-directed curriculum. In fact, various young people spent far more time making presentations to the group than did the teachers.

Carrying out the Unit

As indicated by the previous discussion and tables, our group chose the theme *Living in the Future* from the several they had identified. This theme

123

had been suggested by the many questions the young people had about their personal futures as well as their concerns for the future of the world. Table 7.4 displays the activities the group had planned to do. Here we will describe how these activities actually took shape. Activities were of varying durations and overlapped one another across the calendar. Most of the young people predicted that they would stay in Madison so our group decided to focus our hopes for the future on that community. While initial questions had asked what the future would be like, it was further decided that what would be asked was, What do we want the future to be like? This revised question led us to design a plan for Madison in the year 2020 (roughly when the young people in the group would be the age of the teachers). What came to be known as the "Madison 2020 Project" turned out to be our largest activity and ran across the entire unit.

To do this project, the whole group first brainstormed specific planning areas and then divided into groups focused on environment/waste management, buildings, cultural makeup, recreation, government/education, housing/population, economy/transportation, and medicine/health. Each group was responsible for researching their area and making recommendations to the whole group. The latter activity involved three rounds of discussion and debate as the whole group tried to integrate the work of smaller groups. As a culminating activity for the Madison 2020 Project, we invited a city planner to listen to our recommendations and interact with us about them.

A second activity involved finding out what other young people might forecast for the future. Here we constructed a survey and mailed it to seven other middle schools around the country. We then tabulated the responses to scaled items (e.g., mean, median, mode), clustered and summarized open-ended responses, and graphed results. Small groups then wrote summaries of responses for various sections of the survey.

After the theme was identified, a new question emerged regarding what predictions had been made in the past for our own times. Using an article by John Watkins, "What May Happen in the Next 100 Years," that appeared in *The Ladies' Home Journal* in 1900 (reprinted in the October 1982 issue of *The Furturist*), each person took one prediction and researched whether it had come true and what Watkins may have seen around him in 1900 that would have led to the prediction. Finally, each person gave a short oral report on what they had discovered and answered questions from other group members about their research.

A fourth activity was used to answer the question, How long will I live? While this question was obviously impossible to answer, we did decide that we could learn something from studying our family histories. Here, each person in the group gathered information about lifespans of family members, causes of death, health histories, and other factors that could enter into their own health future. We then discussed the meaning of such information and how it might be used to care for one's own health.

A fifth activity, and perhaps the most clever in the unit, was used in conjunction with the question, What will I look like when I am older? At first we talked about finding out whether each of us supposedly looked like an older relative when she/he was our age, checking young pictures of that person to be sure, and then drawing our conclusions. In the end, one of the teachers contacted an artist who explained how facial features change over time and then sketched each person in the group (this was a very popular activity).

In addition to these types of activities, during the course of the unit we had many spontaneous discussions and debates, talked with a guidance counselor about making personal plans and decisions, and more. As is usually the case though, we came up against time problems. Originally we were to have two hours each day for the unit, but for three weeks we were involved in another program for all eighth graders and so were limited to only one hour per day. As a result we were almost always pressed for time and on several occasions the bell rang just as things were heating up. In the end, the consensus of the group was that while we had accomplished a great deal, much more could have been done if we had been able to use larger time blocks including whole days.

Evaluation

At the end of the unit we were faced with the issue of evaluation at two levels. One was the evaluation of the unit itself. The other was evaluation of student work, including the perennial problem of identifying letter grades for individuals.

Early on, the school principal visited with our group and raised questions about what we were doing and how we interpreted it as an educational experience. The positive comments of young people even at that point, revealed valuable evaluation information as well as encouragement to keep going. During the course of the unit the young people did some journal writing aimed at reflecting on their own work and that of the group.

In the end, we constructed a survey form that included questions about what people had liked best and least about the unit, how this educational experience compared to others they had had, and what recommendations they would make for other units in the future. Each person was also asked to write about the activities he/she had been involved in and what each had learned. Finally, students were asked to say what letter grade they deserved and why. This self-evaluation then served as the basis for assigning grades. While this method may be unpopular in some places, the feeling of the teachers involved in this project was that it was consistent with the general philosophy of constructing meaning and empowering young people that lay behind our approach.

125

Summary

Skeptics of this curriculum experiment might raise two major points that can be anticipated and answered here. First it is true that the group consisted of only twenty-six young people and four teachers. On the other hand, that number of teachers was possible because the group included both "learning disabled" and "emotionally disturbed" students who otherwise would have been in very small pull-out groups with two of the teachers. By including these young people in the group, these teachers were also available. Ironically, a few of the "learning disabled" students turned out to be the most visible leaders in the group.

Another anticipated point of skepticism is the claim that some teachers already do units like this, even with the same theme and activities. This may very well be true, but with at least one major exception. That is, in those units, the theme and activities are almost always identified entirely by the teachers. In our experiment these aspects of the unit were identified by the young people and drawn from their initial open-ended responses to questions and concerns they had about themselves and their world. Thus the activities were directed toward answering the questions of young people rather than "learning" what the teachers felt was important. Although we do not want to demean or underestimate the significant work of those other teachers, this difference is clearly one of kind rather than degree, in that it is a quite different way of viewing the curriculum and its sources.

Certainly other points might be raised but, as in the two previously mentioned, the most important thing to remember is that we were a small group of teachers who had made a deliberate decision to experiment with the curriculum in the way we have described here. In doing so we made necessary arrangements, bent extraneous requirements, and constructed our own sense of what we ought to do. We were trying to get a sense of what doing this felt like and what the possibilities were. We were not out to prove the desirability of what we were doing or to create some master "model" that others ought to imitate. Nor do we want to leave the impression that each and every day was a trouble-free curriculum "high." We had our ups and downs, moments of satisfaction and confusion. After all, Marquette is a real school and the teachers and students are real people. Yet we learned a great deal from our experiment and will learn more as we implement this approach again.

Lessons Learned

That was our first experience with this particular approach to the curriculum. Since then we have personally used the same arrangement with sixth- and seventh-grade students in time blocks up to four hours, in a re-source room for students labeled "emotionally disturbed," and in an alterna-tive school program involving young people from middle and high schools. Moreover, we have worked with teachers from many other schools in the United States and elsewhere at elementary, middle, and high school levels, in-cluding leading their students through the planning process described above.

In the remainder of this chapter we want to reflect on lessons we have learned from those experiences. Our approach is to use the title of this book, *The Curriculum: Problems, Politics, and Possibilities*, to structure three questions:

What are the problems when doing this kind of curriculum work?
What are the politics of doing this kind of curriculum work?
What are the possibilities of this kind of curriculum work?

Each of the three authors responded to these questions and after reading each other's work for both different or recurring themes, we jointly decided which responses should be included.

What are the Problems When Doing this Kind of Curriculum Work?

Gary: While I am convinced that the thematic integrative curriculum is in the best interest of the students, it is important to note that this approach is not without problems. Teaching this way is, at times, exhausting for both teachers and students. The planning stages can be especially draining since students are used to answering questions, not posing them. This role reversal can cause confusion and even tension. Patience and restraint are two qualities teachers must have in order to allow students to truly and effectively plan their curricu-lum. The temptation to alter or even completely take over the student con-structions of concepts and activities often seems overwhelming. To do so would destroy the democratic process that is at the heart of this philosophy.

Essentially, what needs to happen is that teachers must give up some of their actual control, or at least the illusion of control, within their classrooms. (I say the illusion of control because I am not completely convinced that teachers can control a classroom.) Allowing students to have a voice in their learning is scary for many teachers. The teacher-controlled "empty vessel" analogy appears to be alive and well in the minds of many educators. I con-tinue to be amazed and alarmed by colleagues who, after being given explana-tions of what we did, respond by saying, "So you mean you just walk into your classroom and say, 'Okay kids, what should we do today?'" It is difficult to re-move this conception and disheartening to know that it often results in de-fending one's professional judgment. Therefore, it is critical for teachers who use this philosophy to feel secure and confident in their abilities.

Barb: The first problems that come to mind are the ones that impact me personally as a teacher: who my teaching partners are, their competence, commitment, and understanding of the big picture; which would include wanting them to pay attention to issues that relate to issues of justice and the unequal distribution of "power" across race, class, and gender. The second kind of problem concerns the physical space, materials, and resources available, and school schedules that I will have to work within and around. The third has to do with people—parents, other colleagues, and finally, tests and grades.

Jim: Along those lines, the lack of appropriate resources to support an integrative curriculum is a huge challenge. Textbooks and other resources are almost always organized by separate subjects and thus are often unsuitable for work on problems and issues that call for integration of content and skills. Moreover, school district resource allocations are almost always spent on those kinds of materials since their organization and content aligns well with the subject-centered curriculum. For these reasons, teachers (and students) who use an integrative approach typically spend an unusual amount of time seeking out resources, both materials and people, to support their work. Along with other things, this makes integrative teaching more exhausting than it already is.

Barb: It was also exhausting in its intensity. There were times when the teachers and students became so involved in the seriousness of our work that teachers forgot our students were, after all, children. We needed to step back and have some fun, to recapture some of the joy of working together.

Gary: While these difficulties are not unique to an integrative curriculum, they seem intensified because of the strain placed on people and resources while students are engaged in the construction of knowledge, as opposed to the regurgitation of facts. Room space, library time, computer lab time, field trips, and guest speakers are always weekly needs. Competition for these resources with other classrooms often results in student and teacher frustration.

Barb: The issue of separate-subject teaching is so ingrained that many teachers can't see another way of doing things. I believe that a lot of teachers would agree that providing connected learning experiences is what we should be after, but I would say that many of these teachers do not want to put in the kind of work this kind of teaching requires. Work intensification is a reality.

Also, so many teachers and administrators truly don't have a clue about curriculum integration or cooperative planning. This is not being taught at many colleges and universities so there aren't enough people who can teach others how to do curriculum integration. I just assume that I can do this and that it will all work out. Maybe all these problems—lack of sufficient knowledge, work intensification, and insufficient resources—are the real reasons that more teachers don't get involved with this kind of work.

What are the Politics of Doing this Kind of Curriculum?

Jim: Since the overwhelming majority of schools use a separate-subject approach, even in self-contained elementary classrooms, most people apparently believe that approach to be the one and only. If not, there are plenty of academicians and high-culture conservatives to remind them in no uncertain terms. Add to this mix the way in which such things inside schools as space and schedule preferences are tied to perceived status among the various subjects and the ways in which teacher self-definition is tied to subject certification areas.

Barb: Some parents, usually of brighter kids coming from middle- to upper-middle-class homes, wanted their kid to be doing the best the *old* way; they didn't want their kid to lose out. It was hard to convince them what we were doing was "better" for their kids, that, in fact, when using the old way we didn't always have as high expectations for the kids, or challenge them at a high/difficult enough level. Kids want to learn hard and easy stuff. But these parents weren't necessarily looking at each individual activity or assignment to offer constructive criticism, rather they wanted pre-algebra.

Gary: Along those same lines, my experience has been that certain parents, administrators, and teachers believe that math must be taught as a separate subject and should be ability grouped. As a result of this belief, a select few middle school students are granted entry into algebra and/or pre-algebra classes. This separation destroys the purpose of integrative curriculum and creates artificial, institutional barriers among students, as well as disrupting the team aspect critical for this type of teaching.

Jim: While such an objection is likely to be raised by many individuals and groups, it takes on a particular importance when raised by nonprivileged groups who have historically been treated most harshly by the testing system. For this reason, those who use an integrative approach must be careful to communicate how their thematic work includes "test knowledge." Failure to do so not only disrespects the concerns of those groups but threatens a retreat to the remedial, skill-drill curriculum that has deadened their children's school experiences for so long.

Gary: An issue that I am concerned with focuses on the question of how the students view the democratic process within the classroom. Is the democracy we as a group construct a reflection of the democracy outside of the

129

classroom, complete with all of marginalizing "isms" within our society? If so, how do the students of color perceive our attempts at improving the educational process? If not, is "our" democracy a type of educational fantasy that sets students up for failure when they encounter the harsh realities provided by high schools? An even more immediate question is, how do students adjust from our classroom to classrooms in which their voices are limited or even nonexistent, as they change rooms throughout the day?

Jim: And let's not forget the political challenge that emerges from the fundamentalist right wing. This, too, is not surprising since the integrative curriculum, as we define it, places a premium on critical ethics and inquiry in relation to themes that usually involve serious social issues. Moreover, there is conscious emphasis on democratic arrangements and respect for the dignity of young people. Either one of these, let alone both, is enough to send shivers up the spines of fundamentalists. Interestingly, though, the challenge from the Right does not always get to that level since the very term *integrated* is among the collection that is seen as departing from the traditional, basic-skills curriculum that fundamentalists seem to love and protect so much. The name alone is taken as enough to challenge the approach and thus to scare many education officials right back to where they were before. To their credit, perhaps, it may be that many right-wing fundamentalists understand better than most educators that an integrative curriculum is more than a method.

Barb: We did not have to deal with the conservative right, back-to-the-basics movement, so I can't speak from much personal experience. The threat that I would feel would be one coming from grade level tests or covering specific content—that if the kids don't have it they will be penalized in future classes. It then becomes political in new ways. Do I stand my ground and let the kids take their chances, or do I compromise so much that I go back to the old way and not provide the kind of learning experience that I believe to be best for kids?

Let's not forget the politics inside the school. Many other teachers were not really willing to learn about curriculum integration for a variety of reasons, but the everyday politics of this were that they would criticize without being fully informed, and they were unwilling to have a go at it so that they could use personal professional experience to make intelligent evaluative observations. They would ignore our work or make comments behind our backs. I did not feel there was any real support from them or the administration.

Jim: It is not surprising, then, that teachers who use an integrative approach often find themselves under attack by affluent parents who fear for their children's privilege, colleagues who want to protect their space and schedules, and students who have learned their lessons well about how the curriculum is supposed to be organized.

What are the Possibilities of This Kind of Curriculum?

Gary: I am quite sure that the integrative curriculum, like any other curriculum, cannot absolutely ensure success for all students. However, I believe that it provides a few important conditions that improve everyone's chances to learn, and especially those students who have been given exceptional educational labels. These conditions are, in my opinion, fundamental human rights that are frequently unavailable in traditional curriculum and teaching systems but here are introduced in the planning process and nurtured during the daily classroom interactions. I identify them as the following:

- validation of self and experiences. The students are encouraged to share their concerns and questions with their peers, and have them recognized and validated by others.
- sense of control and ownership. The issues that drive the curriculum originate from the concerns, discussions, and, ultimately, the consensus of the students.
- democracy in practice. Each student has a voice and an almost limitless choice in selecting methods for the construction and sharing of knowledge.

Jim: Another possibility involves further understanding of the democratic uses of knowledge. For example, knowledge is organically integrated in the context of real problems and issues. In this sense it is put to use for serious purpose rather than simply accumulated as cultural ornamentation. Moreover, the knowledge is called for by the problem at hand rather than by special interests. And, since the integrative curriculum engages young people in a search for answers to questions and concerns that they have about themselves and their world, they have an opportunity to construct their own knowledge rather than simply accepting the meanings of others. This, by the way, is well beyond the superficial kind of "constructivism" that is really a thinly veiled excursion to the teacher's answer.

Barb: This model of curriculum theory works actively to promote the ideas of dignity, democracy, and diversity in the classroom, with the optimistic expectation that these ideas might then extend into society through the lives of young people. This is what we want to happen for each student. Elsewhere, people have written about work intensification, teacher proof curricula, loss of teacher efficacy, and so on. It is my personal experience, and I believe that of others, that when curriculum work like that described here is undertaken, the ideas of dignity, democracy, and diversity are restored for the teacher as well, taking back part of what was lost over the years.

Teachers who do this work often say they could not go back to the "old" way of teaching where they stand up in the front, making all the decisions. We believe they, like us, have had a profound experience forever changing the way we teach, rejecting how we were taught to teach, or the way we were teaching as a result of the kind of texts being used or the teaching observed going on around us. In this kind of work the teacher is required to use all that was learned about how to be a teacher, and more. There is no script, no traditional teacher's guide. Rather the teacher must draw upon all her diverse abilities, experience, and knowledge to facilitate the learning of students. Two of us had been special education teachers and often felt marginalized, probably feeling like many young people feel. This work has helped redefine our views of self as teacher and has helped us close the gap between what we know to be right and want to do and what is actually being done.

Teachers and students begin to interact with each other as whole people and not as incomplete actors. As this happens trust and respect are obvious results, creating an environment that allows both students and teachers to ask the kind of questions that truly promote a critical analysis of the world. With this new kind of teacher-student relationship, challenging questions can be asked without fear. Answering many of these questions is intense, serious work and in many ways the teachers' workload does intensify. It has been our experience that in this kind of a classroom more students are engaged in learning, and if they are doing more the teacher must do more. Somehow the increased workload is worth the effort because of the results we are seeing.

Certainly the possibilities for students are incredible. The learning situation could provide students a chance to see why and how their school education experiences really could benefit them. They would be able to see that what they are learning is useful now and could have some relationship with their lives outside of school. They would have chances to do things and to feel proud of what they had accomplished. Students would live a diverse learning encounter, working to respect and celebrate differences in the people around them. They would live democracy in action.

Notes

1. The four were Barbara Brodhagen, Gary Weilbacher, James Dunn, and James Beane.

2. Lydia Bertrand, Tom Bremer, Warren Cain III, John Conlon, Angela Diamond, Andy Flesch, Ben Houtman, Mark Jaeger, Sara Johnson, Moe Jones, Pat Kosinski,

Melinda Kroneman, Shannon McDaniel, Jason Meyers, Beth Moody, Tina Moon, Erin Peschel, Jeremy Rednour, Tara Reyes, Mike Seibel, Melissa Spaeni, Michelle Walsh, Cristina Will, Kim Wonderlin, Zach Ziln, Micaela Zitske.

3. James A. Beane, *A Middle School Curriculum: From Rhetoric to Reality*, Columbus, Ohio: National Middle School Association, 1990; rev. ed., 1993.

4. This questioning was adapted from James A. Beane and Richard P. Lipka, *Self-Concept, Self-Esteem and the Curriculum*, New York: Teachers College Press, 1986.

III
Curriculum and Knowledge Selection

EIGHT

Curriculum Platforms and Moral Stories

Thomas E. Barone and *Donald S. Blumenfeld-Jones*

Introduction

Curricularists have historically conceived of the curriculum planning process in rather narrow terms. The focus has been on the task of development—whether as a linear, theory-driven, Tylerian process, or *apres* Schwab, as the practical activity of deliberation. Mutations of the Tyler model seem omnipresent, and the process of deliberation remains intriguing to many curriculum scholars. Without denying the importance of continued attention to the nature of planning and policymaking episodes, especially to the analysis of deliberative engagements, we want to consider how curriculum workers can prepare for such engagements. In this chapter, we concern ourselves less with what curriculum developers do in the development process than with what they bring to it. We are fascinated less with the strategies and maneuvers of curriculum designers, and more with *how they become who they are*. More specifically, we are interested in how they might become people who are more sensitive to issues surrounding the relationship between school curricula and social justice.

137

Our thoughts spring from a notion that Decker Walker, in delineating his "naturalistic model" for curriculum development two decades ago, referred to as the *platform* of the designer. For Walker, "the word platform is meant to suggest both a political platform and something to stand on. The platform includes an idea of what is and a vision of what ought to be, and these guide the curriculum developer in determining what he should do to realize his vision."[1]

Walker's metaphor is insufficient insofar as it conveys an image of a fixed, enduring structure rather than a fragile nexus of vague attitudes, tentative beliefs, complex dispositions, and ideologies perhaps only partially congealed, within which most curriculum workers operate. Nevertheless, the concept is enormously helpful as a reminder that the entire process of curriculum planning or policy making must be contingent upon those individually held conceptions of what is (in Walker's words) educationally "good, true, and beautiful." Indeed, Purpel reinforces this idea by speaking to the "dimly viewed and rarely articulated . . . cluster of visions" which are brought to the process of curriculum design.[2] These visions relate the curriculum worker to a wide dimension of human experience, including conceptions of "the universe, of human potential, and of our relationships to the cosmos."[3] They provide us with theoretical windows that enable us to see facets of the world in particular ways. In turn, the course of our daily lives, including our preferences among educational theories and practices, is shaped by what we view.

The formation of images of educational virtue is, therefore, an enormously complex process occurring within the entire fund of experiences that constitute a biography. Still, the movement of curriculum planners, policy makers, and practitioners toward the articulation of personal educational theory—the erection of a platform, if you will—surely lies at the heart of what those of us who are educators of teachers and of other curriculum workers continually attempt to accomplish. And so we want to imagine what kinds of activities are likely to promote this movement. In particular, we are wondering about how the activity of engaging with the texts of stories can help to foster the platform articulation process. Moreover, we are focused on the influences of certain kinds of stories on platform development. These are stories that are thematically concerned with issues of power and social justice.

Achieving a Self

How does a curriculum worker become who s/he is? How does s/he develop a self-identity, a personal stance, a set of curricular beliefs? We suggest that this development occurs within a *hermeneutical* process; self-understanding comes about through acts of interpretation. *What* is interpreted are the phenomena that, in the course of our daily lives, we *experience*.

John Dewey distinguished between two concepts of experience.[4] There is, first, the stream of consciousness that is part of one's ongoing everyday existence. The second notion involves episodes within this mundane course of events, episodes that provide heightened awareness inasmuch as they are composed, rounded out, and therefore stand apart from the inchoate flow of experience. Following such episodes—Dewey's examples include solving a problem, eating a meal, playing a game, writing a book, and taking part in a political campaign—we say that we have had "an experience."

Experience is, therefore, simultaneously part and whole; the phenomena that are confronted within experience are never self-referential. That is, to be meaningful these phenomena cannot stand in isolation from each other, or from phenomena that are recollected in memory from either generalized or heightened experience. Instead, we tend to make sense of the incidents in our lives by placing them within the context of previous instants of awareness. Eating *this* meal, playing *this* game, participating in *this* political campaign, arranging *this* curriculum material, these are events that accrue meaning only in the light of previous experience, only in the presence of accumulated memories that are elements of a background against which the interpretive process is played out. Moreover, each instant of awareness then becomes part of the mosaic within the experiential backdrop, contributing to the patterned mass of memories against which future experiences and actions will be regarded.

Kerby has noted that this interpretive process can occur—meaning can accrue—only when the interpreter is aware that the background elements are indeed memorial.[5] That is, the present act of recollection must be viewed as temporally distinct from that which is recalled. The interpretive process demands an oscillation between the poles of past and present, and cannot proceed without awareness of the distinction between current activity and a cumulative mass of previous experiences. And it is not only the presently experienced phenomena that are candidates for interpretation; the mosaic of remembrances is also rearranged in the process. Memories themselves are altered. In time, *through* time, with each new hermeneutical act, new insights are achieved, meanings of past events are shifted, and our sense of our selves is revised.

Or, more accurately, we revise our sense of our selves. The active tense underscores the point that the securing and growth of identity is, in part, a purposeful act replete with our own agendas and biases for understanding ourselves in particular ways. The experience that supplies the basis for self-understanding is enacted as well as undergone. The actor moves forward onto the environment in accordance with personal needs and desires, finding people and things within it that respond in various and complex ways. The person constructs a version of a coherent self-identity out of these interactions, these experienced phenomena, by interpreting them and integrating them into an historical unity, a notion of "who I am as one who acts in relation to others in the world."

Indeed, as George Herbert Mead described the self, it is neither material substance nor a spiritual "soul" but an *idea* that is constructed by a conscious human organism. From Mead's pragmatist vantage point "I" am not an existential isolate who arrives at a static self-identity, but rather my identity is an *achievement*, gained and modified through a process of moving upon and reacting to a world in which others are simultaneously achieving their own identities.[6]

Self-Construction and Narrative Expression

Selfhood, therefore, is achieved through acting and reacting within an environment of time and memory. The persona of each of us is, in other words, constructed and reconstructed, crafted and recrafted, continuously shaped and reshaped within the course of securing the meanings from our purposeful transactions with the world. These meanings achieve expression in a form that is called *narrative*.

Narrative, explained Polkinghorne, is the "form of hermeneutic expression in which human action is understood and made meaningful. Action itself is the living narrative expression of a personal and social life . . . and its organization manifests the narrative organization of human experience."[7] "A primary act of mind" is the way Carr defined narrative, "our primary way of organizing and giving coherence to our experience."[8] And as Brooks described it, narrative is "one of the . . . systems of understanding that we use in our negotiations with reality, specifically, . . . with the problems of temporality: man's time-boundedness, his consciousness of existence within the limits of mortality."[9]

Paul Ricoeur has linked the organization and coherence within a self-narrative to that of a literary narrative (either historical or fictional). He reminded us that the construal of meaning in our present negotiations is contingent on understanding those negotiations as part of an ongoing *story*. Indeed, stated Ricoeur, an event is "not only an occurrence, something that happens, but a narrative component" within one's experience.[10] These narrative components are, in the course of living, gathered together in a meaningful whole that reveals their relationship to each other. For Ricoeur, this relationship is the *plot* of a life story, "a way of connecting event and story. A plot is made out of events, to the extent that plot makes events into a story."[11]

The plot of each story that we tell about ourselves-in-the-world organizes and unifies life actions, events, and experiences into a cognizable whole. For Heidegger this wholeness defines the self by distinguishing it from the nothingness from which it emerges and into which it will disappear.[12] The plot of one's life offers a discourse structure as past, present, and possible future actions become expressions through which a singular existence is constructed. These expressions are part of the determinate form of the kind of story identified by Aristotle—one that has a beginning, a middle, and an end. Polkinghorne put it more precisely:

> The self is that temporal order of existence whose story begins with birth, has as its middle the episodes of a lifespan, and ends with death. It is the plot that gathers together these events into a coherent and meaningful unity, and thereby gives context and significance that the individual episodes make toward the overall configuration that is the person.[13]

Narrative, Culture, and Virtue

Acting, as narrative theorists insist, is indeed like writing the story of one's life. But the curriculum worker, as actor, is writing a story, living a life, that is not yet finished. As actor s/he is not merely fashioning together information confronted in the past about who his or her self must *be*. Since s/he is still alive, his/her story is, to some extent, open-ended; s/he is still constructing and discovering who s/he wants to *become*. S/he is in the midst of a process of developing a platform for living, attempting to gather together that "cluster of visions" which serve to illuminate the wide dimension of human experience of which Macdonald and Purpel spoke. What is truth?, s/he asks. What actions are aesthetic and virtuous? What is the good life? And how do I act in accordance with those ideals, so that I might compose a life narrative of high quality?

Even as s/he lives and acts, the curriculum worker—as a human being—is indeed attempting to discover how to do so in a positive fashion, how, that is, to grow a worthy self. Among latter-day thinkers it is Alasdair MacIntyre and Charles Taylor[14] who have most forcefully argued that the growth of the self is inevitably freighted with questions of virtue and morality. It is growth that, as Taylor has insisted, must take place within "a moral space, a space in which questions arise about what is good or bad, what is worth doing and what is not, what has meaning and importance . . . and what is trivial and secondary."[15] Human action is indeed "valorized action."[16] It involves deliberation, choice, value-based decisions about how we, as engaged human agents, might act with ever greater integrity and coherence. Narrative, argued MacIntyre, enables us to articulate our life as an organic whole so that we may see more clearly the purposes and values undergirding those decisions.[17]

The question of virtue does indeed hover over the project of self-construction—even when viewed from a Nietzschean position. Neitzsche's concern was for existential wholeness and integrity, for exertion of the individual will toward self-autonomy and idiosyncrasy.[18] For Nietzsche a good life is like a good original story insofar as disparate thoughts and actions are consciously shaped into a unique narrative or aesthetic form. For Nietzsche, however, this narrative must be purely one's own; to accept someone else's description of oneself was the mark of failure as a human being.

We prefer to couch the issue of ethical living in terms that recognize the intersections with fellow human beings, each of whom is similarly and simultaneously grasping for meaning within the milieu of a culture. We believe that the erection of a sturdy personal platform inevitably occurs within a sociocultural matrix, that the moral space of which Taylor[19] spoke is simultaneously personal and communal. In innumerable ways, from birth onward, we become acculturated through our social existence. Indeed, the genesis of the self (to borrow a phrase from Mead)[20] is an inherently social event, and its moral dimension should not be misunderstood as pertaining solely to the fulfillment of individual potential at the expense of becoming a responsible citizen of a shared community. Put another way, the emplotment of our own lives inevitably entangles us in the plots of other selves; we must move outward to attend to and care for the stories of others in order to enrich our own.

Empathy and Narrative

One important element in this move outward is empathy. Empathetic understanding is the ability to participate vicariously in the story of another life. Its practice rests on certain ordinary if implicit assumptions, namely, that the object of attention and care is a fellow human being; that there is a shared reality in which all of us participate because we are persons; that we can and do in fact imagine ourselves in other situations. Empathetic understanding is more than mere intuition or feeling because what is striven for is not purely emotional identification but rather an *idea of another self*. The process of acquiring this idea is deeply connected with understanding one's own life text as "[e]very hermeneutic [interpretation] is . . . explicitly or implicitly, self-understanding by means of understanding others."[21] Thus, empathy and self-understanding are reciprocally connected. Through interpreting meaning, as Wilhelm Dilthey put it, we apprehend "the vital unity maintained in the structural relations and processes in an individual life . . . seeing all its parts and aspects in relation to the vital movement of the whole."[22] Thus, in empathy we discover and construct our own version of the life narrative of another self and reconstruct our own.

Two paths to the achievement of empathetic understanding come to mind, one more direct and perhaps more powerful than the other. The first is being with other people in the course of everyday living. Knowing an "other" requires interpretation of the relationship between particular actions and the structured life process of that person. This involves reading those actions against the backdrop of what is already known about that person's perspective, and the cultural milieu in which the actions occur. This reading, as with self-construction, also involves recognizing our own purposes and biases, recognizing that our understanding is an amalgam of who we are and what is "out there." The second path to empathy is an indirect one: it is the path of storytelling.

Stories range in complexity from the casual anecdote to the arduously composed work of "high" literature. Whatever its genre, however, each story possesses the potential for promoting a kind of vicarious participation in the lives of others. The story enables the reader to perceive, through vivid, contextually detailed observations, the meaning and significance of actions and events from the characters' (and of course the author's) points of view. Building on each other, the dabs of narrative paint reproduce the plots of others' life stories.

The reader/curriculum worker is thereby dramatically introduced to new forms of life, forms that once were largely alien, beyond what Gadamer called the reader's *horizon*, or the "range of vision that includes everything that can be seen from a particular vantage point."[23] Within this horizon lie the purposes for the reader attending to a story in the first place. A prime motivation for reading is the possibility that a text may suggest answers to questions about a platform for living, that it may involve the kind of hermeneutical practice that Ricouer called the "restoration of meaning."[24] Engaging in this sort of hermeneutics brings greater meaning and coherence to our own life narrative.

For curriculum workers who are seeking a coherent platform it is especially helpful to understand empathetically the students for whom a particular curriculum is intended, or as Dewey would say, to know "where the child is coming from."[25] But it is also important to become familiar with those who have already lived a significant portion of their lives. In particular, if stories are to serve as vehicles for the restoration of meaning in their own personal and professional lives, then curriculum workers must become acquainted with the narratives of people—children and adults—with whom it is difficult to identify, "selves" who are looked upon as aliens living, as Rorty put it, "outside of the range of 'us.'"[26] This empathetic goal of storytelling resonates with Geertz's hope for ethnographic texts which engender awareness "between people quite different from one another in interest, outlook, wealth, and power."[27] To us, it seems particularly important—and profoundly moral—for relatively privileged educators to discover and construct ideas of the selves of the less privileged, to hear the voices of those "aliens" who have lived their lives on society's margins, to confront the "quite different" narratives of the disenfranchised.

But, for educators who intend to lead students outward from where they are, empathy does not equate with wisdom; such leadership requires a sense of direction in which to move. In other words, to empathize is not to validate. The ethics of developing a personal platform, of discovering and constructing a personal sense of what is virtuous (educationally and otherwise), requires a second element in the movement outward from one's self, namely, a critical evaluation of storied selves in the light of cultural/political conditions in which they take form.

Moral Stories and Inherited Scripts

This second element in the move outward requires recognition that the self is shaped in and through culture. Heidegger wisely noted that humans do not speak language (a primary cultural artifact), rather language speaks humans; and not only do we make history, wrote Marx, history also makes us.[28] Speaking language and making history are activities situated within what Willinsky referred to as an *inherited script*. An inherited script consists of the cultural formations "that sustain and give meaning to individual actions."[29]

An inherited script serves to position us *vis à vis* the available resources of the culture. It also differentially distributes power over those resources, and suggests action in accordance with that unequal distribution. The script is, therefore, inherently *political*. And, in our culture, the script is specific in its political dimension, making categories such as race, gender, ethnicity, age, class, and sexual orientation the significant attributes through which our humanness is mediated. The script is marked by domination and control, legitimating social forces that tend to privilege and empower members of certain categories over the members of others.

The move outward must entail an effort to establish a connection between these social forces and the lives of the people they impact. Certain kinds of stories can aid in such an effort. These are *moral stories*,[30] stories that build upon empathy, the vicarious participation with what Fay called the "intentions and desires of dissatisfied actors." But moral stories move the reader further outward to understandings of how particular "irrationalities of social life . . . are causing the dissatisfaction."[31]

Moral stories engender understandings which lead to moral agency. "Moral agency requires some kind of reflexive awareness of the standards one is living by."[32] When we question a piece of inherited script (exploring, for example, the manner in which schools as institutions disempower schoolpeople) we practice what he called *strong evaluation*. *Weak evaluation* is, to the contrary, defined by our tendency to live our daily lives through habit, to think and act pragmatically, in whatever manner will achieve present desires. Kerby has noted that certain cultural narratives such as myths, fables, and legends foster a kind of myopia.[33] The most formidable among such stories are those which Belsey called *declarative*.[34] These are works of propaganda that support the cultural script, authoritative stories that tell us in a dogmatic fashion how to live our lives; they identify "correct" endings and scripted purposes for living. Such narratives undercut the possibility of moral agency, of strong evaluation, for they foster an inability to distance oneself from the prevailing value nexus, and therefore to examine with a critical eye the "irrationalities of social life."

But moral stories encourage us to engage more authentically in the process of creating our own values, revealing the presence and consequences of the inherited script, and how we might reposition ourselves in relation to it. They help us to define ourselves as responsible social beings. Moral stories are, moreover, tentative and localized, heuristic, provocative, and ambiguous in their suggestions about the meanings of specific incidents and events. They include daily anecdotes we tell to ourselves and to each other, as well as historical and fictional literature. What they share is a tendency to transgress against prevailing cultural and personal assumptions, to arouse the reader from a moral slumber resulting from the anesthesia of convention and habit. Inasmuch as moral stories challenge absolutes considered sacred and beyond interrogation, they are "gestures fraught with risk."[35] They offer (sometimes) radical alternatives for thinking about the world and acting within it. They can suggest alternative descriptions of the lives of those who hear and read them, stimulate novel readings about how their lives have been buffeted by cultural forces, offer new interpretations of self-identity, even alter life directions. They promote greater degrees of integrity, responsibility, and morality in a curriculum worker's platform.

We can think of at least two kinds of moral stories. The first type we will call *socially committed narratives*. A second has been identified by bell hooks as *narratives of struggle*.[36] The two types are classified according to the social positions of the author and reader *vis-à-vis* the story characters.

Socially committed narratives consist of stories by privileged writers or storytellers told on behalf of members of oppressed classes who are still largely unable to speak for themselves. When they take the form of novels, plays, or journalistic accounts, they fall within a written narrative tradition identified by Sartre as *engaged literature (literatture engagee)*.[37] Prominent (and privileged) novelists who have published stories of disempowered characters include Charles Dickens, Victor Hugo, John Steinbeck, Upton Sinclair, and Nadine Gordimer. Inside the educational sphere works by Kozol, Sparkes, and Barone are examples of engaged literature.[38]

145

Works of engaged literature are usually intended for privileged audiences. Transgressing against the status quo, they aim to promote empathy with downtrodden protagonists, to portray vividly the historically constituted structures of oppression in which people are enmeshed, and thereby to challenge the complacency, threaten the moral equilibrium, of the privileged. They suggest to readers their own implication in an unjust system, compel them to "take stock of their responsibilities"[39] to reconstruct the part of their personal platform that supports tired notions about the character of oppression, and to act to transform an unjust social system into one that is more democratic. Think of *Uncle Tom's Cabin*, of *Oliver Twist*, and more recently, of *Savage Inequalities*. Or think of the small, informal tales of local injustices against people you know as told to you by your privileged but sympathetic peers. All of these are stories of the underprivileged related by and to compassionate and committed strangers.

Narratives of struggle, on the other hand, are emancipatory-minded stories in which the writer speaks as a member of an oppressed group. The selves that these narrators revisit are their own, or those within their oppressed category of race, ethnicity, class, gender, or sexual orientation. These self-revisions point in a specific political direction, for they arise out of a "coming to consciousness in the context of a concrete experiential struggle for self-actualization and collective . . . self-determination."[40] Consider Manlio Argueta's *One Day of Life*, Toni Morrison's *The Bluest Eye*, Nora Zeale Hurston's *Their Eyes Were Watching God*, Mary Brave Bird's *Lakota Woman*.[41] In the field of education, there is Mike Rose's *Lives on the Boundary*, Basil Johnston's *Indian School Days*, and Richard Rodriguez's *Hunger of Memory*.[42] Such stories promote and enrich struggles of resistance as the tellers, through a "language of democratic imagery"[43] imagine their oppressed selves otherwise.

Moral Stories, Imagination, and Courage

But we feel obliged to emphasize that the understandings that lead to moral agency are not acquired easily. Much anxiety surrounds the movement outward toward a redescription of who one is. The uncertainty that accompanies awareness of difficult moral dilemmas can cause us to yield to falsely moralistic forces within society that offer bogus comfort in their righteous certitude. The dilemma is clear: weak evaluation results in replicating the existing situation and strong evaluation sometimes demands what seems to be extraordinary courage. But moral stories can challenge readers to rethink an inherited script even as they simultaneously reassure them of the feasibility of a reconstructed self.

Good stories do indeed pose a threat to our equilibrium in their capacity to persuade us to choose a life course (sometimes dramatically) different from the one down which we have been traveling. Some moral stories, for example, offer even more than empathic insight and the demystification of prevailing social practices. They transgress against what is by evoking what can be: they adumbrate more enticing visions of, suggest more expansive options for, the future. These images offer hope and courage to those of us who are, in Kermode's words, "in the middest"—in the middle of history, in the middle of our lives.[44]

When we recognize that death will someday end the writing, we become eager for clues as to how best to compose the next chapter of our personal histories. We may each wish to create the best possible self, the most autonomous and responsible, most aesthetic and ethical of possible life stories, one that has exhibited personal fulfillment through social commitment. But envisioning the final version of that story is often beyond our capabilities, requiring, as it does, our imagining a description of an ideal self at the story's ending, at the time of our own death. Those of us—including curriculum workers—who are continuously examining and revising our selves stand in awe of the gap between our present life position and where we might some day finally rest. Equally awesome is imagining an ideal cultural script (including an educational utopia) and the most effective means for achieving it. So we struggle to transform at once so much dissonance and tension into the kind of stability, consonance, and equilibrium that marks a meaningful closure to a life. Given this formidable task, how can we act at all? We can rely on moral stories written by others for guidance in composing our own worthy life narrative.

First, consider certain formal attributes of the moral story. As Bruner recently reminded us, all stories begin with trouble.[45] At the outset the reader may recognize a familiar dilemma, be pulled into an intriguing situation. The plot thickens until the central crisis is tentatively and ambiguously (never, in a good story, finally, never definitively, never "correctly") resolved. So the satisfaction afforded by an aesthetic closure is simultaneously accompanied by both the disturbing recognition of all that was problematized by the story and the implication that different endings might be satisfactorily achieved. Still, the closure is, like the rest of the story, ersatz, virtual, vicariously (not actually) lived, and the story ends while the reader lives on. A moral story can therefore suggest that advancing toward a more just and equitable world, and therefore toward an ethical closure to the story of one's own self, is not an insurmountable task.

Stories also function to place the reader/curriculum worker in an alienated or distanced position from her/his own life and culture, allowing a critical view of previously taken-for-granted elements of an inherited script. This distancing is central to strong evaluation. Consider Erich Auerbach's landmark work of literary criticism authored in exile from Germany.[46] Auerbach understood that the project would have been impossible had he written it at home.[47] Immersed in the minutiae and current canons of his practice, he could never have seen so broadly or deeply. So too with story: it is as if the reader/curriculum worker is living in another land from which s/he may look back upon her/his own circumstances with clarity. The reader/curriculum worker can be awakened to the taken-for-granted values, ideologies, and practices sanctioned within an inherited script through vivid descriptions of the irrational conditions constraining the life of a storied character, and (sometimes) alternative images of more democratic social arrangements. The reader may thereby imaginatively don new realities before committing to purchasing and wearing them. In this manner moral stories offer visions without resorting to the heavy-handedness of propagandistic declarative texts.

Tales of Our Own

To recapitulate: The deliberative positions taken by a curriculum worker will necessarily be conditioned by personal values and beliefs, by the narrative woven to describe and explain what s/he stands for, and therefore who s/he is. His/her own sense of self will in turn be shaped by direct and vicarious participation in the stories of other people. Occasionally these (reading/viewing/listening) encounters will demand a strong evaluation of notions of who s/he is in relation to those people and the culture at large, and especially of prevailing attitudes toward victims and conditions of injustice and alienation.

We, the authors of this chapter, know this because we are readers/educators who have ourselves experienced firsthand the power of moral stories to problematize inherited scripts, challenge social imaginations relative to issues of oppression and disenfranchisement, and thereby prompt revisions in personal narratives. In order to illustrate this personal platform development and its bearing upon the stance assumed in the curriculum deliberation process, we will each share an intimate account of a life-altering event that transformed our sense of who each of us is.

Donald's Story

When I was seven years old, my parents bought a record album of a stage play called "The World of Sholom Aleichem," which contains an I. L. Peretz story entitled "Bontche Schweig" (Bontche the Silent). This narrative of struggle struck me then and strikes me now as profoundly important for the development of my moral Jewish consciousness as Peretz, himself a Jew, gave me access into "the most oppressed layer of human society, the lowest level of the pyramid."[48]

This moral story portrays a wretchedly poor Jew who bore, in silence and without a word of protest, all the terrible misfortunes a Jew could experience in nineteenth-century Eastern Europe. The story is set in the Heavenly Court where, upon Bontche's death, he is to be judged so that he might take his appropriate place in Heaven. After the counsel for the defense recounts all of the terrible happenings of Bontche's life, it is the prosecuting attorney's turn to speak.

> "Gentlemen!" began a sharp, piercing voice, and stopped.
> "Gentlemen!" it began again, but somewhat softer, and stopped again.
> Finally there issued from the same throat a voice that was almost friendly:
> "Gentlemen, he was silent! I will be silent, too."[49]

God turns to Bontche and tells him that his silence is admirable, although had he chosen to cry out against the injustices of his life Heaven would have heard and acted immediately. He invites Bontche to speak and ask for whatever he desires. All of Heaven is his for the asking. Bontche replies:

> "Takeh?" [Really?] he asked in a doubtful, timid voice.
> "Certainly," answered the Supreme Judge firmly. "I tell you, all is yours. Everything in Heaven belongs to you. Gather whatever you want. You are only taking from yourself."
> "Really?" asked Bontche again, but now with a little more assurance.
> "Really, really, really," they answered him from all sides.
> "Well, if it's really so," answered Bontche, with a smile, "then I want, every morning, a hot roll with fresh butter."
> Judges and angels looked down, ashamed. The prosecuting attorney broke into a laugh.[50]

For me, Bontche's tragedy is that he bore all this in silence. In my inherited script of the Jewish tradition we are responsible here and now for justice and equity, we must not bear degradation and indignity in silence and we must see to it that our fellow beings are free. In short, we must make the earth a place of social justice. I was young and middle class, with no understanding of what poverty and silence might do to the spirit of a person. (This, too, was part of my inherited script.) Here was a person, apparently good and decent and, even, caring, whose sense of self was so thoroughly diminished by such experience. It is not that he should have suddenly demanded to be wealthy but that he could conceive of no greater comfort for his existence: this was the fault of silence which burdened his life but brought him the admiration of God and yet destroyed him for all eternity. Silence was wrong.

The dilemma for me, however, extended into silence for I also felt a love for this man's mildness and willingness to help others. These were admirable qualities and connected to silence. For silence, too, was an injunction of Judaism as I understood it. (My parents left the Jewish religion behind entirely but kept intact the social ethic of the culture which is connected to the shtetl life of great personal danger for the revolutionary.) How to prevent such social injustice and yet retain the decency, which seemed bound up with silence, of this person? Thus, this story brought me the moral problematic of action and quietude which are fused and always connected with social issues.

No story "works" merely on the level of plot. It was the quality of the actor's voices, the sound of the trumpets, the musical setting, the "aesthetic narrative" of the portrayal. Eventually I saw the stage production both on television and in the theater, but this first experience, which I would almost call sacred, was the central one. Whenever I think of the story I hear the trumpets, the voices, and feel the same ineffable love and loss I felt then. To this day I read the story as a touchstone and have, recently, obtained the original album to play for my own children. Its attraction remains strong for me and no telling of the plot can convey what I feel and will feel when next I listen.

The experience of the story is clearly multi-dimensional from the curriculum platform perspective. First, and most obvious, is its presentation, in infinite pity and empathy, of the plight of the poor for whom the world metes out no justice. The question is: what can we, as curricularists, do about this? Second, the experience does not deliver a definitive answer to this question. Were Bontche to have railed and clawed in his life, he would not be revered by the angels or God. Yet, his silence doomed him in the mortal sphere and, as the angels learn, dooms him for eternity. And yet again, they, and I, love him precisely for that silence. What must I recommend for myself? Railing makes me an awful person to live with; silence condones the injustice; silence with Bontche's love of all beings creates a sterling heart. How can I conjoin the oppositions to fight the oppression yet find the heart? This story remains a way into the dilemma, if not a resolution to it. It is a center around which to create the necessary dialogue for deliberating this crucial, inevitably moral, curricular question.

Tom's Story

My story is also one of hurting and growing. A story about becoming more wide awake to certain features of my own life and the lives of one category of others, it remains painful to recall and especially to tell. It describes a moment of empathizing with another person while reading a piece of socially committed literature. The other person was my mother, now deceased. The literary work was *Main Street*, by Sinclair Lewis.[51]

When I was twenty years old, my father announced to my mother, my younger brother, and me, that he was leaving our home to live with a woman with whom he had been having a protracted affair. While my brother and I managed to absorb the shock and cope with the grief each in our own fashion, my mother was simply devastated. She had always been a highly conventional person, a traditional woman, a housewife maximally devoted to and supremely dependent upon a domineering husband. Pop psychologists of a later day might have called their relationship dysfunctional, wherein a wife forgoes a sense of self, holding herself captive to society's vision of her role as ever-obedient and loyal servant to her mate.

In the months following my father's departure, my mother's emotional condition deteriorated. My father's promises of financial support were broken, and now the pain of separation was mingling with fears of poverty. My mother had raised two children and maintained a household for twenty-three years, but her official resume was skimpy: her only outside work had been that of weekend waitress in the restaurant owned and managed by my father, uncle, and grandfather. But now she would need to find a job.

It was during this period that my mother's story became most prominent in my own. I was a college sophomore then and could only afford to live at home. So I was often in proximity to her despair as she returned from a day of pounding the pavement in search of work. Sometimes I could hear her crying in her room for hours.

I moved into her story partly out of my own experiences. I had smelled for myself the frustration and humiliation of job hunting, even if only for part-time, summer employment, cash to rattle around with. But I understood that her very life—the abruptly devalued life of an "unskilled," fiftyish, Kennedy-era divorcee—was at stake. Standing so close to the searing pain of a loved one must inevitably alter the plot of own's own life. But my understanding of my mother's predicament was furthered by the story of another woman—a fictional one named Carol Kennicott, imagined by a male author—that I happened to be reading at the time.

Main Street is (the reader may recall) the portrait of a woman struggling against an inherited script. Carol Kennicott is a young person in early 1900s America. Sophisticated and well read, she marries a physician who brings her to the stultifying environment of Gopher Prairie, a small Midwestern town. There she feels trapped by the smugness and complacency of the townspeople, by the vicious monotony of daily life, by the town's pervasive aesthetic and moral drabness. She also feels powerless in her role as loyal spouse. Much of the book vividly chronicles Carol's discontentment, dissects her dispiriting marriage, and details her subtle forms of resistance. After drifting into an extramarital affair, Carol finally flees to Washington, D.C., where she feels liberated while working in a government bureau:

> Not to have to apologize for her thoughts to the Jolly Seventeen [Gopher Prairie social club], not to have to report to Kennicott at the end of the day all that she had done or might do, was a relief which made up for the office weariness. She felt that she was no longer one-half of a marriage but the whole of a human being.[52]

For this reader the fascination with *Main Street* stopped there, for I found its social criticism blunted by an ending that finds Carol returning to Gopher Prairie, reconciled with Doctor Kennicott. Although still eager for change, she is now more tolerant of the conventional, willing to compromise outwardly even as she declares victory through her inwardly held hopes for future generations of women. To her husband:

> If you Tories were wise, you wouldn't arrest anarchists; you'd arrest all these children while they're asleep in their cribs. Think what that baby will see and meddle with before she dies in the year 2000! She may see an industrial union of the whole world, she may see aeroplanes going to Mars.[53]

My mother died in 1977, but first she found her way to her own Washington, D.C., finally landing a job as a receptionist for an insurance firm. Her friends and relatives noticed a new self, independent, confident, intellectually curious—the whole of a human being. In a sense I traveled with her as she emerged from her cultural and personal cocoon. And while the parallels between their two personae are hardly exact, the details of Carol Kennicott's grief and redemption resonated with those of my mother's.

Taken together as a single dose, these two stories (one a piece of socially committed literature, the other a directly confronted narrative of struggle) changed fundamentally who I was and am. They enhanced my empathy with others who had been previously outside the range of "me." They forced me to examine closely the politics of life as a member of a less privileged social category, enticed me to evaluate strongly the nuances of a cultural script that would have the lives of women left unfulfilled. They helped further a general critical disposition toward modernist institutions that distribute power so inequitably, and they greatly stimulated my own imaginings about the character of society (and schools) in a postpatriarchal world.

Today I bring that disposition with me as I deliberate with others the curriculum of, for example, an alternative track to my college's preservice teacher education program. And while I would never presume to speak for any feminist woman in the group, I know that my sense of who I am in relation to them surely affects the tone and quality of those deliberations.

Closure: Narrative, Deliberation, Action

We close where we began, with an insistence that the formation of a life narrative, the creation of a story of who one is, is a fundamental process of human understanding. Embedded in that narrative is a personal (and, by extension, professional) platform, consisting of clusters of (often) partially articulated beliefs related to large concerns such as human potential, and a nexus of attitudes toward political matters such as who does and does not deserve power. The shape of that platform is forged over the course of a lifetime, in the crucible of direct and vicarious experience, shaped by intimate knowledge of the stories of others. Dramatic revisions in a platform may appear during moments that Denzin has called *epiphanies*, conversion experiences, such as the ones described above, that fundamentally alter self-identity.[54]

In our experience it is quite rare for such epiphanies to occur during, or to flow from, deliberative episodes of curriculum making. Indeed, truly significant acts of self-definition and platform construction are precursors to rational thought and reflection, and therefore foreshadow the shape of the theoretical positions that an educator carries into an Aristotelian-style episode of practical reasoning. Or as McLaren put it, "the narratives we live by are not only evident in the way we reflect upon and analyze the past, present, and future, but are ingrained in the very theoretical formulations, paradigms, and principles, that constitute the models for such reflection and analysis."[55] What curriculum worker has ever witnessed a fundamental paradigm shift in the midst of debate and discussion, watched, for example, as a lifelong educational conservative is transformed into a proponent of critical democracy through schooling?

We have never been present at such an event. Still, we are convinced that the business of entertaining alternative moral visions is essential to the enlargement of democratic living. A social imagination seems particularly crucial for those of us who are charged with educating the next generation of American citizens. We consider it essential that curriculum workers— whether members of marginalized groups, or concerned representatives of the more privileged—learn to recognize the troubles arising from the maldistribution of power and resources within our schools and society.

For that reason we suggest that a curriculum for educators—the life curriculum and/or the formal school (especially college of education) curriculum—include the kinds of stories that emerge out of those troubles caused by irrationalities in the culture. It is our belief that such stories can entice curriculum workers into the reconstruction of their personal and professional platforms as they confront concrete images of social arrangements that alleviate these problems. Indeed, moral stories can promote a new idea of one's self as an advocate of, and activist for, democratic ideals. As curriculum workers we should seek out such stories, read, recommend, discuss them, and—figuratively, at least—carry them with us into our deliberative engagements.

Notes

1. Decker Walker, "A Naturalistic Model for Curriculum Development," *School Review* 80 (1971):52.

2. David Purpel, "Curriculum and Planning: Visions and Metaphors," in *Curriculum: An Introduction to the Field*, James Gress with David Purple, eds. (Berkeley: McCutchan, 1988), p. 319.

3. Ibid., p. 319.

4. See John Dewey, *Art as Experience* (New York: Capricorn Books, 1934/1958).

5. Anthony P. Kerby, *Narrative and the Self* (Bloomington: Indiana University Press, 1991).

6. George Herbert Mead, *Mind, Self, and Society* (Chicago: University of Chicago Press, 1934).

7. Donald E. Polkinghorne, *Narrative Knowing and the Human Sciences* (Albany: State University of New York Press, 1988), p. 142.

8. Davis Carr, *Time, Narrative, and History* (Bloomington: Indiana University Press, 1986), p. 65.

9. Peter Brooks, *Reading for the Plot: Design and Intention in Narrative* (New York: Vantage, 1985), p. xi.

10. Paul Ricouer, "On Interpretation," in *Philosophy in France Today*, Alan Montfiore, ed. (Cambridge: Cambridge University Press, 1983), p. 178.

11. Paul Ricoeur, "The Human Experience of Time and Narrative," *Research in Phenomenology* 9 (1979):24.

12. Martin Heidigger, *Being and Time*, J. Macquarrie and Edward Robinson, trans. (New York: Harper and Row, 1962).

13. Pokinghorne, op. cit., p. 152.

14. See Alasdair MacIntyre, *After Virtue: A Study in Moral Theory* (Notre Dame, Ind.: University of Notre Dame Press, 1984); Charles Taylor, *Human Agency and Language: Philosophical Papers I* (Cambridge: Cambridge University Press, 1985) and *Sources of the Self* (Cambridge, Mass.: Harvard University Press, 1991).

15. Taylor, *Sources of the Self*, op. cit., p. 28.

16. Kerby *Narrative and the Self*, op. cit., p. 54.

17. MacIntyre, op. cit.

18. Friedrich Wilhelm Nietzsche, *The Will to Power*, Walter Kaufmann and R. J. Hollingdale, trans. (New York: Vinatge, 1968).

19. Taylor, *Sources of the Self*, op. cit.

20. Mead, op. cit.

21. Paul Ricoeur, *The Conflict of Interpretations: Essay in Hermeneutics*, Don Ihde, trans. (Evanston, Ill.: Northwestern University Press, 1974), p. 17.

22. Cited in Herbert A. Hodges, *Wilhelm Dilthey: An Introduction* (New York: Oxford University Press, 1944), p. 159.

23. Hans-Georg Gadamer, *Truth and Method*, Garrett Barden and John Cumming, trans. and eds. (New York: Seabury, 1975).

24. Paul Ricoeur, *Freud and Philosophy: An Essay on Interpretation*, Denis Savage, trans. (New Haven, Conn.: Yale University Press, 1970), p. 28.

25. John Dewey, *Experience and Education* (New York: Collier, 1938/1963).

26. Richard Rorty, *Contingency, Irony, and Solidarity* (Cambridge: Cambridge University Press, 1989).

27. Clifford Geertz, *Works and Lives: The Anthropologist as Author* (Stanford: Stanford University Press, 1988), p. 147.

28. Martin Heidegger, "Building Dwelling Thinking," in *Poetry, Language, Thought*, Albert Hofstadter, trans. (New York: Harper and Row, 1971).

29. John Willinsky, "Getting Personal and Practical with Personal Practical Knowledge," *Curriculum Inquiry* 19, 3 (1989):251.

30. Robert Stone, "The Reason for Stories: Toward a Moral Fiction," *Harper's* 276 (1988).

31. Brian Fay, *Social Theory and Political Practice* (London: G. Allen & Unwin, 1975), p. 98.

32. Taylor, *Human Agency and Language*, op. cit., p. 34.

33. Kerby, op. cit., p. 58.

34. Catherine Belsey, *Critical Practice* (London: Methuen, 1980).

35. Michel Foucault, *Discipline and Punish* (New York: Pantheon, 1977).

36. bell hooks, "Narratives of Struggle," in *Critical Fictions: The Politics of Imaginative Writing*, Philomena Mariani, ed. (Seattle, Wash.: Bay Press, 1991).

37. Jean-Paul Sartre, *What Is Literature? and Other Essays* (Cambridge: Cambridge University Press, 1948/1988).

38. See Jonathan Kozol, *Savage Inequalities: Children in America's Schools* (New York: Harper Collins, 1991); A. Sparkes, "Life Histories and the Issue of Voice: Reflections on an Emerging Relationship," *International Journal of Qualitative Studies in*

Education, 1994; and Thomas Barone, "Ways of Being at Risk: The Case of Billy Charles Barnett," *Phi Delta Kappan* 71, 2 (1989).

39. Sartre, op. cit., p. 80.

40. hooks, op. cit., p. 54.

41. Manlio Argueta, *One Day of Life*, translated by Bill Brow (New York: Vintage, 1983); Toni Morrison, *The Bluest Eye: A Novel* (New York: Holt, Rinehart, and Winston, 1970); Zora N. Hurston, *Their Eyes Were Watching God* (New York: Perennial Library, 1937/1990); and Mary Brave Bird, *Lakota Woman* (New York: G. Weidenfeld, 1990).

42. Mike Rose, *Lives on the Boundary* (New York: Penguin, 1989); Basil Johnston, *Indian School Days* (Norman: University of Oklahoma Press, 1988); and Richard Rodriguez, *Hunger of Memory: The Education of Richard Rodriguez* (Boston: David R. Godine, 1982).

43. Jesse Goodman, *Elementary Schooling for Critical Democracy* (Albany: State University of New York Press, 1992), p. 174.

44. Frank Kermode, *The Sense of an Ending: Studies in the Theory of Fiction* (London: Oxford University Press, 1967). First, consider certain formal attributes of the moral story. As Bruner (1994) recently reminded us, all stories begin with trouble.

45. Jerome Bruner, *Four Ways to Make Meaning*. Paper presented at the annual meeting of the American Educational Research Association, New Orleans, La., 1994.

46. Erich Auerbach, *Mimesis: The Representation of Reality in Western Literature*, trans. Willard Trask (Princeton, N.J.: Princeton University Press, 1953/1968).

47. Edward Said, "Secular Criticism," in *Critical Theory Since 1965*, Hazard Adams and Leroy Searle, eds. (Tallahassee: Florida State University Press, 1986).

48. M. Samuel, "Silent Bontche," in *Prince of the Ghetto* (Philadelphia: Jewish Publication Society of America, 1948), p. 75.

49. Ibid., p. 82.

50. Ibid., p.83.

51. Sinclair Lewis, *Main Street* (New York: Harcourt, Brace, Jovanovich, 1920/1961).

52. Ibid., p. 408.

53. Ibid., p. 432.

54. Norman Denzin, *Interpretive Interactionism* (Newbury Park, Calif.: Sage, 1989).

55. Peter McLaren, "Border Disputes: Multicultural Narrative, Identity Formation, and Critical Pedagogy in Postmodern America," in *Naming Silenced Lives: Personal Narratives and the Process of Educational Change*, Daniel McLaughlin and William G. Tierney, eds. (New York: Routledge, 1993), p. 207.

NINE

The Culture and Commerce of the Textbook

Michael W. Apple

We can talk about culture in two ways, as a lived process, as what Raymond Williams has called a "whole way of life," or as a commodity.[1] In the first, we focus on culture as a constitutive social process through which we live our daily lives. In the second, we emphasize the products of culture, the very thingness of the commodities we produce and consume. This distinction can, of course, be maintained only on an analytic level, because most of what seem to us to be things—like lightbulbs, cars, records, and, in the case of this chapter, books—are really part of a larger social process. As Marx, for example, spent years trying to demonstrate, every product is an expression of embodied human labor. Goods and services are relations among people, relations of exploitation often, but human relations nonetheless. Turning on a light when you walk into a room is not only using an object, it is also to be involved in an anonymous social relationship with the miner who worked to dig the coal burned to produce the electricity.

This dual nature of culture poses a dilemma for those individuals who are interested in understanding the dynamics of popular and elite culture in our

This chapter is an updated version of one that appeared under the same name as chapter 4 in my *Teachers and Texts: A Political Economy of Class and Gender Relations in Education* (New York: Routledge, 1988).

society. It makes studying the dominant cultural products—from films, to books, to television, to music—decidedly slippery, for there are sets of relations behind each of these "things." And these in turn are situated within the larger web of the social and market relations of capitalism.

Although there is a danger of falling into economic reductionism, it is essential that we look more closely at this political economy of culture. How do the dynamics of class, gender, and race "determine" cultural production? How is the organization and distribution of culture "mediated" by economic and social structures?[2] What is the relationship between a cultural product— say, a film or a book—and the social relations of its production, accessibility, and consumption? These are not easy questions to deal with, in at least two ways. First, the very terms of these questions and the concepts we use to ask them are notoriously difficult to unpack. That is, words such as *determine, mediate, social relations of production*, and so on—and the conceptual apparatus that lies behind them—are not at all settled. There is as much contention over their use currently as there has ever been.[3] Thus, it is hard to grapple with the issue of the determination of culture without at the same time being very self-conscious of the tools one is employing to do it.

Second—and closely related to the first, perhaps because of the theoretical controversies surrounding the topic—there have been fewer detailed and large-scale empirical investigations of these relations recently than is necessary. While we may have interesting ideological or economic analyses of a television show, film, or book,[4] there are really only a few well-designed empirical studies that examine the economics and social relations involved in films and books in general. Because of this, it is hard to get a global picture.

This hiatus is a problem in sociological analysis in general, and yet it is even more problematic in the field of education. Even though the overt aim of our institutions of schooling has more than a little to do with cultural products and processes, with cultural transmission, only in the last decade or so have the politics and economics of the culture *actually* transmitted in schools been taken up as a serious research problem. It was almost as if Durkheim and Weber, to say nothing of Marx, had never existed. In the area that has come to be called the sociology of the curriculum, however, steps have been taken to deal with this issue in some very interesting ways. A good deal of progress has in fact been made in understanding whose knowledge is taught and produced in our schools.[5]

While not the only topics with which we should be concerned, it is clear that major curriculum issues have to do with content and organization. What should be taught? In what way? Answering these is difficult. The first, for example, involves some very knotty epistemological issues—e.g., what should be granted the status of knowledge?—and is a politically loaded question as well. To borrow the language of Pierre Bourdieu and Basil Bernstein, the "cultural capital" of dominant classes and class segments has been considered the most legitimate knowledge.[6] This knowledge, and one's "ability" to deal with it, has served as one mechanism in a complex process in which the economic and cultural reproduction of class, gender, and race relations is accomplished. Therefore, the choice of particular content and of particular ways of approaching it in schools is related both to existing relations of domination and to struggles to alter these relations. Not to recognize this is to ignore a wealth of evidence—in the United States, England, Australia, France, Sweden, Germany, and elsewhere—that links school knowledge, both commodified and lived, to class, gender, and race dynamics outside as well as inside our institutions of education.[7]

The recognition of the political nature of the curriculum, by itself, does not solve all of our problems. The statement that school knowledge has some (admittedly complex) connections to the larger political economy merely restates the issue. It does not in itself answer how these connections operate. Although the ties that link curricula to the inequalities and social struggles of our social formation are very complicated, research occasionally becomes available that helps to illuminate this nexus, even when it is not aimed, overtly, at an educational audience. I want to draw on this research to help us begin to uncover some of the connections between curriculum and the larger political economy. The most interesting of this research deals with the culture and commerce of publishing. It wants to examine the relationship between the ways in which publishing operates, internally—its social relations and composition—and the cultural and economic market within which it is situated. What do the social and economic relations within the publishing industry have to do with schools, with the politics of knowledge distribution in education? Perhaps this can be made clearer if we stop and think about the following question.

How is this "legitimate" knowledge made available in schools? By and large it is through something to which we have paid much too little attention—the textbook. Whether we like it or not, the curriculum in most American schools is not defined by courses of study or suggested programs, but by one particular artifact, the standardized, grade-level-specific text in mathematics, reading, social studies, science (when it is even taught), and so on. The impact of this on the social relations of the classroom is also immense. It is estimated, for example, that 75 percent of the time elementary and secondary students are in classrooms and 90 percent of their time on homework is spent with text materials.[8] Yet, even given the ubiquitous character of the textbook, it is one of the things we know least about. While the text dominates curricula at the elementary, secondary, and even college levels, very little critical attention has been paid to the ideological, political, and economic sources of its production, distribution, and reception.[9]

In order to make sense out of this, we need to place the production of curricular materials such as texts back into the larger process of the production of cultural commodities—such as books—in general. There are approximately forty thousand books published each year in the United States.[10] Obviously, these are quite varied, and only a small portion of them are textbooks. Yet, even with this variation, there are certain constants that act on publishers.

We can identify four "major structural conditions" that by and large determine the shape of publishing currently in the United States. As Coser, Kadushin, and Powell state:

> (I) The industry sells its products—like any commodity—in a market, but a market *Culture and Commerce of the Textbook* that, in contrast to that for many other products, is fickle and often uncertain. (2) The industry is decentralized among a number of sectors whose operations bear little resemblance to each other. (3) These operations are characterized by a mixture of modern mass-production methods and craft-like procedures. (4) The industry remains perilously poised between the requirements and restraints of commerce and the responsibilities and obligations that it must bear as a prime guardian of the symbolic culture of the nation. Although the tensions between the claims of commerce and culture seem to us always to have been with book publishing, they have become more acute and salient in the last twenty years.[11]

These conditions are not new phenomena by any means. From the time printing began as an industry, books were pieces of merchandise. They were, of course, often produced for scholarly or humanistic purposes, but before anything else their prime function was to earn their producers a living. Book production, hence, has historically rested on a foundation where from the outset it was necessary to "find enough capital to start work and then to print only those titles which would satisfy a clientele, and that at a price which would withstand competition." Similar to the marketing of other products, then, finance and costing took an immensely important place in the decisions of publishers and booksellers.[12] Febvre and Martin, in their analysis of the history of book printing in Europe, argue this point exceptionally clearly:

> One fact must not be lost sight of: the printer and the bookseller worked above all and from the beginning for profit. The story of the first joint enterprise, Fust and Schoeffer, proves that. Like their modern counterparts, fifteenth-century publishers only financed the kind of book they felt would sell enough copies to show a profit in a reasonable time. We should not therefore be surprised to find that the immediate effect of printing was merely to further increase the circulation of those works which had already enjoyed success in manuscript, and often to con-

sign other less popular texts to oblivion. By multiplying books by the hundred and then thousand [compared to, say, the laborious copying of manuscripts], the press achieved both increased volume and at the same time more rigorous selection.[13]

Drawing upon Pierre Bourdieu's work, we can make a distinction between two types of "capital"—*symbolic* and *financial*. This enables us to distinguish among the many kinds of publishers one might find. In essence, these two kinds of capital are found in different kinds of markets. Those firms that are more commercial, that are oriented to rapid turnover, quick obsolescence, and to the minimization of risks, are following a strategy for the accumulation of financial capital. Such a strategy has a strikingly different perspective on time, as well. It has a short time perspective, one that focuses on the current interests of a particular group of readers. In contradistinction to those publishers whose market embodies the interests of finance capital, those firms whose goal is to maximize the accumulation of symbolic capital operate in such a way that their time perspective is longer. Immediate profit is less important. Higher risks may be taken, and experimental content and form will find greater acceptance. These publishers are not uninterested in the "logic of profitability," but long-term accumulation is more important. One example is provided by Beckett's *Waiting for Godot*, which sold only ten thousand copies in the first five years after its publication in 1952, yet then went on to sell sixty thousand copies as its rate of sales increased yearly by twenty percent.[14]

The conceptual distinction based on varying kinds of capital does not totally cover the differences among publishers in the kinds of books they publish, however. Coser, Kadushin, and Powell, for example, further classify publishers according to the ways in which editors themselves carry out their work. In so doing, they distinguish among trade publishers, text publishers, and finally the various scholarly monograph or university presses. Each of these labels not only refers to editorial policy, but also speaks to a wide array of differences concerning the kind of technology employed by the press, the bureaucratic and organizational structures that coordinate and control the day-to-day work of the company, and the different risks and monetary and marketing policies of each. Each label also refers to important differences in relations with authors, in scheduling, and ultimately in defining what counts as "success."[15] Behind the commodity, the book, stands indeed a whole set of human relations.

These structural differences in organization, technology, and economic and social relations structure the practices of the people involved in producing books. This includes editors, authors, agents, and, to a lesser extent, sales and marketing personnel. Digging deeper into them also enables us to understand better the political economy of culture. By integrating analyses of internal decision-making processes and external market relations within publishing we can gain a good deal of insight into how particular aspects of popular and elite culture are presented in published form.

Let us set the stage for our further discussion historically. From the period just after the Civil War to the first decade of the twentieth century, fiction led in the sheer quantity of titles that were published. We can see this if we take one year as an example. In 1886, *Publishers Weekly* took the nearly 5,000 books published in the United States and broke them down into various categories. Those ten categories with the most volumes were: fiction (1,080), law (469), juvenile (458), literary history and miscellaneous (388), theology (377), education and language (275), poetry and drama (220), history (182), medical science (177), and social and political science (174).[16] These data do not account for the many informal political booklets and pamphlets that were published. But who the readership actually was, what the rates of literacy were between particular classes and genders, and what the economic conditions of publishing and purchasing were—all of this had an impact on what was published.

These figures have tended to change markedly over the years. Yet it is not just the type of book published that is of import historically or currently. Form and content have been subject to the influences of the larger society as well. To take one example, market constraints have often had a profound impact on what gets published and even on what authors will write. Again, certain aspects of the writing and publishing of fiction offer an interesting case in point. Wendy Griswold's analysis of the manner in which different market positions occupied by various authors and publishers had an impact documents this nicely.

In the nineteenth century, topics treated by European writers had a distinct market advantage in the United States, due to the oddities of our copyright laws. As Griswold states:

> During most of the nineteenth century, American copyright laws protected citizens or permanent residents of the United States but not foreign authors. The result was that British and other foreign works could be reprinted and sold in the United States without royalties being paid to their authors, while Americans did receive royalty payments. Many interests in the United States benefitted from this literary piracy and lobbied to maintain the status quo. (Actually piracy is something of a misnomer, for the practice was perfectly legal.) The nascent printing industry was kept busy. Publishers made huge profits from reprinting foreign books. Readers had available the best foreign literature at low prices; for example, in 1843 *A Christmas Carol* sold for c.06 in the United States and the equivalent of $2.50 in England.[17]

Clearly, such a situation could lead to some rather difficult circumstances for authors. American publishers had little inducement to publish "original native works" because a copyright had to be paid to their authors. The American author was largely left, then, unable to earn his or her living as a fiction writer because he or she was excluded from the fiction market. This also had an impact on the very content of writing as well. Discouraged from dealing with subjects already treated in the cheaper editions of European works, American authors often had to stake out a different terrain, areas that were unusual but would still have enough market appeal to convince publishers to publish them.[18]

These influences did not constitute a new phenomenon. In fact, the growth of particular genres and styles of books themselves has been linked closely to similar social forces operating earlier. As Ian Watt and Raymond Williams have argued, the rise of something as common today as the novel is related to changes in political economies and class structures and to the growth of ideologies of individualism, among other things.[19] In the eighteenth century in Europe, for instance, "the rapid expansion of a new audience for literature, the literate middle class, especially the leisured middle-class women," also led to novels focusing on "love and marriage, economic individualism, the complexities of modern life, and the possibility of personal morality in a corrupting world." The economic conditions of publishing also changed a good deal. A decline in patronage was accompanied by the growth of the bookseller who combined publishing, printing, and selling. Authors were often paid by the page. The speed of writing and amount of pages written was of no small value, as one might imagine.[20]

These small examples give a sense of the historical complexity of the influences on publishing and on its content, readership, and economic realities. Book publishing today lives in the shadow of this past and the social, ideological, and economic conditions that continued their development out of it. This is particularly the case in understanding the commercial and cultural structures involved in the publication of textbooks for schools. An excellent case in point is the production of texts for tertiary level courses. As we shall see, the "culture and commerce" of college-text and other text production can provide some important insights into how the process of cultural commodification works.

Textbook Publishing as Commerce

While we may think of book publishing as a relatively large industry, by current standards it is actually rather small compared with other industries. The *entire* book-publishing industry, with its 65,000 or so employees, would rank nearly forty to fifty positions below a single one of the highest grossing and largest employing American companies. While its total sales in 1980 were approximately six billion dollars and this does in fact sound impressive, in many ways its market is much less certain and is subject to greater economic, political, and ideological contingencies than other, larger companies.

Six billion dollars, however, is still definitely not a pittance. Book publishing is an industry, one divided up into a variety of markets. Of the total, $1.2 billion was accounted for by reference books, encyclopedias, and professional books; $1.5 billion came from the elementary, secondary, and college-text market; $1 billion was taken in from book clubs and direct mail sales; books intended for the general public—what are called trade books—had a sales level of $1 billion; and, finally, nearly $660 million was accounted for by mass-market paperbacks. With its $1.5 billion sales, it is obvious that the text-book market is no small segment of the industry as a whole.[21]

The increasing concentration of power in text publishing has been marked. There has been more and more competition recently, but this has occurred among a smaller number of larger firms. The competition has also reduced the propensity to take risks. Instead, many publishers now prefer to expend most of their efforts on a smaller selection of "carefully chosen 'products.'"[22]

Perhaps the simplest way to illuminate part of this dynamic is to quote from a major figure in publishing, who, after thirty-five years of involvement in the industry; reflected on the question, How competitive is book publishing? His answer, succinct and speaking paragraphs was only one word— "Very."[23]

A picture of the nature of the concentration within text publishing can be gained from a few facts. Seventy-five percent of the total sales of college textbooks was controlled by the ten largest text publishers, with 90 percent accounted for by the top twenty. Prentice-Hall, McGraw-Hill, the CBS Publishing Group, and Scott, Foresman—the top four—accounted for 40 percent of the market.[24] In what is called the "Delhi" (elementary and high school) market, the figures are also very revealing. It is estimated that the four largest textbook publishers of these materials account for 32 percent of the market. The eight largest firms control 53 percent. And the twenty largest control over 75 percent of sales.[25] This is no small amount, to be sure. Yet concentration does not tell the entire story. Internal factors—who works in these firms, what their backgrounds and characteristics are, and what their working conditions happen to be—also play a significant part.

What kind of people make the decisions about college and other texts? Even though many people find their way into publishing in general by accident, as it were, this is even more the case for editors who work in firms that deal with, say, college texts. "Most of them entered publishing simply because they were looking for some sort of a job, and publishing presented itself."[26] But these people are not all equal. Important divisions exist within the houses themselves.

In fact, one thing that recent research makes strikingly clear is the strength of sex-typing in the division of labor in publishing. Women are often found in subsidiary rights and publicity departments. They are often copy editors. While they outnumber men in employment within publishing as a whole, this does not mean that they are a powerful overt force. Rather, they largely tend to be hired as "secretaries, assistants, publicists, advertising managers, and occupants of other low- and mid-level positions." Even though there have been a number of women who have moved into important editorial positions in the past few years, by and large women are still not as evident in positions that actually "exercise control over the goals and policy of publishing." In essence, there is something of a dual labor market in publishing. The lower-paying, replaceable jobs, ones with less possibility for advancement, form the "female enclaves."[27]

What does this mean for this particular discussion? Nearly 75 percent of the editors in college-text publishing either began their careers as sales personnel or held sales or marketing positions before being promoted to editor.[28] As there are many fewer women than men who travel around selling college or other level texts or holding positions of authority within sales departments that could lead to upward mobility, this will have an interesting effect on the people who become editors and on the content of editorial decisions as well.

These facts have important implications. Most editorial decisions dealing with which texts are to be published—that is, concerning that which within particular disciplines is to count as legitimate content which students are to receive as "official knowledge"—are made by individuals who have specific characteristics. The vast majority of these editors will be male, thereby reproducing patriarchal relations within the firm itself. Second, their general background will complement the existing market structure that dominates text production. Financial capital, short-term perspectives, and high profit margins will be seen as major goals.[29] A substantial cultural or educational vision and the concerns associated with strategies based on symbolic capital will necessarily take a back seat, where they come into play at all.

Coser, Kadushin, and Powell recognize the influence of profit, the power of what they call commerce, in text production. As they note about college-text publishing, the major emphasis is on the production of books for introductory level courses that have high student enrollments. A good deal of attention is paid to the design of the book itself and to marketing strategies that will cause it to be used in these courses.[30] Yet, unlike most other kinds of publishing, text publishers define their markets not in terms of the actual reader of the book but in terms of the teacher or professor.[31] The purchaser, the student, has little power in this equation, except where his or her views may influence a professor's decision.

Based on the sense of sales potential and on their "regular polling of their markets," a large percentage of college-text editors actively search for books. Contacts are made, suggestions given. In essence, it would not be wrong to say that text editors create their own books.[32] This process is probably cheaper in the long run.

In the United States, it is estimated that the production costs of an introductory text for a college-level course is usually between $100,000 and $250,000. Given the fact that text publishers produce a relatively small number of books compared with large publishers of, say, fiction, there is considerable pressure on the editorial staff and others to guarantee that such books sell.[33] For the Delhi market, the sheer amount of money and risks involved are made visible by the fact that, nearly a decade ago, for every $500,000 invested by a publisher in a text, it had to sell 100,000 copies just to break even.[34] Publishers of basal reading textbooks may perhaps play for the highest stakes here, as their start-up costs range from $10 million to $40 million. Such high costs give current basal publishers a virtual monopoly over the market.[35]

These conditions have an impact on the social relations within the firm besides that of the patriarchal structure noted earlier. Staff meetings, meetings with other editors, meetings with marketing and production staff to coordinate the production of a text, and so on—these kinds of activities tend to dominate the life of the text editor. As Coser and his coauthors so nicely phrase it, "text editors practically live in meetings."[36] Hence, text publishing will be much more bureaucratic and will have decision-making structures that are more formalized. This is partly due to the fact that textbook production is largely a routine process. Formats do not markedly differ from discipline to discipline. And, as I mentioned, the focus is primarily on producing a limited number of *large sellers* at a comparatively high price compared to fiction. Lastly, the emphasis is often on marketing a text with a standard content, a text that—with revisions and a little bit of luck—will be used for years to come.[37]

All of these elements are heightened even more in another aspect of text publishing that contributes to bureaucratization and standardization, the orchestrated production of "managed" texts. These volumes are usually written by professional writers, with some "guidance" from graduate students and academics, although such volumes often bear the name of a well-known professor. Closely coordinated are text and graphics, language and reading levels, and the main text and an instructor's manual. In many ways, these are books without formal authors. Ghostwritten under conditions of stringent cost controls, geared to what will sell, not necessarily to what is most important to know, managed texts have been finding a place in many college classrooms. While the dreams of some publishers that such texts will solve their financial problems have not been totally realized, the managed text is a significant phenomenon and deserves a good deal of critical attention not only at the college level but also in elementary and secondary schools, since the managed text is not at all absent in these areas, to say the least.[38]

Even with the difficulty some managed texts have had in making the anticipated high profits, there will probably be more centralized control over writing and over the entire process of publishing material for classroom use. The effect, according to Coser, Kadushin, and Powell, will be "an even greater homogenization of texts at a college level,"[39] something we can expect at the elementary and high school level as well.[40] In fact, even after reviewing different sets of basal series extensively for many weeks, teachers and administrators often find it very difficult to tell one set from another, because of the similarity of organization and content.[41]

These points demonstrate some of the important aspects of day-to-day life within publishing. With all the meetings, the planning, growing sampling of markets, the competition, and so forth, one would expect that this would have a profound impact on the content of volumes. This is the case, but perhaps not quite in the way one might think. We need to be very careful here about assuming that there is simple and overt censorship of material. The process is much more complicated than that. Even though existing research does not go into detail about such things within the college-text industry specifically, one can infer what happens from its discussion of censorship in the larger industry.

In the increasingly conglomerate-owned publishing field at large, censorship and ideological control as we commonly think of them are less a problem than might be anticipated. It is not ideological uniformity or some political agenda that accounts for many of the ideas that are ultimately made or not made available to the larger public. Rather, it is the infamous "bottom line" that counts. As Coser, Kadushin, and Powell state: "Ultimately . . . if there is any censorship, it concerns profitability. Books that are not profitable, no matter what their subject, are not viewed favorably."[42]

This is not an inconsequential concern. In the publishing industry as a whole, only three out of every ten books are marginally profitable; only 30 percent manage to break even. The rest lose money.[43] Further, it has become clear that sales of textbooks in particular have actually been decreasing. If we take as a baseline the years of 1968 to, say, 1976, costs had risen considerably, cut sales at a college level had fallen 10 percent. The same is true for the "Delhi" text market; coupled with rising costs was a drop in sales of 11.2 percent[44] (this may have changed for the better given recent sales figures). If we speak specifically of basal textbooks, beyond the leading five basal publishers, which control over 80 percent of the market,[45] ten publishers compete for the remaining $8 million.[46] With start-up costs so high and with revision costs estimated at between $5 million to $8 million,[47] issues of profit are in fact part of a national set of choices within corporate logic.

If this is the case for publishing in general, and probably—in large part—for college-text production, is this case generalizable to those standardized secondary and, especially, elementary textbooks I pointed to earlier? Are market, profit, and internal relations more important than ideological concerns? Here we must answer: only in part.

The economics and politics of elementary- and secondary-school text production are somewhat more complicated. While there is no official federal government sponsorship of specific curriculum content in the United States (as there is in those countries where ministries of education mandate a standard course of study), the structures of a national curriculum are produced by the marketplace and by state intervention in other ways. Perhaps the most important aspect of this is to be found in the various models of state adoption now extant.

As many know from personal experience, in quite a few states—most often in the southern tier around to the western sunbelt—textbooks for use in the major subject areas must be approved by state agencies or committees, or they are reviewed and a limited number are selected as recommended for use in schools. If local school districts select material from such an approved list, they are often reimbursed for a significant portion of the purchase cost. Because of this, even where texts are not mandated, there is a good deal to be gained by local schools in a time of economic crisis if they do in fact ultimately choose an approved volume. The cost savings here, obviously, are not inconsequential.

Yet it is not only here that the economics of cultural distribution operates. Publishers themselves, simply because of good business practice, must by necessity aim their text-publishing practices toward those states with such state adoption policies. The simple fact of getting one's volume on such a list can mean all the difference in a text's profitability. Thus, for instance, sales to California and Texas can account for over 20 percent of the total sales of any particular book—a considerable percentage in the highly competitive world of elementary- and secondary-school book publishing and selling. Due to this, the writing, editing, promotion, and general orientation and strategy of such production is quite often aimed toward guaranteeing a place on the list of state-approved material. Since this is the case, the political and ideological climate of these primarily southern states often determines the content and form of the purchased curriculum throughout the rest of the nation. And since a textbook series often takes years to both write and produce and, as I noted earlier, can be very costly when production costs are totaled, "publishers want [the] assurance of knowing that their school book series will sell before they commit large budgets to these undertakings."[48]

Yet even here the situation is complicated considerably, especially by the fact that agencies of the state apparatus are important sites of ideological struggle. These very conflicts may make it very difficult for publishers to determine a simple reading of the needs of "financial capital." Often, for instance, given the uncertainty of a market, publishers may be loath to make decisions based on the political controversies or "needs" of any one state, especially in highly charged curriculum areas. A good example is provided by the California "creationism versus evolutionism" controversy, where a group of "scientific creationists" supported by the political and ideological Right, sought to make all social studies and science texts give equal weight to creationist and evolutionary theories.

Even when California's Board of Education, after much agonizing and debate, recommended "editorial qualifications" that were supposed to meet the objections of creationist critics of the textbooks, the framework for text adoption was still very unclear and subject to many different interpretations. Did it require or merely allow discussion of creation theory? Was a series of editorial changes that qualified the discussions of evolution in the existing texts all that was required? Given this ambiguity and the volatility of the issue in which the "winning position" was unclear, publishers "resisted undertaking the more substantial effort of incorporating new information into their materials."[49] In the words of one observer: "Faced with an unclear directive, and one that might be reversed at any moment, publishers were reluctant to invest in change. They eventually yielded to the minor editorial adjustments adopted by the board, but staunchly resisted the requirement that they discuss creation in their social science texts."[50] Both economic and ideological forces enter here in important ways, both between the firms and their markets and undoubtedly within the firms themselves.

Notice what this means if we are to fully understand how specific cultural goods are produced and distributed for our public schools. We would need to unpack the logic of a fairly complicated set of interrelationships. How does the political economy of publishing itself generate particular economic and ideological needs? How and why do publishers respond to the needs of the "public"? Who determines what this "public" is?[51] How do the internal politics of state adoption policies work? What are the processes of selecting people and interests to sit on such committees? How are texts sold at a local level? What is the actual process of text production from the commissioning of a project to revisions and editing to promotion and sales? How and for what reasons are decisions on this made? Only by going into considerable detail with each of these questions can we begin to see how a particular group's cultural capital is commodified and made available (or not made available) in schools throughout the country.[52]

My discussion of the issues of state adoption policies and my raising of the questions above are not meant to imply that all of the material found in our public schools will be simply a reflection of existing cultural and economic inequalities. After all, if texts were totally reliable defenders of the existing ideological, political, and economic order, they would not be such a contentious area currently. Industry and conservative groups have made an issue of what knowledge is now taught in schools precisely because there *are* progressive elements within curricula and texts.[53] This is partly due to the fact that the authorship of such material is often done by a particular segment of the new middle class, with its own largely liberal ideological interests, its own contradictory consciousness, its own elements of what Gramsci might call good and bad sense, ones that will not be identical to those embodied in profit maximization or ideological uniformity. To speak theoretically, there will be relatively autonomous interests in specific cultural values within the groups of authors and editors who work for publishers. These values may be a bit more progressive than one might anticipate from the market structure of text production. This will surely work against total standardization and censorship.[54]

These kinds of issues—concerning who writes and edits texts, whether they are totally controlled by the complicated market relations and state policies surrounding text publishing, and what the contradictory forces are at work—all clearly need further elaboration. My basic aim has been to demonstrate how recent research on the ways in which culture is commodified can serve as a platform for thinking about some of our own dilemmas as teachers and researchers in education who are concerned with the dynamics of cultural capital.

The Relative Autonomy of the Text

So far, I have employed some of the research on book publishing to help understand an issue that is of great import to educators—how and by whom the texts that dominate the curriculum come to be the way they are. As I mentioned at the very outset of this chapter, however, we need to see such analyses as a serious contribution to a larger theoretical debate about cultural processes and products as well. In this concluding section, let me try to make this part of my argument about the political economy of culture clear.

External economic and political pressures are not somewhere "out there" in some vague abstraction called "the economy." As recent commentators have persuasively argued, in our society hegemonic forms are not often imposed from outside by a small group of corporate owners who sit around each day plotting how to "do in" workers, women, and people of color. Some of this plotting may go on, of course. But just as significant are the routine bases of our daily decisions, in our homes, stores, offices, and factories. To speak somewhat technically, dominant relations are reconstituted on an ongoing basis by the actions we take and the decisions we make in our own local and small areas of life. Rather than an economy being out there, it is right here. We rebuild it routinely in our social interaction. Rather than ideological domination and the relations of cultural capital being something that is imposed on us from above, we reintegrate them within our everyday discourse merely by following our commonsense needs and desires as we go about making a living, finding sustenance and entertainment, and so on.[55]

These abstract arguments are important to the points I want to make. For while a serious theoretical structure is either absent or hidden within the data presented by the research I have drawn upon, a good deal of this research does document some of the claims made in these abstract arguments. As Coser, Kadushin, and Powell put it in their discussion of why particular decisions are made:

> For the most part, what directly affects an editor's daily routine is not corporate ownership or being one division of a large multi-divisional publishing house. Instead, on a day-to-day basis, editorial behavior is most strongly influenced by the editorial policies of the house and the relationship among departments and personnel *within* the publishing house or divisions.[56]

This position may not seem overly consequential, yet its theoretic import is great. Encapsulated within a changing set of market relations that set limits on what is considered rational behavior on the part of its participants, editors and other employees have "relative autonomy." They are partly free to pursue the internal needs of their craft and to follow the logic of the internal demands within the publishing house itself. The past histories of gender, class, and race relations, and the actual "local" political economy of publishing, set the boundaries within which these decisions are made and in large part determine who will make the decisions. To return to my earlier point about text editors usually having their roots in the sales department, we can see that the internal labor market in text publishing, the ladder on which career mobility depends, means that in these firms, sales will be in the forefront ideologically and economically. "Finance capital" dominates, not only because the economy out there mandates it, but because of the historical connections among mobility patterns within firms, because of rational decision making based on external competition, political dynamics, and internal information, and thus because of the kinds of discourse that tend to dominate the meetings and conversations among all the people involved within the organizational structure of the text publisher.[57] This kind of analysis makes it more complicated, of course. But surely it is more elegant and more grounded in reality than some of the more mechanistic theories about the economic control of culture, theories that have been a bit too readily accepted. This analysis manages to preserve the efficacy of the economy while granting some autonomy to the internal bureaucratic and biographical structure of individual publishers, and at the same time recognizes the political economy of gendered labor that exists as well.

Many areas remain that I have not focused on here, of course. Among the most important of these is the alteration in the very technology of publishing. Just as the development and use of print "made possible the growth of literary learning and journals" and thereby helped to create the conditions for individual writers and artists to emerge out of the more collective conditions of production that dominated guilds and workshops,[58] so too would one expect that the changes in the technology of text production and the altered social and authorial relations that are evolving from them will have a serious impact on books. At the very least, given the sexual division of labor in publishing, new technologies can have a large bearing on the deskilling and reskilling of those "female enclaves" I mentioned earlier.[59]

Further, even though I have directed my attention primarily to the "culture and commerce" surrounding the production of one particular cultural commodity—the standardized text used for tertiary- and elhi-level courses—it still remains an open question as to exactly how the economic and ideological elements I have outlined work through some of the largest of all text markets, those for the elementary and secondary schools. However, in order to go significantly further we clearly need a more adequate theory of the relationship between the political and economic (to say nothing of the cultural) spheres in education. Thus, the state's position as a site for class, race, and gender conflicts, how these struggles are "resolved" within the state apparatus, how publishers respond to these conflicts and resolutions, and ultimately what impact these resolutions or accords have on the questions surrounding officially sponsored texts and knowledge—all of these need considerably more deliberation.[60] The recent work of Carnoy and Dale on the interrelations between education and the state, and Offe's analyses of the state's role in negative selection, may provide important avenues of investigation here.[61]

This points to a significant empirical agenda, as well. What is required now is a long-term and theoretically and politically grounded ethnographic investigation to follow a curriculum artifact such as a textbook from its writing to its selling (and then to its use). Not only would this be a major contribution to our understanding of the relationship among culture, politics, and economy, it is also absolutely essential if we are to act in ways that alter the kinds of knowledge considered legitimate for transmission in our schools.[62] As long as the text dominates curricula, to ignore it as simply not worthy of serious attention and serious struggle is to live in a world divorced from reality.

Notes

1. Raymond Williams, *Marxism and Literature* (New York: Oxford University Press, 1977), p. 19. See also, Michael W. Apple and Lois Weis, eds., *Ideology and Practice in Schooling* (Philadelphia: Temple University Press, 1983), especially chap. 1.

2. Janet Wolff, *The Social Production of Art* (London: Macmillan, 1981), p. 47.

3. I have described this in more detail in Michael W. Apple, ed., *Cultural and Economic Reproduction in Education: Essays on Class, Ideology and the State* (Boston: Routledge and Kegan Paul, 1982). For further analysis of this, see Williams, *Marxism and Literature*; Colin Sumner, *Reading Ideologies* (New York: Macmillan, 1979); G. A. Cohen, *Karl Marx's Theory of History: A Defense* (Princeton, N.J.: Princeton University Press, 1978); and Paul Hirst, *On Law and Ideology* (London: Macmillan, 1979).

4. See Todd Gitlin, "Television's Screens: Hegemony in Transition," in Apple, ed., *Cultural and Economic Reproduction in Education*. The British journal *Screen* has been in the forefront of such analyses. See also, Will Wright, *Sixguns and Society* (Berkeley, Calif.: University of California Press, 1975). An even greater number of investigations of literature exist, of course. For representative approaches, see Terry Eagleton, *Marxism and Literary Criticism* (Berkeley, Calif.: University of California Press, 1976).

5. Michael W. Apple, *Ideology and Curriculum*, 2d ed. (Boston: Routledge and Kegan Paul, 1990). It is important to realize, however, that educational institutions are *not* merely engaged in transmission or distribution. They are also primary sites for the *production* of technical/administrative knowledge. The contradiction between distribution and production is one of the constitutive tensions educational institutions try to solve, usually unsuccessfully. For arguments about the school's role in the production of cultural capital, see Michael W. Apple, *Education and Power*, revised ARK Edition (Boston: Routledge and Kegan Paul, 1985), especially chap. 2.

6. Pierre Bourdieu and Jean-Claude Passeron, *Reproduction in Education, Society and Culture* (Beverly Hills, Calif.: Sage, 1977); and Basil Bernstein, *Class, Codes and Control*, vol. 3 (Boston: Routledge and Kegan Paul, 1977).

7. For an analysis of recent theoretical and empirical work on the connections between education and cultural, economic, and political power, see Apple, *Education and Power*.

8. Paul Goldstein, *Changing the American Schoolbook* (Lexington, Mass.: D. C. Heath, 1978), p. 1. On which subjects are taught the most, see John I. Goodlad, *A Place Called School* (New York: McGraw-Hill, 1983).

9. I do not want to ignore the importance of the massive number of textbook analyses that concern themselves with, say, racism and sexism. Although significant, these are usually limited to the question of balance in content, not the relationship between economic and cultural power. Some of the best analyses of the content and form of educational materials can be found in Apple and Weis, eds., *Ideology and Practice in Schooling*. See also Sherry Keith, "Politics of Textbook Selection," Institute for Research on Educational Finance and Governance, Stanford University, April 1981. Among the best recent critical studies of textbooks are Allan Luke, *Literacy, Textbooks and Ideology* (Philadelphia: Falmer, 1988); and

Patrick Shannon, *Broken Promises: Reading Instruction in Twentieth-Century America* (Granby, Mass.: Bergin and Garvey, 1989).

10. Lewis Coser, Charles Kadushin, and Walter Powell, *Books: The Culture and Commerce of Publishing* (New York: Basic, 1982), p. 3.

11. Ibid., p. 7.

12. Lucien Febvre and Henri-Jean Martin, *The Coming of the Book* (London: New Left Books, 1976), p. 109. As Febvre and Martin make clear, however, in the fifteenth and sixteenth centuries printers and publishers also acted as "the protectors of literary men," published daring books, and frequently sheltered authors accused of heresy. See p. 150.

13. Ibid.

14. Ibid., p. 44.

15. Ibid., p. 54

16. Wendy Griswold, "American Character and the American Novel: An Expansion of Reflection Theory in the Sociology of Literature," *American Journal of Sociology* 86 (January 1981):742.

17. Ibid., p. 748.

18. Ibid., pp. 748–49.

19. See Ian Watt, *The Rise of the Novel* (Berkeley, Calif.: University of California Press, 1974); and Raymond Williams, *The Long Revolution* (London Chatto and Windus, 1961).

20. Griswold, "American Character and the American Novel," p. 743.

21. Leonard Shatzkin, *In Cold Type* (Boston: Houghton and Mifflin, 1982), pp. 1–2. For estimated figures for the years after 1980, see John P. Dessauer, *Book Industry Trends, 1982* (New York: Book Industry Study Group, 1982).

22. Coser, Kadushin, and Powell, *Books*, p. 273. While I will be focusing on text production here, we should not assume that texts are the only books used in elementary, secondary, and college markets. The expanding market of other material can have a strong influence in publishing decisions. In fact, some mass-market paperbacks are clearly prepared with both school and college sales in the forefront of their decisions. Thus, it is not unusual for publishers to produce a volume with very different covers depending on the audience for which it is aimed. See Benjamin M. Compaine, *The Book Industry in Transition: An Economic Study of Book Distribution and Marketing* (White Plains, N.Y.: Knowledge Industry Publications, 1978), p. 95.

23. Shatzkin, *In Cold Type*, p. 63.

P24.   Coser, Kadushin, and Powell, *Books*, p. 273.

25. Goldstein, *Changing the American Schoolbook*, p. 61.

26. Coser, Kadushin, and Powell, *Books*, p. 100.

27. Ibid., pp. 154–55.

28. Ibid., p. 101.

29. Coser, Kadushin, and Powell, however, do report that most editors, no matter what end of house they work for, tend to be overwhelmingly liberal. Ibid., p. 113.

30. Ibid., p. 30.

31. Ibid., p. 56.

32. Ibid., p. 135.

33. Ibid., pp. 56–57.

34. Goldstein, *Changing the American Schoolbook*, p. 56.

35. Kenneth Goodman et al., *Report Card on Basal Readers* (Katonah, N.Y.: Richard C. Owen, 1988), pp. 45–50.

36. Coser, Kadushin, and Powell, *Books*, p. 123.

37. Ibid., p. 190.

38. Keith, "Politics of Textbook Selection," p. 12.

39. Coser, Kadushin, and Powell, *Books*, p. 366.

40. I have discussed this at greater length in Michael W. Apple, "Curriculum in the Year 2000: Tensions and Possibilities," *Phi Delta Kappan* 64 (January 1983):321–26.

41. Roger Farr, Michael Tully, and Deborah Powell, "The Evaluation and Selection of Basal Readers," *Elementary School Journal* 87 (January 1987):267–81.

42. Coser, Kadushin, and Powell, *Books*, p. 181.

43. Compaine, *The Book Industry in Transition*, p. 20.

44. Ibid., pp. 33–34.

45. Goodman et al., *Report Card on Basal Readers*.

46. R. Auckerman, *The Basal Reading Approach to Reading* (New York: John Wiley, 1987).

47. James Squire, "A Response to the *Report Card on Basal Readers*," paper presented at the Annual Meeting of the National Council of Teachers of English, Los Angeles, California. November 1987.

48. Keith, "Politics of Textbook Selection," p. 8.

49. Goldstein, *Changing the American Schoolbook*, p. 47.

50. Ibid., pp. 48–49.

51. For an interesting discussion of how economic needs help determine what counts as the public for which a specific cultural product is intended, see the treatment of changes in the radio sponsorship of country music in Richard A. Peterson, "The Production of Cultural Change: The Case of Contemporary Country Music," *Social Research* 45 (Summer 1978):292–314. See also Paul DiMaggio and Michael Unseem, "The Arts in Class Reproduction," in Apple, ed., *Cultural and Economic Reproduction in Education*, pp. 181–201.

52. I have discussed the relationship between the commodification process and the dynamics of cultural capital at greater length in Apple, *Education and Power*.

53. Ibid., especially chap. 5.

54. A related argument is made in Douglas Kellner, "Network Television and American Society," *Theory and Society* 10 (January 1981):31–62. See also Philip Wexler, "Structure, Text and Subject: A Critical Sociology of School Knowledge," in Apple, ed., *Cultural and Economic Reproduction in Education*, pp. 275–303.

55. This is discussed in greater detail in Apple, ed., *Cultural and Economic Reproduction in Education*.

56. Coser, Kadushin, and Powell, *Books*, p. 185.

57. Wexler's argument that texts need to be seen as the result of a long process of transformative activity is clearly related here. In essence, what I have been attempting to demonstrate is part of the structure in which such transformations occur and which makes some more likely to occur than others. See Wexler, "Structure, Text and Subject," and Philip Wexler, *Social Analysis and Education* (New York: Routledge, 1987).

58. Wolff, *The Social Production of Art*, p. 36.

59. The relationship among deskilling, reskilling, and the sexual division of labor is treated in more depth in Michael W. Apple, *Teachers and Texts* (New York: Routledge, 1988). See also David Gordon, Richard Edwards, and Michael Reich, *Segmented Work, Divided Workers: The Historical Transformation of Labor in the United States* (New York: Cambridge University Press, 1982).

60. See. for example, Apple, *Education and Power*; Roger Dale, Geoff Esland, Ross Furguson, and Madeleine MacDonald, eds., *Education and the State*, vol. I (Barcombe, England: Falmer, 1981); Michael W. Apple, "Common Curriculum and State Control," *Discourse* 2, 4 (1982):1–10; and Michael W. Apple, "Social Crisis and Curriculum Accords," *Educational Theory* 38 (Spring 1988):191–201.

61. I am indebted to Dan Liston for documenting the possible power of Offe's work. See Daniel Liston, *Capitalist Schools* (New York: Routledge, 1989); Martin Carnoy, "Education, Economy, and the State," in Apple, ed., *Cultural and Economic Reproduction in Education*, pp. 79–126; Roger Dale, "Education and the Capitalist State: Contributions and Contradictions," in Apple, ed., *Cultural and Economic Reproduction in Education*, pp. 127–61; and Roger Dale, *The State and Education Policy* (Bristol, Pa.: Open University Press 1989).

62. I do not want to imply that what is "transmitted" in schools is necessarily what is in the text. Nor do I want at all to claim that what is taught is wholly "taken in" by students. For analyses of teacher and student rejection, mediation, or transformation of the form and/or content of curriculums see Paul Willis, *Learning to Labour* (Westmead, England: Saxon House, 1977); Robert Everhart, *Reading, Writing and Resistance* (Boston: Routledge and Kegan Paul, 1983); Michael W. Apple, *Teachers and Texts*; and the chapters by Linda McNeil, Andrew Gitlin, and Lois Weis, in Apple and Weis, eds., *Ideology and Practice in Schooling*.

TEN

Democracy and the Curriculum

George H. Wood

As other selections in this collection have made clear, the curriculum arises as a product of choice. Further, choosing from among many curricular possibilities is always first and foremost a political act.

Political debates are usually generated by competing views of the way the world "should" be. Thus, we argue for competing conceptions of the curriculum (or school organization, pedagogy, control, etc.) on the basis of our view of a just society and good life. What this means is that behind arguments for particular curricula is more than the intention that students gain particular academic skills. In addition, each proposed curricular formation carries with it a distinct social outcome—a notion of what body of knowledge, skills, attitudes, and values students should gain in order to live in a particular social order. This essence of the curriculum leads to the vociferous debates over what schools should do.

These questions become especially difficult in a democracy, given democracy's essentially fluid character. Primary to any sense of democratic life is the notion that individuals are free to remake the social order in ways that best suit collective needs. On the other hand, concern is always present regarding the stability of the social order which requires that citizens accept the status quo in terms of social organization. These are questions not faced in terms of education in more centralized political orders. Autocracies, monarchies, and dictatorships all are preoccupied with stability and have little concern with the ability of the general populace to be self-governing. A democracy, however, faces directly the need for the democratic empowerment of its citizens.

In the early days of the Republic, Thomas Jefferson laid out the rationale for public schooling in a democratic society.

> In every government on earth is some trace of human weakness, some germ of corruption and degeneracy, which cunning will discover, and wickedness insensibly open, cultivate and improve. Every government degenerates when trusted to the rulers of the people alone. The people themselves therefore are its only safe depositories. And to render even them safe, their minds must be improved to a certain degree.[1]

Jefferson's ideas have been criticized for their elitism and limited view of the public. Yet within his proposals for free, public education are the seeds of the most important task before the school—to be the site where democratic citizens are empowered.

Indeed, the ongoing debate over schooling in America has historically focused on the school's social mission. The question is how can we best meet a democracy's need for informed, active, and productive citizens? Of course, this invokes a series of prior issues as well, most importantly the issue of how we are to define democracy and citizenship within it.

The resolution of this debate is central to thinking about and formulating educational decisions—including those regarding the school curriculum. Simply put, we need to know *what* we intend to do before we try and do it. Only after we are sure we undestand the school's role in a democracy can we begin to approach the question of curriculum. Only after we understand what it means to be a citizen, to participate democratically, can we begin to sort out the shape and scope of the curriculum.

Unfortunately, the contest over a curriculum for empowerment or control in a democratic society is often lost in curricular debates. We assume that the way the world as it currently exists is the way it should be; the curriculum is, thus, merely a tool to prepare students to fit into the existing social order. However, this begs the question of what it means to live and act democratically. This chapter addresses the meaning of democracy and its centrality as an organizing principle for curricular action.

In particular, three issues are explored. First, what do we mean by democracy and why should it be invoked as an organizing principle for schooling? Second, what can we say about the nature of many current curricular reforms in light of this discussion of democracy? And finally, what would a curriculum for democratic empowerment, as opposed to social control, look like?

The Meaning of Democracy

What do we mean when we say the purpose of schooling is to prepare democratic citizens? Certainly much of what we mean is found in how we define democracy. Often, the definition invoked is merely a reflection of current social and political practices. However, other choices are possible when deciding whether to judge a system or action democratic. In fact, there are ways to conceive of democracy which run directly counter to our present practices. A discussion of educating for democracy thus must begin with a clear understanding of democracy itself.

In the last thirty years a concerted effort has been made to bring definitions of democracy into line with its contemporary practice. Intended here was a move away from direct public participation in governance to making representation democracy's central characteristic.[2] These theories of democracy, referred to as either "weak" or "protectionist" theories, argue that we all engage in politics, or governance, only when we have personal interests to protect. Thus, we elect representatives to protect those interests from being violated.

To justify this vision of democracy, contemporary theorists of democracy draw on a variety of sources. First, the argument is made that the populace is composed of people who generally do not possess either the democratic attitudes or the intellectual capacity needed for self-governance. We are not willing, the argument goes, to invest the time necessary for democratic self-governance. Beyond that, the intellectual skills needed to resolve the problems of governance are not widely found in the general population. Therefore, democratic politics should be primarily a process of our choosing those who will make decisions rather than making decisions ourselves. Democracy is to be a competition between social and/or intellectual elites for the right to govern.[3]

Given this model, the central criterion for judging a system democratic is a system of open and free elections. If some public system exists through which social or political elites can compete for the right to represent individuals and their interests, that system must be judged democratic. As for those who do not vote, they also play a vital political role.

The positive contribution of political apathy is twofold. First, it demonstrates the general level of satisfaction with the system—it is simply assumed that those who do not vote are satisfied with the way things are. The second function of apathy is to keep to a minimum the demands on the system. Some individuals will refrain from voting not because they are satisfied, but because no elite is articulating their interests. This implies that the interests held by the individual are not widely shared, and thus do not deserve a place on the ballot.

179

This second function of political apathy is the key to understanding the main concern of proponents of protectionist democracy's stability. Any political system that claims to be "by, of, and for" the people does have inherent in it some instability. The greatest fear of those who advocate protectionist democracy is that this instability will be carried as far as it was in the Weimar Republic in Germany. As George Will states:

> In two presidential ballotings in Germany in 1932, 86.2 and 83.5 percent of the electorate voted. In 1933, 88.8 percent voted in the Assembly election swept by the Nazis. Were the 1932 turnouts a sign of the health of the Weimar Republic? The turnout reflected the unhealthy stakes of politics then; elections determined which mobs ruled the streets and who went to concentration camps.
>
> The fundamental human right is to good government. The fundamental problem of democracy is to get people to consent to that, not just to swell the flood of ballots. In democracy, legitimacy derives from consent, but nonvoting is often a form of passive consent. It often is an expression not of alienation but contentment . . . the stakes of our elections, as they affect the day-to-day life of the average American, are agreeably low.[4]

An alternative, "strong" or "participatory" conception of democracy, focuses on public participation as opposed to representation. This classical notion has posited that democracy, in the words of John Dewey, "is more than a form of government; it is primarily a mode of associated living, of conjoint communicated experiences."[5] That is, democracy is a way of living in which we collectively deliberate over our shared problems and prospects. It is conceived as a system in which decisions are made by those who will be directly effected by the decision.

The rationale for this notion of democracy comes from Rousseau's *The Social Contract*: (1) Participatory systems are self-sustaining because the very qualities required of citizens if such a system is to work are those that participation itself fosters; (2) participation increases one's "ownership" over decisions, thus making public decisions more acceptable to individuals; and (3) participation has an integrative function—helping integrate individuals into the social order.[6] These premises were further developed by John Stuart Mill and G. D. H. Cole.[7] Mill argued that the primary consideration in judging a society or government to be good was the effect that system had on individuals. Rather than concern himself with efficiency, Mill argued that participatory democracy fostered within individuals the psychological attributes needed in self-governance. In addition, Mill and Cole argued that these characteristics are best developed at the local level. Through such local participation, citizens come to formulate and take seriously decisions made on an immediate level, and develop those skills and attitudes necessary for self-governance at the national level.

What in particular is meant in referring to attributes needed for self-governance? J. S. Mill argued that an active character would emerge from participation and Cole suggested that a nonservile character would be generated. What this means is that individuals should have the confidence that they are fit to govern themselves. Such a state is often known as a *sense of political efficacy*. That is, the belief that individual political action does have an impact on decision making; therefore, performing one's civic duties is worthwhile.

Empirical evidence suggests that participation does enhance feelings of political efficacy. Studies by Almond and Verba, Carnoy and Shearer, and those cited by Wirth, point out that participatory models in local governments, workplaces, and associations do lead to higher levels of participation in national politics. In all of these studies, local participation in self-governance increased a sense of control over the immediate political environment and a concurrent desire emerged to participate in controlling the national political agenda.[8]

Let me clarify what these theories and studies mean when the term *participation* is used. Three conditions must be obtained: First, the participants must be in the position of decision maker rather than decision influencer; second, all participants must be in possession of, or have access to, the requisite information on which decisions can be reached; and third, full participation requires equal power on the part of participants to determine the outcome of decisions. When individuals experience participation in this sense at a local level, the research suggests that they will gain a greater sense of political efficacy in the national arena.[9]

This implies, contrary to claims made by protectionist theorists, that democracy best functions as a lived process of participation, a process in which citizens do not merely choose between elites but actually transform themselves through debate and contestation over public issues. This was the original vision of democracy upon which the foundations of our political practice were laid. Additionally, as has been pointed out in Wirth's review of workplace democracy, it is a vision of democracy that continus to be relevant as it humanizes shared social spheres, empowers democratic citizens, and leads to more effective and efficient decision making. Ongoing debate into the way such participation is facilitated in our evolving society is necessary. The point here is that *participatory theory* holds us closer to a democratic society than does *protectionist theory*.[10]

Educators should realize that the social role they play depends on the conception of democracy, participatory or protective, they choose. On the one hand rests a conception of democracy within which the participation of the minority elite is crucial and the nonparticipation of the apathetic ordinary individual is necessary to maintain the system's stability. On the other hand, democracy is conceived as encompassing the broadest participation of the people working to develop political efficacy and a sense of belonging in order to further extend and enhance more participation.

Schooling and Protectionist Democracy

Given the above outline, it seems clear that the most broadly publicized and debated of the current reports on curricular reform are based on protectionist democracy. Both in substance and implementation, recommendations for change seem destined to limit democratic participation rather than expand it. It is important to see how this happens before turning to curricular action based upon participatory democracy.

Perhaps the most glaring democratic indictment of the reform effort of the 1980s was its top-down nature. A simple survey of the makeup of commissions that have issued curricular proclamations demonstrates the elite makeup of the recommending committees: In the six most publicized and promoted reports, 132 individuals played a part, among whom were three teachers.[11] This top-down reform is carried out in the best traditions of protectionist democracy, with self-selected elites choosing the curriculum to be followed by teachers and students. Perhaps Susan O'Hannian's biting sarcasm most clearly summarizes the nature of such curricular mandates:

> The good gray managers of the U.S., the fellows who gave us Wonder Bread, the Pinto, hormone-laden beef wrapped in Styrofoam, and *People* magazine—not to mention acid rain, the Kansas City Hyatt, $495 hammers, and political campaigns—are now loudly screaming that we teachers should mend our slothful ways and get back to excellence.[12]

Such curricular action is a continuation of the trend to "teacher-proof" the curriculum; that is, a desire to standardize and routinize the curriculum in ways that dictate teacher behaviors, leaving little or no room for creativity, individuality, or spontaneity. Only in that way will the top-down reformers be assured that they, not teachers, are in control.[13]

Additionally, these reforms are to be implemented by state or national mandate. Most of the national commissions do not see a need for local control of, or diversity in, the curriculum. Rather, standardization is to be imposed on teachers from the highest levels of the educational bureaucracy. Again, the theme is centralization of both power and control as opposed to any notion of public participation and community control. If this is how reform is to be implemented, what end does it serve?

The answer to this seems to be the narrowing of what counts as worthwhile knowledge, linking schooling to work, and avoiding issues of equity in pursuing what is loosely called *excellence*. Some examples of each of these trends are in order here.

In each report, the sentiment is that it is time to get back to the basics. All focus on what is believed to be a set of basic skills to be mastered and then tested on standardized measures. The Twentieth Century Fund calls for a core of reading, writing, and calculating; technical capability in computers; training in science and foreign languages; and knowledge of civics. The National Science Board (NSB) couples the "three R's" with communication and higher problem-solving skills, and scientific and technological literacy. The President's Commission on excellence in Education's much discussed report, *A Nation at Risk*, calls for concentrating in the "Five New Basics," English, mathematics, science, social studies, and computer literacy.

Objecting to the notion that these should all be valued components of any curricular reform is difficult. However, upon careful examination, two problems of intent arise. First, these proposals all seem to define narrowly what is considered *an education*. Under the guise of returning to "basics," a great deal is eliminated—such as the arts, music, and humanities in their broadest sense. Of course, given that these proposals all carry with them an intent to test student achievement, we can expect a narrowing even within the basics. In English, for example, the ability to find a verb in a list of words becomes more important than crafting a clear sentence or paragraph. Given the very nature of standardized testing, the process of teaching to the test forces a narrowing of the curriculum.

But the curriculum always has some intent—and the intent in these reports is clearly to produce a steady source of workers. The concern that motivates each report is with the failure of American industrial strength: "Our once unchallenged preeminence in commerce, industry, science, and technological innovation is being overtaken by competitors throughout the world."[14] "Japan, West Germany, and other relatively new industrial powers have challenged America's position on the leading edge of change and technical innovation."[15] "Already the quality of our manufactured products, the viability of our trade, our leadership in research and development, and our standards of living are strongly challenged. We must not let this happen; America must not become an industrial dinosaur."[16]

Given these problems, the need for "more skilled young people [is greater] than every before."[17] And the origination of these demands for well-trained workers comes directly from business: "Business will require, to an increasing degree, people who are knowledgeable about science and technology."[18] The purpose of these reforms, the motivation behind the narrowing of the curriculum, is simply to prepare children for work (and, in *A Nation at Risk*, for the military).

In analyzing this trend, David Cohen has called it part of the "Toyota Problem."

> We have not always had Toyotas, but schools have long had the problem of improving productivity, or efficiency, or both—at least schools have long thought they had that problem. Since the 1890s we have thought of schools as a chief means for making America more productive, more efficient, more competitive. This is an idea that becomes increasingly problematic the deeper one digs into the relationship between education and productivity, yet few seem inclined to question the notion that schools are responsible for the many failures of General Motors, or Ford, or Chrysler. It is odd since schools never were praised for causing earlier success in that industry.[19]

It is important at this point to note that this is not a new trend. Rather, it derives directly from the scientific management ethos forced on schooling in the early 1900s. The attempt in these early decades was to mold the schools in the model of scientifically managed industry. Here, work was fragmented into small parts with each worker a cog in a larger machine controlled by the foreman. Workers did not control either the speed or nature of their work because the goal was a tightly controlled process which generated the greatest amount of production in the shortest time possible.

Schooling, molded in this image, was a process of mass producing workers in the most cost-effective, or efficient, manner. Minimum standards were set both for job performance and student achievement. Teaching was to be controlled by an administrative hierarchy applying the latest techniques of scientific measurement and analysis. The results of this "cult of efficiency," as Raymond Callahan has called it, depended on where one sat.[20] Ellwood P. Cubberly, an administrator and proponent of the application of scientific management to schooling, saw the movement this way in 1916:

> The [efficiency] movement indicates the growth not only of a professional consciousness as to the need of some quantitative units of measurement, but also, to a limited extent, of a public demand for a more intelligent accounting by school officers for the money expanded for public education.[21]

As opposed to this in 1911, Margaret Haley, an elementary teacher and organizer of the Chicago Teacher's Association, saw the "Factory System" of education as needing "only the closing time whistle to make complete its identification with the great industrial plants."[22]

Indeed, as Arthur Wirth and others have recounted, the attempts to scientifically control education, to mandate from the top down, worked to limit the educative function of schooling. Rote learning was valued over critical thinking, group recitation took the place of individual inquiry, and bland, standardized textbooks replaced reading the classics or the legitimate literature of the day. This is not to suggest that there was some "Golden Age" of schooling that the scientific management craze displaced. Rather, while alternatives did exist (often in school districts under more localized and populist, as opposed to bureaucratic and professional, administrative forms) they were eliminated in the name of science.

To return to the theme of this chapter, it could also be claimed that such school reform was profoundly antidemocratic. School control was removed from the public and put in the hands of administrators (never teachers). The curriculum was structured to meet national or local manpower needs, not the preparation of active citizens. Lessons learned focused on rote repetition, obedience, and compliance as opposed to inquiry, self-government or control, and active involvement. All in all, it was schooling for passive control, not for democratic involvement.

The mainstream reform documents of today seem to echo the words of these scientific management educators and efficiency experts. (Exceptions to this are highlighted in the following section.) As opposed to restructuring the antidemocratic nature of many curricular practices, including rote memorization, passive learning, and tightly controlled school environments, we hear calls for more of the same. More is frequently the actual prescription: more days, more hours, more homework, more tests, more, more, more.[23] Additionally, control of the curriculum is to continue to be centralized—mandated by state or professional bodies and carried out by the lowly teacher (worker). In this new manifestation of schooling for work, the scientific management of the curriculum enters not a new, but a merely expanded, phase.

The consequence of schooling that seeks merely to respond to the demands of the workplace seems all too clear: Individuals patterned to take their place unthinkingly in a world that operates beyond their control with no respect for their needs. We become cultural and political isolates—with little sense of community or cooperative effort. And most essentially, we adopt a position of passivity, waiting to be "done to" rather than acting ourselves.

The broadest, most public agenda for schooling is thus abandoned. The issue of preparing a public to live democratically, to share in collective decision making, to participate broadly in public affairs, is lost to the simple memory tasks of mandated minimum competencies. It is not simply an ignorance of the school's democratic mission that brings about these trends. Rather, it is a decidedly antidemocratic spirit that motivates reforms designed to keep the public ignorant and passive as opposed to enlightened and active. "The public schools of America have not been corrupted for trivial reasons," writes Walter Karp.

> Much would be different in a republic composed of citizens who could judge for themselves what secured or endangered their freedom. Every wielder of illicit or undemocratic power, every possessor of undue influence, every beneficiary of corrupt special privilege woud find his position and tenure at hazard. Republican education is a menace to powerful, privileged, and influential people, and they in turn are a menace to a republican education. . . . Merit pay, a longer school year, more home work, special schools for "the gifted," and more standardized tests will not even begin to turn our public schools into nurseries of "informed, active, and questioning citizens." They were not meant to. When the authors of *A Nation at Risk* called upon schools to create an "educated work force," they are merely sanctioning the prevailing corruption, which consists precisely in the reduction of citizens to credulous workers.[24]

A Curriculum for Democratic Empowerment

Is it possible for public schooling to achieve its democratic promise? Rejecting recent reform proposals is not enough if schooling is to take a democratic direction. Additionally, parameters (as opposed to prescriptions) of what would count as democratic curriculum, school organization, and pedagogy need to be set forth. In what follows we consider solely the issue of the curriculum. Yet this does not mean curricular reform can stand alone. If the curriculum is to become a source of democratic empowerment, it will need the support of changing administrative and pedagogic structures. But these are beyond the scope of this chapter. Here, my concern is with the notions of democratic empowerment, democratic values, and a democratic curriculum.

Historically, the assumption was that a liberal arts curriculum was all that was required to educate for democratic citizenship. The political tools were there to be utilized by those literate enough to engage in political matters. This is no longer a viable approach to public education for democratic life for two reasons. First, the complexity of the issues that face the public often seem to paralyze popular democratic action. We turn too often to technical experts to solve what are more genuinely political problems. Second, strong, antidemocratic forces are at work today that must be contained if democratic life is to have a future. Institutionally, we are witnessing broad areas of public concern (foreign policy, local economic development, the environment) coming under increasingly private or, if public, bureaucratic control. Attitudinally, vast numbers of citizens refuse to participate politically due to despair, apathy, or a refusal to take responsibility. The complexity and antidemocratic nature of our social lives will not be overcome by traditional liberal arts curricula, as valuable as they may be.

This is not to suggest that the alternative curricula proposed herein for democratic empowerment will resolve all of the foregoing problems. Certainly, the revitalization of democratic life requires action in a variety of spheres—economic, cultural, social, and political, as well as educational. Yet the value of engendering a democratic disposition among youth in schools cannot be underestimated. If Dewey and the pragmatic philosophers are correct, if indeed we learn what we experience, then the only way to guarantee a reservoir of democratic sentiment in the culture is to make public schooling a center of democratic experience.

What is meant when we speak of a curriculum for democratic empowerment? To begin with, let us define what is meant by democratic empowerment. Gaining a sense of democratic empowerment involves the following cognitive, personal, and communal skills and understandings:

1. believing in the individual's right and responsibility to participate publicly;
2. having a sense of political efficacy, that is, the knowledge that one's contribution is important;
3. coming to value the principles of democratic life—equality, community, and liberty;
4. knowing that alternative social arrangements to the status quo exist and are worthwhile; and
5. gaining the requisite intellectual skills to participate in public debate.

A wide body of literature, as well as actual curricular practices, have recently focused on school reform geared to democratically empower students. There have been proposals, such as those from the American Educational Studies Association (AESA) and the Public Education Information Network, that argue for more democratic school structures.[25] In both cases, the argument is that autocratic forms of school organization foster passive, nonparticipatory models of citizenship. Students, with no role to play in decision making within the institution, learn through experience that the role of the good citizen is to passively obey, not to question.

Opposed to this are offered models of school organization that actively engage students in making decisions about their lives. From the AESA document:

> Moreover, a democratic commitment demands a pedagogy which does more than effectively transmit the cultural heritage, extend bodies of knowledge, or vocational skills. It must teach students how to think, how to order their own affairs

rationally, how to function as competent citizens, and how to accept, value, and respect others. It must develop the exercise of those capacities central to understanding one's own interests, those of others, and how to effect decisions. . . .

It is unreasonable to expect school graduates to behave responsibly unless they have learned to exercise the judgment that yields such behavior and to practice the examining and choosing of alternative courses of action. . . . If we want adults who can outgrow the bonds of their personal dependency, and who are capable of the freedom a democratic society expects them to exercise, the school must explicitly concern itself with the development of individual autonomy.[26]

Other proposals focus on reforming the curriculum in ways that would better equip students to participate democratically. They argue against ability-segregated school organization that creates a political underclass through differentiated knowledge acquisition. Furthermore, they suggest that the entire curriculum should target political and social as opposed to vocational life. Such is the argument of curricular proposals put forth by a wide range of individuals, from Mortimer Adler to John Goodlad and Ernest Boyer.

The one-track system of schooling *The Paideia Proposal* advocates has the same objectives for all without exception. These objectives are not now aimed at in any degree by the lower tracks onto which a larger number of our underprivileged children are shunted—an educational dead end. It is a dead end because these tracks do not lead to the result that the public schools of a democratic society should seek, first and foremost, for all its children—preparation to go on learning, either at advanced levels of schooling, or in adult life, or both.[27]

Civic literacy is decreasing, and unless we find better ways to educate ourselves as citizens, we run the risk of drifting unwittingly into a new kind of Dark Age—a time when, increasingly, specialists will control knowledge and the decision making process. In this confusion, citizens would make critical decisions, not on the basis of what they know, but on the basis of blind belief in one or another set of professed experts.[28]

At the center of all five proposals is some sense, more explicit in the first two, of educating for democratic empowerment. They set forth the broad outlines of the necessary schooling arrangements to generate the social, intellectual, personal, and cultural skills to embrace democratic citizenship. The issue now is to move more directly to what a curriculum for democratic empowerment would look like. Such a curriculum includes critical literacy skills, developing student's stock of cultural capital, actively engaging students in decision making, providing for social alternatives, and embracing democratic values. Each of these is set forth in what follows.[29]

Critical Literacy

Any curriculum focusing on democratic empowerment must find at its base a foundation in critical literary skills. This does not mean, however, the limited "back to basics" approach that dominates so much of the literacy literature. The workbook, basal approach to reading, writing, and speaking presents only a fragmented and technical approach to these skills. Not only do these approaches not work, they restrict the ways children come to see literacy as a tool for their own empowerment. Language is seen as a decoding device, useful for understanding what we are told, but not for making our own voices heard.

In opposition to that prescription, a curriculum for democratic empowerment needs to enhance critical literacy skills that give children personal and political facility with the language. Critical literacy involves the ability to evaluate what is read or heard with respect to the interests being served or the positions taken. Furthermore, critical literacy enhances the ability to mold one's own world through naming and constructing models of preferred social and personal life.

What this means in practice is helping students come to see the written word as something other than truth incarnate—working toward an understanding that all writing and speaking is nothing more, and nothing less, than an attempt to communicate and persuade—a process open to all. Several examples help illuminate this process.

For younger children, critical literacy involves building reading skills around students' own reading agendas. Having them read about things in which they have an interest and helping them write their own reading material are key components in this process. Several teachers with whom I work approach this in a variety of ways. One has children extend the books they read, either writing new endings or going beyond the ending to continue the story. Another builds entire curricular units around topics of student interest. Called *webbing*, the teacher and students gather real books, not basals, on the topic at hand and read, share, write about, construct models, present plays, and so forth on topics based on their readings. Moving beyond webbing, one teacher has students write their own textbooks in the academic areas, drawing together student learning in their own words.

At the elementary level, some of this is just sound teaching practice. Reading and writing, when taught as interconnected processes and not just technical skills, become things students enjoy and continue to engage in over time. Beyond that, these children are learning that they can control words so as to build their own reality. They do not have to rely on the words and images of others.[30]

With older children, critical literacy means interrogating the text and writing about the real. In one social studies class, the teacher has students read competing accounts of the same event. The questions then addressed are why these accounts differ, what counts as a trustworthy source, and whose interests these competing accounts serve. Several English teachers are engaged in a project involving students writing about community affairs. Students research issues in their communities that concern them and then write about them for publication from an advocacy position.

Such activities develop critical literacy skills in two ways. First, students come to see that what is written down is never "plain truth" but rather attempts to persuade. Second, they find their own voices to speak and persuade others. In so doing, they move well beyond basic skills and become what Moffit has termed "dangerously and democratically literate."[31]

Cultural Capital

The term *cultural capital* means that stock of cultural awareness that an individual possesses about his or her own history, and this knowledge makes acting as autonomous human beings possible.[32] As Black history advocates have so clearly argued, without a sense of one's roots it is hard to act in ways that are in one's self—or group—interest. Feminists as well have worked to rediscover the historic, social, political, and economic contributions of women, in order to foster a deeper sense of possibility and unity among women.

What this means for a democratic curriculum is the use of students' own histories as the focus of historical inquiry. Rather than the endless parade of great white men and large-scale wars, history should contain a focus on the daily lives and contributions of the average citizen. Already available are commercially prepared history texts for older students focusing on the contributions of citizens' groups and popular protest.[33] More important is the example of the *Foxfire* program in Rabun Gap, Georgia.[34] In what began as an English curriculum, students explore local folk ways through oral interviews and publish those in the now highly successful *Foxfire Magazine* and books. This English curriculum has branched out to include music and radio/television work. Many additional examples of such a localized approach to history or English can be found.[35]

With younger students, the focus is often on their own lives and surroundings. In the *"Perspectives"* series, produced by Educators for Social Responsibility, a text entitled *Making History* provides ways of students understanding and investigating their own histories.[36] From personal to family to community frameworks, the focus is on expanding the historical investigation while maintaining a personal sense of location within that history.

Teachers who have worked on such projects find their students have a new sense of empowerment and possibility. For example, one young student summarized the feelings of an entire class when she expressed shame at her racism in the face of her own town's history of involvement in the underground railway during the Civil War. Other students have felt and acted on a sense of personal power when they connect their own concerns with those of ongoing movements for social justice or change in their own communities. Perhaps nothing is more personally inspiring than finding in one's own family history an example of democratic participation in order to make the world a better place.

Such approaches to social studies, history, English, the arts, and other areas all have as their focus one agenda—personal empowerment. To participate democratically requires a sense of political efficacy—the belief that each individual's engagement is both required and has an effect. One side of efficacy is a historical sense of being part of a larger participatory tradition. The other is practical experience in decision making.

Student Decision Making

The literature on efficacy clearly states that the desire to engage in democratic participation is generated by actual experiences with decision making. Beginning at the local level, when individuals participate in decisions that directly effect them, they develop the confidence that such action is possible as well as the desire to participate in even broader public debates. Harry Boyte and Sara Evans have recently called sites of such participation "free spaces" where "people are able to learn a new self-respect, a deeper and more assertive group identity, public skills, and values of cooperation and civic virtue."[37] I return to this larger notion of free spaces later, but here it is the focus on exercising control in such environments that concern us.

Students often have little, if any, control over their lives inside the institution called school. Curriculum, school rules, time schedules, texts, and on and on are all set long before students arrive inside the schoolhouse door. There are usually no free spaces within which students can practice and thus develop the skills needed for public participation in decision making.

Any curriculum with democracy at its heart needs to include expanding spheres of free spaces for decision making on the part of students. Perhaps the most straightforward way to approach this is to suggest that whenever the teacher has the latitude to make a decision, an opportunity is also present for students to enter into the decision making process themselves. In conversations with and observations of classroom teachers, I have learned that the possibilities here are endless.

With younger children, seemingly simple issues like room decoration provide excellent free spaces to begin the development of decision-making skills and potential. Additionally, such activities as choosing reading materials, group activities, and the focus of reading webs, are all well within the abilities of children. As students get older, spheres of decision making can expand to include room management, curricular focus (as seen earlier with local history and writing), and the organization of social life in the school.

A word needs to be said here about classroom management. The way a classroom or school is run has a great deal to do with the way students perceive their place in the life-world of the school. Recently, an entire school of classroom management has developed that argues for a reassertion of the teacher's power to dominate and control the classroom. The most widely embraced of these models is Assertive Discipline which operates from a behavior modification agenda in stipulating that behavior rules and punishments (sometimes awards) are to be set by the teacher and followed by the students. Aside from *not* teaching self-discipline, this system takes away the experience of decision making and disempowers students who face almost total institutional control.

As an alternative to such antidemocratic schemes, a variety of collaborative possibilities have been offered as ways of enhancing both self-discipline and decision making. While I do not have space to catalogue all of these suggestions here, their broadest outlines can be traced. First, they all argue that developing genuine self-discipline comes from the experience of making and holding oneself to rules that are collectively established. Second, the parameters of behavior can only be set in an atmosphere of cooperation between all parties, including the adult teacher who plays the role of facilitator and guide. Finally, rules must be flexible enough to allow for change as participants learn more about the consequences of their actions. In such settings, classroom management becomes a collaborative, democratic experience as opposed to an autocratic, antidemocratic one.[38]

Coupled with a sense of personal and community history, such decision-making structures offer the possibility of developing genuine personal efficacy. The curriculum develops both personal power and participatory skills within a collaborative environment. Within such free spaces students learn to act for the common good.

Social Alternatives

However, if students are to act for the common good, they need some notion that such action is likely to yield results—that alternatives to the way we currently organize social life exist. The curriculum is often presented to students as a given, a set of established facts. There seem to be only one answer to each question and only one approach to each problem—the right one. If students are to make decisions, which of course involve choices, they need to be aware of the range of choices they face.

Teachers concerned with such choices operate in two ways. First, the curriculum can offer choices to students. For example, the teaching of science

192

can offer multiple approaches to uncovering the same principles. The teaching of writing can consist of a variety of ways to learn the rules of grammar through students' own modes of expression. Throughout the curriculum, using multiple sources as opposed to a textbook format exposes students to the notion that multiple approaches to a variety of ends are possible.

In addition, students deserve to see that the ways in which we order our social lives are not written in stone. Rather, they are human choices which, in a democracy, are always open to change. The point then is to present to students, through the curriculum, alternatives to the existing order. Herbert Kohl states:

> The most important thing we can do is have our students understand that socialism, communism, anarchism, and other noncapitalist forms of organizing human life are serious, and must be thought about; and that people have a right to choose the social systems they believe will meet their needs and the needs of their communities. Young people also ought to be given an opportunity to know that people fight for such abstractions as justice and for such concretions as the elimination of poverty and oppression.[39]

Peter Dreier additionally suggests that students be exposed to attempts in the Third World to transform a harsh reality into a humane society as examples of what people, through cooperative action, can accomplish.[40] Making the connection between the Third World and our technological society can be enhanced by exploring examples of similar social alternatives in our society. Such examples range from the publicly owned and operated plants and utilities in the United States to such large-scale projects as Canadian socialized health systems, England's nonprofit housing system, and Sweden's mass-transit system. Coupling these two sets of examples provides alternatives to the existing order and demonstrates the means by which such alternatives arise and take their place in a transformed social order. It further confronts students with a variety of concepts of the "social good," offering choices around which decisions can be made.

Democratic Values

Finally, the curriculum should be structured so as to embrace the values of democratic life. These include the essential values of equality, liberty, and community. All of these are best taught through lived experiences as opposed to the disembodied accounts in textbooks of the founding fathers' pronouncements regarding freedom, liberty, justice, and similar concepts. We have already discussed liberty in the context of student decision making. Here I turn more explicitly to issues of equality and community.

As for equality, curricular practices that are based on notions of inequality should be abolished. First and foremost, this means eliminating from the curriculum all ability grouping and tracking. Not only is this practice clearly antidemocratic, it simply does not work. As Jeannie Oakes states:

> [T]racking is *not* in the best interests of most students. It does not appear to be related to either increasing academic achievement or promoting positive attitudes and behaviors. Poor and minority students seem to have suffered most from tracking—and these are the very students on whom so many educational hopes are pinned. If schooling is intended to provide access to economic, political, and social opportunity for those who are so often denied such access, school tracking appears to interfere seriously with this goal. Yet, despite what we know about the effects of tracking, the practice persists.[41]

Of course, beyond this is the clearly inegalitarian and thus antidemocratic bias in ability grouping. The practice of ability grouping segregates students and prepares them for decidedly different futures. In so doing, the clear message is that some students should have access to higher-status knowledge because they will be expected to occupy higher-status social positions. The notion of political equality, fundamental to a democracy, gets lost in the rush to label and segregate young learners. Alternatives to such inegalitarian, antidemocratic practices are those that focus on the classroom as a cooperative community. A wide variety of approaches to the curriculum are available that embrace community and cooperation over competition and tracking, including grouping students by interest as opposed to ability in all subjects. In elementary grades, this can be as simple as reading groups based on topics in which a wide range of ability-level texts are available. In upper grades, collaborative projects such as those involved in the Foxfire Program can be undertaken. The point in all of these is to structure the classroom so that cooperation is valued over individualistic competition. As Johnson and Johnson have argued, it is only in classrooms directed toward cooperative learning that those interpersonal skills necessary for democratic life will be developed. Furthermore, it is only in cooperative settings that higher-order cognitive skills are obtained. According to Johnson and Johnson:

> When the instructional task is some sort of problem-solving activity, a cooperative goal structure clearly results in higher achievement than does a competitive or an individual goal structure. There is evidence that factual material will be remembered better if it is discussed in a cooperatively structured group. Cooperative goal structures also facilitate mastery of concepts and principles and of creative processes (such as divergent thinking, risk-taking thinking, and entering into controversy). They are effective in developing verbal and problem-solving

skills, cooperative skills, and the ability to see a situation from someone else's perspective (an ability that is essential to empathy, social adjustment, communication and autonomous moral judgment). In turn, the development of cooperative skills is essential to a person's self-actualization, i.e., the development of one's potentialities and the utilization of those potentialities.[42]

Certainly, students will only cooperate well when the teacher takes the time to structure the curriculum so that it requires cooperation and prepares students for the task. Given the cognitive and social benefits of such an effort it seems undemocratic and miseducative to do anything else.

Conclusion

How we school is a direct reflection of what we believe our social life should be. I have argued that fundamental to our best social intentions is a participatory form of democratic life. If we are to live democratically, the way we induct the young into the culture must be democratic as well. The emphasis on protectionist democracy currently a part of reform efforts in education must be resisted.

In terms of the curriculum, this suggests that both in content and form we embrace democracy. In content, we provide students with the tools to live a democratic life and the visions of what is possible in our shared social context. In terms of form, the curriculum should engage students in actual decision making in a shared community of equality and justice.

What this suggests is that schools, and the classrooms within them, become islands of democracy. Locations where, in an often undemocratic society, children gain a strong sense of both their own autonomy as well as interconnectedness. That is, there should be the type of free space Boyte and Evans described—one where students gain a sense of self-respect, assertiveness, democratic values, and public skills that enable them to act democratically. It is only in so doing that they will come to value their own right and obligation to participate publicly, without which democracy has no future.

Notes

1. Andrew A. Lipscomb, ed., *The Writings of Thomas Jefferson*, vol. 2 (Charlottesville, Va.: Thomas Jefferson Memorial Association, 1903), p. 207.

2. For a more detailed discussion of democratic theory see Carole Pateman, *Participation and Democratic Theory* (Cambridge: Cambridge University Press, 1970); and Benjamin Barber, *Strong Democracy* (Berkeley, Calif.: University of California Press, 1984).

3. See, for example, R. A. Dahl, *Preface to Democratic Theory* (Chicago: University of Chicago Press, 1956).

4. George Will, "In Defense of Non-Voting," *Newsweek*, October 10, 1983.

5. John Dewey, *Democracy and Education* (New York: Macmillan, 1916), p. 87.

6. Pateman, op. cit.

7. John Stuart Mill, *Essays on Politics and Culture* (Toronto: University of Toronto Press, 1965); John Stuart Mill, *Collected Works* (Toronto: University of Toronto Press, 1963); and G. D. H. Cole, *Social Theory* (London: Methuen, 1920).

8. G. A. Almond and S. Verba, *The Civic Culture* (Boston: Little, Brown, 1945); Martin Carnoy and Derek Shearer, *Workplace Democracy: The Challenge of the 1980s.* (White Plains, N.Y.: M. E. Sharp, 1980); Arthur Wirth, *Productive Work—In Industry and Schools* (New York: University Press of America, 1983).

9. See also Harry Boyte, *The Backyard Revolution* (Philadelphia: Temple University Press, 1980).

10. To claim one vision or theory of democracy to be "truer" to the original intent of our cultural heritage is most certainly tenuous business. For example, in practice our democratic origins excluded women and Blacks from the political process. If, however, it is fair to claim that our entire cultural heritage is based on the expansion of political rights and freedoms, then participatory theory does seem to have a more legitimate claim to our loyalties. Organizing social life along the lines of participatory democracy moves us along a continuum toward the more as opposed to the less democratic. Social institutions come under more direct as opposed to representative control and the process of governing is broadened to embrace the widest possible number of participants. Certainly this comes closer to a government of, by, and for the people than do notions of an elected autocracy.

11. The commissions, their reports, and membership were as follows: National Commission on Excellence in Education (*A Nation at Risk*)—18 members, 1 teacher; Twentieth Century Fund (*Making the Grade*)—11 members, no teachers; National Science Foundation (*Educating Americans for the Twenty-first Century*)—20 members, 1 teacher; Education Commission of the States (*Action for Excellence*)—41 members, 1 teacher; The Paideia Group (*The Paideia Proposal*)—22 members, no teachers.

12. Susan Ohanian, "Huffing and Puffing and Blowing the School Excellent," *Phi Delta Kappan* (January 1985):316.

13. Michael W. Apple, "Curricular Form and the Logic of Technical Control," in Michael W. Apple, ed., *Cultural and Economic Reproduction in Education* (London: Routledge & Kegan Paul, 1982); Henry Giroux, *Theory and Resistance in Education* (South Hadley, Mass.: Bergin and Garvey, 1983).

14. National Commission on Excellence in Education, *A Nation at Risk* (Washington, D.C.: Government Printing Office, 1983), p. 5.

15. Education Commission of the States, *Action for Excellence* (Washington, D.C.: Education Commission of the States, 1983), p. 13.

16. National Science Foundation, *Educating America* (Washington, D.C.: National Science Foundation, 1983), p. v.

17. Twentieth Century Fund, *Making the Grade* (New York: The Twentieth Century Fund, 1983), p. 3.

18. National Science Foundation, *Educating Americans*, op. cit., p. 44.

19. David Cohen, ". . . the condition of teachers' work . . ." *Harvard Educational Review* 54, 1 (February 1984):11–12.

20. Due to space restraints, the historic origins of scientific management as applied to schooling cannot be discussed fully. For a detailed analysis see Arthur Wirth, *Productive Work in Industry and Schooling* (Lanthan, N.Y.: University Press of America, 1983); Raymond Callahan, *Education and the Cult of Efficiency* (Chicago: University of Chicago Press, 1962); and the chapters by Kliebard and Carlson herein.

21. Ellwood P. Cubberly, *Public School Administration* (Boston: Houghton Mifflin, 1916), p. 325.

22. Margaret Haley, "The Factory System," *The New Republic*, November 12, 1924, p. 19.

23. Christopher Lasch points out how these are actually calls for more mediocrity and operate against education for citizenship. See "'Excellence' in Education: Old Refrain or New Departure?" *Issues in Education* III, 1 (Summer 1985):1–12.

24. Walker Karp, "Why Johnny Can't Think," *Harpers* (June 1985):73.

25. Public Education Information Network, *Education for a Democratic Future* (St. Louis: Public Education Information Network, 1985), p. 3. Mary Ann Raywid; Charles A. Tesconi, Jr.; Donald R. Warren, *Pride and Promise* (Westbury, N.Y.: American Educational Studies Association, 1984), p. 10.

26. Raywid et al., op. cit., pp. 11, 12.

27. Mortimer J. Adler, *The Paideia Proposal* (New York: Macmillan, 1982), p. 15.

28. Ernest Boyer, *High School* (New York: Harper and Row, 1983), p. 105. See also John Goodlad, *A Place Called School* (New York: McGraw Hill, 1984).

29. I am indebted to the teachers involved in the Institute for Democracy in Education for their work with democratic alternatives that have provided me with the examples in the following sections of this chapter.

30. See Marcia M. Burchby, *The Whole Language Alternative to Basal Instruction*. Occasional Paper #1, Institute for Democracy in Education Series (Athens, Ohio: Institute for Democracy in Education, 1986). For information about these or other materials mentioned herein, please contact the Institute for Democracy in Education, 372 McCracken Hall, Ohio University, Athens, Ohio 45701.

31. James Moffitt, "Hidden Impediments to the Teaching of English," *Phi Delta Kappan* (September 1985):50–56.

32. It is important to note that by *autonomous individuals* I am not arguing for an individualized or privatized notion of the citizen. Rather, what is suggested is the notion of autonomy within a community—the ability to be a free and equal con-

tributor to collective and collaborative social life. For an extensive discussion of this concept, see Landon E. Beyer and George H. Wood, "Critical Inquiry and Moral Action in Education," *Educational Theory* 36, 1 (Winter 1986):1–14.

33. See, for example, D. Cluster, *They Should Have Served That Cup of Coffee: Seven Radicals Remember the 1960s* (Boston: South End Press, 1979): R. Cooney and H. Michalowski, *The Power of the People: Active Nonviolence in the United States* (Culver City, Pa.: Peace Press, 1977); and H. Zinn, *A People's History of the United States* (New York: Harper and Row, 1980).

34. Eliot Wigginton, *Sometimes a Shining Moment: The Foxfire Experience* (New York: Anchor Press, 1985).

35. The best compendium of such examples are published in *Hands On: Newsletter for Cultural Journalism*. Published by the Foxfire Fund, Rabun Gap, Ga., 30568.

36. See the "Perspectives" series, especially the volumes *Taking Part, Making History*, and *Investigations: Toxic Wastes*, published by Educators for Social Responsibility, 23 Garden St., Cambridge, Mass., 02138.

37. Harry Boyte and Sara Evans, *Free Spaces* (New York: Harper and Row, 1986), p. 17.

38. See Albert Alschuler, *School Discipline: A Socially Literate Solution* (New York: McGraw Hill, 1980); Rudolf Dreikurs, Bernice Grunwald, and Floy C. Pepper, *Maintaining Sanity in the Classroom*, 2d ed. (New York: Harper and Row, 1982) and "Teaching Self-Discipline," special issue of *Theory into Practice* 24, 4 (Autumn 1984).

39. H. Kohl, "Can the School Build a New Social Order?" *Journal of Education* 162, 3 (Summer 1980):63.

40. P. Dreier, "Socialism and Cynicism," *Socialist Review* 10, 5 (September–October 1980).

41. J. Oakes, *Keeping Track: How American Schools Structure Inequality*. (New Haven, Conn.: Yale University Press), p. 2.

42. D. Johnson and R. Johnson, *Learning Together and Alone* (Englewood Cliffs, N.J.: Prentice-Hall, 1975), pp. 32–32. See also Johnson and Johnson, *Circles of Learning: Cooperation in the Classroom* (Alexandria, Va.: Association for Supervision and Curriculum Development, 1984).

IV
Curriculum and the Work of Teachers

ELEVEN

Toward a Theory of Culturally Relevant Pedagogy

Gloria Ladson-Billings

Teacher education programs throughout the nation have coupled their efforts at reform with revised programs committed to social justice and equity. Their focus has become the preparation of prospective teachers who support equitable and just educational experiences for all students.[1]

Currently, there are debates in the educational research literature concerning both locating efforts at social reform in schools[2] and the possibilities of "reeducating" typical teacher candidates for the variety of student populations in U.S. public schools.[3] Rather than looking at programmatic reform, this article considers educational theorizing about teaching itself and proposes a theory of culturally focused pedagogy that might be considered in the reformation of teacher education.

Shulman's often-cited article, "Knowledge and Teaching: Foundations of the New Reform,"[4] considers philosophical and psychological perspectives, underscored by case knowledge of novice and experienced practitioners. Although Shulman's work mentions the importance of both the knowledge of learners and the characteristics and knowledge of educational contexts, it generally minimizes the culturally based analyses of teaching

A previous version of this chapter was published in the *American Educational Research Journal* 32, 3 (Fall 1995).

that have preceded it. In this chapter, I attempt to build on the educational anthropological literature and suggest a new theoretical perspective to address the specific concerns of educating teachers for success with African American students.

Teaching and Culture

For more than a decade, anthropologists have examined ways that teaching can better match the home and community cultures of students of color who have previously not had academic success in schools. Au and Jordan termed "culturally appropriate" the pedagogy of teachers in a Hawaiian school who incorporated aspects of students' cultural backgrounds into their reading instruction.[5] By permitting students to use "talk-story," a language interaction style common among Native Hawaiian children, teachers were able to help students achieve at higher than predicted levels on standardized reading tests.

Mohatt and Erickson conducted similar work with Native American students.[6] As they observed teacher-student interactions and participation structures, they found that teachers who used language interaction patterns that approximated the students' home cultural patterns were more successful in improving student academic performance. Improved student achievement also was evident among teachers who used what they termed "mixed forms"[7]—a combination of Native American and Anglo language interaction patterns. They termed this instruction, "culturally congruent."[8]

Cazden and Leggett and Erickson and Mohatt used the term *culturally responsive* to describe similar language interactions of teachers with linguistically diverse and Native American students, respectively.[9] Later, Jordan, as well as Vogt, Jordan, and Tharp began using the term *culturally compatible* to explain the success of classroom teachers with Hawaiian children.[10]

By observing the students in their home/community environment, teachers were able to include aspects of the students' cultural environment in the organization and instruction of the classroom. More specifically, Jordan discusses cultural compatibility in this way:

> Educational practices must match with the children's culture in ways which ensure the generation of academically important behaviors. It does not mean that all school practices need be completely congruent with natal cultural practices, in the sense of exactly or even closely matching or agreeing with them. The point of cultural compatibility is that the natal culture is used as a guide in the selection of educational program elements so that academically desired behaviors are produced and undesired behaviors are avoided.[11]

These studies have several common features. Each locates the source of student failure and subsequent achievement within the nexus of speech and language interaction patterns of the teacher and the students. Each suggests that student "success" is represented in achievement within the current social structures extant in schools. Thus, the goal of education becomes how to "fit" students constructed as "other" by virtue of their race/ethnicity, language, or social class into a hierarchical structure that is defined as a *meritocracy*. However, it is unclear how these conceptions do more than reproduce the current inequities. Singer suggests that, "cultural congruence is an inherently moderate pedagogical strategy that accepts that the goal of educating minority students is to train individuals in those skills needed to succeed in mainstream society."[12]

Three of the terms employed by studies on cultural mismatch between school and home—*culturally appropriate*, *culturally congruent*, and *culturally compatible*—seem to connote accommodation of student culture to mainstream culture. Only the term *culturally responsive* appears to refer to a more dynamic or synergistic relationship between home/community culture and school culture. Erickson and Mohatt suggest their notion of culturally responsive teaching can be seen as a beginning step for bridging the gap between home and school:

> It may well be that, by discovering the small differences in social relations which make a big difference in the interactional ways children engage the content of the school curriculum, anthropologists can make practical contributions to the improvement of minority children's school achievement and to the improvement of the everyday school life for such children and their teachers. Making small changes in everyday participation structures may be one of the means by which more culturally responsive pedagogy can be developed.[13]

For the most part, studies of cultural appropriateness, congruence, or compatibility have been conducted within small-scale communities—for example, Native Hawaiian and Native Americans. However, an earlier generation of work considered the mismatch between the language patterns of African Americans and the school in larger, urban settings.[14] Villegas challenged the microsocial explanations advanced by sociolinguists by suggesting that the source of cultural mismatch is located in larger social structures and that schools as institutions serve to reproduce social inequalities. She argued that

> as long as school performs this sorting function in society, it must necessarily produce winners and losers. . . . Therefore, culturally sensitive remedies to educational problems of oppressed minority students that ignore the political aspect of schooling are doomed to failure.[15]

Although I agree with Villegas's attention to the larger social structure, other scholars in the cultural ecological paradigm are ahistorical and limited,[16] particularly in their ability to explain African American student success.[17] The long history of African American educational struggle and achievement is well documented.[18] This historical record contradicts the glib pronouncements that "Black people don't value education."

Second, more recent analyses of successful schooling for African American students[19] challenge the explanatory power of the cultural ecologists' caste-like category. They raise questions about what schools can and should be doing to promote academic success for African American students.[20]

Despite their limitations, the microanalytic work of sociolinguists and the macrostructural analysis of cultural ecologists both are important in helping scholars think about their intersections and consider possible classroom/instructional adjustments. For scholars interested in the success of students of color in complex, urban environments, this work provides some important theoretical and conceptual groundwork.

Irvine developed the concept of "cultural synchronization" to describe the necessary interpersonal context that must exist between the teacher and African American students to maximize learning.[21] Rather than focus solely on speech and language interactions, Irvine's work describes the acceptance of students' communication patterns, along with a constellation of African American cultural mores such as mutuality, reciprocity, spirituality deference, and responsibility.[22]

Irvine's work on African American students and school failure considers both micro- and macroanalyses, including teacher-student interpersonal contexts, teacher and student expectations, institutional contexts, and the societal context. This work is important for its break with the cultural deficit or cultural disadvantage explanations which led to compensatory educational interventions.[23] A next step for positing effective pedagogical practice is a theoretical model that not only addresses student achievement but also helps students to accept and affirm their cultural identity while developing critical perspectives that challenge inequities that schools (and other institutions) perpetuate. I term this "culturally relevant pedagogy."

Several questions, some of which are beyond the scope of this discussion, drive this attempt to formulate a theoretical model of culturally relevant pedagogy. What constitutes student success? How can academic success and cultural success complement each other in settings where student alienation and hostility characterize the school experience? How can pedagogy promote the kind of student success that engages larger social structural issues in a critical way? How do researchers recognize that pedagogy in action? And, what are the implications for teacher preparation generated by this pedagogy?

The Illusion of Atheoretical Inquiry

Educational research is greeted with suspicion both within and outside of the academy. Among practitioners, it is regarded as too theoretical.[24] For many academicians, it is regarded as atheoretical.[25] It is the latter notion that I address in this section.

Clearly, much of educational research fails to make explicit its theoretical underpinnings.[26] However, I want to suggest that, even without explicating a theoretical framework, researchers do have explanations for why things "work the way they do." These theories may be partial, poorly articulated, conflated, or contradictory, but they exist. What is regarded as traditional educational theory—theories of reproduction[27] or neoconservative traditional theory[28]—may actually be a *default* theory that researchers feel no need to make explicit. Thus, the theory's objectivity is unquestioned, and studies undergirded by these theories are regarded as truth or objective reality.

Citing the ranking, or privileging, of theoretical knowledge, Code observes:

> Even when empiricist *theories* of knowledge prevail, knowledgeable *practice* constructs positions of power and privilege that are by no means as impartially ordered as strict empiricism would require. Knowledge gained from practical (untheorized) experience is commonly regarded as inferior to theoretically derived or theory-confirming knowledge, and theory is elevated above practice.[29]

In education, work that recognizes the import of practical experience owes an intellectual debt to scholars such as Smith, Atkin, Glaser and Strauss, and Lutz and Ramsey, who explored notions of grounded theory as an important tool for educational research.[30] Additionally, work by scholars in teacher education such as Stenhouse, Elliott, Carr and Kemmis, Zeichner, and Cochran-Smith and Lytle illuminates the action research tradition where teachers look reflexively at their practice to solve pedagogical problems and assist colleagues and researchers interested in teaching practice.[31] Even some scholars in the logical positivist tradition acknowledged the value of a more experientially grounded research approach in education.[32] More fundamental than arguing the merits of quantitative versus qualitative methodology[33] have been calls for broader understanding about the limits of any research methodology.[34] In using selected citations from Kuhn, Patton, Becker, and Gouldner,[35] Rist helps researchers understand the significance of research paradigms in education. For example:

Since no paradigm ever solves all of the problems it defines and since no two paradigms leave all the same problems unsolved, paradigm debates always involve the question, Which problems is it more significant to have solved?

A paradigm is a world view, a general perspective, a way of breaking down the complexity of the real world. As such, paradigms are deeply embedded in the socialization of adherents and practitioners, telling them what is important, what is reasonable.

The issue is not research strategies, *per se*. Rather, the adherence to one paradigm as opposed to another predisposes one to view the world and the events within it in profoundly differing ways.

The power and pull of a paradigm is more than simply a methodological orientation. It is a means by which to grasp reality and give it meaning and predictability.[36]

It is with this orientation toward the inherent subjectivity of educational research that I have approached this work. In this next section, I discuss some of the specific perspectives that have informed my work.

The Participant Observer Role for Researchers Who are "Other"

Increasingly, researchers have a story to tell about themselves as well as their work.[37] I, too, share a concern for situating myself as a researcher—who I am, what I believe, what experiences I have had, all impact what, how, and why I research. What may make these research revelations more problematic for me is my own membership in a marginalized racial/cultural group.

One possible problem I face is the presumption of a "native" perspective as I study effective practice for African American students.[38] To this end, the questions raised by Narayan seem relevant:

"Native" anthropologists, then, are perceived as insiders regardless of their complex backgrounds. The differences between kinds of "native" anthropologists are also obviously passed over. Can a person from an impoverished American minority background who, despite all prejudices, manages to get an education and study her own community be equated with a member of a Third World elite group who, backed by excellent schooling and parental funds, studies anthropology abroad, yet returns home for fieldwork among the less privileged? Is it not insensitive to suppress the issue of location, acknowledging that a scholar who chooses an institutional base in the Third World might have a different engagement with Western-based theories, books, political stances, and technologies of written production? Is a middle-class white professional researching aspects of her own society also a "native" anthropologist?[39]

This location of myself as native can work against me.[40] My work may be perceived as biased or, at the least, skewed, because of my vested interest in the African American community. Thus, I have attempted to search for theoretical grounding that acknowledges my standpoint and simultaneously forces me to problematize it. The work of Patricia Hill Collins on Black feminist thought has been most helpful.[41]

Briefly, Collins's work is based on four propositions: (1) concrete experiences as a criterion of meaning, (2) the use of dialogue in assessing knowledge claims, (3) the ethic of caring, and (4) the ethic of personal accountability. Below, I briefly describe the context and methodology of my study and then attempt to link each of these propositions to a three-year study I conducted with successful teachers of African American students.

Issues of Context and Methodology

While it is not possible to fully explicate the context and method of this study in this chapter, it is necessary to provide readers with some sense of both for better continuity. I have provided more elaborate explanations of these aspects of the work in other writings.[42] Included here is a truncated explanation of the research context and method.

In 1988, I began working as a lone investigator with a group of eight teachers in a small (less than three thousand students), predominantly African American, low-income elementary school district in Northern California. The teachers were identified through a process of "community nomination"[43] with African American parents (in this case, all mothers) who attended local churches suggesting who they thought were outstanding teachers. The parents' criteria for teaching excellence included being accorded respect by the teacher, student enthusiasm toward school and academic tasks, and student attitudes toward themselves and others. The parents' selections were cross-checked by an independent list of excellent teachers generated by principals and some teaching colleagues. Principals' criteria for teaching excellence included excellent classroom management skills, student achievement (as measured by standardized test scores), and personal observations of teaching practice. Nine teachers' names appeared on both the parents' and principals' lists and were selected to participate in the study. One teacher declined to participate because of the time commitment. The teachers were all females: five were African American and three were White.

The study was composed of four phases. During the first phase, each teacher participated in an ethnographic interview[44] to discuss her background, philosophy of teaching, and ideas about curriculum, classroom management, and parent and community involvement. In the second phase of the study, teachers agreed to be observed by me. This agreement meant that the teachers gave me carte blanche to visit their classrooms. These visits were not scheduled beforehand. I visited the classrooms regularly for almost two years, an average of three days a week. During each visit, I took field notes, audio taped the class, and talked with the teacher after the visit, either on-site or by telephone. The third phase of the study, which overlapped the second phase, involved videotaping the teachers. I made decisions about what to videotape as a result of my having become familiar with the teachers' styles and classroom routines.

The fourth and final phase of the study required that the teachers work together as a research collective or collaborative to view segments of one another's videotapes. In a series of ten two- to three-hour meetings, the teachers participated in analysis and interpretation of their own and one another's practice. It was during this phase of the study that formulations about culturally relevant pedagogy that had emerged in the initial interviews were confirmed by teaching practice.

My own interest in these issues of teaching excellence for African American students came as a result of my desire to challenge deficit paradigms that prevailed in the literature on African American learners.[45] Partly as a result of my own experiences as a learner, a teacher, and a parent, I was convinced that, despite the literature, there were teachers who were capable of excellent teaching for African American students. Thus, my work required a paradigmatic shift toward looking in the classrooms of excellent teachers, *through* the reality of those teachers. In this next section, I discuss how my understanding of my own theoretical grounding connected with the study.

Concrete Experiences as a Criterion of Meaning

According to Collins, "individuals who have lived through the experiences about which they claim to be experts are more believable and credible than those who have merely read and thought about such experience."[46]

My work with successful teachers of African American students began with a search for expert assessment of good teachers. The experts I chose were parents who had children attending the schools where I planned to conduct the research. The parents were willing to talk openly about who they thought were excellent teachers for their children, citing examples of teachers' respect for them as parents, their children's enthusiasm and changed attitudes toward learning, and improved academics in conjunction with support for the students' home culture. In most cases, the basis for their assessments was comparative, both from the standpoint of having had experiences with many teachers (for each individual child) and having had several schoolage children. Thus, they could talk about how an individual child fared in different classrooms and how their children collectively performed at specific grade levels with specific teachers.

The second area where concrete experiences as a criterion of meaning was evident was with the teachers themselves. The eight teachers who participated in this study had from twelve to forty years of teaching experience, most of it with African American students. Their reflections on what was important in teaching African American students were undergirded by their daily teaching experiences.

The Use of Dialogue in Assessing Knowledge Claims

This second criterion suggests that knowledge emerges in dialectical relationships. Rather than the voice of one authority, meaning is made as a product of dialogue between and among individuals. In the case of my study, dialogue was critical in assessing knowledge claims. Early in the study, each teacher participated in an ethnographic interview.[47] Although I had specific areas I wanted to broach with each teacher, the teacher's own life histories and interests determined how much time was spent on the various areas. In some cases, the interviews reflect a teacher's belief in the salience of his or her family background and education. In other instances, teachers talked more about their pedagogical, philosophical, and political perspectives. Even after I began collecting data via classroom observations, it was the teachers' explanations and clarifications that helped to construct the meaning of what transpired in the classrooms.

Additionally, after I collected data from classroom observations and classroom videotaping, the teachers convened as a research collaborative to examine both their own and one anothers' pedagogy.[48] In these meetings, meaning was constructed through reciprocal dialogue. Instead of merely accepting Berliner's notions that "experts" operate on a level of automaticity and intuition that does not allow for accurate individual critique and interpretation—that is, they cannot explain how they do what they do[49]—together the teachers were able to make sense of their own and their colleagues' practices. The ongoing dialogue allowed them the opportunity to reexamine and rethink their practices.

The Ethic of Caring

Much has been discussed in feminist literature about women and "caring."[50] Other feminists have been critical of any essentialized notion of women and suggest that no empirical evidence exists to support the notion that women care in ways different from men or that any such caring informs their scholarship and work.[51] I argue that Collins's use of caring refers not merely to affective connections between and among people but to the articulation of a greater sense of commitment to what scholarship and/or pedagogy can mean in the lives of people.

For example, in this study, the teachers were not all demonstrative and affectionate toward the students. Instead, their common thread of caring was their concern for the implications their work had on their students' lives, the welfare of the community, and unjust social arrangements. Thus, rather than the idiosyncratic caring for individual students (for whom they did seem to care), the teachers spoke of the import of their work for preparing the students for confronting inequitable and undemocratic social structures.

The Ethic of Personal Accountability

In this final dimension, Collins addresses the notion that *who* makes knowledge claims is as important as *what* those knowledge claims are. Thus, the idea that individuals can "objectively" argue a position whether they themselves agree with the position, as in public debating, is foreign. Individuals' commitments to ideological and/or value positions are important in understanding knowledge claims.

In this study, the teachers demonstrated this ethic of personal accountability in the kind of pedagogical stands they took. Several of the teachers spoke of defying administrative mandates in order to do what they believed was right for students. Others gave examples of proactive actions they took to engage in pedagogical practices more consistent with their beliefs and values. For example, one teacher was convinced that the school district's mandated reading program was inconsistent with what she was learning about literacy teaching/learning from a critical perspective. She decided to write a proposal to the school board asking for experimental status for a literacy approach she wanted to use in her classroom. Her proposal was buttressed by current research in literacy and would not cost the district any more than the proposed program. Ultimately, she was granted permission to conduct her experiment, and its success allowed other teachers to attempt it in subsequent years.

Although Collins's work provided me with a way to think about my work as a researcher, it did not provide me with a way to theorize about the teachers' practices. Ultimately, it was my responsibility to generate theory as I practiced theory. As previously mentioned, this work builds on earlier anthropological and sociolinguistic attempts at a cultural "fit" between students' home culture and school culture. However, by situating it in a more critical paradigm, a theory of culturally relevant pedagogy would necessarily propose to do three things—produce students who can achieve academically, produce students who demonstrate cultural competence, and develop students who can both understand and critique the existing social order. The next section discusses each of these elements of culturally relevant pedagogy.

Culturally Relevant Pedagogy and Student Achievement

Much has been written about the school failure of African American students.[52] However, explanations for this failure have varied widely. One often-cited explanation situates African American students' failure in their "caste-like minority" or "involuntary immigrant" status.[53] Other explanations posit *cultural difference* as the reason for this failure and, as previously mentioned, locate student failure in the cultural mismatch between students and the school.[54]

Regardless of these failure explanations, little research has been done to examine academic success among African American students. The effective schools literature[55] argued that a group of schoolwide correlates were a reliable predictor of student success.[56] The basis for adjudging a school "effective" in this literature was how far above predicted levels students performed on standardized achievement tests. Whether or not scholars can agree on the significance of standardized tests, their meaning in the real world serves to rank and characterize both schools and individuals. Thus, teachers in urban schools are compelled to demonstrate that their students can achieve literacy and numeracy.[57] No matter how good a fit develops between home and school culture, students must achieve. No theory of pedagogy can escape this reality.

Students in the eight classrooms I observed did achieve. Despite the low ranking of the school district, the teachers were able to help students perform at higher levels than their district counterparts. In general, compared to students in middle-class communities, the students still lagged behind. But, more students in these classrooms were at or above grade level on standardized achievement tests.[58] Fortunately, academic achievement in these classrooms was not limited to standardized assessments. Classroom observations revealed a variety of demonstrated student achievements too numerous to list here. Briefly, students demonstrated an ability to read, write, speak, compute, pose and solve problems at sophisticated levels—that is, pose their own questions about the nature of teacher- or text-posed problems and engage in peer review of problem solutions. Each of the teachers felt that helping the students become academically successful was one of their primary responsibilities.

Culturally Relevant Teaching and Cultural Competence

Among the scholarship that has examined academically successful African American students, a disturbing finding has emerged—the students' academic success came at the expense of their cultural and psychosocial well being.[59] Fordham and Ogbu identified a phenomenon called "acting White," where African American students who were academically successful were ostracized by their peers.[60] Bacon found that, among African American high school students identified as gifted in their elementary grades, only about half were continuing to do well at the high school level.[61] A closer examination of the successful students' progress indicated that they were social isolates, with neither African American nor White friends. The students believed that it was necessary for them to stand apart from other African American students so that teachers would not attribute to them the negative characteristics they may have attributed to African American students in general.

The dilemma for African American students becomes one of negotiating the academic demands of school while demonstrating cultural competence.[62] Thus, culturally relevant pedagogy must provide a way for students to maintain their cultural integrity while succeeding academically. One of the teachers in the study used the lyrics of rap songs as a way to teach elements of poetry.[63] From the rap lyrics, she went on to more conventional poetry. Students who were more skilled at creating and improvising raps were encouraged and reinforced. Another teacher worked to channel the peer-group leadership of her students into classroom and schoolwide leadership. One of her African American male students who had experienced multiple suspensions and other school problems before coming to her classroom demonstrated some obvious leadership abilities. He could be described as culturally competent in his language and interaction styles and demonstrated pride in himself and his cultural heritage. Rather than attempt to minimize his influence, the teacher encouraged him to run for sixth-grade president and mobilized the entire class to organize and help run his campaign. To the young man's surprise, he was elected. His position as president provided the teacher with many opportunities to respond to potential behavior problems. This same teacher made a point of encouraging the African American males in her classroom to assume the role of academic leaders. Their academic leadership allowed their cultural values and styles to be appreciated and affirmed. Because these African American male students were permitted, indeed encouraged, to be themselves in dress, language style, and interaction styles while achieving in school, the other students, who regarded them highly (because of their popularity), were able to see academic engagement as "cool."

Many of the self-described African-centered public schools have focused on this notion of cultural competence.[64] To date, little data has been reported on the academic success of students in these programs. However, the work of African American scholars and others indicates that African-centered education does develop students who maintain cultural competence and demonstrate academic achievement.[65]

Culturally Relevant Teaching and Cultural Critique

Not only must teachers encourage academic success and cultural competence, they must help students to recognize, understand, and critique current social inequities. This notion presumes that teachers themselves recognize social inequities and their causes. However, teacher educators have demonstrated that many prospective teachers not only lack these understandings but reject information regarding social inequity.[66] This suggests that more work on recruiting particular kinds of students into teaching must be done. Also, we are fortunate to have models for this kind of cultural critique emanating from the work of civil rights workers here in the United States[67] and the international work of Freire[68] that has been incorporated into the critical and feminist work currently being done by numerous scholars.[69] Teachers who meet the cultural critique criteria must be engaged in a critical pedagogy that is

> a deliberate attempt to influence how and what knowledge and identities are produced within and among particular sets of social relations. It can be understood as a practice through which people are incited to acquire a particular "moral character." As both a political and practical activity, it attempts to influence the occurrence and qualities of experiences.[70]

Thus, the teachers in this study were not reluctant to identify political underpinnings of the students' community and social world. One teacher worked with her students to identify poorly utilized space in the community, examine heretofore inaccessible archival records about the early history of the community, plan alternative uses for a vacant shopping mall, and write urban plans, which they presented before the city council.

In a description of similar political activity, a class of African American middle school students in Dallas identified the problem of their school's being surrounded by liquor stores.[71] Zoning regulations in the city made some areas dry while the students' school was in a wet area. The students identified the fact that schools serving White, upper middle-class students were located in

213

dry areas, while schools in poor communities were in wet areas. The students, assisted by their teacher, planned a strategy for exposing this inequality. By using mathematics, literacy, and social and political skills, the students were able to prove their points with reports, editorials, charts, maps, and graphs. In both of these examples, teachers allowed students to use their community circumstances as official knowledge.[72] Their pedagogy and the students' learning became a form of cultural critique.

Theoretical Underpinnings of Culturally Relevant Pedagogy

As I looked (and listened) to exemplary teachers of African American students, I began to develop a grounded theory of culturally relevant pedagogy. The teachers in the study met the aforementioned criteria of helping their students to be academically successful, culturally competent, and sociopolitically critical. However, the ways in which they met these criteria seemed to differ markedly on the surface. Some teachers seemed more structured or rigid in their pedagogy. Others seemed to adopt more progressive teaching strategies. What theoretical perspective(s) held them together and allowed them to meet the criteria of culturally relevant teaching?

One of the places I began to look for these commonalties was in teachers' beliefs and ideologies. Lipman has suggested that, despite massive attempts at school reform and restructuring, teacher ideologies and beliefs often remain unchanged, particularly toward African American children and their intellectual potential.[73] Thus, in the analysis of the teacher interviews, classroom observations, and group analysis of videotaped segments of their teaching, I was able to deduce some broad propositions (or characteristics) that serve as theoretical underpinnings of culturally relevant pedagogy.

I approach the following propositions tentatively to avoid an essentialized and/or dichotomized notion of the pedagogy of excellent teachers. What I propose represents a range or continuum of teaching behaviors, not fixed or rigid behaviors that teachers must adhere to in order to merit the designation "culturally relevant." The need for these theoretical understandings may be more academic than pragmatic. The teachers themselves feel no need to name their practice culturally relevant. However, as a researcher and teacher educator, I am compelled to try to make this practice more accessible, particularly for those prospective teachers who do not share the cultural knowledge, experiences, and understandings of their students.[74]

The three broad propositions that have emerged from this research center around the following:

214

- the conceptions of self and others held by culturally relevant teachers,
- the manner in which social relations are structured by culturally relevant teachers,
- the conceptions of knowledge held by culturally relevant teachers.[75]

Conceptions of Self and Others

The sociology of teaching literature suggests that, despite the increasing professionalization of teaching, the status of teaching as a profession continues to decline.[76] The feeling of low status is exacerbated when teachers work with what they perceive to be low-status students.[77] However, as I acted as a participant-observer in the classrooms of exemplary teachers of African American students, both what they said and did challenged this notion. In brief, the teachers

- believed that all the students were capable of academic success,
- saw their pedagogy as art—unpredictable, always in the process of becoming,
- saw themselves as members of the community,
- saw teaching as a way to give back to the community,
- believed in a Freirean notion of "teaching as mining" or pulling knowledge out.[78]

The teachers demonstrated their commitment to these conceptions of self and others in a consistent and deliberate manner. Students were not permitted to choose failure in their classrooms. They cajoled, nagged, pestered, and bribed the students to work at high intellectual levels. Absent from their discourse about students was the "language of lacking." Students were never referred to as being from a single-parent household, being on AFDC (welfare), or needing psychological evaluation. Instead, teachers talked about their own shortcomings and limitations and ways they needed to change to ensure student success.

As I observed them teach, I witnessed spontaneity and energy that came from experience and their willingness to be risk takers. In the midst of a lesson, one teacher, seemingly bewildered by her students' expressed belief that every princess had long blond hair, swiftly went to her book shelf, pulled down an African folk tale about a princess, and shared the story with the students to challenge their assertion. In our conference afterward, she commented:

> I didn't plan to insert that book, but I just couldn't let them go on thinking that only blond-haired, White women were eligible for royalty. I know where they get those

ideas, but I have a responsibility to contradict some of that. The consequences of that kind of thinking are more devastating for our children. (sp-6, field notes)[79]

The teachers made conscious decisions to be a part of the community from which their students come. Three of the eight teachers in this study live in the school community. The others made deliberate efforts to come to the community for goods, services, and leisure activities, demonstrating their belief in the community as an important and worthwhile place in both their lives and the lives of the students.

A final example I present here is an elaboration of a point made earlier. It reflects the teachers' attempt to support and instill community pride in the students. One teacher used the community as the basis of her curriculum. Her students searched the county historical archives, interviewed long-term residents, constructed and administered surveys and a questionnaire, and invited and listened to guest speakers to get a sense of the historical development of their community. Their ultimate goal was to develop a land-use proposal for an abandoned shopping center that was a magnet for illegal drug use and other dangerous activities. The project ended with the students making a presentation before the City Council and Urban Planning Commission. One of the students remarked to me, "This community is not such a bad place. There are a lot of good things that happened here, and some of that is still going on." The teacher told me that she was concerned that too many of the students believed that their only option for success involved moving out of the community, rather than participating in its reclamation.

Social Relations

Much has been written about classroom social interactions.[80] Perhaps the strength of some of the research in this area is evidenced by its impact on classroom practices. For example, teachers throughout the nation have either heard of or implemented various forms of cooperative learning: cross-aged, multi-aged, and heterogeneous ability groupings.[81] While these classroom arrangements may be designed to improve student achievement, culturally relevant teachers consciously create social interactions to help them meet the three previously mentioned criteria of academic success, cultural competence, and critical consciousness. Briefly, the teachers

- maintain fluid student-teacher relationships,
- demonstrate a connectedness with all of the students,
- develop a community of learners,

- encourage students to learn collaboratively and be responsible for one another.

In these teachers' classrooms, the teacher-student relationships are equitable and reciprocal. All of the teachers gave students opportunities to act as teachers. In one class, the teacher regularly sat at a student's desk, while the student stood at the front of the room and explained a concept or some aspect of student culture. Another teacher highlighted the expertise of various students and required other students to consult those students before coming to her for help: "Did you ask Jamal how to do those math problems?" "Make sure you check with Latasha before you turn in your reading." Because she acknowledged a wide range of expertise, the individual students were not isolated from their peers as teacher's pets. Instead, all of the students were made aware that they were expected to excel at something and that the teacher would call on them to share that expertise with classmates.

The culturally relevant teachers encouraged a community of learners rather than competitive, individual achievement. By demanding a higher level of academic success for the entire class, individual success did not suffer. However, rather than lifting up individuals (and, perhaps, contributing to feelings of peer alienation), the teachers made it clear that they were working with smart classes. For many of the students, this identification with academic success was a new experience. "Calvin was a bad student last year," said one student. "And that was last year," replied the teacher, as she designated Calvin to lead a discussion group. Another example of this community of learners was exemplified by a teacher who, herself, was a graduate student. She made a conscious decision to share what she was learning with her sixth graders. Every Friday, after her Thursday evening class, the students queried her about what she had learned.

A demonstration of the students' understanding of what she was learning occurred during the principal's observation of her teaching. A few minutes into a discussion where students were required to come up with questions they wanted answered about the book they were reading, a young man seated at a table near the rear of the class remarked with seeming disgust, "We're never gonna learn anything if y'all don't stop asking all of these low-level questions!" His comment was evidence of the fact that the teacher had shared Bloom's *Taxonomy of Educational Objectives*[82] with the class. At another time, two African American boys were arguing over a notebook. "What seems to be the problem?" asked the teacher. "He's got my metacognitive journal!" replied one of the boys. By using the language of the teacher's graduate class, the students demonstrated their ability to assimilate her language into their own experiences.

To solidify the social relationships in their classes, the teachers encouraged the students to learn collaboratively, teach each other, and be responsible for the academic success of others. These collaborative arrangements were not necessarily structured like those of cooperative learning. Instead, the teachers used a combination of formal and informal peer collaborations. One teacher used a buddy system, where each student was paired with another. The buddies checked each other's homework and class assignments. Buddies quizzed each other for tests, and, if one buddy was absent, it was the responsibility of the other to call to see why and to help with makeup work. The teachers used this ethos of reciprocity and mutuality to insist that one person's success was the success of all and one person's failure was the failure of all. These feelings were exemplified by the teacher who insisted, "We're a family. We have to care for one another as if our very survival depended on it—actually, it does!"

Conceptions of Knowledge

The third proposition that emerged from this study was one that indicated how the teachers thought about knowledge—the curriculum or content they taught—and the assessment of that knowledge. Once again, I will summarize their conceptions or beliefs about knowledge:

- Knowledge is not static; it is shared, recycled, and constructed.
- Knowledge must be viewed critically.
- Teachers must be passionate about knowledge and learning.
- Teachers must *scaffold*, or build bridges, to facilitate learning.
- Assessment must be multifaceted, incorporating multiple forms of excellence.

For the teachers in this study, knowledge was about doing. The students listened and learned from one another as well as the teacher. Early in the school year, one teacher asked the students to identify one area in which they believed they had expertise. She then compiled a list of "classroom experts" for distribution to the class. Later, she developed a calendar and asked students to select a date that they would like to make a presentation in their area of expertise. When the students made their presentations, their knowledge and expertise was a given. Their classmates were expected to be an attentive audience and to take seriously the knowledge that was being shared by taking notes and/or asking relevant questions. The variety of topics the students offered included rap music, basketball, gospel singing, cooking, hair braiding, and babysitting. Other students listed more school-oriented areas of expertise such as reading, writing, and mathematics. However, all students were required to share their expertise.

Another example of the teachers' conceptions of knowledge was demonstrated in the critical stance the teachers took toward the school curriculum.

Although cognizant of the need to teach certain things because of a districtwide testing policy, the teachers helped their students engage in a variety of forms of critical analyses. For one teacher, this meant critique of the social studies textbooks that were under consideration by a state evaluation panel. For two of the other teachers, critique came in the form of resistance to district-approved reading materials. Both of these teachers showed the students what it was they were supposed to be using along with what they were going to use and why. They both trusted the students with this information and enlisted them as allies against the school district's policies.

A final example in this category concerns the teachers' use of complex assessment strategies. Several of the teachers actively fought the students' *right-answer* approach to school tasks without putting the students' down. They provided them with problems and situations and helped the students to ask aloud the kinds of questions they had in their minds but had been taught to suppress in most other classrooms. For one teacher, it was the simple requiring of students to always be prepared to ask, Why? Thus, when she posed a mathematical word problem, the first question usually went something like this: "Why are we interested in knowing this?" Or, someone would simply ask, "Why are we doing this problem?" The teacher's response was sometimes another question: "Who thinks they can respond to that question?" Other times, the teacher would offer an explanation and then ask, "Are you satisfied with that answer?" If a student said "Yes," she might say, "You shouldn't be. Just because I'm the teacher doesn't mean *I'm* always right." The teacher was careful to help students to understand the difference between an intellectual challenge and a challenge to the authority of their parents. Thus, just as the students were affirmed in their ability to "code switch"—or move with facility between African American language and a standard form of English—they were supported in the attempts at role switching between school and home.

Another teacher helped her students to choose both the standards by which they were to be evaluated and the pieces of evidence they wanted to use as proof of their mastery of particular concepts and skills. None of the teachers or their students seemed to have test anxiety about the school district's standardized tests. Instead, they viewed the tests as necessary irritations, took them, scored better than their age-grade mates at their school, and quickly returned to the rhythm of learning in their classroom.

Conclusion

I began this chapter arguing for a theory of culturally relevant pedagogy. I also suggested that the tensions that surround my position as a native in the research field force me to face the theoretical and philosophical biases I bring to my work in overt and explicit ways. Thus, I situated my work in the context of Black feminist thought. I suggested that culturally relevant teaching must meet three criteria: an ability to develop students academically, a willingness to nurture and support cultural competence, and the development of a sociopolitical or critical consciousness. Next, I argued that culturally relevant teaching is distinguishable by three broad propositions or conceptions regarding self and other, social relations, and knowledge. With this theoretical perspective, I attempted to broaden notions of pedagogy beyond strictly psychological models. I also have argued that earlier sociolinguistic explanations have failed to include the larger social and cultural contexts of students, and the cultural ecologists have failed to explain student success. I predicated the need for a culturally relevant theoretical perspective on the growing disparity between the racial, ethnic, and cultural characteristics of teachers and students along with the continued academic failure of African American, Native American, and Latino students.

Although I agree with Haberman's assertion[83] that teacher educators are unlikely to make much of a difference in the preparation of teachers to work with students in urban poverty unless they are able to recruit "better" teacher candidates, I still believe researchers are obligated to reeducate the candidates we currently attract toward a more expansive view of pedagogy.[84] This can be accomplished partly by helping prospective teachers understand culture (their own and others) and the ways it functions in education. Rather than add on versions of multicultural education or human relations courses[85] that serve to exoticize diverse students as "other," a culturally relevant pedagogy is designed to problematize teaching and encourage teachers to ask about the nature of the student-teacher relationship, the curriculum, schooling, and society.

This study represents a beginning look at ways that teachers might systematically include student culture in the classroom as authorized or official knowledge. It also is a way to encourage praxis as an important aspect of research.[86] This kind of research needs to continue in order to support new conceptions of collaboration between teachers and researchers (practitioners and theoreticians). We need research that proposes alternate models of pedagogy, coupled with exemplars of successful pedagogues. More importantly, we need to be willing to look for exemplary practice in those classrooms and communities that too many of us are ready to dismiss as incapable of producing excellence.

The implication of continuing this kind of work means that research grounded in the practice of exemplary teachers will form a significant part of the knowledge base on which we build teacher preparation. It means that the research community will have to be willing to listen to and heed the "wisdom of practice" of these excellent practitioners.[87] Additionally, we need to consider methodologies that present more robust portraits of teaching. Meaningful combinations of quantitative and qualitative inquiries must be employed to help us understand the deeply textured, multilayered enterprise of teaching.

I presume that the work I have been doing raises more questions than it answers. A common question asked by practitioners is, Isn't what you described just "good teaching"? And, while I do not deny that it is good teaching, I pose a counterquestion: Why does so little of it seem to occur in classrooms populated by African American students? Another question that arises is whether or not this pedagogy is so idiosyncratic that only "certain" teachers can engage in it. I would argue that the diversity of these teachers and the variety of teaching strategies they employed challenge that notion. The common feature they shared was a classroom practice grounded in what they believed about the educability of the students. Unfortunately, this raises troubling thoughts about those teachers who are not successful, but we cannot assume that they do not believe that some students are incapable (or unworthy) of being educated. The reasons for their lack of success are far too complex for this discussion.

Ultimately, my responsibility as a teacher educator who works primarily with young, middle-class, White women is to provide them with examples of culturally relevant teaching in both theory and practice. My responsibility as a researcher is to move toward a theory of culturally relevant pedagogy.[88]

Notes

1. See Judith S. Kleinfeld, "Learning to Think Like a Teacher: The Study of Cases," in *Case Methods in Teacher Education*, Judith H. Shulman, ed. (New York: Teachers College Press, 1992); K. Noordhoff, "Shaping the Rhetoric of Reflection for Multicultural Settings," in *Encouraging Reflective Practice in Education*, Renee T. Clift, Robert Houston, and Marleen C. Pugach, eds. (New York: Teachers College Press, 1990); K. Noordhoff and Judith S. Kleinfeld, *Preparing Teachers for Multicultural Classrooms: A Case Study in Rural Alaska*, paper presented at the Annual Meeting of the American Educational Research Association, Chicago, April, 1991; Joyce King and Gloria Ladson-Billings, "The Teacher Education Challenge in Elite University Settings: Developing Critical Perspectives for Teaching in a Democratic and Multicultural Society," *European Journal of Intercultural Studies* 1, 1 (1990); Landon E. Beyer, *Creating Democratic Classrooms: The Struggle to Integrate Theory and Practice* (New York: Teachers College Press, 1996); Peter Murrell, *Cultural Politics in Teacher Education: What's Missing in the Preparation of African American Teachers*, paper presented at the Annual Meeting of the American Educational Research Association, Boston, April, 1990; and Peter Murrell, *Deconstructing Informal Knowledge of Exemplary Teaching in Diverse Urban Communities: Apprenticing Presence Teachers as Case-Study Researchers in Cultural Sites*, paper presented at the Annual Meeting of the American Educations Research Association, Chicago, April, 1991.

2. Thomas S. Popkewitz, *A Political Sociology of Educational Reform* (New York: Teachers College Press, 1991).

3. See Carl A. Grant, "Urban Teachers: Their New Colleagues and Curriculum, *Phi Delta Kappan* 70 (1989); Martin Haberman, "The Rationale for Training Adults as Teachers," in *Empowerment Through Multicultural Education*, Christine E. Sleeter, ed. (Albany: State University of New York Press, 1991); and Martin Haberman, "Can Cultural Awareness Be Taught in Teacher Education Programs?" *Teaching Education* 4 (1991).

4. Lee Shulman, "Knowledge and Teaching: Foundations of the New Reform," *Harvard Educational Review* 63 (1987).

5. Kathryn Hu-Pei Au and Cathie Jordan, "Teaching Reading to Hawaiian Children: Finding a Culturally Appropriate Solution," in *Culture and the Bilingual Classroom: Studies in Classroom Ethnography*, Henry Trueba, Grace Pung Guthrie, and Kathryn Hu-Pei Au, eds. (Rowley, Mass.: Newbury House, 1981).

6. Gerald Mohatt and Frederick Erickson, "Cultural Differences in Teaching Styles in an Odawa School: A Sociolinguistic Approach," in *Culture and the Bilingual Classroom: Studies in Classroom Ethnography*, op. cit.

7. Ibid., p. 117.

8. Ibid., p. 110.

9. See Courtney B. Cazden and Ellen L. Leggett, "Culturally Responsive Education: Recommendations for Achieving Lau Remedies II," in *Culture and the Bilingual Classroom: Studies in Classroom Ethnography*, op. cit.; and Frederick Erickson and Gerald Mohatt, "Cultural Organization and Participation Structures in Two Classrooms of Indian Students," in *Doing the Ethnography of Schooling*, George Spindler, ed. (New York: Holt, Rinehart & Winston, 1982), p. 167.

10. See Cathie Jordan, "Translating Culture: From Ethnographic Information to Educational Program." *Anthropology and Education Quarterly* 16 (1985); and Leonard Vogt, Cathie Jordan, and R. Tharp, "Explaining School Failure, Producing School Success: Two Cases," *Anthropology and Education Quarterly* 18 (1987).

11. Jordan, Ibid., p. 110.

12. Eliot A. Singer, *What Is Cultural Congruence, and Why Are They Saying Such Terrible Things about It?* (East Lansing, Mich.: Institute for Research on Teaching, 1988), p. 1.

13. Erickson and Mohatt, op. cit, p. 170.

14. See Geneva Gay and Roger D. Abrahams, "Talking Black in the Classroom," in *Language and Cultural Diversity in American Education*, Roger D. Abrahams and Rudolph C. Troike, eds. (Englewood Cliffs, N.J.: Prentice-Hall, 1972); William Labov, "The Logic of Nonstandard Negro English," in *Linguistics and the Teaching of Standard English*, James E. Alatis, ed. (Washington, D.C.: Georgetown University Press, 1969); and Ann Piestrup, *Black Dialect Interference and Accommodation of Reading Instruction in First Grade* (Berkeley: Language Behavior Research Laboratory, 1973).

15. Ana Maria Villegas, "School Failure and Cultural Mismatch: Another View," *The Urban Review* 20, 4 (1988).

16. See John Ogbu, "Black Education: A Cultural-Ecological Perspective," in *Black Families*, Harriette Pipes McAdoo, ed. (Beverly Hills: Sage, 1981); and John Ogbu, "Minority Status and Schooling in Plural Societies," *Comparative Education Review* 27 (1983).

17. T. Perry, *Toward a Theory of African American School Achievement* (Boston, Mass.: Wheelock College, Center on Families, Communities, Schools, and Children's Learning, 1993). It should be noted here that although issues of culturally relevant teaching can and should be considered cross culturally, this chapter looks specifically at the case of African American students.

18. See James Anderson, *The Education of Blacks in the South, 1860–1935* (Chapel Hill: University of North Carolina Press, 1988); Andrew Billingsley, *Climbing Jacob's Ladder: The Enduring Legacy of African American Families* (New York: Simon & Schuster, 1992); Horace Mann Bond, *Negro Education in Alabama: A Study in Cotton and Steel* (New York: Octagon Books, 1969); Henry A. Bullock, *A History of Negro Education in the South from 1619 to the Present* (Cambridge, Mass.: Harvard University Press, 1967); Reginald Clark, *Family Life and School Achievement: Why Poor Black Children Succeed or Fail* (Chicago: Chicago University Press, 1983); Vincent Harding, *There Is a River: The Black Struggle for Freedom in America* (Harcourt Brace Jovanovich, 1981); Violet Harris, "African American Conceptions of Literacy: a Historical Perspective," *Theory into Practice* 3 (1992); C. Johnson, "The Education of the Negro Child," *American Sociological Review* 1 (1936); John Rury, "The New York African Free School, 1827–1836: Conflict over Community Control of Black Education," *Phylon* 44 (1983); Carter G. Woodson, *The Education of the Negro Prior to 1861* (Washington, D.C.: Associated Publishers, 1919); and Meyer Weinberg, *A Chance to Learn: The History of Race and Education in the United States* (New York: Cambridge University Press, 1977).

19. See Joyce King, "Unfinished Business: Black Student Alienation and Black Teachers' Emancipators Pedagogy," in *Readings on Equal Education*, M. Foster, ed. (New York: AMS Press, 1991); Gloria Ladson-Billings, "Liberatory Consequences of Literacy: A Case of Culturally Relevant Instruction for African American Students," *The Journal of Negro Education* 61 (1992); Gloria Ladson-Billings, *The Dreamkeepers: Successful Teaching for African American Students* (San Francisco: Jossey-Bass); and Emilie V. Siddle-Walker, "Caswell County Training School, 1933–1969: Relationships Between Community and School," *Harvard Educational Review* 63, 2 (1993).

20. It is interesting to note that a number of trade books have emerged that detail the rage and frustration of academically successful, professional, middle-class, African American adults, which suggests that, even with the proper educational credentials, their lives continue to be plagued by racism and a questioning of their competence. Among the more recent books are Jill Nelson, *Volunteer Slavery* (Chicago: Noble, 1993); Brent Staples, *Parallel Time: Growing Up in Black and White* (New York: Pantheon); and Ellis Cose, *The Rage of a Privileged Class* (New York: Harper Collins, 1993).

21. Jacqueline Jordan Irvine, *Black Students and School Failure: Policies, Practices, and Prescriptions* (Westport, Conn.: Greenwood Press, 1990).

22. Joyce Elaine King and Carolyn Ann Mitchell, *Black Mothers to Sons: Juxtaposing African American Literature with Social Practice* (New York: Peter Lang, 1990).

23. It should be noted that the "cultural deficit" notion has been reinscribed under the rubric of "at-risk"; see Larry Cuban, "The 'At-risk' Label and the Problem of Urban School Reform," *Phi Delta Kappan* 70 (1989). Initially, the U.S. Commission on Excellence in Education defined the nation as at risk. Now, almost ten years later, it appears that only some children are at risk. Too often, in the case of African American students, their racial/cultural group membership defines them as at risk.

24. Carl F. Kaestle, "The Awful Reputation of Educational Research," *Educational Researcher* 22, 1 (1993).

25. Jeffrey Katzer, Kenneth H. Cook, and Wayne W. Crouch, *Evaluating Information: A Guide for Users of Social Science Research* (Reading, Mass.: Addison-Wesley, 1978).

26. See Chris Argyris, *Inner Contradictions of Rigorous Research* (New York: Academic Press, 1980); and Ron Amundson, Ronald C. Serlin, and Richard Lehrer, "On the Threats That Do *Not* Face Educational Research," *Educational Researcher* 21, 9 (1992).

27. See, for example, Michael W. Apple and Lois Weis, *Ideology and Practice in Schooling* (Philadelphia: Temple University Press, 1983); Samuel Bowles, "Unequal Education and the Reproduction of the Social Division of Labor," in *Power and Ideology in Education*, Jerome Karabel and A. H. Halsey, eds. (New York: Oxford University Press, 1977); and Kathleen Weiler, *Women Teaching for Change* (New York: Bergin & Garvey, 1988).

28. This is described in Robert Young, *A Critical Theory of Education: Habermas and Our Children's Future* (New York: Teachers College Press, 1990).

29. Lorraine Code, *What Can She Know? Feminist Theory and the Construction of Knowledge* (Ithaca, N.Y.: Cornell University Press, 1991), p. 243.

30. See Lou M. Smith, "An Evolving Logic of Participant Observation, Education Ethnography, and Other Case Studies," in *Review of Research in Education*, Lee Shulman, ed. (Itasca, Ill.: Peacock/AERA, 1978); J. M. Atkin, "Practice-Oriented Inquiry: A Third Approach to Research in Education," *Educational Researcher* 2, 7 (1973); Barney G. Glaser and Anselm L. Strauss, *The Discovery of Grounded Theory: Strategies for Qualitative Research* (Chicago: Aldine, 1967); and F. Lutz and M. Ramsey, "The Use of Anthropological Field Methods in Education," *Educational Researcher* 3, 10 (1974).

31. Lawrence Stenhouse, "The Relevance of Practice to Theory," *Theory into Practice* 22 (1983); John Elliot, *Action Research for Educational Change* (Philadelphia: Open University Press, 1991); Wilfred Carr and Stephen Kemmis, *Becoming Critical: Education, Knowledge and Action Research*, rev. ed. (Victoria, Australia: Deakin University Press, 1986); Kenneth M. Zeichner, "Preparing Teachers for Democratic Schools," *Action in Teacher Education* 11 (1990); and Marilyn Cochran-Smith and Susan Lytle, *Inside/Outside: Teachers, Research, and Knowledge* (New York: Teachers College Press, 1992).

32. Lee J. Cronbach, "Beyond the Two Disciplines of Scientific Psychology," *American Psychologist* 30 (1975).

33. See, for example, Nathaniel Lees Gage, "The Paradigm Wars and Their Aftermath," *Educational Researcher* 18, 7 (1989).

34. Ray Rist, "On the Relations among Educational Research Paradigms: From Disdain to Detentes," in *Education and Society: A Reader*, K. Dougherty and F. Hammack, eds. (New York: Harcourt Brace Jovanovich, 1990).

35. Thomas S. Kuhn, *The Structure of Scientific Revolutions*, 2d ed., enlarged (Chicago: University of Chicago Press, 1970); Michael Q. Patton, *Alternative Evaluation Research Paradigm* (Grand Forks: University of North Dakota Press, 1975); H. S. Becker, "Whose Side Are We On?" *Social Problems*, 14 (1967); and Alvin Gouldner, *The Coming Crisis in Western Sociology* (New York: Basic Books, 1970).

36. Rist, op. cit., p. 83.

37. See K. Carter, "The Place of Story in the Study of Teaching and Teacher Education," *Educational Researcher* 22, 1 (1993); and A. Neumann and P. Peterson, *Learning from our Lives: Women, Research, and autobiography in education* (New York: Teachers College Press, 1997).

38. See James A. Banks, "African American Scholarship and the Evolution of Multicultural Education," *The Journal of Negro Education* 61 (1992); K. Narayan, "How Native Is a 'Native' Anthropologist?" *American Anthropologist* 95 (1993); A. Padilla, "Ethnic Minority Scholars, Research, and Mentoring: Current and Future Issues," *Educational Researcher* 23, 4 (1994); and Renato Rosaldo, *Culture and Truth: The Remaking of Social Analysis* (Boston: Beacon, 1989).

39. Narayan, Ibid., p. 677.

40. Banks, op. cit., and Padilla, op. cit.

41. Patricia Hill Collins, *Black Feminist Thought: Knowledge, Consciousness, and the Politics of Empowerment* (New York: Routledge, 1991).

42. See my, "Like Lightning in a Bottle: Attempting to Capture the Pedagogical Excellence of Successful Teachers of Black Students," *International Journal of Qualitative Studies in Education* 3 (1990); "Liberatory Consequences of Literacy," op. cit.; "Reading Between the Lines and Beyond the Pages: A Culturally Relevant Approach to Literacy Teaching," *Theory into Practice* 31 (1992); and *The Dreamkeepers*, op. cit.

43. M. Foster, "Constancy, Connectedness, and Constraints in the Lives of African American Teachers," *National Women's Studies Journal* 3 (1991).

44. See James P. Spradley, *The Ethnographic Interview* (New York: Holt, Rinehart and Winston, 1979).

45. Benjamin S. Bloom, Allison Davis, and Robert Hess, *Compensatory Education for Cultural Deprivation* (New York: Holt, Rinehart & Winston, 1965).

46. Collins, op. cit., p. 209.

47. Spradley, op. cit.

48. The research collaborative met to view portions of the classroom videotapes that I, as researcher, selected for common viewing.

49. David Berliner, *Implications of Studies of Expertise in Pedagogy for Teacher Education and Evaluation. New Directions in Teacher Assessment*. Conference proceedings of the ETS Invitational Conference (Princeton, N.J.: Educational Testing Service, October, 1988).

50. See Carol Gilligan, *In a Different Voice* (Cambridge: Harvard University Press, 1982); Nel Noddings, *Caring* (Berkeley: University of California Press, 1984); and Nel Noddings, "Stories in Dialogue: Caring and Interpersonal Reasoning," in *Stories Lives Tell: Narrative and Dialogue in Education*, Carol Witherell and Nell Noddings, eds. (New York: Teachers College Press, 1991).

51. See, for example, Weiler, op. cit.

52. African American Male Task Force, *Educating African American Males: A Dream Deferred* (Washington, D.C.: Author, 1990); R. Clark, op. cit.; James Comer, "Home School Relationships as They Affect the Academic Success of Children," *Education and Urban Society* 16 (1984); Irvine, op. cit.; Ogbu, "Black Education: A Cultural-Ecological Perspective," op. cit.; and D. Slaughter and V. Kuehne, "Improving Black Education: Perspectives on Parent Involvement," *Urban League Review* 11 (1988).

53. Ogbu, "Minority Status and Schooling in Plural Societies," *Comparative Education Review* 27 (1983), p. 171.

54. See Frederick Erickson, "Transformation and School Success: The Politics and Culture of Educational Achievement," *Anthropology and Education* 18 (1987); and "Transformation and School Success: The Politics and Culture of Educational Achievement," in *Minority Education: Anthropological Perspectives*, Evelyn Jacob and Cathie Jordan, eds. (Norwood, N.J.: Ablex, 1993); and Piestrup, op. cit.

55. Wilbur Brookover, "Can We Make Schools Effective for Minority Students?" *The Journal of Negro Education* 54 (1985); Wilbur Brookover, et al., *School Social Systems and Student Achievement: Schools Can Make a Difference* (New York: Praeger, 1979); and Ronald Edmonds, "Effective Schools for the Urban Poor," *Educational Leadership* 37, 1 (1979).

56. These correlates include a clear and focused mission, instructional leadership, a safe and orderly environment, regular monitoring of student progress, high expectations, and positive home-school relations.

57. Lisa Delpit, "Acquisition of Literate Discourse: Bowing Before the Master?" *Theory into Practice* 31 (1992).

58. Students in this district took the California Achievement Test (CAT) in October and May of each school year. Growth scores in the classrooms of the teachers in the study were significantly above those of others in the district.

59. Michelle Fine, "Why Urban Adolescents Drop into and out of High School," *Teachers College Record* 87 (1986); and Signithia Fordham, "Racelessness as a Factor in Black Student's School Success: Pragmatic Strategy or Pyrrhic Victory?" *Harvard Educational Review* 58 (1988).

60. Signithia Fordham and John Ogbu, "Black Students' School Success: Coping with the Burden of Acting White," *The Urban Review* 18 (1986):176.

61. M. Bacon, *High Potential Children from Ravenswood Elementary School District*, follow-up study (Redwood City, Calif.: Sequoia Union High School District , May, 1981).

62. This is not to suggest that cultural competence for African American students means being a failure. The problem that African American students face is the constant devaluation of their culture both in school and in the larger society. Thus, the styles apparent in African American youth culture—e.g., dress, music, walk, language—are equated with poor academic performance. The student who identifies with "hip-hop" culture may be regarded as dangerous and/or a gang member for whom academic success is not expected. He (and it usually is a male) is perceived as not having the cultural capital (Bourdieu, 1984) necessary far academic success. See Pierre Bourdieu, *Distinctions: The Social Critique of the Judgment of Taste* (Cambridge: Harvard University Press, 1984).

63. An examination of rap music reveals a wide variety of messages. Despite the high profile of gansta rap, which seems to glorify violence, particularly against the police and Whites, and the misogynistic messages found in some of this music, there is a segment of rap music that serves as cultural critique and urges African Americans to educate themselves because schools fail to do so. Prominent rap artists in this tradition are Arrested Development, Diggable Planets, KRS-1, and Queen Latifah.

64. I am indebted to Mwalimu Shujaa for sharing his working paper, "A Afrikan-Centered Education in Afrikan-Centered Schools: The Need for Consensus Building," which elaborates tile multiplicity of thinking on this issue extant in the African-centered movement.

65. See Joan Davis Ratteray, "The Search for Access and Content in the Education of African Americans," in *Too Much Schooling, Too Little Education*, Mwalimu J. Shujaa, ed. (Trenton, N.J.: Africa World Press, 1994); Carol D. Lee, "African-Centered Pedagogy: Complexities and Possibilities," in Shujaa, op. cit.; Asa Hilliard, "Behavioral Style, Culture, and Teaching and Learning," *The Journal of Negro Education* 61 (1992); Peter Murrell, "Afrocentric Immersion: Academic and Personal Development of African American Males in Public Schools," in *Freedom's Plow: Teaching in the Multicultural Classroom*, Theresa Perry and James W. Fraser, eds. (New York: Routledge, 1993); and Molefi K. Asante, "The Afrocentric Idea in Education," *Journal of Negro Education* 60 (1991).

66. See Grant, 1989, op. cit.; Haberman, "Can Cultural Awareness be Taught in Teacher Education Programs?" op. cit.; Joyce King, "Dysconscious Racism: Ideology, Identity, and the Miseducation of Teachers," *The Journal of Negro Education* 60 (1991); King and Ladson-Billings, op. cit.; and Kenneth M. Zeichner, *Educating Teachers for Cultural Diversity* (East Lansing, Mich.: National Center for Research on Teacher Learning, 1992).

67. See L. Aaronsohn, "Learning to Teach for Empowerment," *Radical Teacher* 40 (1992); Aldon D. Morris, *The Origins of the Civil Rights Movement: Black Communities Organizing for Change* (New York: Free Press, 1984); S. Clark, "Literacy and Liberation," *Freedomways* (1964, First Quarter); and S. Clark with C. Brown, *Ready from Within: A First Person Narrative* (Trenton N.J.: Africa World Press, 1990).

68. Paulo Freire, *Education for Critical Consciousness* (New York: Seabury, 1973); and *Pedagogy of the Oppressed* (New York: Seabury, 1974).

69. See, for example, Elizabeth Ellsworth, "Why Doesn't This Feel Empowering? Working Through the Repressive Myths of Critical Pedagogy," *Harvard Educational Review* 59 (1989); Henry Giroux, *Theory and Resistance: a Pedagogy for the Opposition* (Hadley, Mass.: Bergin & Garvey, 1983); bell hooks, *Talking Back, Thinking Feminist, Thinking Black* (Boston: South End, 1989); Patti Lather, "Research as Praxis," *Harvard Educational Review* 56 (1986); and Peter McLaren, *Life in Schools* (White Plains, N.Y.: Longman, 1989).

70. Henry Giroux and Roger Simon, "Popular Culture and Critical Pedagogy: Everyday Life as a Basis for Curriculum Knowledge," in *Critical Pedagogy, the State, and Cultural Struggle*, Henry Giroux and Peter McLaren, eds. (Albany: State University of New York Press, 1989), p. 239.

71. R. Robinson, "P. C. Anderson Students Try Hand at Problem Solving," *Dallas Examiner*, February 25, 1993, pp. 1, 8.

72. Michael W. Apple, *Official Knowledge* (New York: Routledge, 1993).

73. P. Lipman, *The Influence of Restructuring on Teachers Beliefs about and Practices with African American Students*, unpublished doctoral dissertation, University of Wisconsin–Madison.

74. Martin Haberman, "Redefining the 'Best and the Brightest,'" *In These Times*, January 24, 1994.

75. Readers should note that I have listed these as separate and distinct categories for analytical purposes. In practice, they intersect and overlap, continuously.

76. Kenneth Strike, "Professionalism, Democracy, and Discursive Communities: Normative Reflections on Restructuring," *American Educational Research Journal* 30 (1993).

77. Herbert L. Foster, *Ribbin', Jivin' and Playin' the Dozens: The Persistent Dilemma in Our Schools* (Cambridge, Mass.: Ballinger, 1986).

78. Freire, 1974, op. cit., p. 76.

79. These letters and numbers represent codes I employed to distinguish among the interview data and field notes I collected during the study.

80. See, for example, Jere Brophy and Thomas Good, "Teachers' Communication of Differential Expectations for Children's Classroom Performance," *Journal of Educational Psychology* 61 (1970); Ray Rist, "Student Social Class and Teacher Expectations: The Self-Fulfilling Prophecy in Ghetto Schools," *Harvard Educational Review* 40 (1970); and K. Wilcox, "Differential Socialization in the Classroom: Implications for Equal Opportunity," in *Doing the Ethnography of Schooling*, George Spindler, ed. (Prospect Heights, Ill.: Waveland, 1982).

81. See E. Cohen and J. Benton, "Making Groupwork Work," *American Educator* (Fall, 1988); and Robert Slavin, "Cooperative Learning and the Cooperative School," *Educational Leadership* 45 (1987).

82. Benjamin Bloom, *Taxonomy of Educational Objectives* (New York: Longman, 1956).

83. Haberman, "Can Cultural Awareness be Taught in Teacher Education Programs?" op. cit.

84. Lilia I. Bartolome, "Beyond the Methods Fetish: Toward a Humanizing Pedagogy," *Harvard Educational Review* 64, 2 (1994).

85. See Kenneth M. Zeichner, *Educating Teachers for Cultural Diversity*, op. cit.

86. Lather, op. cit.

87. Shulman, op. cit.

88. I am grateful to the National Academy of Education's Spencer postdoctoral fellowship program for providing me with the funding to conduct this research. However, the ideas expressed here are my own and do not necessarily reflect those of the National Academy of Education or the Spencer Foundation.

TWELVE

Teaching, Gender, and Curriculum

Sara E. Freedman

Hurry up, hurry up, hurry up." I would stand in my classroom and hear myself repeating that phrase to the students, over and over again, several times a day. Hearing myself say those words set me trying to figure out why: What was compelling me to force myself and my students to think faster, to move faster, to tidy up faster, quietly to stand at the door faster? The "hurry up, hurry up, hurry up" in my own mind implied that somehow what we were doing within our own four tight walls had to catch up with the world outside the classroom. I was obviously anxious to make sure we made those connections in time, even as I sensed that the world outside would never know how we had reached the correct stage at the appropriate time, nor how we had changed in the process. No one came in and stood by my side to see what page we were on in the workbook, and no one timed my reading groups to calculate the speed of the children's reading, or how quickly they answered comprehension questions or completed their SRA worksheets. I simply knew that that phrase had become part of the day's lessons, and that I was now recognizing the presence of something whose shape and origin were invisible and utterly domineering, yet so impersonal that I did not know its shape, its voice, or its demands.

The major thing I did know was that it had to do with the school work—either it was not being done fast enough or it was not being put away quickly enough or there was time wasted between one activity and another. There were moments of unproductivity in the classroom, times when children were not concentrating intensely on reading or writing or learning their multiplication tables.

Of course I felt bad. Not so much about those lapses of productivity, which did not seem to cause lower year-end test scores. My own education had made me appreciate the moments between "time on task." I cherished the students who would come up to me two hours after a classroom discussion and say, "Does that mean . . . ?" obviously having continued to mull over a whole new concept of life, relishing the chance to tell me what they had been trying to figure out for the last hour or so when they were supposedly sharpening pencils or filling in the blanks in their workbooks.

What made me feel bad was that I could not help pushing them away from that kind of thinking, away from that kind of personal musing, and away from sharing of the moment when teacher and student sense that a new leap has been taken. Those connections—between myself and the students, between past ways of thinking and an emergent understanding—sprang out of a particular classroom discussion, and the desire to share with one who had participated in it the sense of excitement that had sparked thought. Those connections, as well as the discussions that led to them, simply had less and less place in my classroom. Why? What was taking their place? What ideas about how learning should take place were constraining life in the classroom? Where were those ideas coming from?

This chapter is an attempt to answer these questions. I have come to believe that considering them seriously can challenge both the way curriculum is defined and who does the defining. For those of us who want to transform the schools, such a redefinition is essential.

Two major ways of defining curriculum exist within current educational literature, each with its own group of adherents. One group sees curriculum as a body of knowledge that is divided by subject matter and complexity according to the ability levels of students who, moving through the divisions in order, will master the whole body of knowledge by the time they finish school. This camp sees curriculum eroded by the other group: educational technocrats, who replace the emphasis on knowledge with one on methods and form.

Both of these emphases take knowledge to be a product, either a body of knowledge I was supposed to have mastered myself or a set of discrete steps and procedures that, if carefully studied and followed, would ensure that my students learned a body of knowledge. In both definitions, curriculum is something developed *outside* the classroom. It may be refined and tested within classrooms but the purpose of the testing is not to modify it so that it is specific to that classroom, but rather to ensure that it can be moved from classroom to classroom, or across state lines, and be recognized everywhere as the same set of ideas or facts.

What goes on in the classroom that is not part of that transportable set of concepts and facts is simply irrelevant by either definition. Missing from both is a recognition that what one learns, and what one teaches, is transformed within the classroom, and to a great extent can only be understood by honoring that context. As a teacher, I was also losing track of that recognition. This chapter attempts to renew it, arguing that to define curriculum as an object, something that can be abstracted from a specific group of people, trivializes the role of the teacher and the pupil in shaping curriculum, and causes much of the resistance curriculum reformers face when they attempt to introduce yet another set of books, concepts, or schedules.

For the one thing they do *not* consider part of *curriculum* is the personalized adaptation of those ideas or stories by the teacher and her students, the establishment of a rhythm and a tone that matches that special time and place. Curriculum designers see those rhythms as corruptions, or at best as slight modifications by a gifted or assertive teacher. When such personalizing takes over, the results cannot be cross tabulated, they are hard to measure, they mess up time tables and schedules, and they raise the possibility that what goes on in the classroom is as important as, and potentially as exciting, as what happens in the university curriculum laboratory or textbook company.

When curriculum experts do allow that "classroom climate" can contribute to pupil progress (i.e., enhanced test scores), they generally credit the teacher with providing the emotional sustenance, the reassurance, and the personal incentive that makes learning possible. Conversely, when they see learning as arrested, they often cite the teacher's personal traits as obstacles to student progress. She has withheld approval, been overindulgent, neglectful, or too demanding. In short, she has *burned out*—a phrase that emphasizes the teacher's emotional makeup, implying that the teacher has become too numb to feel and that the core of who she used to be has somehow evaporated due to a reckless disregard for self-preservation. (The idea that a teacher's dissatisfaction might be tied to a lack of intellectual stimulation and/or recognition in schools is generally absent from the numerous discussions of burnout, underlining the common assumption that the ability of a teacher to use her mind is irrelevant to her self-esteem as a teacher.)

So curriculum people define teachers, successful as well as failed, as the emotional components, the heart if you will, of learning. The curriculum and those who develop it are the mind, contributing the intellect, the abstract concepts, and the clearly delineated sequences. To use the language of schools, teachers provide "affect," the personal, emotional, spontaneous, in-stinctual, private, and therefore secretive dimension. Those who work outside the classroom provide the curricula: the "cognitive," intellectual, abstract, public, rational dimension.

It is crucial to recognize that the division between affect—thought to be rooted in classroom life—and cognition—imported into the classroom—is structurally embodied in schools in a very clear-cut way. The principal adult actors *inside* the classroom are women, while the principal actors *outside* the classroom are men. This arrangement has held since the beginning of the common school movement. Nor is the belief that men and women properly have different and separate roles an anamoly of the educational system. Schools replicate and publicly sanction the division of labor and the power structure that distinguish men's and women's spheres of influence outside of schools. Bringing this knowledge to bear on a discussion of curriculum helps understand how curriculum has developed, what role it plays in schools, and how to change it.

A large and growing body of scholarship describes this division of labor, which is known in the literature as the *doctrine of the separate spheres*. The eco-nomic basis for this division of labor, with its accompanying difference of val-ues and ideological supports, was the rise of modern industrial capitalism. New economic conditions removed the father from the home, required him to earn a wage in factory or office, assigned the responsibility for raising the family solely to the mother, thereby dividing life into the *public sphere* of the market and the *private sphere* of the home. "As fathers moved off the farm into wage labor in factories and offices, women's maternal instincts were 'discov-ered,' and mothers became increasingly associated with child care."[1] The di-visions were both mutually reinforcing and antagonistic. "Life would now be experienced as divided into two distinct spheres: a *public* sphere of endeavor governing ultimately by the Market; and a *private* sphere of intimate relation-ships and individual biological existence."[2] In the home, people were valued "for themselves rather than for their marketable qualities"[3] and women were expected to provide to family members the sense of self-worth and unques-tioned duty missing from the market place. In contrast, the definition of mas-culinity, at least for the rising bourgeoisie, was increasingly linked to managerial ideologies and practice. "The two spheres stand, in respect to their basic values, opposed to each other, and the line between them . . . charged with moral tension."[4]

The belief in women's maternal destiny affected not only mothers by confining them within their families, it also provided the ideological justifica-tion for encouraging women to export their supposed natural qualities of nur-turance outside the home.

Women's maternal destiny now seemed to educators' satisfaction to prove their fitness as instructors and influencers of youth. Emma Willard argued not only that women were "naturally" suited to teach but that they could be hired at lower salaries in the common schools and that their employment would free more men to increase the wealth of the nation. In Joseph Emerson's estimation, the schoolroom ranked next to the home as a sphere of women's work. He "suspected" that nature had designed the teaching profession to be women's, since the law, medicine, religion, and politics were exclusively (and appropriately) men's. Catherine Beecher drew tighter the link between motherhood and schoolteaching by asserting that "women's profession," inside and outside the family, was to form pure minds and healthy bodies. Along with an increasing host of educators, Beecher believed that the most direct path to the regulation of conscience and reason ran through the "affections," or "heart," the realm in which women's influence reigned. In these natural facts she discerned the efficacy of training women to be teachers.[5]

Beecher's arguments were eventually accepted by the architects of the common school movement, who desperately needed to expand the teaching workforce to accommodate the growing number of children now required to attend school.

Women filled a desperate need created by the challenge of the common schools, the ever-increasing size of the student body, and the westward growth of the nation. America was committed to educating its children in public schools, but it was insistent on doing so as cheaply as possible. Women were available in great numbers, and they were willing to work cheaply. The result was another ideological adaptation: in the very period when the gospel of the home as woman's only proper sphere was preached most loudly, it was discovered that women were the natural teachers of youth, could do the job even better than men, and were to be preferred for such employment. This was always provided, of course, that they would work at the proper wage differential—30 to 50 percent of the wages paid male teachers was considered appropriate.[6]

Being identified with nurturance gave middle-class women entry to one of the few wage-earning jobs open to them, and let many working-class women move up. Once hired, however, they found it was not so much their "natural" abilities with children as their willingness to work for lower wages and their supposed acceptance of male authority that made them so attractive to school committees and school bureaucrats. The latter supervised their work strictly, making sure they taught prescribed curriculum, following mandated techniques.

234

While today there is more of a willingness to nostalgically grant old-time teachers a degree of intelligence assumed lacking from present recruits, to the teachers themselves, their now much vaunted intelligence was never mentioned. Instead their "natural ability" to work with children was emphasized, a trait that earned teaching the label "women's true profession." The emphasis on nurturing, as distinct from intelligence and analytical ability, if not their opposite, made irrelevant any discussion of the intellectual abilities of teachers.

Philip W. Jackson, in *Life in Classrooms*, provides a more updated insight into the role divisions between teachers and administrators/educational experts. In describing a group of teachers he has chosen to interview on the basis of their ability to work effectively with children, he states:

> If teachers sought a more thorough understanding of their world, insisted on a greater rationality in their actions, were completely open-minded in their consideration of pedagogical choices, and profound in their view of the human condition, they might well receive greater applause from intellectuals, but it is doubtful that they would perform with greater efficiency in the classroom. On the contrary, it is quite possible that such paragons of virtue, if they could be found to exist, would actually have a deuce of a time coping in any sustained way with a class of third graders in a playyard full of nursery tots.[7]

This quotation shocks us today in its patronizing attitude. Yet it baldly exemplifies a still-common belief in the necessary distinction between "pedagogical choices"—here equated with rationality and open mindedness—and the unique, personal, and idiosyncratic wisdom of teachers, considered essential for "coping with" children. Furthermore, the quote suggests that these two ways of viewing the world cannot be found in the same person. Indeed their combined presence in one person or group of individuals would make life in schools extremely problematic. Jackson suggests that here he has the teachers' own interests at heart. They would make their lives easier by just accepting the curriculum that is imported into the classroom and adjusting the students to it.

But if so, what does that tell us about what counts as learning in our schools? Can we actually separate what is taught from who does the teaching and who does the learning? Can a curriculum be devised outside the classroom that will work inside the classroom? And if so, who benefits from such a system and who suffers?

To address these questions, I now turn to the way teachers themselves view these divisions and the effect of the divisions on their work both in and out of classrooms. At first glance, some teachers appear to agree with those who say that teaching is fundamentally emotional labor, and intrinsically distinct from intellectual pursuits.

"It's funny. You don't use your mind when you're teaching kids. Now, I know that sounds really dumb, but you don't. It's not intellectual. It's a lot of emotion. I'd put out a tremendous amount of emotional energy when I work with the kids, but it's not intellectual."[8]

Yet the same teacher, when talking about what children learn in her classroom, gives a rather different view of her own contribution to their learning, and in the process questions the way curriculum is normatively defined. This teacher explains that the skills she uses in her present position, and that she sees as essential, are individual to her classroom. For her, the official curriculum of the school system is abstract, it is not a "lived" curriculum. Even when a curriculum emphasizes such issues as social awareness or cultural diversity, there is pressure to implement it through a factual, teacher-manual type of approach:

> The affective kinds of things that I did with my kids aren't in the curriculum. The health curriculum talks about self-identity and finding yourself as a person, but I always felt it went much deeper than that and I spent a lot of time and a lot of energy getting kids to be good to each other and good to themselves by talking about their differences and similarities. That's not in the curriculum. Because the core curriculum deals with content—short *a* says *a*, Boston is the hub of the commonwealth, that type of thing. That's different from the kinds of things I thought were going on in my classroom that you just don't find in curriculums.[9]

Experts see the books, not the teacher, as defining the curriculum and determining the education—or miseducation—of the child. If the teacher adheres strictly to the text, the child should learn. But frequently there is a price to pay, both intellectually and emotionally, like my own "hurry-up" voice. Another teacher says:

> I think sometimes I get into a panic and panic the kids, cramming work down their throats in an effort to get them up to grade level. One of the problems I have is that I've got to complete all this work. I do feel that their books have gotten harder. The basal uses language arts a lot. A lot of adjectives, synonyms, naming words, action words. They are very much concerned with the technicalities, with sentences, periods, question marks. I have to introduce the vocabulary from that book, so whatever I do with them whether it's in the basal reader or outside the basal reader I still have to make sure that they can pick up the "green book" in the next grade. If I don't, no matter how great their vocabularies are, then the second grade teacher will say, "Hey, they didn't get this specific skill and they don't know these specific words." I think they'd be able to tell.[10]

Still another teacher, on the theme of pace and panic:

> The principal started another program in kindergarten that he wanted to adopt, working with small groups, using electronic equipment like head sets and things, very carefully planned individualizing instruction with the children. He was structuring, planning 15-minute segments. He wanted to try something new. We would have one-half hour of concentrated teaching in small groups. so you worked on listening to sounds or you worked on your workbooks in small groups and then after 15 minutes it was [clap hands] change groups. And no matter what, you had to stop at that point. There was one little girl in my room who had had kidney surgery who really wasn't learning and had a lot of problems and I felt couldn't sit and do the work like that. And I remember one day when I said, "You know, she just had kidney surgery." He said, "I'm tired of hearing about her kidney surgery. I'm tired of hearing emotional things blamed for reading problems." It's a very cut-and-dried thing.[11]

As speed-up and imposed structure increase, teachers, one would suppose, need less and less education to work well at the job, even though—ironically—they need more and more to get it in the first place. Needless to say, this disparity has exacerbated teacher alienation and increased resistance to curriculum reforms.

A teacher with a master's degree in reading talks about her efforts to use her experience both with curriculum and with a particular child to improve his learning.

> The director [who has no experience in elementary education] has sent word down to the building that everybody is supposed to be reading in the Ginn series and if they're not, he wanted the names of teachers and children sent to the office. So he was keeping in touch. I got into hell for saying some kids couldn't read that book and I wanted to use the other one, that I knew really worked. He kept saying, "No, put 'em in the Ginn." He wanted them in that book and that was the end of it. He doesn't take his own teachers' expertise into consideration at all. Maybe he really believes his own teachers don't have any expertise or at least he doesn't value it.[12]

That belief seems implicit in the more and more common practice of mandating a basal reading series for an entire school or school system.

> We were mandated to develop a program that within the building we had to use the same text. So we had to find a reading system that quote unquote met the needs of every kid in that building, kindergarten through eighth grade. Well, we chose a textbook that was excellent for teaching skills in the primary grades, but

was not a good transitional text. I developed a transitional reading program for my classroom, and I wasn't unique in that. Our kids weren't ready to begin that fourth grade reader. And the answer was, "Directive number such and such from the school department dictates that there must be one basal reading series in the building, so therefore you must order materials."[13]

Teachers are told that these books are the most educationally sound on the market but the grapevine sometimes suggests other reasons:

They hired a new reading coordinator. He was a writer for the American Book Company. He wanted to bring workbooks into the school for the kindergarten. I said I didn't want reading readiness workbooks. He said. "Studies have shown that children who use books do better later," and he kept quoting those studies. So the second year, he introduced the American Book Company books, K through 6. All the other books were thrown out.[14]

Even when no crass interest of this sort is present, the impulse is toward uniformity:

Some neat things might be happening next door with two teachers, but [administrators can't boast] this is what we're doing for the whole school or the whole town—so it doesn't have as much value. So, they're under pressure to show the community that this is how we are handling curriculum development. The easiest way is to use commercial materials such as a beautiful SCIS kit, lovely, big expensive kits, and easier to do it like that.[15]

Children learn, of course, that the knowledge they possess comes from and is only legitimately validated by the anonymous authority of the textbook. When they fill in the blanks, they are not responding to their own needs but to that of an authority whose interest in the child is not personal. Tacit acceptance by teacher and child that their skills are simply reactive is a strong means of control. Without an awareness of their own contributions, and without the public's awareness, they are easily blamed for any breakdown, and hiring a teacher becomes a question of choosing the person who will most strictly adhere to the one best system.

Even when teachers' work has created a major program their contribution appears publicly as negligible, secondary, or an exception to the rule. Their isolation from each other is perpetuated by the need to funnel any request or information up through the levels of the hierarchy and back down again rather than directly to each other. This prevents teachers from using their special knowledge of classroom life, which they alone possess, as a basis for determining systemwide, or even schoolwide, policies.

> After working for months on the fourth grade reading curriculum, we brought it up to the Assistant Superintendent. We had put a blanket statement at the beginning stating that we would assume that the teachers would be responsible by consulting the textbooks and other resource materials and their expertise and so on. . . . He made it quite clear that he didn't think they were capable of going over anything by themselves, finding the materials, using them appropriately. . . . We're smart enough to do all the busy work but not smart enough to carry it out. . . . All the teachers did all the work, but I haven't seen any acknowledgment of that publicly or any published words of praise for the teachers.[16]

In fact, teachers' ability to innovate frequently depends upon their skill in concealing their originality, even their successes, so that they do not appear to consider their own judgment on intellectual matters equal to that of principals or other administrators.

Many teachers, however, do develop imaginative, creative, and intellectually rigorous curricula. How do they fare within the educational system? Some teachers, who can more openly acknowledge their curricular efforts, depend on a benevolent principal who is usually seen by other administrators and by the teachers themselves as the exception to the rule. Teachers' efforts are tolerated, for instance, in affluent school systems with access to enrichment resources or in situations that include students from more privileged backgrounds, or in pilot programs, or in environments comprised of an unusually cohesive group of pupils. Yet there is a danger that such teachers will be seen as an example and a rebuke to other teachers.

> I was hired originally because open classrooms were popular at the time, and was interested in that kind of thing, even though I really didn't know what it was. I did try all kinds of things, and I was lucky because I also had an unusually bright classroom. The principal used to send all of the newspaper reporters to my classroom and I got my picture in the paper and full-page write-ups. I had no idea how this was affecting other teachers. Years later I discovered that the second-grade teacher had fallen apart because she had been the principal's pet teacher for the last few years, and all of a sudden her very tightly controlled style was no longer in favor. In fact, the principal sent her into my classroom to observe my methods, and I was a first-year teacher in that school and she had been there for ten years! After that, she worked incredibly hard, but her way just wasn't what sold newspapers anymore. It was only after I left that school, and went to another school district where my style was no longer popular, that I learned how devastating it can be when you have to prove constantly that you are competent, when

that isn't taken for granted, and where the assumption is you are mediocre until you can prove otherwise. Of course, you become, at least I felt I was becoming, mediocre because I was so afraid to take chances for fear I would fail and prove them right.[17]

Administrators cite such "superteachers" not to encourage other teachers to innovate within their own classrooms, but to limit the number of innovative teachers, requiring others to copy the method of the teacher currently in favor or to encourage even the innovative teacher to hold on to a sure thing else they disappoint, and jeopardize their favored status. The tendency of the system thus is to encourage standardization, inevitably encouraging mediocrity and conformity as the general, and safer, way of continuing one's teaching career amid the many curricular changes demanded periodically of teachers.

When I first started teaching 17 years ago, I believed in a very child-centered, developmental approach for kindergarten; I still do, but over the years my teaching style has changed because of feedback I've gotten from different principals, pushing me to rely more on workbooks and things like that which I never would have done on my own. When this new reading coordinator came in one day, I was working with a group in workbooks and my aid was working with another group in workbooks and everything was quiet, and we had exactly what my first principal would have loved. And she thought it was terrible. So what can I do? [she laughs] *Finally*, I accomplished what they wanted me to do, and it's hard to change tools. It's not that easy because they're habits you've formed over the years, and I got to like the other way because that's the way I've been doing it. I wouldn't mind going back, but I'm not sure that the reading coordinator will stay very long and I'm not sure that even that superintendent will stay very long.[18]

Even teachers deemed capable by one principal of developing curriculum may find that the next principal disagrees:

There was one particular teacher who really was turned on to language experience teaching, a terrific teacher, so she set up a whole language experience program in her class. Well, we got a change of principals. Principals tend to be threatened by things they don't understand or can't control because they're more dependent upon the person, not a system. It's always easier to go by a traditional reading program. Well, she got a lot of flack from the principal. He completely belittled her efforts, even though her results, and the feel of her classroom, were fantastic. She withdrew, isolated herself. Her classroom was not exciting anymore. The kids were in straight rows. She does what she thinks is expected of her. She goes home at 3:30 and that's it. She's just waiting to retire.[19]

240

For a teacher to have influence outside her own classroom, the curriculum she has developed must be cleansed of any individualistic traits peculiar to the teacher originating it, making it a commodity suitable for sale outside the classroom.

> I think generally teachers would want to share with other teachers and feel good about it and do it. I think next door or even in another school somebody is doing something, and they become very excited about it and that excitement is transmitted to another person, and I think they're very apt to try it. My own feeling is that when I get a pile of things that somebody else has made it's lovely and I may use some of it, but it's not mine. But I think teachers resent that administrators who are supposed to be helping us come in and ask us to give them copies of things we've done in our room. The administration's assumption is that now I'm going to be so committed to it—the whole curriculum—that you will go and you will sit and you will listen and you will learn and you will go back to your classroom and implement it.[20]

Researchers have been arguing for some time that teachers are subjected to such intrusions because they lack a shared body of professional knowledge. It is true that many teachers are not willing to lay down specific formulae for raising reading scores or teaching math facts or even lining children up to go out to recess. It does not necessarily follow that teachers lack concrete knowledge or that they have not demonstrated to themselves and other teachers the success of many techniques and strategies they have devised.

Teachers consistently report that their major and most reliable source of information inside the classroom is their personal interactions with their students, even if these interactions are not usually classified as part of the curriculum.

> Discussion is not part of the core curriculum because it's not something you can write down and give back in a test. There's no way that you can empirically prove that a kid's attitude or opinion has developed and changed, except that the kid seems to be a different kid then he was before. We know he's cjamged because we can look at the kid and we can hear the way he communicates. We know that this is different. I think that teachers get so caught up with producing something that proves the kid scored one point on his reading test and that means he's now four months above his grade level—that type of thing. We have to have some way almost of justifying what we've been doing in our classrooms and talking about things. Somehow you can't justify an hour spent talking about why you feel the way you do because you can't empirically prove it later on a report card.[21]

Teachers also report that outside the classroom their most trusted source for new techniques and strategies, as well as feedback and confirmation, is the discussion they carry on with other teachers during break time between speakers at an in-service workshop, at crosstown meetings with teachers at the same grade level, or by a frank request for help in the teachers' room. The informal nature of these discussions, the low institutional and social status accorded the participants, the fact the issues are embedded in specific contextual situations, and the pressing need for immediate help, mask the fact that teachers do possess a great deal of knowledge and expertise about curricular as well as classroom management issues. An administrator or researcher, more comfortable with abstract and no-fault solutions, may not recognize these discussions as demonstrating knowledge or expertise but for the teacher the fact that someone who is really "in there" suggested these alternatives is the most solid reason for trying them out.

Teachers know how mistakes and false judgments made in the past have led to present choices. But they also know they can never be sure, because this year's class is so different from last year's. Curriculum must respond to what the teacher experiences each year.

Perhaps if children's emotions could be easily defined, diagnosed, and treated, with the just the proper "treatment" given to each child—a treatment that had been agreed upon by experts on the basis of sample behaviors of children—then teachers could simply choose the right treatment, and the child would fall into line. Alas, or fortunately, that is not the case, as anyone who has spent time actually working with children can tell you. Instead, teachers must, and good ones do, depend on their empathy, their observation, their acceptance of each child as particular, when they teach them, talk to them, prepare them for the next grade level. The identification of good teaching with nurturing, while at the same time trivializing the importance of nurturing by categorizing it as a mindless, low-level skill, serves to restrict teachers to their classrooms by convincing them it is in their own and their pupils' best interests.

Creating a bureaucracy in schools does allow some people to distance themselves from students, teachers, and others—formalizing relationships and setting up specific times and timetables for when they will sit down and work with someone. That does not mean everyone in a school, however, has the luxury of such clear boundaries of time and emotions. Just as a husband can leave home and expect the wife to clear up any emotional loose ends that arise, some school people can set the rules while others are expected to continue the daily, intimate involvement that is required to put those or a reasonable facsimile of those rules into practice. It is easy for a principal to believe that it is the rules, and the clear expectations and boundaries that create adherence to them, that create school successes. That is because he does not see all the negotiating that makes them work (sometimes), all the recourse to individual ties that appear at a distance like standardized results.

Talk of "teacherproof" materials, for example, carries with it the assumption that if teachers are allowed to teach idiosyncratically and with a degree of emotional involvement, they will inevitably be led to make distinctions among their pupils, distinctions that would inhibit rather than enhance the equal opportunity, or simply the just rewards, of all. The belief that curriculum specialists and administrators, the great majority of whom are White males, are less prone to prejudice and stereotypes than classroom teachers, is fundamentally racist, classist, and sexist. Numerous examples of blatantly racist, sexist, and/or classist texts or curriculum packages that practice the benign neglect of simply projecting White middle-class values and experiences as national standards are found.

Today, a teacher who wishes a more active role in curriculum reform is forced to step out of the classroom and to become a specialist who devises curriculum for other people's classrooms. She cannot combine nurturing pupils, seen as essentially an idiosyncratic, personalized role, with the abstract analytic skills considered crucial to the development of curriculum. The often-heard remark, intended as a compliment, "What are you still doing in the classroom? You're so bright!" indicates the degree of popular contempt for the majority of teachers and the general unwillingness to believe that a large number of teachers could, and do—when given honest and sustained encouragement—create exciting curricula.

Removing curriculum reform from the individual classroom is doomed to failure. Teachers will resist such reform, either overtly or covertly, consciously or unconsciously; and so too will students, in an attempt to assert the significance of their own experience to what and how they want to learn. Good curriculum reform can come about only through a rethinking of the division between affect and cognition, between the heart and the mind, between the personalized and the abstract, between the public and the private. By analyzing how, and why, these divisions are embedded in our society, we can perhaps begin to understand what our society is trying to learn, and whether it is worth learning it.

Notes

1. Leonore Weitzman, *The Marriage Contract* (New York: Macmillan, 1981), p. 100.

2. Barbara Ehrenreich and Deirdre English, *For Her Own Good, 150 Years of the Experts' Advice to Women* (New York, Anchor Press, Doubleday, 1978), p. 9.

3. Ibid., p. 9.

4. Ibid., p. 9.

5. Nancy Cott, *The Bonds of Womanhood: "Woman's Sphere" in New England, 1780–1835* (New Haven, Conn.: Yale University Press, 1977), pp. 121–22.

6. Gerda Lerner, "The Lady and the Mill Girl: Changes in the Status of Women in the Age of Jackson, 1780–1840," in *A Heritage of One's Own*, Nancy F. Cott and Elizabeth H. Pleck, eds. (New York: Simon and Schuster, 1979), pp. 188–89.

7. Philip W. Jackson, *Life in Classrooms* (New York: Holt, Rinehart & Winston, 1969) p. 149.

8. Sara E. Freedman, Jane Jackson, and Katherine Boles, interview transcriptions from the research report, *The Effects of the Institutional Structure of Schools on Teachers* (Final report, NIE Grant No. NIE-G-81-0031, Boston Women's Teachers' Group, P.O. Box 169, W. Somerville, Mass. 02144, 1982).

9. Ibid., p. 23.

10. Ibid., p. 45.

11. Ibid., p. 67.

12. Ibid., p. 25.

13. Ibid., p. 17.

14. Ibid., p. 89.

15. Ibid., p. 92.

16. Ibid., p. 87.

17. Sara E. Freedman, *Personal Journal* (1979).

18. Freedman, Jackson, and Boles, op. cit.

19. Ibid., p. 104.

20. Ibid., p. 123.

21. Ibid., p. 57.

THIRTEEN

Schooling for Democracy: What Kind?

Landon E. Beyer

An array of potential options surround teachers as they engage in classroom activities. The expectations others hold of teachers—students, colleagues, administrators, parents, and local and state policy-making agencies—are equally wide ranging and at times conflicting. At the same time, and in spite of the repeated call for more autonomy,[1] teachers often have comparatively little input into school policies and day-to-day decisions. In short, the demands on teachers are often not accompanied by a corresponding level of freedom to explore, invent, and engage in analysis and inquiry. Such freedom is essential if teachers are to conceptualize a variety of educational possibilities and act on them with their students.

Daily decisions become more consequential when we recognize that teaching and curriculum deliberation cannot be carried on in isolated and technical ways. Questions and issues regarding pedagogy and curriculum intersect with the political, moral, economic, and cultural domains of society. Educational choices frequently respond to, and help reinforce, some set of values, priorities, and perspectives that have the effect of furthering some interests while hampering others. Teachers as a result confront several difficult, complex issues: What values should guide the establishment of some kind of

245

classroom climate? What modes of analysis, ways of thinking, and kinds of experiences should be encouraged, which hampered? What attitudes and expectations should be encouraged or altered among students? What modes of interaction should be promoted or curtailed in the classroom? What forms of knowledge are most worth perpetuating? In short, for teachers there is no neutral place to stand, as decisions that are made every day in classrooms—or, just as likely, made by others outside classrooms—support certain normative beliefs and assumptions, ideals and convictions. Such beliefs and assumptions must be critically scrutinized and analyzed by teachers, and by those preparing to teach.

The normative dimensions of education differentiate teaching from most other professions. Even as the autonomy of teachers continues to be both worked for and contested, and even when that autonomy is constricted, teachers can influence the students in their care, and those students' futures, in ways that speak in the broadest sense to the political nature of teaching and schooling. In addition to "providing a service" to the public, and beyond an obsession with "the bottom line" that infects both the "private sector" and an increasingly privatized neo-public one, teachers affect the hopes, dreams, attitudes, and perspectives of their students, and because of that the future of the society in which they and their students live.

There are at least three contemporary tendencies that may lead us to doubt the impact of teaching, and the influence of teachers, in promoting ideas, perspectives, and ways of thinking among students that will promote social progress. First, at least in some quarters there is increased skepticism about the very notion of *public* education as a social undertaking. This may be related to anxiety about our sons' and daughters' economic and social futures, to the problems associated with school and social service funding cutbacks, or to the number of social problems—the use of drugs and the instances of physical and emotional abuse, the problems associated with teenage pregnancies, and the like—with which teachers must often deal. Second, as already noted, it remains the case for many teachers that state guidelines, school district directives, the culture of the school itself, and the daily demands on teachers' time serve to curtail some classroom activities that might be beneficial. Combating these tendencies requires political action of a public character that aims, among other things, at changing the culture of the school and the nature of teacher preparation.[2] Third, and ironically, aspects (or, in some cases, misreadings) of the critical educational literature, as well as some postmodern writings, appear to leave little room for hope or optimism regarding the possibility of making significant changes in schools and their surrounding social and cultural contexts.[3] If schools and teachers are narrowly constrained by larger social, economic, and cultural forces that are hegemonic, or if a loss of

246

"modernist" certainty leads to forms of relativism that make all educational choices seem equally plausible, the teacher may come to see herself as both powerless and incapable of grounding decisions in a set of convictions and principles that are efficacious.

This chapter focuses on the practice of possibility as it may be aided by rediscovering the radical-progressive potential of democratic ideas and values, and democratic participation, in schooling and curriculum. The political and moral dimensions of participatory democracy not only dovetail with a recurrent theme of this volume, but also resonate with a central value on which modern social systems have presumably been based. Within education, discussions regarding the possible role of U.S. schools in promoting a democratic social order are as old as attempts to establish a system of publicly supported education. From Thomas Jefferson's proposals for a system of schools in Virginia, to Horace Mann's call for school reform in the second quarter of the nineteenth century, to the report of the National Commission on Excellence in Education, to the recommendations of the Eisenhower Leadership Group, America's schools have been called upon to advance a variety of purportedly democratic purposes.[4]

One problem—both conceptual and ideological—that has repeatedly plagued discussions about schooling and democracy is that the meaning of democratic discourse, practice, and values continues to undergo substantial, periodic revision. Curricular changes have, in fact, been initiated in an attempt to redefine the meaning of democratic life and the social and political choices consistent with it. A variety of interest groups and those in positions of power have suggested one vision of democracy or another that is consistent with their larger ideological agenda. Powerful segments of U.S. society affiliated with what has been called "the conservative restoration"[5] and the "Republican revolution" are attempting to reassert an agenda that caricatures or simply denies the existence of those progressive strands of democratic thought and practice that they oppose. Clearly, important conceptual and ideological differences exist among those urging that we adopt or invigorate democratic practices, values, and institutions. Understanding these differences is crucial if we are to articulate a vision of social possibility for schools.

The latter portion of this chapter outlines the relevance of teaching for helping rebuild forms of moral discourse and action, and in recreating genuine communities, as these are required for a progressive notion of democracy. The outlines of an alternative approach to schooling that is consistent with a progressive, participatory democracy will be offered here. An important part of the argument of this chapter is that we need to reconstitute democracy as founded on a set of cultural and moral principles, ideas, and practices that infuse day-to-day social and classroom life.

Traditions of Democratic Thought

The meaning and import of democracy cannot be separated from a vision of what is constituted by "the good life," or from an analysis of what currently prevents us from realizing that vision. Beyond current social ills and possible social redirections, democracy, however construed, has an intimate relationship with moral values and related normative frameworks. Democracy is promoted in significant part for the ways in which it advances particular values that are held in high regard; an analysis of those values is thus central if we are to evaluate competing claims concerning the nature of democracy. In addition, particular economic and cultural practices, and patterns of power and influence, are related to varying conceptions of democracy. These practices and patterns too must be considered as we consider the democratic purposes of education. Considering competing conceptions of democracy, in short, is a multifaceted undertaking, which can only be sketched here.[6]

The New Right

In 1996, the Republican Party nominated Bob Dole and Jack Kemp for the highest political offices in the land. Celebrating the previous "victories" of Ronald Reagan, Richard Nixon, and others, party faithful touted the advantages of a reduced federal government, individual striving and the importance of one's character, lower income and capital gains taxes, reduced social spending for our most needy populations, school choice programs that would end public education as we have known it, greater incentives for capitalist expansion, and related political initiatives. Such ideas, while not new, outline a set of values, beliefs, and ideologies that have become well known over the past few years in the United States—consolidated into what has come to be known as the new right agenda.[7]

For members of the new right, the societal ills that dampen national progress are the result of weaknesses that lie within individuals—weaknesses that are multiplying and portend a social crisis. Chester Finn[8] and William Bennett,[9] for example, portray us as a nation of individuals who have lost our determination and nerve. Not all of "us," to be sure, are equally culpable in this new right scenario. America's poor, this view goes, no longer exhibit self-discipline or commitment. The way to change this reality is clear, and speaks to some interesting convictions of this group:

> It's hard to estimate what self-discipline and the ability to commit to a task could bring about if every child in America had them. At least they would eliminate

248

much remedial education, much of our drop-out problem and much social pathology among the poor. But one cannot simply wave a wand and create virtue and social character in people.[10]

In the absence of a "magic wand," we may use the schools to infuse character, commitment, self-discipline, and the proper convictions in the populace. If this is done well, we may remedy the individual behavioral ills that constrain us as a nation.

Yet the public schools—especially teachers' unions and a massive bureaucracy—are now part of the cause of the social problems we confront. Schools have become "tyrannical" bureaucratic machines that ignore their consumers (i.e., students) and end up serving the "educrats" (bureaucratic educational administrators) who run them. As Bennett maintains, instead of confronting its internal problems,

> the education establishment—that wide array of professional organizations putatively representing teachers, administrators and other educators—by and large offers a steady stream of defenses, denials, ultimatums, and repeated calls for more money. . . . Too often this education establishment itself is the single greatest obstacle to education reform.[11]

In response to this situation, the new right suggests that teachers must emphasize content and character in the classroom. To accomplish this teachers need to return to the foundational features of the curriculum—for example, to the provision of shared background knowledge that provides an important element in our shared cultural identity. As E. D. Hirsch (1983) writes:

> Without appropriate, tacitly shared background knowledge, people cannot understand newspapers. A certain extent of shared, canonical knowledge is inherently necessary to a literate democracy.
>
> For this canonical information I have proposed the term *cultural literacy*. It is the translinguistic knowledge on which linguistic literacy depends. You cannot have the one without the other. . . . School materials contain unfamiliar materials that promote the "acculturation" that is a universal part of growing up in any tribe or nation. Acculturation into a national literate culture might be defined as learning what the "common reader" of a newspaper in a literate culture would be expected to know.[12]

Beyond the lack of acculturation through schools, adherents to new right ideology commonly claim that the decline in America is due to a deterioration in "traditional American values." As Bennett puts it, in the 60s and 70s, we saw a sustained attack on traditional American values and the place where those values had long had a comfortable and congenial home—the school. Many of the [liberal] elite correctly understood that civilization's major task is the upbringing of children; if they could alter the ways we raised children by changing the way we teach them, they could then alter American society to suit their view of the world. Academics provided much of the intellectual heavy artillery—citing how endemically corrupt and sick America is. Once the traditional teachings were discredited and then removed, the vacuum was filled by faddish nonsense, and the kids lost.[13]

Bennett and other new right spokespeople stress that students must learn (or at least internalize) "our" traditional values. Wynne, for example, baldly asserts that, "on the whole, school is and must be inherently indoctrinative."[14] Teachers should indoctrinate students into the "great tradition," which emphasizes "good habits of conduct as contrasted with moral concepts or moral rationales."[15] Bennett further claims that

there are values that all American citizens share and that we should want all American students to know and to make their own: honesty, fairness, self-discipline, fidelity to task, friends, and family, personal responsibility, love of country and belief in the principles of liberty, equality and the freedom to practice one's own faith.[16]

Character education proposals have been forwarded by a number of new right advocates. They clearly and unambiguously follow the general analysis of the new right in focusing on the individual. Amidst social disorder and moral decay the new right maintains that students need to be initiated into larger moral communities. They assume that in spite of the dominance of the social disorder and the moral decay they decry, worthwhile and valuable moral communities exist into which students ought to be initiated.

These educational and cultural views are in keeping with the "radical individualism" that is inherent in the new right's perspective.[17] For members of the new right, the social good is revealed in and through the actions of independent, self-motivated individuals—especially as they engage in economic exchanges. This doctrine is one of the legacies of Adam Smith:

As every individual . . . endeavours as much as he can both to employ his capital in the support of domestic industry, and so to direct that industry that its produce may be of the greatest value; every individual necessarily labours to render the annual revenue of the society as great as he can. He generally, indeed, neither intends to promote the public interest, nor knows how much he is promoting it. By preferring the support of domestic to that of foreign industry, he intends only his own security; and by directing that industry in such a manner as its produce may be of the greatest value, he intends only his own gain, and he is in this, as in many other cases, led by an invisible hand to promote an end which was no part of his intention. . . . By pursuing his own interest he frequently promotes that of the society more effectually than when he really intends to promote it.[18]

In maximizing our own private, individual economic interests, we assist the accumulation of capital by those enterprises we support, increasing in turn the total wealth of a nation. Self-interest and the social good are, on this view, coextensive. From Adam Smith's "invisible hand" in the eighteenth century to Ronald Reagan's "trickle down economics" of the twentieth, many have held that regulatory activities imposed by government agencies are unnecessary and destructive. The important point for our purposes is that given this perspective, the state is not to play a role in mediating economic exchanges or in infringing on the economic transactions through which the social good will be spontaneously generated. Convictions about the nature of social justice, or initiatives aimed at redressing economic and social ills, thus have little or no room in the minimalist state that the new right envisions. Instead, expanded opportunities made possible through increased access to the capitalist marketplace make state intervention unnecessary; simultaneously, such intervention is seen by the new right as one of the prime examples of infringement on individual rights. The notion that the state has a responsibility to articulate and uphold a vision of social and economic justice thus loses out to a view of social life as founded in personal strivings bounded by a "negative freedom"[19] or freedom from constraint orientation that is consistent with the new right's ideology of radical individualism.

The center of human existence for the new right is in critical respects the sphere of economic exchange. Restricted only by our level of individual merit, capitalism offers the opportunity of pursuing whatever occupation we find meaningful. Free from outside constraint—by individuals or the state—we may enjoy those labors that provide intrinsic satisfaction and/or that generate the level of material wealth necessary to procure ends we have individually chosen. Thus do we enact the explicit promise of our Declaration of Independence that we can pursue (if not necessarily attain) our individually defined sense of happiness.

The market mechanisms entailed in the processes of production and consumption (pricing, competition, the division of labor, and so on) underscore our individual liberties and collectively ensure the social good. Combined with the unfolding of individual activities that are spontaneously productive of a common good, our actions further our material interests and free us to choose in our private lives whatever conceptions of the good life we find compelling—provided they do not infringe on the freedoms of others. The freedoms to produce, consume, and act as we see fit, are to be accompanied by procedurally fair, socially neutral rules that maintain social order. Such rules may be established to enforce the contractual market obligations voluntarily entered into, to protect the individual rights of other people, to guarantee forms of national sovereignty and domestic tranquility that are required for the exercise of liberty, and to provide for certain elements of the infrastructure required to maintain commerce.

Democracy within the orientation of the new right takes on a particular meaning. The role of government officials is largely to protect the private, individual prerogatives of people, and to guarantee those inalienable rights specified in our country's founding documents. The work of politicians is limited to generating neutral, fair procedural rules that leave questions of distributive justice to a disinterested market economy. A representative government composed of people we elect to protect our individual interests is best suited to such a society.

The new right's educational orientation, discussed earlier, helps maintain the democratic, cultural, and social perspectives they advance. Dedicated to reviving character traits that have all but been abandoned by public schools and colleges alike, emphasizing skills and forms of knowledge that will make the United States once again a competitive force in the increasingly global economic realm, and restoring a common culture and value system, schools are central social institutions that support the ideology of the new right. Within public schools, an emphasis on "the facts," cultural literacy and moral character, increased constraints on student behavior, and more rigorous academic standards will serve our national/economic needs and the traditional values of education. In the process, the "weak democracy" favored by the new right will be promoted.[20]

A Progressive Alternative

The new right is correct in claiming that there is a social crisis in the United States that needs concerted attention. Yet their explanation for this crisis, and their proposals to deal with it, are inadequate, aligned with deep-seated ideologies that further the cultural and economic prerogatives of capitalism rather than respond to the predicaments of actual people who continue to be marginalized within our society. They also fail to acknowledge alternative democratic traditions that could transform the social order and the schools of which they are a part.

For members of the new right, as we have seen, people are first or "naturally" isolated, atomistic individuals. We do, presumably for reasons of necessity or convenience, form social bonds from time to time. But such bonds have little value or place outside family life. Instead, we form larger social collectives primarily to avoid conflicts—whether personal or social. We do not, on this view, form communal bonds to become virtuous, fully developed, humane people. Given their commitment to individualism, and their allegiance to a view of the state as minimally "intrusive" and amoral, the new right is unable to grasp either the social sources of moral decay or the benefits that accrue from enhancing the moral value of communities. They refuse, for example, to examine how the disparities of income and wealth, and the systemic inequities of class, race, and gender, have themselves been partially responsible for the loss of communities and the moral decay they rail against. They are unable to consider the extent to which the very development of a free-market economy is implicated in this process of decay. Yet it is clear, whatever else we may think about a market economy, that capitalism requires a hierarchical division of labor, and is built on economic inequality. Adam Smith himself recognized that, "for one very rich man there must be at least five hundred poor, and the affluence of the few supposes the indigence of the many."[21] Dealing with the roots of the current social crisis demands looking at the sources of social inequality—including the dynamics of a market economy. While the inequalities of race and gender predate the appearance of capitalism, it has been able to utilize those inequalities in furthering its expansion. Members of the new right are unable to recognize or respond to such realities, inasmuch as they are caught up in an untenable individualism, and in either a posture of moral neutrality or a commitment to moral conservatism. They bemoan any substantial attention to larger social realities because it would allegedly undermine individual responsibility.

Contrary to the presumptions of the new right, a society dedicated to creating moral principles by which citizens can live, and through which they can attain the communal identity necessary for the development and exercise of liberty, must not focus simply on so-called characterless students. As Dewey for example noted, all education is both psychological and social. It is the *social* quality of experience, the values people acquire *in virtue of living within particular social institutions*, and the dynamics of power that impinge on daily life, that the new right overlooks. As Bowles and Gintis put it:

> In rejecting the premise of exogenous interests, we argue that an adequate conception of action must be based upon the notion that people produce themselves and others through their actions. According to this conception, action is neither instrumental toward the satisfaction of given wants nor expressive of objective interests, but it is an aspect of the very generation of wants and specification of objective interests. Individuals and groups, accordingly, are not merely to *get* but to *become*. The politics of becoming, we believe, provides a central corrective to both the normative and the explanatory dimensions of traditional political theory.[22]

We become who we are, develop character and virtues of one sort or another, in the daily experience of living in social settings. We *become* free through the creation of robust, challenging social circumstances. Schools and other social institutions therefore have no choice but to exhibit and encourage the adoption of perspectives deemed morally worthwhile and defensible. The society in which they function must be supportive of moral communities of a sort that have been eroded by the consequences of inequality, individualism, and domination that are in significant part the effects of the economic system the new right seeks to defend and further.

In contrast to new right ideology, people form identities within determinate social situations. In and through engagement with other people, institutional structures, cultural practices, and political situations, people become who they are, and sometimes become other than they used to be. Individuals do of course need to be held accountable for their actions—including corporate executives who engage in leveraged buyouts that result in workers' losing their jobs. But members of the new right are unable to see that a lack of character is more than an individual failing, and is related to the ways of life, cultural values and goods, economic patterns, and so on, that people engage in and that in significant measure form their character.

To the extent that we regard people as forming collegial and social attachments only to avoid the perils of living among other individuals whose greater power may overwhelm us, it is not surprising that any notion of a common or social good will wither. And this is how contemporary members of the new right regard people.

When members of the new right claim their views are based on "Natural law," or refuse to acknowledge the socially constructed, value-laden nature of their perspectives, we must reject their pretensions to neutrality. Such pretensions discount the reality of power as it is exercised in unequal societies. As Barber puts this point:

> Where is there genuine neutrality in a society riven with differences in power and status? And if apparent neutrality is always belied in the real world by power relations that privilege some speakers before they open their mouths— theirs are the dominant paradigms, they belong to the groups that make the rules, their speech is already part of the background for all speaking, they are privileged by previous education and eloquence—then how can there be genuine equality?[23]

To deal with the real predicaments of people's lives—and that "moral decay" decried by the new right—we must attend to the social, economic, and cultural disparities of power that continue to exist (and, at least in the case of economic inequality, increase).[24] We must also note the injurious consequences of an individualism that isolates people and deforms character while making collective action to redress common problems more problematic. We must see the virtue, and moral necessity, of creating genuine, participatory communities that not only allow but *value* dissent and challenge. An emphasis on dissent and on the development of pedagogical sensitivities leads to an openness to the other, to debate, to intellectual conflict, to challenges and responses, and to the kind of empathy that permits us to see the world through others' eyes.

These ideas are related to a number of provocative observations made by Jean Bethke Elshtain in *Democracy on Trial*.[25] She recognizes and understands the mistrust contemporary Americans have expressed in their elected leaders, in governmental institutions, and indeed in democratic practices as these continue to be lived out. She suggests as a response to this cynicism that we undertake to construct "a new covenant." The terms of this covenant simultaneously recognize the need for some form of common good while valuing disagreement. As Elshtain puts this:

> Unless Americans, or the citizens of any faltering democracy, can once again be shown that they are all in it together; unless democratic citizens remember that being a citizen is a *civic* identity, not primarily a private sinecure; unless government can find a way to respond to people's deepest concerns, a new democratic social covenant has precious little chance of taking hold. . . . The social covenant is not a dream of unanimity or harmony, but the name given to a hope that we can draw on what we hold in common even as we disagree.[26]

This sort of openness to disagreement and collegial discontent, however, is not sufficient to establish community bonds of the sort that can support a new commitment to a common good. In addition, people must see that they have interests in common and, more importantly, that there is the possibility of joint, collaborative actions that will further those interests, and through which they will attain freedom and personhood, and develop character.

Also central to reviving community is the development of normative frameworks and support for forms of moral discourse that can serve as a valuative center for practical action. This valuative center must itself be open to reinterpretation, critical appraisal, and alteration. Now in part because of a loss of moral discourse in the United States, keeping such a valuative center open to reconsideration will likely be among the most difficult of the responsibilities we have in recreating communities. Yet there are examples of this recreation of communities in which a moral center has been influential. Consider the activities of environmental groups to stop the contamination of drinking water, efforts to reform schools through parental and community involvement, and neighborhood organizing to "take back the night" and make the streets safer, especially for women and young girls.

The difficulties inherent in this reassertion of collective, reciprocal discourse and action are compounded by the very reasons for the collapse of moral discourse in the United States. Beyond the assumption of individualism that denies a common good, many, including members of the new right as well as others, have tended to regard value disputes as essentially relativistic. In addition to these kinds of situations, the moral consequences of a consumptive ethic that infuses capitalist economies must be critically considered as an impediment to moral reflection and action. As more and more products are generated and available, "the good life" becomes increasingly associated with what we are capable of purchasing and consuming. Our social status becomes tied to the kind of automobile we can afford, the sort of house we have, the number of televisions and appliances we "benefit" from, the technological cutting-edge computers and related equipment we own, and so forth. Our identity, our worth, thereby become associated with these commodities and our ability to purchase them. This makes it seem as if our value as a person is intimately connected to our purchasing power, to the kinds of things we can buy and presumably enjoy. A cult of consumerism is developed as a part of the commodification process that erodes larger claims to moral imperatives. Similarly, a vast array of choices and actions tend to be "marketized" as they become seen as commodities to be produced, inserted in some kind of market, consumed, and then discarded. The culture of capitalism, accordingly, tends to generate a sense of temporariness, a belief that both things and commitments are there for the taking (and then, just as readily, for the "consuming"), after which we move on to the next consumable item or position. When we see even matters of moral choice as equivalent in some ways to options concerning what clothes to try on and then discard when our tastes change, those choices become debased and misshapen. Both material things and valuative decisions become tangential, surface-level "goods" to be tried on, perhaps worn for a time, and replaced by newer, more fashionable "goods." Such cultural-economic realities will not be changed through an emphasis on acculturation or indoctrination in schools, or by a return to "traditional values."

If we are to challenge and replace the new right's emphasis on individualism, if we are to establish moral discourse and action as something more than expressions of personal preference, if we are to counter a consumerist ethic and drive, we must revive a sense of community, of shared commitments that are open to alternative forms of discourse and understandings. Part of the value of such communities is that they provide opportunities for positive actions in the world. They provide avenues for acting in ways that go beyond freedom as merely the absence of constraint, and for considering virtue as something more than the purchase of the latest commodities.

Understanding democracy in a rather narrow sense of embedded in activities associated with electoral politics (voting, seeking or supporting others for political office, participating in candidate forums, keeping abreast of political issues and proposals, and the like) is too limited as a basis for revitalizing communities and social action. Instead democracy provides a moral and broadly social framework that has implications for interpersonal as well as institutional actions and decisions that must be made on a day-to-day basis. As Dewey put it, democracy is "more than a form of government; it is primarily a mode of associated living, of conjoint communicated experience."[27] The way we live with each other, the way we treat one another in our daily interactions and relationships, is central to this understanding of democracy and its implications. Thinking about democracy as only a way of making electoral choices—as important as these may be—allows undemocratic practices like those associated with a capitalist economy to seem outside the pale of democratic inquiry—as if a democratic critique of the economic apparatus involves making something like a category mistake. As a moral and social force, democratic values provide frameworks and guidelines for how we should live, and how our social institutions—including the economy—should be organized and run.

Any sort of wide-ranging participatory democracy is only possible if we adopt something like the proposals sketched above that may reinvigorate a sense of community. This in turn requires, and is supported by, a grasp of the possibilities for a common good, collectively decided by people engaged in open, moral discourse with others, within which a commitment to equality is central.[28] We need a broadly based cultural vision for democratic practice in which daily activities and interactions, a search for the common good, the reinvigoration of community, and an openness to dissent and difference, mutually support each other, and allow for new forms of life and decision making to emerge.

These ideals resonate with Freire's emphasis on "integration" with the world, rather than "adapting" to it. As Freire puts it, "integration results from the capacity to adapt to reality *plus* the critical capacity to make choices and to transform that reality."[29] To become an integrated person is not only to understand the social, physical, and political worlds in which we live and work, but to develop the attitudes and forms of consciousness that will allow people to take part in shaping and reshaping that world. This emphasis on critiquing current realities, on participating in the recreation of our worlds, is a central part of a progressive understanding of democracy.

A democratic community must, accordingly, enable people to develop values and ideas that outline alternative possibilities. Equally important, such a community must generate concrete practices that enact a moral vision—a vision not reducible to any set of present realities and yet not simply an Idealist construction. A democratic community encourages its members to become participants in civic discussions that require concerted, collaborative actions in the name of social justice and structural change.

The importance of the material conditions of social life, as these may alter people's character and day-to-day actions, leads to a reconsideration of the role of education and the shape of the school curriculum. Teachers—supported by parents, students, administrators, university faculty members, and others—must be the central players in the ultimate design, crafting, and implementation of the public school curriculum. But all too often they are allowed to pay only minimal attention to curricular matters, and frequently these are accomplished alone. Yet given the social, moral, and democratic ideas outlined above, making connections among students, knowledge, and the larger social contexts in which schools function is a central responsibility of teachers. This is obviously a large-order task. Even when substantial and clearly articulated curricular frameworks are in place the planning and deliberative process can be arduous and time consuming.

The deliberative process of curriculum design must attempt to balance and integrate an attention to the child, rich understandings of and skillful accomplishments in the world, *and* an awareness of the larger societal dynamics and life contexts in which these children live and to which they may very well return. Whereas Dewey decried the false dichotomy between the child and the curriculum and wanted to bring the two together, a third element is central to curriculum design and planning—the social, political, and cultural context.

Dewey understood knowledge to be the outcome of past and present human efforts to deal with and come to terms with the worlds in which we live. For Dewey children were beings actively engaged in attempts to understand and become more skillful in the world in which they lived. What has been missing (or perhaps inadequately emphasized) in the nominal Progressive educational movement, something that George Counts underscored in his talk to the Progressive Education Association,[30] was an articulated direction in which this educational endeavor should head. Early on Counts criticized the progressive movement as lacking a valued direction. Counts maintained that,

If an educational movement, or any other movement, calls itself progressive, it must have orientation; it must possess direction. The work itself implies moving forward, and moving forward can have little meaning in the absence of clearly defined purposes. . . . Here, I think, we find the fundamental weakness, not only of Progressive Education, but also of American education generally. Like a baby shaking a rattle, we seem to be utterly content with action, provided it is sufficiently vigorous and noisy. . . .

The weakness of Progressive Education thus lies in the fact that it has elaborated no theory of social welfare, unless it be that of anarchy or extreme individualism. In this, of course, it is but reflecting the viewpoint of the members of the liberal-minded upper middle class who send their children to the Progressive schools—persons who are fairly well-off . . . who pride themselves on their open-mindedness and tolerance, who favor in a mild sort of way fairly liberal programs of social reconstruction, who are full of good will and humane sentiment . . . who are genuinely distressed at the sight of unwonted forms of cruelty, misery and suffering, . . . but who, in spite of all their good qualities, have no deep and abiding loyalties, possess no convictions for which they would sacrifice over-much . . . are rather insensitive to the accepted forms of social injustice, [and] are content to play the role of interested spectator in the drama of human history.[31]

In short, Counts maintained that the progressive movement needed to "come to grips with life in all of its stark reality, establish an organic relation with the community, [and] develop a realistic and comprehensive theory of welfare."[32] This is an important part of what is meant by adding to the child-curriculum dualism a third element—the social context. When we add the societal context to the child-curriculum progressive design, and a set of moral, political, and cultural values that provides the direction Counts advocated, we have a more adequate basis for articulating a curricular direction. Such a direction includes a conception of a life worth living and an understanding of the dynamics that might harm people in an effort to achieve that better life. This context is part and parcel of any student's life and an element in the rich understandings and skillful accomplishments that constitute the formal curriculum. Just as Dewey saw the child and the curriculum as integrally interconnected, the child, the curriculum, and the larger context (both the current one and a future one that is possible) comprise three essential and interrelated design elements in any defensible outline of curriculum deliberation.

Toward a Different Future

The curricular orientation outlined here is guided by a commitment to radical democracy as it may provide avenues for reconceiving social institutions and practices, guided by a populism in form, and dedicated to structural change. Such change may be brought about by a reinvigoration of communities in which genuine participation, moral discourse, and the common good fuel actions in the world. Seeing the various components of our worlds as susceptible to alteration through collaborative actions that build on our sociability; articulating moral values in open settings in which dissent is expected and valued that can guide those actions; and altering hierarchical structures and inequalities that demean and disempower, and that, contrary to the new right, deny liberty and opportunity, form basic elements of the vision articulated here.

We don't, obviously, live in that kind of society now. Rather, we live in a democratic-capitalist social order in which commodity fetishism, the rule of the market, patriarchy, and White supremacy constrain, distort, and oppress the expression of many individuals' humanity and their ability to act democratically. This affects adults and children. A concrete example will help illustrate these ideas.

In heading toward an education that is democratically empowering and cognizant of the harms and brutish outcomes of our current setting, we need to engage students in a meaningful and challenging education. Such an education recognizes the real, complex identity of students, provides knowledge and understandings that will enable them to become skilled adult participants and fully engaged human beings, and readies them for an adult life that, unchanged, may neither engage their skills nor their human capacities. For example, many African American inner-city youth do not find schooling engaging, challenging, or rewarding. For these students public education tends to provide little substance worthy of engaging. A progressive educational agenda for these students needs to understand them, their family, and the community from which they come. It must find ways to instruct students that fit with and build on the patterns and norms of their community, offer knowledge, understandings, and skilled practices that both recognize the students' strengths and the demands of mainstream discourse. "Character education" that is founded on a blame-the-victim mentality and that overlooks the causes of cultural and social malaise, as favored by the new right, misses the point. As Lisa Delpit argues, students need to acquire the ability to function in a dominant discourse, though that need not

> mean that one must reject one's home identity and values, for discourses are not static, but are shaped, however reluctantly, by those who participate within them and by the form of their participation. . . . Today's teachers can help economically disenfranchised students and students of color, both to master the dominant discourse and to transform them.[33]

To accomplish this task Delpit argues that teachers must "acknowledge and validate students' home language without using it to limit students' potential"; "recognize the conflict . . . between students' home discourses and the discourse of the school"; and "acknowledge the unfair 'discourse-stacking' that our society engages in" by openly discussing the "injustices of allowing certain people to succeed, based not upon merit but upon which family they were born into, upon which discourse they had access to as children."[34] In this vision and in these suggestions Delpit brings together the child, the curriculum, and the society. Such a vision is consistent with the emphasis on a progressive democracy founded on participation, moral reasoning, social justice, and action in and on the world, sketched above. It provides an alternative to the thin democracy sketched by the new right, and hope for those now harmed by the inequalities that continue to thrive and grow in the United States. It also offers hope for significant change, in society and in classrooms where democratic values may be enacted.

Notes

1. See Peter Grimmett and Galen Erickson, *Reflection in Teacher Education* (New York: Teachers College Press, 1988); Donald Schön, *The Reflective Practitioner* (New York: Basic, 1983) and *Educating the Reflective Practitioner* (San Francisco: Jossey-Bass, 1987); John Smyth, "Developing and Sustaining Critical Reflection in Teacher Education, *Journal of Teacher Education* 40, 2, (1989):2–9; Landon E. Beyer, *Critical Reflection and the Culture of Schooling: Empowering Teachers* (Victoria: Deakin University Press, 1989); and Kenneth M. Zeichner and Daniel P. Liston, "Teaching Student Teachers to Reflect," *Harvard Educational Review* 57, 1:23–48.

2. See Landon E. Beyer, *Creating Democratic Classrooms: The Struggle to Integrate Theory and Practice* (New York: Teachers College Press, 1996), especially chapter 1.

3. For an example of the pessimism associated with certain postmodern writers, see Henry A. Giroux, *Border Crossings: Cultural Workers and the Politics of Education* (New York: Routledge, 1992). For discussions of the limitations of postmodern analysis, see Leonard J. Waks, *The Character of Contemporary Life: An Analysis of "Post Order" Theories*, paper presented at the annual meeting of the American Educational Research Association, April, 1995; Svi Shapiro, "Postmodernism and the Crisis of Reason: Social Change or the Drama of the Aesthetic?" *Educational Foundations* 5, 4 (1991); and Landon E. Beyer and Daniel P. Liston, "Discourse or Moral Action? A Critique of Postmodernism," *Educational Theory* 42, 4 (1992).

4. See Gordon C. Lee, *Crusade Against Ignorance: Thomas Jefferson on Education* (New York: Teachers College Press, 1991), National Commission on Excellence in Education, *A Nation at Risk: The Imperative for Educational Reform* (Washington, D.C.: U.S. Government Printing Office, 1983); Eisenhower Leadership Group, *Democracy at Risk: How Schools Can Lead* (College Park, Md.: Center for Political Leadership and Participation, May, 1996).

5. See Michael W. Apple, *Official Knowledge: Democratic Education in a Conservative Age* (New York: Routledge, 1993).

6. Some of the ideas in this section are developed more fully in Landon E. Beyer and Daniel P. Liston, *Curriculum in Conflict: Social Visions, Educational Agendas, and Progressive School Reform* (New York: Teachers College Press, 1996).

7. "The new right," while not a neatly definable or completely monolithic group, includes such Republican platform ideas, together with a general desire to curtail or dismantle the welfare state, return significant decision making to state and local governments, and promote the interests of capital accumulation. They are related in sometimes direct ways to the seventeenth- and eighteenth-century tradition of "classical liberalism," which highlighted the importance of individual sovereignty as well as a number of related philosophical, religious, and political ideas. I do not deal in this chapter with social conservatives or the religious right, who share some ideas of the new right while holding sometimes dramatically different perspectives.

8. See Chester Finn, "Narcissus Goes to School," *Commentary* 89 (June 1990); and *We Must Take Charge* (New York: Free Press, 1991).

9. See William Bennett, "Moral Literacy and the Formation of Character," *National Association of Secondary School Principles Bulletin* 72 (1988); and *The De-valuing of America: The Fight for Our Culture and Children* (New York: Summit, 1992).

10. Bennett, *The De-Valuing of America*, op. cit., p. 199.

11. Ibid., pp. 43–44; see also Finn, *We Must Take Charge*, op. cit.

12. E. D. Hirsch, "Cultural Literacy," *The American Scholar* 52, 2 (1983), pp. 165–66.

13. Bennett, *The De-valuing of America*, op. cit., pp. 51–52.

14. Edward Wynne, "The Great Tradition in Education: Transmitting Moral Values," *Educational Leadership* 43, 4 (1985/86), p. 9.

15. Ibid., p. 6.

16. Bennett, *The De-valuing of America*, op. cit., p. 58.

17. See Robert N. Bellah, Richard Madsen, William M. Sullivan, Ann Swidler, and Steven M. Tipton, *Habits of the Heart: Individualism and Commitment in American Life* (Berkeley: University of California Press, 1985).

18. Adam Smith, *An Inquiry into the Nature and Causes of the Wealth of Nations, Volume 1* (New York: E. P. Dutton, 1910), p. 400.

19. See Isaiah Berlin, *Four Essays on Liberty* (New York: Oxford University Press, 1969).

20. See Benjamin Barber, *Strong Democracy* (Berkeley: University of California Press, 1984).

21. Adam Smith, *An Inquiry into the Nature and Causes of the Wealth of Nations, Volume 2* (New York: E. P. Dutton, 1910), p. 199.

22. Samuel Bowles & Herbert Gintis, *Democracy & Capitalism: Property, Community, and the Contradictions of Modern Social Thought* (New York: Basic Books, 1987), p. 22.

23. Benjamin R. Barber, *An Aristocracy of Everyone: The Politics of Education and the Future of America* (New York: Ballantine, 1992), p. 96.

24. See Benjamin M. Friedman, *Day of Reckoning: The Consequences of American Economic Policy* (New York: Vintage, 1989).

25. Jean Bethke Elshtain, *Democracy on Trial* (New York: Basic, 1995).

26. Ibid., pp. 30–31.

27. John Dewey, *Democracy and Education: An Introduction to the Philosophy of Education* (New York: Free Press, 1916), p. 87.

28. See Ann Bastian, Norm Fruchter, Marilyn Gittell, Colin Greer, and Kenneth Haskins, *Choosing Equality: The Case for Democratic Schooling* (Philadelphia: Temple University Press, 1985).

29. Paulo Freire, *Education for Critical Consciousness* (New York: Seabury, 1973), p. 4.

30. See George S. Counts, *Dare the Schools Build a New Social Order?* (New York: John Day, 1932).

31. Ibid., pp. 4–5.

32. Ibid., p. 7.

33. Lisa Delpit, *Other's People's Children: Cultural Conflict in the Classroom* (New York: New Press, 1995), p. 163.

34. Ibid., pp. 163–65.

V
Curriculum and Technology

FOURTEEN

The Regime of Technology in Education

Douglas D. Noble

Public schooling is once again ripe for colonization by the powerful forces behind technological development in this country.[1] Corporate marketeers and technocratic politicians, joined by an eager stable of high-tech researchers and sycophantic educators, are now more determined than ever to refine the means and to redefine the ends of public schooling according to their visions of a technology-driven economy. And their seductive technological excursions in the classroom once again reflect not so much the use of technology in the service of education as the usurpation of education in the service of technological enterprise.

In recent years, countless reformers have decried the regime of U.S. public schooling, with its exasperating historical, cultural, bureaucratic, and pedagogical barriers to technological innovation. Yet little critical attention has been paid to the cultural character and the political economy of another regime, made up of those institutional forces fueling the ongoing impulse to change the public schools through technology. What is this regime of technology in education? What is its history? Who are the key players driving and shaping the use of computers and telecommunications in schools? And what are their visions for education? The story, of course, is a complex one, reflecting a confluence of many agendas and many visions. Some are alarmingly hard edged, seemingly antihuman, while others appear seductively progressive and humane, when contrasted with the current conditions of public schooling. Despite these deceptive differences, the intersection of interests is sufficient for us to begin to identify this loose amalgam as a regime, a regime of technology in education. In this chapter, I situate this regime of technology within the larger historical and institutional contexts responsible for the persistent impulse to align education with technology.

I must note at the outset that the place of technology in education is as ambiguous as the place of sexuality in private life: Each is marginal and incidental, yet also somehow pervasive and definitive. When I talk to my teacher friends in public schools, or when I offer to conduct workshops on issues related to educational technology for teachers and teacher educators, I'm reminded again and again how relatively insignificant for them are issues of technology, amid the range of pressing concerns in urban education. One meets, of course, the occasional enthusiast among teachers, someone whose desk overflows with the latest software packages, or who is involved in a truly innovative project in school computer use—by one account, as rare as whale sightings.[2] Occasional surveys, too, find that most teachers nationwide celebrate the importance of computers in schools, while other surveys find that most teachers still have never used one. By and large, however, despite the several billions spent in the last decade on school computers, most educators I know are focused elsewhere—on diminishing state resources, fragmented and deteriorating health- and child-support services, massive racial and class inequities, ongoing family disintegration, rampant drug abuse and violence. In fact, because of these more pressing, often seemingly insurmountable, priorities, I was at first reluctant to write still another essay on educational technology. Attention paid to technology seemed a luxurious distraction from, if not an abandonment of, the real concerns and deeper purposes of public education. Yet this is precisely the point to be made here.

Computer technology represents for many powerful interests the solution to, if not an escape from, the social, political, cultural, and economic dilemmas ravaging public education. Indeed, for key corporate and political interests, ongoing research and development in computer technology offers the potential (and potential profit) of dramatically "reinvented" means of educational delivery. For these interests, such technological research and development signals, as well, a redefinition of the very meaning and purpose of education, now seen as part of the technical infrastructure, the human capital supply system, for advanced technological society.

So while technology remains in many respects still quite marginal to public education despite decades of haphazard implementation and massive public expenditure, it nevertheless occupies center stage for key political and corporate architects of education policy in the 1990s, many of whom have reached the point of exasperation with the continuing intransigence of public schooling. We are entering a phase of education policy in which technology will be called upon increasingly to "break the mold," to end the "gridlock," of public schooling, and to ensure an efficient delivery system of "human resources" with the generic, technical, "problem-solving" skills required within technological systems of the new global economy. Technology has become the centerpiece of the redesign and reinvention of public education by outside forces, serving both as the impetus for this redesign and, increasingly, as its lever.

Of course, public education is in need of reshaping, and prominent progressive educators have been active over the past decade in programs and coalitions intended to disengage public schooling from the structural legacies that inhibit more humane approaches and purposes. Ted Sizer, Henry Levin, James Comer, Deborah Meier, and others have all been involved, in one form or another, with this educational "restructuring," which, at its best, enhances autonomy, flexibility, collaboration, equity, and holistic approaches to children's learning. This is also a moment of efflorescence for progressive impulses in education—whole language, authentic assessment, site-based management, and antiracist curricula. In some cases, technology is employed to further these agendas, and an appreciation of the changing technological landscape of the workplace and the economy often serves as a backdrop for such efforts, especially for economists such as Levin, who has contributed substantially to our understanding of these changes. Despite this backdrop, however, the pivotal concerns of these educators are equity and empowerment—the education of all children, not so much to function in some future technological scenario (within which, almost by definition, most have already been written off) as to understand and to engage the present circumstances of their individual and collective lives, and to help forge a humane technological landscape for the future.

Seductively aligned with these efforts, in rhetoric if not also in practice, is an array of corporate promoters and technologists whose agendas, ultimately, have less to do with issues of equity or even of education, broadly conceived, than with furthering technological development (and potential profit) through research and development in the public arena, through the merchandising of hardware and software, and through the reshaping of educational systems both to facilitate their technological colonization and to ensure the training of a reliable cadre of adaptable "problem solvers" and technicians. These agendas come with an abundance of resources—both financial and political—that dwarf those available to progressive educators unwilling to adorn their efforts with technological or vocational trappings. Consequently, many adopt these trappings, hoping all the while to maintain the scope and integrity of their visions, just as, early in this century, John Dewey and other progressives hoped vainly to forge a humane response to industrialism by turning the powerful vocational impulse of a National Association of Manufacturers coalition to their own progressive ends. Once again we are at a crossroads in American education, with child-centered advocates of humane alternatives to a broken school system joining forces with the "educational engineers," inheritors of a century-long enterprise whose legacy includes vocationalism, standardized testing, a cult of administrative efficiency, behaviorist and now cognitivist learning theory, and an arsenal of technologies from programmed instruction to teaching machines.

It is necessary here to introduce the principal forces behind the alignment of technology and education, if we are to gauge their motives and become more vigilant in our partnerships to restructure education for the twenty-first century. Technology in education is not simply a matter of multimedia presentations and computers in schools; for over thirty years its promoters have been telling us that it is about a fundamental redefinition of the means and ends of education. In the current educational environment in which corporate partnerships abound, in which the line between public and private blurs steadily, in which talk of redesign and reinvention of public schooling is common fare, in which a resurrected vocationalism for a technological age ("tech prep") is rampant, in which public schooling is in desperate straits, the time is ripe for a technology-driven escapade in educational engineering the scope of which we have not seen before. What follows is a scorecard of some of the key players.

The Military Legacy

First, some history. Although it is not widely understood, military research in what is called "human engineering"—training, human factors in weapons design, personnel classification and selection—has been the prime incubator, catalyst, and sponsor of educational technology throughout this century, from the intelligence tests of World War I, to programmed instruction and teaching machines in the 1960s, to the sophisticated computer-based multimedia and tutoring systems of today. Decades of military training research have also provided the impetus behind the development of criterion-referenced testing, mastery learning, and the refined use of behavioral objectives in instruction. Military agencies have been the source of three-fourths of all funding for educational technology research over the past three decades, and within government agencies, the military spends seven dollars for every civilian dollar spent on educational technology research. Each year the military spends as much on educational technology research as the Department (formerly Office) of Education has spent in a quarter-century.[3]

Since the late 1950s military research has been the pivotal player in advancing the state-of-the-art of computer-based education, and its influence continues today, at the cutting edge of new developments in the field. As I have traced in my book, *The Classroom Arsenal*, computer-based education grew out of military research and development in the late 1950s at the juncture of two fields: training science and what is now called computer science. Within training science the field arose from a military fascination with what was labeled "automated teaching," involving programmed instruction, teaching machines, and other training devices and simulators. With rapid turnover of personnel and rapid technological obsolescence, the automation of ongoing technical training has long been a military priority. Computer-based training began as an attempt to embed "on-line" training into weapon systems and command-and-control systems themselves, which could then train their "human components" as the need arose, automatically. Human beings were considered the "personnel subsystem" of an increasingly sophisticated military technological infrastructure, which was and continues to be of primary concern within the military.

This trend toward dissolving training functions within systems operations, eliminating the distinction between training and job performance, remains central today. Training technology is increasingly seen as merely one among many "engineering" functions serving high-performance systems, providing the automated technical training of a steadily diminishing number of required human components. The ultimate military technological fantasy calls for total automation of military high-performance technology, eliminating any need for training, for instructors, or for people generally—the fulfillment of the longstanding ideal of the totally automated battlefield, "war without men."

Indeed, within nascent computer science in the 1950s, the field of computer-based education grew out of research on troublesome "human factors" problems arising within military computer-based command-and-control and weapon systems. These problems generated interest in how best to improve or to supplant human capacities for processing information within large computer-based systems characterized by superhuman performance speeds and overwhelming information loads. Military research in this area gave birth to the twin fields of information-processing cognitive psychology and artificial intelligence, now merged under the rubric "cognitive science," still largely military funded. Through computer simulation of human intelligence, the military has striven to develop an array of "smart" weapon systems, from intelligent bombs and aircraft, to tanks that might fix themselves and "perceive" terrain, to totally automated battlefield management systems. Short of this, artificial intelligence and cognitive science research in the military has also been directed toward the development of a codified map of "human cognitive

271

performance for defense use" and an arsenal of "intelligent tutoring systems" for embedded training. The birth of computer-based training and cognitive science occurred simultaneously within the same military projects in air defense in the late 1950s, and the field of computers in education remains wedded to computer-based research on human cognition, intelligence, and learning today, still funded substantially by the military. Many of the principal players in computer-based education research and development, as well as many of the most prominent educational researchers in cognitive science and learning research, originally cut their teeth in military research and continue to find much support for their work from military agencies. These individuals include such leading figures in computer education research as National Academy of Education member John Seeley Brown, of Xerox and its Institute for Research on Learning; Seymour Papert of the MIT Artificial Intelligence Lab and Media Lab, and developer of LOGO (originally funded by the Office of Naval Research); and Roger Schank, founder of the Institute for Learning Sciences at Northwestern, lavishly funded by military agencies, as well as by such high-tech corporations as IBM, Ameritech, and Arthur Andersen.

The work of a virtual who's who of cognitive science and educational research has been shaped in whole or part by military contracts, including the work of such luminaries of the National Academy of Education as Robert Gagne and Robert Glaser, who continue to work on military projects on human performance, and Lauren Resnick, director of the Learning Research and Development Center at the University of Pittsburgh and a pivotal figure in current efforts to reform education through national standards. (By no surprise Resnick's 1987 presidential address to the American Education Research Association was cosponsored by the Office of Naval Research.) Other educational researchers engaged in current reform efforts who have also, often simultaneously, been engaged in military-funded research on human performance and cognition or "learning science" include Allan Collins, Richard Shavelson, Richard C. Anderson, Richard Snow, and M. C. Wittrock.

These hybrid activities of key educational researchers have substantially colored the complexion of research in education, from an earlier focus on behavioral objectives and criterion-referenced testing, to more recent emphases on "problem-solving" skills, "learning strategies," and "performance" measures. To cite just a few recent examples, the largest coordinated effort in the area of "authentic" performance assessment, now the rage in education, has not taken place in the schools; rather, it has been the multimillion dollar Joint-Service Job Performance/Enlistment Standards Project, conducted over the past decade by the Department of Defense, with educational researchers Glaser, Shavelson, and others on board.[4] Many educational researchers now codifying "workforce skills" for high school students also have career histories winding through military laboratories and funding agencies.[5] And the codification of "computer literacy" skills for schools was entrusted by the Department of Education to the Human Resources Research Organization, originally the principal human factors laboratory of the U.S. Army. Though rarely noted, the overriding emphasis on student performance in recent educational reform is in part a direct reflection of this wider military/industrial emphasis on job performance skills and measures.

Among the institutions playing seminal roles within the military history of computer-based education research since the late 1950s have been the RAND Corporation, progenitor of Air Force R&D and architect of "systems design" experiments for education since the 1960s; the high-tech research firm of Bolt, Beranek, and Newman (BBN), a major military contractor; and IBM. Each of these conducted pioneering research on computer-based training within the context of military "man-machine" and human performance research for air defense systems. They continue as pivotal players in recent excursions on the cutting edge of educational technology and education reform.

For example, consider the New American Schools Development Corporation (NASDC), the corporate-funded centerpiece of President George Bush's America 2000 education agenda, which was created to fund "design teams" to "reinvent" education through "break-the-mold" schools. Consultants from RAND orchestrated the selection process for NASDC, whose board includes the heads of such military contractors and high-tech firms as Boeing, Martin Marietta, Kodak, Honeywell, AT&T, and BellSouth.[6] No wonder Secretary of Education Lamar Alexander referred to the design teams as "the defense contractors of the education industry."[7] Little wonder, too, that the editors of the journal *Educational Technology* declared "technology . . . the big winner" in the final selection of eleven design teams, which include such partners as IBM, Xerox, and AT&T.[8] The most technology-intensive design teams include one directed by BBN, and one headed by the National Center on Education and the Economy (NCEE). A key partner in both of these has been Apple Computer Corporation—no surprise since John Sculley, former CEO of Apple, was chair of NCEE, and Allan Collins of BBN is a principal scientist for Apple's school computer research initiative, Apple Classrooms of Tomorrow (ACOT).

It seems strange, in a discussion on educational technology and school reform, to be paying so much attention to military research and technology. But the accumulated military legacy, still very much alive, must be taken into account for a deeper understanding of technology in education. This legacy includes the use of computers in schools for "command and control" of instruction, from "integrated learning systems," to the continuous monitoring of student performance, to nationwide databases and information networks linking schools, employers, and government agencies. The military legacy also includes a massive research enterprise on human cognitive performance and learning within technological systems, engendering cognitivist incursions in schooling as well as the ongoing codification of job performance skills for the twenty-first century.

Perhaps the most seductive efforts in educational computing involve the military legacy of artificial intelligence (AI) researchers such as Seymour Papert, Allan Collins, John Seeley Brown, and Roger Schank, all prominent in recent education reform. Their progressive agenda celebrates higher-order "thinking" of children as constructors of their own learning. At bottom, though, they seem to harbor an ideal vision of children as clones of themselves: as designers of new realities and automated wizardry, either building robotic Legos or creating new onscreen species of fantastic animals. This constructivist agenda explicitly designed to nurture "children as AI scientists"[9] appears progressive, especially in contrast to the typical mind-numbing school experience. However, the celebration of such mindgames as a paradigm for education is actually a seductive distortion of progressive education, encouraging the hubris of militarized child fantasy in the place of a more substantive struggle for meaning and character and understanding.

Another legacy of military researchers in educational technology and cognition is this: Again and again, from the 1960s to the present, they have used the public schools as a refuge. In some cases, as in the development of the military-funded PLATO system at the University of Illinois, interest in computer-based education projects first arose out of researchers' need to find alternative sources of funding for technology development when military money dried up. Lavish federal funding for education in the mid-1960s attracted many such excursions into schools, as federal education labs and centers provided researchers a bridge from military to civilian research. We are at such a time again, with post–Cold War demilitarization resulting in accelerating the "transfer" of military research, technology, and personnel into public education.[10]

Finally, public schools, with their "captive" student population, have served as laboratory sites for ongoing research on technology, learning, and human performance. As a pioneer in military training research observed over thirty years ago, "The final difficulty that . . . must be faced in the attempt to integrate the science of learning and the technology of education is that of gaining access to children of school age for . . . experimental investigations."[11] Most recently, Apple's Classrooms of Tomorrow and similar corporate high-tech excursions in the classroom are billing themselves as "research and development" efforts, as distinct from sales or marketing ventures.[12] This approach defuses suspicions of underlying commercial motives. It also continues a thirty-year tradition among educational technologists of forestalling critics by perpetually prolonging the "research phase" of their efforts. Such corporate research in schools—on learning, cognitive performance, technological development, instructional design—has now acquired the veneer of legitimacy and philanthropy. Yet we must begin to ask whether this research truly serves the interests of children and schools, or whether it serves, instead, corporate interests in human performance, product development, and public relations, while providing yet another refuge for a cadre of technologists and cognitive researchers.

Recent Corporate Agendas

Corporate America is the latest patron for researchers pushing advanced technologies into the schools. Corporate interest in brokering school reform and in penetrating substantial school markets now coincides as never before with the agendas of researchers of technological innovation. Several major electronics and communications corporations attempted unsuccessfully to exploit education markets in the 1960s with teaching machines and other gadgetry, and computer companies have flooded the schools with their wares since the mid-1980s, with marginal impact. But in this new decade, with its urgent attention to school reform, its massive cutbacks in state funding, and its general approbation of American business despite the recession, the welcome mat is out for widespread corporate intervention in education. The moment is especially ripe for renewed attempts by major corporate interests to transform the schools through advanced technology.

This corporate offensive takes a number of forms. First, of course, major computer and telecommunications companies have continued flooding the public schools with hardware and software, lending technological expertise along with their products, providing publicity and support for computer-related projects, sponsoring all sorts of teacher and student awards, and spinning tantalizing visions of the future for their partners in education.

One need only walk into a suburban school or scan the advertisements by IBM, Apple, and other computer vendors splashed over the pages of teacher magazines to appreciate the ubiquity of the high-tech presence in the business of education.

But there are two less obvious, though more significant, inroads of high-tech corporations into public schooling. For one, the CEOs of major high-technology companies have become influential brokers in state and federal education policy, shaping the direction of school reform to their interests. For another, major high-tech corporations are busy underwriting new public school experiments and new private, for-profit, education schemes aimed at the technology-intensive "reinvention," or abandonment, of public schooling. A closer look at each of these is in order.

First, leaders of major high-tech companies have assumed influential positions in education policy. To note just a few, David Kearns, former CEO of Xerox and catalyst for its Institute for Research on Learning, served as Deputy Secretary of Education under President Bush. John Akers, former CEO of IBM, has been a member of Bush's Education Policy Advisory Committee and chair of the Business Roundtable's Education Task Force. The CEOs of such major multinational high-technology companies as AT&T, Kodak, Boeing, BellSouth, Honeywell, and Martin Marietta were key board members of Bush's New American Schools Development Corporation, a powerful new force shaping educational research. And John Sculley, CEO of Apple Computer, served as chairman of the National Center on Education and the Economy, perhaps the single most influential organization shaping education policy for the Clinton Administration.[13] This high-tech corporate presence on the federal level of education policy is echoed on state and local levels, through affiliates of the Business Roundtable and the U.S. Chamber of Commerce, and through the influence of these companies in their home states and regions.

Among the principal features of the education agenda of these corporate leaders is an emphasis on performance standards and national examinations, on a resurrected vocationalism and school-to-work transitions, on intensified mathematics and science instruction, on organizational restructuring for accountability, and on enhanced productivity—through longer school days and years, and through the use of advanced technologies. Their model for education reform is the restructured, high-performance, technology-intensive corporation, epitomized by Xerox (and, despite the hype, characteristic of still less than 10 percent of American companies).[14] According to their vision, successful schools will model this high-performance structure and will produce students with the "high skills" required to enter the high-performance workplace of the twenty-first century. For anyone familiar with recent state and federal education policy legislation, the principal agendas of these corporate leaders and their business organizations have provided the code words for the latest top-down education reform initiatives across the country.

A second front in the corporate high-tech offensive on public education involves the underwriting of new public and private "designs" for the "reinvention" of schooling for the twenty-first century. Some such experimentation is taking place within the public schools, as is the case with the much-celebrated "design teams" sponsored by the New American Schools Development Corporation (and also heavily funded by such corporations as Xerox, IBM, AT&T, and Apple). Other examples abound. Ameritech Corporation, one of the Baby Bells, has announced a $750,000 awards competition encouraging schools in the Midwest to find creative, innovative ways to use electronic communication to improve education. IBM recently completed its sponsorship of a $25 million competition in university-school partnerships for technology instruction in teacher education. Other corporations, among them Honeywell and BellSouth (another Baby Bell), have established their own technology-rich experimental schools in their home regions. And Apple Computer has been a partner of the computer-saturated "Saturn School" in St. Paul, Minnesota, made famous by President Bush's visit on the announcement of his America 2000 education plan.

Major computer and telecommunications corporations have most recently begun to underwrite the development of for-profit schools, as in the substantial investment by Time Warner and Philips Electronics in Chris Whittle's Edison Project, the celebrated proposal to set up a private school system heavily dependent on advanced technology for cost effectiveness.[15] Education Alternatives, Inc. (EAI) is another celebrated for-profit initiative, which contracted for the management and instruction of schools in Dade County, Florida, and in Baltimore. EAI's president, the former superintendent of schools in St. Paul, was a key promoter of the "Saturn School." The ideas behind EAI were extracted from research conducted by Control Data Corporation, until recently the proprietor of the military-developed PLATO system, whose total systems control philosophy informs EAI's approach. In alliance with Computer Curriculum Corporation (or CCC, itself an early pioneer in instructional systems technology), EAI emphasizes continuous, computer-controlled monitoring of student and teacher performance. Meanwhile, IBM provides EAI with its latest hardware and software in exchange for EAI's agreement to provide feedback for IBM product developments.[16] The Edison Project and EAI are two of the more visible efforts by high-tech firms to privatize cost-effective, for-profit schooling through technological innovation; interestingly, their largest partners, respectively Time Warner and Paramount Communications (which owns CCC), are giant communications conglomerates whose multimedia visions for education are, by all indications, another harbinger of things to come.

How might we make sense of this burgeoning presence of high-technology corporations in the schools, in educational R&D, and in education policy? Some answers come readily to mind: School markets for computers and telecommunications remain as strong as ever. There are substantial profits to be made if cost-effective "learning growth" can be guaranteed through technological gadgetry (as CCC guarantees). Also, high-technology corporations claim an ongoing need for a cadre of sophisticated, technically trained individuals in their workforce. Corporate intervention in failing schools affords an excellent opportunity for high-profile community contribution. Corporate leaders are eager to extend to the schools their experience with advanced technology and with organizational "restructuring." Corporate leaders view schools as the last major labor-intensive industry ripe for colonization and modernization. Public schools, finally, represent for them an expensive public monopoly overcome by bureaucratic inefficiency and abysmal productivity. For all of these reasons and more, high-technology corporations have become an integral partner in the regime of technology in education.

By far the two rationales most often repeated by the leaders of high-technology corporations have to do with improving educational productivity through organizational "restructuring" and technological innovation, and securing a supply of technologically sophisticated "human capital" for the high-performance workplace. In each of these objectives there is great irony, when one considers the recent history of the high-technology firms most visibly promoting them.

We need only ask what these corporations are doing with their own technology, how they are restructuring, how they are increasing productivity and enhancing their human capital. The answers, in the case of IBM, AT&T, Kodak, Ameritech, BellSouth, Time Warner, Philips Electronics, Apple, Xerox, and most other high-tech firms, is that "restructuring" means massive "retrenchment," or "downsizing"—made possible, in part, by global telecommunications and technological innovation. Under intense competition, IBM reduced its workforce by over 25 percent between 1986 and 1993, and by 40,000 in 1992 alone—despite its highly touted no-layoff policy—resulting in what has been called a "psychological reign of terror" throughout the company.[17] Philips Electronics has laid off 45,000 workers since 1990; Kodak has cut 20,000 workers, a third of its local workforce, in the last decade; AT&T and the Baby Bells have been undergoing equally massive downsizing; and Apple and Xerox have recently undergone sizable though less severe cuts in management ranks. By most accounts, these massive cutbacks are permanent and as yet incomplete, with resulting devastation in employee morale.[18] This is what high-tech corporate "restructuring" has really been about, along with the dismemberment of monolithic bureaucracies into independent units threatened with extinction if they fail to produce. What irony, then, and what a chilling prospect, to read the words of James Dezell, president of IBM's new independent education division EduQuest: "Just as IBM is being restructured, the American educational system is in the midst of an awesome restructuring.[19]

In fact, when one reads between the lines, restructured schools, as envisioned by high-tech corporate leaders, have less to do with the improvement of education than with the easy assimilation of technology into education. Denis Doyle, co-author with ex-Xerox CEO Kearns of the book, *Winning the Brain Race*, writes: "The introduction of technology will totally transform schools. Or perhaps more to the point, schools must be totally transformed to use technology wisely and well."[20] And Allan Collins of Bolt, Beranek, and Newman, a principal researcher for the Apple Classrooms of Tomorrow program, talks about his work in schools as an attempt "to construct a systematic science of how to design educational environments so that new technologies can be introduced successfully."[21] Is this the development of technology in the service of education or the usurpation of education in the service of technological expansionism by high-tech firms desperate for new markets?

Despite the persistent celebration of teachers and teaching in the advertisements of IBM, Apple, and other computer vendors, the use of technology for educational productivity raises the specter of automated instructional delivery on a grand scale, reminiscent of military training agendas discussed earlier. In the words of Doyle:

> We do not yet have the technologies at our disposal to create human capital as readily as we create physical capital. But at some point we will, [and] it will break the mold and eliminate the gridlock of labor-intensive schooling. . . . Schools are actively afraid of, even hostile to, technology because in their bones educators know that technology will replace people. It always has and always will. About this matter educators' hunches and fears are justified.[22]

This agenda of automating education through the use of sophisticated technology is central to the work in "intelligent tutoring systems" of AI guru Roger Schank, whose Institute for Learning Sciences is lavishly bankrolled by Arthur Andersen, Ameritech, IBM, as well as by the Department of Defense. Schank "would replace teachers with computers [since] most teachers . . . are intellectually and temperamentally ill-equipped to deal with schoolchildren." According to one account, "even though Schank would like to see teachers dethroned, he doesn't want them banished from the classroom. Instead, their roles would be considerably diminished so that they'd serve as teaching assistants to computers."[23]

The arrogance and undisguised contempt for educators in these remarks complements perfectly the aggressiveness and "controlled impatience" characteristic of many corporate leaders engaged in school reform.[24] The championing of technology as an alternative to labor-intensive schooling also explains the sudden interest in for-profit schools: "Suddenly, for-profit schools are the subject of intense interest," explains Doyle, "because, first, in the area of technology, there is real promise of a breakthrough [and] . . . whoever unlocks the secrets of educational technology, whoever devises major productivity increases, stands on the threshold of enormous wealth."[25]

Of course, in the business of manufacturing and servicing computers and telecommunications, as in almost every other sector of corporate America, productivity improvement—increased output per worker hour—has been achieved not by taking full advantage of workforce capabilities through technology, but rather through the permanent displacement or disenfranchisement of millions of often highly educated, highly skilled U.S. workers, as advanced technology facilitates automation and global production. Such technology also escalates the pace and multiplies the tasks for those workers remaining on the job, while enabling the meticulous, online monitoring of their job performance, within a workplace "panopticon."[26]

Such is the real meaning of productivity in education, as engineered by corporate leaders frantically rescuing their corporations by streamlining their workforce. This agenda is captured by the words of Norman Augustine, CEO of defense conglomerate Martin Marietta and board member of the New American Schools Development Corporation: "We must accelerate the process of streamlining our society [just as we are] streamlining our economy."[27] Such sentiment is merely the latest echo of a legacy perhaps best captured by the words of military computing legend J. C. R. Licklider, the inspirational leader behind Bolt, Beranek, and Newman: "We are going to retool our industry, and . . . we must, at the same time, retool ourselves."[28]

This helps to explain the otherwise bewildering corporate insistence that schools produce students with "high skills" for the high-performance workplace, even as corporations are busy lopping off millions of present and future high-skill jobs in the name of productivity and competition (while also tapping cheaper skilled labor overseas). This recent corporate celebration of "human capital" reflects a number of corporate concerns about retooling its workforce. For one, corporate leaders have been greatly influenced by (increasingly controversial) studies predicting both a shortage of skilled workers and a burgeoning level of skill required by be high-tech workplace; this dubious double prophecy has generated a torrent of human capital rhetoric in the past few decades, catapulting corporate leaders into school reform.[29]

Corporate human capital concerns also reflect the changing nature of work done by the dwindling cadre of workers on the shop floor or in the office. This work must be "multiskilled," requiring more tasks from fewer people; the work is increasingly "abstract" as technicians and troubleshooters retreat from hands-on production to vigilance in computerized control rooms (always presumed to require higher, "thinking" skills); site-based teamwork and shop-floor decision making are intensified (approaches not without controversy);[30] worker responsibility and loyalty, tending massive capital investment in technology, are at a premium; and, finally, "learning" has become "the new form of labor,"[31] as accelerating production pace and product cycles, continuous technological upgrading, and constantly shifting job tasks force remaining workers continually, defensively, to "retool" themselves, just as those less fortunate scramble to "retrain" for the next array of evanescent job prospects (all this in the name of "lifelong learning").

Above all, high-tech corporate interest in education reform expects a school system that will utilize sophisticated performance measures and standards to sort students and to provide a reliable supply of such adaptable, flexible, loyal, mindful, expendable, "trainable" workers for the twenty-first century. This, at bottom, underlies the corporate drive to retool education and retool human capital. "We in the personal computer industry," notes Apple CEO John Sculley, also chair of the National Center on Education and the Economy, "are really in the behavior changing industry. We have the challenge to create the tools that fundamentally are going to change the way people learn, the way they think, the way they communicate, the way they work."[32] Such is the scope and hubris of the regime of technology in education, a legacy of military fantasy conjoined with the unbridled self-interest of corporate power.

In conclusion, technology in schools must not be thought about piecemeal, as simply a computer here, some fiber optic cable there. Rather, it represents a powerful regime, enjoined by a confluence of forces alien to education, buttressed by the accumulated momentum (if not success) of almost half a century of research and development, and encouraged by the longstanding complicity of increasingly influential sectors of the educational community. There is every indication that the time is ripe for a revitalization of the various agendas this regime represents, signaling the further colonization of schooling in the service of technological enterprise. For those progressive educators interested in the well being of whole children rather than in the modernization of instructional delivery systems for a chimerical high-performance economy, there is ample reason for concern.

Notes

1. A previous version of this chapter was published in *Holistic Education Review* (June 1993):4–13.

2. Quoted in "Computer 'Revolution' on Hold," ASCD Update (November 1990), Association for Supervision and Curriculum Development. For a recent account of computer use in schools, see the articles in the September 1992 issue of *MacWorld*, with the cover title "America's Shame."

3. Unless otherwise noted, the principal reference for this section is my book, *The Classroom Arsenal: Military Research, information Technology and Public Education* (Falmer Press, 1991).

4. See Alexandra K. Wigdor and Bert F. Green, Jr., *Performance Assessment for the Workplace*, vol. 1 (Washington: National Academy Press, 1991).

5. For example, see the recent work at the University of Southern California on the measurement of workforce readiness competencies codirected by veteran military researcher Harold J. O'Neil, Jr.

6. For a detailed account of the business activities and education agendas of corporate board members of the New American School Development Corporation, see my paper, "New American Schools and the New World Order," presented at the Annual Meeting of the American Educational Research Association, April, 1992.

7. Quoted in Troy Segal, "Saving Our Schools," *Business Week* (September 24, 1992), p. 72.

8. Charles Blaschke, "Review of the NASDC Awards," *Educational Technology* (August 1992):4.

9. See, for example, Idit Harel (of the MIT Media Lab), "Expanding the LOGO Environment," American Educational Research Association, Artificial Intelligence and Education Special Interest Group Newsletter (June 1990).

10. Millicent Lawton's article, "E. D., Pentagon Set 'Career Academies,'" in *Education Week* (November 4, 1992), p. 35, describes President Bush's "defense adjustment assistance initiative," calling for increased use of Defense Department resources for education, job training, and other objectives.

11. A. W. Melton, "The Science of Learning and the Technology of Educational Methods," *Harvard Education Review* 29, 2 (1959).

12. See Jane I. David, "Partnerships for Change," ACOT Report No. 12 (1992), Apple Computer, Inc.

13. For an account of the influence of the National Center on Education and the Economy, see my article, "Let Them Eat Skills" in *Rethinking Schools* (October 1992).

14. This was the unexpected finding of a nationwide survey conducted by the Commission on Workforce Skills, sponsored by the National Center on Education and the Economy, in their influential 1990s report, *America's Choice: High Skills or Low Wages!*

15. For a critical account of Whittle's Edison Project, see Jonathan Kozol, "Whittle and Privateers," *The Nation* (September 21, 1992):272–78.

16. For an account of EAIN, see Elizabeth Conlin, "Educating the Market," *Inc.* (July 1991):62–67.

17. See note 5 above.

18. For a recent summary of these circumstances in the business press, see Ronald Henkoff, "Where Will the Jobs Come From?" *Fortune* (October 19, 1992):58–64.

19. Quoted in a recent EduQuest brochure.

20. Denis Doyle, "The Challenge, the Opportunity," *Phi Delta Kappan* (March 1992):519.

21. Allan Collins, "Toward a Design Science of Education," Bolt, Beranek, and Newman, Technical Report No. 1 (January 25, 1990).

22. Doyle, "The Challenge," op. cit., p. 515.

23. See John Blades's article on Schank and the Institute for Learning Sciences, "Thinking Ahead," *Chicago Tribune* (March 24, 1991).

24. P. Michael Timpane and Laurie Miller McNeill, *Business Impact on Education and Child Development Reform* (New York: Committee on Economic Development, 1991), p. 34.

25. Doyle, "The Challenge," p. 515.

26. For discussions about these most prevalent uses of technology in service and industry, see Shoshana Zuboff, *In the Age of the Smart Machine* (New York: Basic, 1988); and Barbara Carson, *The Electronic Sweatshop* (New York: Simon & Schuster, 1988).

27. See note 5 above.

28. Noble, *Classroom Arsenal*, op. cit., p. xiii.

29. For a good summary of the studies and their critics, see Jonathan Weisman, "Some Economists Challenge View that Schools Hurt Competitiveness," *Education Week* (November 13, 1991):1, 14–15. For the latest compendium celebrating human capital, see *Human Capital and America's Future*, David W. Hornbeck and Lester Salamon, eds. (Baltimore: Johns Hopkins University Press, 1991).

30. See, for instance, Mike Parker and Jane Slaughter, *Choosing Sides: Unions and the Team Concept* (Boston: South End, 1988).

31. Zuboff, op. cit. For a more complete critique of high-tech skills, see my chapter "High-tech Skills" in *The Re-education of the American Working Class*, Steven London et al., eds. (New York: Greenwood, 1989).

32. Tom Inglesby, "An Interview with John Sculley," *Manufacturing Systems* (January 1989).

FIFTEEN

A Critical Analysis of Three Approaches to the Use of Computers in Education

Michael J. Streibel

W̲e are currently in the process of introducing microcomputers into our public and private schools at an exponential rate.[1] We are doing this at a time when many are calling for a return to basics in education and for an increase in the productivity of students, teachers, and administrators.[2] These two phenomena are not unrelated because microcomputers are seen as an answer to the "productivity crisis" in education.[3]

With respect to the content and outcome of education, however, microcomputers are not just another neutral "delivery system." Microcomputers are environments within which certain values, biases, and characteristics are played out; for example, calculation and logical operations are central within a computer-based environment. We therefore need to examine the way computers are used in education and the implications of this for the future of education.[4]

The three major approaches to using computers in education are: drill and practice, computer tutoring, and simulation and programming. Each of these approaches is analyzed in the following. Although each has some unique characteristics and a set of accompanying assumptions, a common conceptual framework, which is described throughout the remainder of the chapter binds them all together.

The investigation into the approaches of microcomputer use is shaped by three questions. First, what kind of logic is embedded in each approach and how does this logic express itself in a learning situation? Second, how do the various approaches treat the human learner and what are the consequences? Third, how does the "intellectual tool" use of computers help or hinder us in formulating, understanding, and solving problems?

The answers to these questions form the body of this chapter. They reveal, for example, that computerized drill and practice is designed to produce predictable learning performance. The logic used, however, runs counter to the dialectics of learning. Also, all of the approaches view the learner as a generic information processor. Ultimately, this indicates that a learner's intellectual agency is *decreased* rather than increased in the case of computerized tutorials even though the rhetoric promises the exact opposite.

The other major influences on the body of the text are my own values and assumptions. My background is as a teacher, teacher educator, and scholar in the area of educational technology. I am motivated by a desire to teach others *how* to think about media and computers, and how to become empowered, lifelong learners. In my view, derived from critical theory, knowledge and learning are the result of a social construction of reality.[5] That is, what we *know* to be real is the result of historical and social processes of meaning making, language making, and symbol-system making.[6] This social construction of reality applies to our knowledge of physical reality (i.e., scientific and technological knowledge), as well as to our knowledge of social reality (i.e., what we know about ourselves and others).[7] Both entail a process of human collaboration and dialogic engagement within interpretive communities. This collaboration and engagement creates a "public space" in the minds of the people involved that then leads to the further evolution of shared meanings and shared symbol systems. In a sense, collaboration and engagement within interpretive communities defines our very humanity because we are participating in the creation of our history, our language, and our values.[8]

Formal education is a social process of nurturing cognitive, affective, physical, aesthetic, and moral growth and diversity in children. The latter are dimensions of "meaning making" and therefore can only happen within community. The arguments developed below are therefore based on my belief that acquisition of factual knowledge and skills are important but always subordinate to personal and communal growth and development. A simple way of stating this is to say that dialogue is at the heart of education.[9]

Furthermore, learning is as much a process of accommodation as assimilation.[10] *Accommodation* requires the active creation of new meanings and the active construction of new symbol systems to give expression to these meanings. This clearly requires dialogic engagement with an interpretive community. Although *assimilation* may at first sight seem like an individual psychological activity, it is also an intentional and constructive act. My reason for believing the latter derives from an ontology which views *all* events—both physical and social—as unique, historical, and irreversible.[11] Students who are learning facts or skills are not incorporating meaningless pieces of information or manipulating meaningless puzzles. They are expanding some part of how they make sense of the world. Humans are, in other words, *always* intentional agents and education must respect and foster this agency.

I also believe that our knowledge encompasses more than discrete, objective, rational symbolic representations, and that cognition entails more than formal operations that operate on explicit knowledge structures. An individual's cognitive process are always subordinate to meaning making, and, therefore, are always open to the future and new ways of representing meaning. Even quasiformal systems are never complete.[12]

Formal education is more than a "rationally managed process." Schooling should not be modelled on an industrial assembly line because schooling deals with "meaning making" (and ultimately with "people making") and not with widget production.[13] Predictability and control are appropriate concepts for the efficient production of identical products but human beings are never identical products and should not be treated as such.

In my view, a teacher is a central agent in a dialectical community of learning and one who forms a triadic relationship with the learner and the subject matter. This maintains a learning community that extends backward and forward in time. Teaching is seen as having a craft status—a status that is particularly important today because a technological environment tends to leave most people "powerless" and inarticulate about their state of being.[14]

Finally, a teacher nurtures various types of intelligence in students and facilitates the conception and execution of learning. A teacher is not someone who adopts a theoretical stance toward the learner as does a researcher. Rather, a teacher is a lifelong learner who engages and guides others along a similar path.

I value individual and cultural uniqueness and diversity as well as the knowledge and skills that contribute to the social construction of reality. Maintaining a balance between uniqueness and uniformity (of person, culture, knowledge, and skills) is a daily struggle for a teacher that will be profoundly affected by the computer.[15]

Drill-and-Practice Computer Programs

Introduction to Drill-and-Practice Courseware

Drill-and-practice courseware programs (i.e., computer programs that guide learning with a drill-and-practice instructional strategy) are the dominant use of computers in education today.[16] They currently run on time-sharing computers and microcomputers. As described below, the characteristics of the drill-and-practice approach legitimize behavioral performances over other types of educational goals. Ironically, behaviorally oriented learning cultures must still be created, mediated, and sustained by interpersonal interactions that have the potential for forming alternate cultures (and thereby alternate types of educational goals. Drill-and-practice courseware programs, however, do not permit these alternate goals to develop.

Description and Analysis of Drill-and-Practice Courseware

Drill-and-practice courseware programs make a number of assumptions about instruction:[17]

1. Previous instruction in the concept or skill has already occurred.
2. Regular instruction is only being supplemented and not replaced.
3. Instruction is to follow a controlled, step-by-step linear sequence of subskills according to an algorithm embedded in the computer program. This algorithm does *not* constitute a model of a student or an expert but constitutes a model of:
   a. rote skill building in the case of drill; and,
   b. patterned skill building according to the logic of the content and an instructional theory in the case of practice.[18]
4. A right/wrong answer dichotomy exists in the logic of the content.
5. The basic unit of instructional interaction is a question/answer-branch episode.[19] Continuous learner responses in the form of correct answers are therefore expected.
6. The best feedback by the program from an instructional point of view is an immediate check on a student's responses according to the logic of the content:
   a. positive feedback when the answer is correct; and,
   b. corrective (rather than judgmental) feedback when the answer is incorrect.

The characteristics described above make several things clear: drill-and-practice courseware programs are designed to provide immediate corrective interventions in the learning process when continuously monitored performance measures indicate incorrect responses. The learner is viewed as a "black box" and his or her behaviors are shaped by an external, mechanical process (i.e., by an instructional algorithm that uses feedback mechanisms to guide the learner toward a prespecified behavioral goal). Drill-and-practice courseware programs therefore constitute a deterministic form of behavioral technology.[20] This may be adequate for beginning skill building but may mitigate against higher levels of learning.[21] To understand why, we must examine the concepts of mastery learning, individualized learning, and educational work.

Mastery Learning and Drill-and-Practice Courseware

The mastery-learning paradigm assumes that most students can learn most things to a specific level of competence in varying amounts of time.[22] It therefore associates differences in the *amount* of learner performances at any point in time with differences in the *rates of learning*. Second, the mastery-learning paradigm assumes that instruction can be consciously designed to guarantee specific outcomes. It therefore places a heavy emphasis on the *quality of instructional materials*. Finally, the mastery-learning approach uses criterion-referenced tests that restrict themselves to the level of the objective in order to decide whether a student has met the criterion of success. Success is *not* defined with reference to a higher-level objective.

One can see from this description that the mastery-learning paradigm closely resembles a rationally managed input/output model of educational performance. It therefore makes a number of assumptions about the (1) pedagogical principles, (2) classroom practices, and (3) instructional arrangements involved.[23] These assumptions elaborate the input-output model:

1. Pedagogical Principles

The mastery-learning paradigm assumes that students vary in their aptitude, ability to understand instruction, motivation, and perseverance. These factors are only considered insofar as they affect educational performance. They are not, for example, considered in terms of their contribution to non-performance educational goals (e.g., growth in consciousness, growth in aesthetic appreciation, moral growth, etc.). Finally, the mastery-learning paradigm assumes that all students are able to achieve mastery *given enough time*.

This pedagogical assumption treats learning as a rationally managed process because sufficient time and resources will guarantee predictable performance. Considerations such as the dialectics of learning, accommodation to individual uniqueness, and the possibility of emergent goals have been factored out of the process. Yet these considerations are essential for learning—even at the level of simple skills.

2. Classroom and School Practices

The mastery-learning paradigm manipulates the *time* allowed for learning and the *quality of instructional stimuli* to help students achieve mastery. It therefore entails the rational planning of classroom time, schedules, organization, and conditions of instruction, as well as the rational design of instructional materials.[24] Such design and planning activities are only called rational to the extent that they are guided by the pragmatics of instructional and organizational theories. They are *not* guided by the pragmatics of classroom teaching.[25] For example, predictability and manageability of process and product are prime considerations, not whether some unique classroom event becomes an occasion for further learning. Hence, the *conception* of instructional events is separate from and directs the *execution* of such events.[26] In this scheme of things, we would expect to evaluate teacher performance (and ultimately administrator and even system performance) in terms of student performance because correct student behavior is the ultimate product. However, I will show later that this in fact serves the system's needs more than the learner's needs.

3. Instructional Arrangements

The mastery-learning paradigm follows a number of procedures to guarantee that students will perform at prespecified levels:[27]

a. preinstructional assessment procedures are used to measure the presence or absence of prerequisite knowledge in the learner;
b. initial teaching methods are used to inform the learner of the objectives and prerequisite knowledge;
c. training procedures are used to help the learner acquire the appropriate knowledge and skills;
d. continual assessment procedures are used to ensure the presence or absence of subskills;
e. immediate remediation procedures are used if the subskills are not present; and
f. certification of mastery is added when some predetermined criterion performance is reached by the learner.

One can see from all these techniques that the mastery-learning paradigm conceptualizes the instructional process in quality-control terms. Each step in the paradigm is expressed as a procedure and all instruction is arranged to maximize output. Knowledge is categorized as a hierarchy of prerequisite knowledge such that it becomes illogical to focus on higher-level skills before lower-level skills, and such that higher-level skills are somehow the *sum* of component subskills.

The mastery-learning paradigm described above therefore specifies *what kinds* of things are to be achieved (i.e., measurable performance gains) and *how* these things are to be achieved (i.e., through the manipulation of time and instructional stimuli). Drill-and-practice courseware functions as the training and remediation component within this framework. Although group work is permissible within the mastery paradigm, drill-and-practice courseware is usually individualized.

Individualization and Drill-and-Practice Courseware

Individualization can mean many things: e.g., independent study, individual pacing, individual diagnosis, individual educational outcomes.[28] It arises out of the larger recognition that individuals differ from each other.[29] Within computer-based forms of individualized learning, however, it refers to generic outcomes for generic individuals rather than to personal goals for unique individuals.

The philosophy of individualization contains a number of specific assumptions:[30]

1. A belief that each person has a unique set of characteristics or aptitudes that ultimately influence the *rate* at which competent performance in a particular skill is achieved.
2. A belief that a well-defined and well-structured sequence of instructional events will facilitate progress toward preplanned outcomes.
3. A belief that time and quality of instructional materials will influence successful completion of an objective.
4. A belief that student "needs" and characteristics can indicate a readiness for the objectives by the learner.
5. A belief that an evaluation mechanism can be found for *constantly* monitoring the student's progress toward a preplanned outcome (thereby providing data for the instructional system's performance).
6. A shift in the role of the teacher *from* a pedagogical one *toward* an instructional decision-making one (e.g., placement of students; selection, use, and allocation of space, time, and materials; data collection and report writing).

In some systems of individualized learning such as the Keller Plan, students have a great amount of flexibility in setting schedules, getting help from student tutors, and following any number of paths toward a predefined goal.[11]

Each of these factors is adjusted for the sake of individual rates of learning. In the Skinnerian version of the philosophy of individualization, on the other hand, instruction is broken down into much smaller units, and instructional events are more controlled and automated.[32]

It is this latter version that is most often seen in drill-and-practice courseware, which overwhelmingly uses rate of progress as their major dimension of individualization although they sometimes include level of difficulty. Other dimensions such as cognitive style are often called for but rarely implemented because of the computational complexity involved.[33]

Drill-and-practice courseware programs also break the instructional process into very small steps. They then assess each learner's response and specify a finite number of paths for the learner to follow. They are therefore "individualized" in the narrow sense of allowing individual rates of progress along finite, forced-choice paths that lead to prespecified, measurable outcomes. Because they control both the *presentation of information* as well as the learner's *interactions with that information*, they control the individual's total attention during the time that they are used.

Finally, drill-and-practice courseware programs relegate the teacher to a resource manager or exception handler.[34] This is not to suggest that a teacher is forced by the computer to organize the classroom according to the Skinnerian philosophy of individualization, only that drill-and-practice courseware programs are biased toward such an orientation. In many schools, the shift toward teacher-as-manager has already taken place without the computer.[35]

In many ways, the philosophy of drill-and-practice courseware is consistent with the movement in the curriculum field toward the "technical control" of learning.[36] I will describe this notion under the rubric of the *technological framework* throughout the rest of this chapter. For now, the concept of replicated work will help us begin to understand the concept of *technical control* in courseware.

Courseware as Replicated Work

Victor Bunderson has developed one of the most thorough analyses of the concept of courseware as replicated work.[37] The following discussion expands his analysis.

Computer courseware, he argues, has both a product and a process dimension. As a *product*, courseware consists of the "consumable [materials of instruction] that operate on and with a technologically mediated instructional delivery system." As a *process*, courseware constitutes an "economically replicable and easily portable package that, when used in combination with a technologically mediated instructional delivery system, is capable of performing work related to training and performance improvement."

291

The instructional delivery system consists of both *the physical objects and structures* "designed to perform or facilitate the work necessary to achieve educational and training goals," and a *human culture* of "traditions, values, and habits that inform and constrain the use of the physical artifacts." All components of the ensemble therefore derive their meaning from the instructional delivery system.

We can see from the description above that the technical structure of the delivery system shapes the form and function of the human culture and the physical artifacts. The technical structure also orients these components toward some external goal (i.e., educational performance) and then tries to maximize the levels of this goal. A technological delivery system will therefore ultimately influence the nature of the classroom culture—unless, of course, the classroom is already organized as a work culture.

The technical structure imposed by courseware allows students only pseudocontrol because they can only choose from a finite number of paths toward a predetermined goal. Bunderson acknowledges this somewhat by saying that "learner-centered will emphasize learner productivity, not necessarily learner control." This restricts the meaning of "individualized learning" to that of "individualized productivity level."

Bunderson continues his discussion of educational work by criticizing the inability of current teacher-centered delivery systems to be more "productive." The teacher-centered culture, he argues, has reached the "limits" of [its] improvability." His solution is a technological one: "when education is analyzed into the work that is required, technology is seen as the *only* way to make a fundamental difference." Bunderson's argument is very general and even applies to book-based technology (i.e., a teacher with books can accomplish more than a teacher without books).

By conceiving of the classroom as an instructional delivery system (rather than, say, an instructional setting for the dialectical encounter of mutually respected and unique individuals), Bunderson narrows the debate about what can happen in such a setting. The classroom, in effect, becomes a place for training and development. I mentioned earlier that the mastery-learning paradigm turned the classroom into a workplace for both teachers and students. The concept of the classroom as a workplace is further compounded by highlighting the work potential of classroom technologies.

When teacher-delivered instruction and technology-delivered instruction are conceptualized in similar terms, computer courseware is then seen as a more efficient mechanism. Observation of certain classrooms containing hierarchical authority, rigid schedules, and mindless workbooks may support Bunderson. But even in such classrooms, students still have some opportunity for personal integration of experiences and skills. They can still integrate their drill-and-practice activities with exploration, planning, negotiation, and collaboration—even if it is done as a subterfuge. These latter characteristics are essential for education.[38] In individualized drill-and-practice courseware, on the other hand, where a student's total time, attention, and interactions are controlled by the computer, such integrations are no longer possible.[39] Is this loss worth the price—even for low levels of learning where only the acquisition of procedural rules is involved?

When we examine the actual characteristics of Bunderson's concept of educational work, we find that they all embody the *extensional* side of education (i.e., the measurable and procedural). According to Bunderson, a teacher presents information, models processes, provides students, with trials and feedback, discusses "individual needs" with students uses affective appeals to motivate learning, trains students in how to use the delivery system, assesses student performance, manages the assessed information, and manages classroom interactions. Where, within this analysis, is a teacher's affective and semantic engagement with students beyond maximizing performance gains? All that Bunderson describes are procedural skills and information-processing functions: such functions *can* be carried out more efficiently and effectively by technology (e.g., video, microcomputer, etc.). Efficiency here means maximizing educational productivity at the lowest financial cost. Effectiveness means reliably reproducing the process and the product.[40] In effect, these things are no longer subject to the qualitative criteria of excellence and expertise within a particular subject area but to the quantitative criteria of economics.[41] No wonder teachers cannot compete!

Bunderson's point of view has a fundamental contradiction, however. The rhetoric stresses the "needs" of the individual but the terms of the debate emphasize instructional systems concerns. By shifting the educational interactions away from the intentional logic of interpersonal interactions and toward the extensional logic of procedural skills and information-processing functions, the following criteria are emphasized:

1. *systems efficiency*, maximizing the throughput of students for the time and resources invested rather than developing individual talents;
2. *systems reliability*, emphasizing quality control and replicability of output rather than individual, communal, or cultural diversity; and
3. *systems economy*, "more scholar for the dollar" rather than personally determined pursuit of excellence.

Hence, *only those "individual needs" amenable to systems' logic are served.*

Bunderson's concept of educational work has another contradiction. The very work culture that has to exist in a classroom for a technological instructional system to operate can only come about from intentional human engagement, negotiation, and interaction. Students and teachers are therefore essential and continuous agents in the creation of a classroom work culture.[42] However, the very processes that are required to *produce* the work culture then have to be *denied* because they contradict the technological framework. This is the case because an instructional delivery system embodies a technological culture that tries to shape the human culture to its own ends, whereas human cultures shape their own ends.[43]

This can be seen in the teacher roles that Bunderson believes will predominate in a technological environment: corrector of imperfect and outdated information, illustrator and augmenter of delivered instruction, illustrator and augmenter of the expert algorithms embodied in the instructional system, creator of a technologically acceptable setting, and interpreter of automatically tested and recorded results. Each of these requires insight, understanding, and interpretation on the part of the teacher; yet each reinforces the technological delivery system as the central organizing factor in the classroom. The classroom has thereby been structured as a workplace by someone other than the teacher while at the same time requiring the teacher's unacknowledged labor.[44] A drill-and-practice courseware program is therefore not all that innocent an aid to teaching in a classroom community.[45] In fact, such programs may ultimately conflict with the nature of teaching because teaching is *more* than a highly rational, decision-making affair.[46]

Summary of Drill-and-Practice Courseware

Drill-and-practice courseware programs embody narrow aspects of the mastery-learning paradigm, the philosophy of individualization, and the concepts of educational work and efficiency. They convert the learning process into a form of work that tries to maximize performance gains, and they restrict the meaning of individualization to rate of progress and level of difficulty (and ultimately to individualized levels of productivity). Drill-and-practice courseware programs restrict the type of interaction of learner and computer to a decontextualized performance domain and diminish integration of subskills with higher-level skills. Thus, even though they maximize performance, they may *not* be the best instructional supplement. Finally, drill-and-practice courseware programs are part of a behavioral learning culture that mitigates against non-behavioral goals. Hence, such programs do not lead to critical thinking or personal empowerment. The question therefore arises whether computer-based *tutorials* have such a potential or whether they simply develop the behaviorally oriented learning philosophy in a more sophisticated way. Many authors have argued that computer-based tutorials do in fact solve some of the limitations of drill-and-practice programs.[47]

Tutorial Computer Programs

Introduction to Tutorial Courseware

Tutorial courseware programs go beyond drill-and-practice approaches in that they are *designed* to "take total responsibility for instruction" and to contain a "mixed-initiative dialogue."[48] These terms are examined in depth later. Analyzing the nature of "dialogue" in human-computer interactions is a way of analyzing the nature of tutorial programs, because dialogue is often seen as the basic building block for higher levels of learning.[49] Another critical element to be examined is the *type* of "quality-control" procedures used in computer-based tutorials. Other themes uncovered in my analysis of computerized drill and practice reemerge in computerized tutorials in a more sophisticated form. This will stand in sharp contrast to the rhetoric about tutorial courseware programs, which claims that such tutorials resemble real conversations and real teaching.[50]

Description and Analysis of Tutorial Courseware

The various types of human-computer interactions in tutorial courseware programs are on-line tests, remedial dialogues, and interactive proofs.

On-line tests are initiated by a computer as part of the tutorial interaction. They compare a model of student performance with a model of expert performance. In simpler tutorials, on-line tests only involve a comparison between student performances and prespecified, content-determined performance levels.[51] In both cases, on-line tests provide continual diagnoses of students' performances.

An immediate consequence of having on-line tests in computerized tutorials is that the learner is subject to constant quality control. This does not seem unreasonable because, in interpersonal interactions, humans also check out their inferences about each other.[52] Why should a computer not do the same? Yet, in interpersonal dialogues, such monitoring takes place in the context of semantic engagement and conjoint intentions; in human-computer interactions, such monitoring is guided by an external agent's (i.e., author, instructional designer, or programmer) intentions, which are fixed *for the duration of the interaction*. These external intentions establish preset, nonnegotiable, and measurable performance outcomes *for the learner*. Constant monitoring is therefore not intended to understand the learner and his or her messages (as in interpersonal dialogue) but rather intended to guarantee a behavioral outcome. In drill-and-practice courseware, this was rather obvious. In "mixed-initiative" computer "dialogues," this is not always so evident.

The constancy and immediacy of diagnosis and feedback in on-line tests has several other consequences:

1. It emphasizes accretion learning because the computer is looking for evidence of normal progress toward a prespecified goal. This discourages "messing around" with the subject matter: "messing around behavior" is not evidence that a learner is building toward a quantum leap of understanding.[53]

2. It tends to focus learning on *generic* means in spite of the fact that tutorials are individualized. The computer, in effect, *controls the means as well as the ends* and constitutes a powerful "other" that structures and dominates the entire interaction.[54]

   In interpersonal interactions, learning tends to focus on the ends-in-view and not on the means.[55] Learning here incorporates personally constructed means and meanings, something preempted in on-line tests. This is not to suggest that human teachers cannot dominate an interaction with a learner but only that learners have the opportunity to develop personal ways to reach a particular goal.

3. It tends to accelerate the learning process because it creates a set of temporal expectations where rate of learning is the major dimension of individualization, and faster rates increase the efficiency of the system. This, in turn, biases the tutorial interaction *against* reflectiveness and critical thinking.[56] Some courseware authors have suggested that this bias can be countered by using "individualized" wait loops in the programs.[57] However, reflectiveness is *not* a matter of waiting longer.

Remedial dialogues are initiated by the computer when the learner's performance does not match some prespecified performance criteria.[58] They assume that the student already knows the area and can work with the information presented. This also parallels what happens in interpersonal dialogues but with some very important distinctions:

1. In interpersonal tutorials, remedial dialogues are initiated by a teacher on the basis of his or her tacit knowledge about the unique characteristics of the learner. The teacher tries to understand the learner's state of mind by "thinking like the student" in order to unravel the student's conceptual bind or misunderstanding. This is a unique, constructive, and intentional act of empathy and engagement by the teacher and *only nominally entails the student's behaviors.*

2. In human-computer tutorials, remedial "dialogues" are initiated on the basis of a set of explicit and procedural models (expert or content-related algorithms).[59] The tutorial courseware program, in effect, constitutes a generic, rule-driven process that engages an internal,

generic model of the learner. The actual human agent (i.e., student) in this "dialogue" only provides the data for the computer's formal, generic model of the learner. Remedial "dialogues" therefore do not involve *this* student but rather this *type* of student.

Interactive proofs are a type of computer-based tutorial that permit the learner to make decisions beyond a predefined set of choices.[60] Hence, students can ask for information, work through a variety of examples that embody some concept, and even construct their own models of the problem. However, the very nature of the computing environment still constrains the terms of the debate. The best examples of interactive proofs usually come from mathematics and science where the nature of the content parallels the nature of the computing environment. Of course, even nonmathematical subject areas can be reformulated to be amenable to interactive proofs. Hence, the socio-political problem of hunger can be recast into economic terms and then reduced to a set of formulae that relate an arbitrarily chosen set of variables. The interactive "proof" then proceeds *as if* it were a mathematical problem, treating a problem such as hunger as if it were a computerized numbers game or an "artificial" reality.

Human-Computer "Dialogues" in Tutorial Courseware

The central assumption of computer-based tutorials is that human-computer "dialogues" should resemble interpersonal conversations. Bork has modified this claim somewhat by saying that the student is really conducting a dialogue with the author of the computer tutorial rather than with the computer itself, but this is a facile reformulation. Bork also admits that the author of a computer tutorial is trying to manipulate the student by "stimulat[ing] meaningful responses which contribute to learning."[61] Hence, human-computer "dialogues" are a form of behavioral technology where dialogic interactions are controlled by an author who is *not part of the actual interaction*. Student responses are only meaningful in light of their contribution to educational performance. The actual confrontations between humans and computers are, therefore, one-sided affairs because the computers have fixed-goal structures, interactive strategies, and deductive capabilities.

What *should* human-computer interactions in a tutorial be called? To answer this, we must compare them with interpersonal interactions. Interpersonal dialogues contain an essential component of *conjoint control* (in spite of the power differentials that may exist between students and teachers). In human-computer "dialogues," however, students only control the *rate* (i.e., pacing of predefined sequences), *route* (i.e., any one of a finite number of predefined, or algorithmically-constrained, paths towards a predefined goal), and *timing* (i.e., speed of individual responses). All other control resides in the courseware program, leaving students with a form of pseudocontrol because the actual interaction follows a preplanned, goal-oriented, procedural network. Hence, human-computer tutorial interactions are best called *"utilogs"* rather than "dialogues."[62] Of course, utility here is defined by a courseware author who in turn is restricted to certain categories within the technological framework.[63]

The deeper implications of having interactions in a computer tutorial shaped by the external intentions of an author are summarized below.

1. Humans are Treated as Data-Based, Rule-Following, Symbol-Manipulating Information Processors

This implication emerges from the nature of the computer technology used to carry out the actual tutorial interactions. Machine processes can only operate on explicit information according to algorithmic rules. Computers cannot semantically or affectively engage human beings. Humans therefore have to adapt to the *nature* of the computational environment, although within that framework, computer processes can be designed to adapt to the "individual differences" of humans.

Recall that computers only engage *data* from an individual, not the actual person. This data is organized by the program into a model of the learner (in simpler programs, this is merely a data base of variables and values). The particular model of an individual that the program contains (or builds up) always remains a formal and abstract *type*. Furthermore, this model is a *means* for the computer to carry out the interaction. The human is therefore treated by the computer as a *generic type* and a *means* to an end. This has serious implications for education.

Because human beings develop personal intellectual agency through dialogic interactions,[64] the learner in computer-based tutorial interactions can *never* develop such agency. Furthermore, human beings tend to model the "other" in dialogic interactions,[65] so that computer-based tutorials may actually teach students to treat other dialogic partners as *anthropomorphized processes* and *means* rather than as ends.

In interpersonal dialogic interactions, on the other hand, persons encounter, confront, accept (to a greater or lesser degree), and engage each other as unique individuals. The person in interpersonal dialogues is therefore a *unique ontological entity* (rather than a generic type) and an *end* (rather than a means). This sets the stage for personal agency in learning. Interpersonal dialogue can, of course, become mechanical if the humans involved act on the basis of some stereotypical image about each other. However, the potential for true discourse is *always* present in interpersonal interactions. This potential can *never* exist in human-computer interactions.[66]

Viewing humans as rule-following information processors (as opposed to individuals with unique intentionalities) legitimizes uniform educational goals, methods, and outcomes. Uniformity in education is enforced not only because the instructional systems attempt to shape a uniform product (i.e., prespecified learning outcomes) but also because the very conceptualization of the individual places "semantic and syntactical constraints on acceptable language for the discussion of human beings."[67] This, in turn, makes expressing and legitimizing other conceptions of human beings, educational goals, and methods outside of the technological framework impossible.[68] A simple example of an alternative framework can make this clear.

In order to create a community and carry out community action, we must:[69] (a) unconditionally accept individual uniqueness and diversity; (b) carry out an ongoing dialectical synthesis of opposing viewpoints with the actual members of the community; and (c) respect emergent community goals. The technological framework, on the other hand, builds on the generic characteristics of individuals, a means-ends rationality, and a predetermined set of performance goals. The two opposing sets of assumptions cannot be balanced.

2. Machine Processes Will Eventually Match Human Processes

This second implication derives from the first implication: if humans are ultimately rule-following information processors, then computers will eventually do everything that humans can do. Human-computer interactions will then in fact become dialogues because both sides of the interaction will have identical ontological status.

This statement has some serious implications for education, even if we only restrict ourselves to the cognitive domain. If we as educators accept the responsibility for the growth of young minds, then we are obligated to ask how such minds do in fact grow. Furthermore, if we find that mental development at all levels requires a dialectical synthesis of personally and socially constructed meanings, then we can see that the very ontology of the technological framework (i.e., the world is made up of specifiable and controllable processes) is inadequate for the whole domain of intentions and interpersonal meanings. *Machine processes*, in this case, *will never replace interpersonal interactions!*

Finally, if we find that human skills and knowledge are ultimately based on tacit beliefs and judgments that cannot be analyzed into components, then computational processes (which by their nature reduce similarity *judgments* to computable comparisons of component identities) will never match human processes.[70]

3. Education Will Be Viewed as a Form of Training and Be Subject to Explicit, Extensional Logic

Having an expert author design the goals, rules, and messages for a human-computer interaction means that the logic of prediction and control (the technological framework) is applied to developing preplanned performance outcomes. The whole educational enterprise is then reduced to a means-ends rationality because the ends are specified first and then the most efficient means are employed to guarantee a quality product. The resulting mechanization of interaction is sometimes hard to see when computers carry out the actual interaction because of the sophistication, speed, and variety of media involved. But we should never confuse sophisticated technique with sophisticated instruction.[71] Technique does not have a tacit dimension, whereas all human knowledge and learning does.[72] Technique is solely subject to extensional logic, whereas knowledge is subject to *both* intentional and extensional logic.

We can see the implications of computer-based tutorial interactions for education most clearly when we examine the nature of experiential learning within the technological and nontechnological frameworks.[73] This statement can be explored by comparing the following notions: the nature of experience, events, and activities; the concept of individual; the methods of knowledge; and, the types of thinking involved.

When restricted to a computational environment, "experiences" take on the form of puzzles *of the same type* (i.e., declarative, quantifiable, procedural). Events are nonhistorical because they are reversible and activities are restricted to a nondialectical logic (i.e., formal operations).[74] Furthermore, an individual is only trivially unique (i.e., the variables of a student model in the computer are generic, only the *values* of the variables are unique). Finally, an individual only needs the ability to decode abstract symbols because the "text" and "context" are predetermined by an external agent, and because knowledge is expressed in an explicit, abstract form. Critical and dialectical thinking are not needed because they make too many things problematical, ambiguous, and noncontrollable.

In a natural environment, on the other hand, "experiences" are made up of indefinite *types*. Events are ambiguous, historical, and irreversible.[75] Activity involves a confrontation between persons and events, and meanings are personally and interpersonally constructed. Experiences and actions are dialectical and historical. Furthermore, natural experiences entail an accommodation to, and assimilation of, an indefinite variety of uniqueness in persons, ideas, and events. These, in turn, become the experiential basis for further critical and dialectical thinking. Finally, individuals need interpretive as well as decoding skills because they are forced to construct as well as deconstruct the meanings-in-use of others.[76] Interpersonal dialogue plays a central role here because knowledge is dialectical, historical, and subject to transformation.

In brief, the technological framework places tremendous restrictions on the variety of educational experiences. Computer-based tutorials therefore seem to rule out everything that is of value in the natural and social worlds.

Summary of Tutorial Courseware Programs

Tutorial courseware does go beyond drill and practice because it is a more sophisticated form of interaction, but it also stays well within the bounds of the behavioral and technological framework. Behavioral outcomes are still prespecified by expert agents outside of the actual interaction, quality-control procedures are still used to guarantee that the learner will reach the intended outcomes, and learners are still only given a form of pseudocontrol (i.e., rate, route, and timing). Furthermore, though the interaction is less rigid, it is still constrained by an explicit algorithm, is still focused on maximizing educational performance gains, and still treats the learner as a means toward someone else's end. Computer-based tutorial interactions, therefore, provide an artificial "other" that preempts personal intellectual agency and ultimately inner-directed learning. Computer-based tutorials are also biased against experiential learning outside of the technological framework, quantum leaps in learning, and reflective thinking. Their value in education is therefore very limited.

A question now arises about using computers as "intellectual tools." Does *this* use of computers go beyond the limitations discussed so far? On first reflection, personal intellectual agency seems to be a natural concomitant of the "tool" use of computers, but this conclusion requires a careful analysis.

Computers as Intellectual Tools

Introduction to The Intellectual Dimension of Computers

What are the intellectual dimensions, if any, of computers? To answer this question, we must not focus on the computer as a personal productivity tool (e.g., word processor) but rather as an "object to think with."[77] This brings me into the realm of computer languages and simulations.

Thus far, I have described the way drill-and-practice and tutorial courseware programs introduce a means-end rationality into the learning process. Knowledge acquisition and skill building (the terms themselves are revealing) become subject to efficiency and performance criteria, and learning becomes a systematically designed and rationally managed process. Does such a situation apply to the case where the learner programs his or her own solutions to problems?[78] Surely here we will not see the means-ends rationality of an external agent conceptualizing, designing, and managing the learning process. After all, the *learner* is now in control of the whole process!

Can the student who controls the computer go beyond the technological framework of the computer (the values associated with the computer and the symbol systems that can be manipulated by the computer)? Tools tend to insist that they be used in certain ways and intellectual tools tend to define the user's mental landscape.[79] Computational intellectual tools (i.e., computer programming and simulations) therefore bias our ways of knowing toward the quantitative, declarative, and procedural kinds of knowledge, hiding other kinds of knowledge.

The Computer as an Intellectual Problem-Solving Tool

A computer is basically a box that manipulates symbols (and information) according to a plan. When someone else writes the plan, we are forced to follow his or her set of procedures. When we write the plan, we are forced to use the computer's language. In both cases, we are confronted with a question about the nature of the plans and the types of symbols that the computer can manipulate. We therefore need to explore how programming a problem in a computer language helps us learn and think about that problem.

The symbols a computer manipulates are actually only energy states in an electronic machine which are transformed according to formal, algorithmic rules. Even if a computer manipulates two high-level representational constructs such as "All men are mortal," plus "Socrates is a man," and ends up with, "Therefore Socrates is a mortal," it only manipulates semantically empty energy states (which we call input or data or symbols) according to syntactical rules—regardless how high-level those rules. It is *we* who actively construct and ascribe meaning. A computer language is therefore *not* a language in the traditional sense of the term (i.e., expressive, intentional, and connotative as well as denotative and based on qualitative knowing) but rather a set of syntactical notations to control computer operations.[80] Hence, *a computer's expressive potential only extends over the syntactical dimension of its formal operations.* Of course, for those who equate cognition with computation, the expressive potential of computer languages extends into the semantic domain because "all relevant semantic distinctions [are] mirrored by syntactic distinctions."[81]

Clearly, if humans are going to use computers as intellectual tools, then they must work within the epistemological limitations of these tools.[82] Because computers can only manipulate explicit data and symbols according to formal, syntactical rules, they tend to legitimize those types of knowledge that fit into their framework and delegitimize other types of knowledge.[83]

Hence, computers tend to *legitimize* the following characteristics of knowledge:[84] rule-governed order, objective systematicity, explicit clarity, nonambiguity, nonredundancy, internal consistency, noncontradiction (i.e., logic of the excluded middle), and quantitative aspects. They also tend to legitimize deduction and induction as the only acceptable epistemological methods.

By way of contrast, computers tend to *delegitimize* the following characteristics of knowledge: emergent goals, self-constructed order, organic systematicity, connotation and tacitness, ambiguity, redundancy, dialectical rationality, simultaneity of multiple logics, and qualitative aspects. Finally, they tend to delegitimize the following epistemological methods: abduction, interpretation, intuition, introspection, and dialectical synthesis of multiple and contradictory realities.

The more computers are used as intellectual tools, therefore, the more we rely on the formal characteristics of knowledge and the less we rely on the tacit and interpretative dimensions of knowledge. It is almost as if the technological framework is not only incompatible with other ways of knowing, but inevitably excludes them from our mental landscape as well. Of course, the formal and the tacit dimensions of knowledge can never be separated from each other.[85] The tacit dimension can only become hidden.

Thus, we return to an earlier conclusion: computers force us to act *as if* we were rule-governed information processors. They also force us to construe thinking as "'cognitive problem solving' where the 'solutions' are arrived at by formal calculation, computation, and rational analysis."[86] Even if we are active and constructive and intuitive in our approach to the world, we must still analyze and reduce problems into explicit and procedural terms. The concept of the computer as an intellectual tool is therefore *not* a neutral formulation because it forces us to objectify ourselves as agents of prediction, calculation, and control. Personal intellectual agency has thereby been limited to the technological framework.

Computer Programming and Computer Simulations

We can easily see how programming is a paradigm of *thinking* in the context of the tool use of computers. If the only legitimate knowledge entails objective facts, explicit representations of facts as data, and formal operations on these representations, then programming is the ideal way to process such knowledge. The same can be said of programming as a paradigm for *learning*. If the only way to think about things is through analysis and procedural debugging, then programming is also the ideal way to *learn* how to deal with the world. After all, we are not just learning to act *as if* we were computers, we are developing operational and representational cognitive structures to deal with *any* aspect of the world! Gone are aesthetic, metaphoric, artistic, affective, interpretive, and moral structures for dealing with the world!

We can, therefore, understand how many of the chief advocates of the tool use of computers see computer literacy as the ability to "do computing"[87] and see computer programming as the best way to shape a child's cognitive development.[88] However, in this scheme of things, we can also see that our rational life is thereby reduced to a set of operational, problem-solving skills— to say nothing about our emotional life.

Is there anything positive to be gained from programming aside from the actual technical skills? In several studies, very little positive transfer was found from programming to other domains of cognitive problem solving.[89] However, this conclusion is only tentative because the field is still new.[90] We must therefore fall back on an analysis of the nature of programming in order to see what is possible with this approach.

Computing, as Arthur Luehrmann, one of the chief advocates of programming, argues,

> belongs as a regular school subject for the same reason as reading, writing, and mathematics. Each gives the student a basic intellectual tool with wide areas of application. Each gives the student a distinctive means of thinking about and representing a problem, of writing his or her thoughts down, of studying and criticizing the thoughts of others, whether they are embodied in a paragraph of English, a set of mathematical equations, or a computer program. Students need practice and instruction in all these basic modes of expressing and communicating ideas.[91]

This certainly is an admirable statement because it integrates computing (algorithmic, procedural thinking) into the other "basics" of education (i.e., reading, writing, and arithmetic). Luehrmann's argument also casts programming as an aid to understanding.

What grounds exist for objecting to programming as a school subject? The answer applies to other "distinctive means of thinking and representing a problem": whenever technique is emphasized over grappling with content, then the innermost principles of that content are lost.[92] This is especially true for computer programming because the computer is an instrument of technique par excellence. It can *only* manipulate content-free symbols according to formal procedures. Hence, although computer programming may force one to structure *information* in precise and systematic ways and carry out *logical operations* on abstract representations of that information, it tells us *nothing* about *what* information should be treated in this way nor about the *nature* of the real world. A simple computer-simulation example should make this clear. The same argument applies to programming the simulation.

Oregon Trail is a popular computer simulation that records the problems faced by pioneers crossing the American frontier.[93] It provides a simplified environment for elementary school children where they can make decisions and watch the consequences of their "actions." For example, forgetting to "buy" enough bullets leads to the "death" of the settlers. A student can "win" if he or she keeps a careful record of the "purchases" and analyzes the relationships between events, supplies, and mileage. Yet this is a quantitative, artificial reality with no hint of the lived reality. The simulation, in fact, represents an abstract world of algorithmic logic. Historical logic is incapable of being represented. It would be more justifiable to say that winning here (i.e., solving the problem) is more the result of looking for patterns among the numbers than developing a sense of history. *The simulation is simply a well-disguised numbers game.*

One might object to the foregoing discussion on a number of grounds:

1. The algorithmic logic of simulations does in fact parallel a similar logic in *some* content areas (such as mathematics) so that computer simulations have a place in education.
2. All learning proceeds from the known to the unknown (and from the simple to the complex) so that simulations are a stepping stone to life.
3. Persons can learn to become autonomous inquirers within the limitations of a safe and simple artificial reality—a skill that they can later use in real life.

Each of these objections has an intuitive appeal and therefore warrants our attention.

The first objection is easy to handle. It is certainly the case that many real-world activities contain the same logical and procedural structure that is found in the realm of computation. Learning to subtract can be modelled in a computer program because procedural rules are all there is to the *process* of subtraction. But does it tell you about the *reasons* for subtracting?

Brown and Burton have developed an "intelligent" computer tutor that recognizes more than ninety ways to make a mistake during subtraction.[94] This is certainly a very sophisticated approach and may be very useful in some cases. However, it only elaborates the procedures surrounding subtraction. A logical positivist would say: fine, that's all there is to subtraction. A trainer might also say: fine, this will help establish the automaticity of the subtraction skill more efficiently. But an educator would say: wait a minute—subtraction is not an isolated, decontextualized skill. At a minimum, it should lead to competence in *using* subtraction with real-world problems. At a maximum, it should lead to mathematical understanding. In both cases, it should be

305

connected to experiences that ultimately generate personal expertise, involving judgments as well as calculations. As Dreyfus and Dreyfus conclude:

> At the higher stages of skill acquisition, even if there are rules underlying expertise, the rules that the expert has access to are not the rules that generate his expertise . . . [Hence], trying to find rules or procedures in a domain often stands in the way of learning *even at the earliest stages.*[95] (Emphasis added.)

Developing procedure-following skills, therefore, does *not* facilitate broader learning. This argument applies even more for nonprocedural kinds of expertise and understanding (e.g., historical expertise and understanding).

The second objection is more difficult to handle: all learning proceeds from the known to the unknown and from the simple to the complex. But we have to define simple in a way that does not prejudge the *nature* of the complex. This problem is a perennial concern in the philosophy of science: should we base our scientific concepts on our intuitions and lived experiences, or should we base them on counterintuitive conceptual constructions that happen to fit empirical facts?[96] This problem emerges in education in a number of forms. For example, in science education, should we teach young children to be Aristotelians before Newtonians—let alone, before Einsteinians?[97]

In the context of this discussion, is a simple, context-free, quantitative, and procedural simulation *ever* an adequate preparation for a complex, contextual, qualitative, and nonprocedural lived experience?[98] If we wanted to prepare children to understand and deal with the real world, should we not develop simple learning situations *of the same kind* as those they will later encounter in a more complex form? Is not problem solving, in fact, domain specific regardless how high-level the activity?[99] Using computers to develop problem-solving skills, however, establishes a dichotomy between "*simple* artificial reality" and "*complex* natural reality." Notice that the *artificial-natural* dimension of the above dichotomy is usually hidden in the debate on the matter.[100] Learning to program the computer may therefore *not* be the best way to prepare children for real life.

The final objection is the most difficult to answer: can persons develop analytical and inquiry skills within the limitations of a computational environment that can then be used in real life? After all, analytical and inquiry skills are very general and more like "frames of mind" than simple procedures.[101] The question can be reformulated, however, to reveal what has been hidden: are the analytical and inquiry skills developed within a noncontextual, nondialectical, and judgment-free computational environment useful within a lived environment that requires tolerance for ambiguity, interpersonal construction of new meanings, dialectical thinking, the acceptability of incomplete solutions, and judgment-based actions? A positive answer is now doubtful. The reason is twofold: the computer embodies a technological framework that crowds out other forms of conceptualizing and understanding problems; yet thinking is only ever thinking *about* something. Hence, mature analysis and inquiry can only be the result of a history of dealing with similar *kinds* of things. Flight simulators work so well for this reason—both the simulation and the real-world event are controlled by the same kinds of procedures.

A final answer to the third objection remains to be seen. It does seem, however, that the computer restricts our rational life to utilitarian, problem-solving skills. Although such skills are under our control, they have delegitimized other ways of knowing. Saying that such skills display "intelligence" does not help either because intelligence itself has been redefined in a restricted manner. As Broughton laments,

> one can measure the educational impact of computers, and particularly of learning to program them, in terms of what is lost in the process. To the curriculum is lost the arts and the humanities. To pedagogy is lost the hermeneutic art and language that allows us to ask about the meaning of things and of life, to interpret them in their many and various cultural horizons. To both is lost the self and the autonomous capacity to examine critically what we interpret.[102]

Hence, although problem-solving with a computer appears more desirable and high level than computerized drill and practice, programming still limits us to the technological framework. It is, therefore, a more subtle form of behavioral learning technology, done with the active consent and participation of the learner. It represents, as one author has called it, the "industrialization of intellectual work."[103] This is particularly disturbing because programming (as well as drill-and-practice and tutorial courseware) is being introduced to children in their most plastic and formative years.[104]

Summary of Computers as Intellectual Tools

Computers do help us develop a limited personal intellectual agency by forcing us to structure information in precise, systematic ways and specify logical operations for that information. However, this agency only develops within the computational domain. Hence, we are left with an underdeveloped intellectual agency within the qualitative, dialectical, and experiential domain of natural and social events. Learning to program is therefore only a good way to learn and think about procedural problems—although even here there are some limitations.

The root of the difficulty seems to reside in the nature of computer languages: the expressive potential of computer languages only extends over the syntactical dimension of computer operations. This contrasts sharply with the expressive potential of natural languages which extend over the aesthetic, metaphoric, artistic, affective, and moral domains. Why cannot these various languages coexist? The answer boils down to this: computer languages are part of a technological framework that, when applied to a number of problems, delegitimizes other frameworks. We are then left with a very restricted mental landscape.

Conclusion

Each of the three major approaches to the use of computers in education has serious limitations. The drill-and-practice approach was shown to embody a deterministic, behavioral technology that turned learning into a systematically designed and quality-controlled form of work. Although intended only to supplement instruction, they, in fact, introduced a technological framework into the classroom culture that mitigated against nonbehavioral educational goals. Computerized tutorial programs were shown to extend these limitations. That is, interactions in tutorial courseware programs are still shaped by an external agent's intentions and still constrained by computable algorithms. Furthermore, the human learner is treated as a means toward someone else's ends and only given a form of pseudocontrol in the interaction. Most seriously, computerized tutorial interactions preempted personal intellectual agency and ultimately inner-directed learning. Finally, the use of computer programming and simulations in education was shown to limit the learner's mental landscape to objective, quantitative, declarative, and procedural intellectual tools. This left the learner with an underdeveloped intellectual agency within the qualitative, dialectical, and experiential domains of natural and social events.

Each of the approaches described above may have some short-term benefits associated with it. Taken together, however, they represent a shift toward technologizing education. Drill-and-practice courseware programs alter the nature of subskill acquisition, tutorial courseware programs restrict the full range of personal intellectual agency, and computer programming and simulations delegitimize nontechnological ways of learning and thinking about problems. Is this worth the price?

Notes

1. Henry J. Becker, *School Uses of Microcomputers: Reports from a National Survey* (Baltimore, Md.: Center for Social Organization of Schools, Johns Hopkins University, 1983, 1985).

2. Michael W. Apple, *Education and Power* (Boston: Routledge & Kegan Paul, 1982).

3. Andrew R. Molnar, "The Next Great Crisis in American Education: Computer Literacy," *Journal of Educational Technology Systems* 7 (1972).

4. Douglas Sloan, "On Raising Critical Questions About the Computer in Education," *Teachers College Record* 85, 4 (1984).

5. Jürgen Habermas, *The Theory of Communicative Action. Vol. 1. Reason and the Rationalization of Society* (Boston: Beacon, 1984).

6. Walter J. Ong, *Orality and Literacy: The Technologizing of the Word* (New York: Methuen, 1982).

7. Peter L. Berger and Thomas Luckmann, *The Social Construction of Reality* (New York: Doubleday, 1966).

8. Maxine Greene, "Literacy for What?" *Phi Delta Kappan* 63, 5 (1982).

9. Theodore Roszak, *The Cult of Information* (New York: Pantheon, 1986).

10. Hans G. Furth, *Piaget and Knowledge: Theoretical Foundations* (Englewood Cliffs, N.J.: Prentice-Hall, 1969).

11. Alfred North Whitehead, *The Aims of Education and Other Essays* (New York: Free Press, 1967).

12. Kurt Godel, *On Formally Undecidable Propositions in "Principia Mathematicia" and Related Systems*, R. B. Braithwaite, ed., B. Meltzer, trans. (New York: Basic, 1962).

13. Michael W. Apple, "The Adequacy of Systems Management Procedures in Education," in Ralph A. Smith, ed., *Regaining Educational Leadership* (New York: Wiley, 1975).

14. Jacques Ellul, "The Power of Technique and the Ethics of Non-Power," in Kathleen Woodward, ed., *The Myths of Information* (Madison, Wisc.: Coda, 1980).

15. Ann Berlak and Harold Berlak, *The Dilemmas of Schooling* (New York: Methuen, 1981).

16. Patrick Suppes, "The Uses of Computers in Education," *Scientific American* 215, 3 (1966).

17. David F. Salisbury, "Cognitive Psychology and Its Implications for Designing Drill-and-Practice Programs for Computers," presented at the annual meeting of the *American Educational Research Association*, New Orleans, April 1984.

18. Robert M. Gagne, Walter Wagner, and A. Rojas, "Planning and Authorizing Computer-Assisted Instruction Lessons," *Educational Technology* 21 (1981).

19. J. Richard Dennis, "The Question-Episode: Building Block of Teaching with a Computer," *The Illinois Series on Educational Applications of Computers*, vol. 4e (Urbana, Ill.: College of Education, University of Illinois, 1979).

20. B. F. Skinner, *The Technology of Teaching* (Englewood Cliffs, N.J.: Prentice-Hall, 1968).

21. Hubert L. Dreyfus and Stuart E. Dreyfus, "Putting Computers in Their Proper Place: Intuition in the Classroom," *Teachers College Record* 85, 4 (1984).

22. Benjamin S. Bloom, *Human Characteristics and School Learning* (New York: McGraw-Hill, 1976).

23. Robert Barr and Robert Dreeben, "Instruction in Classrooms," in Lee Shulman, ed., *Review of Research in Education*, Vol. 5 (Ithaca, Ill.: F. E. Peacock, 1978).

24. Ted Nunan, *Countering Educational Design* (New York: Nichols, 1983).

25. Harry F. Wolcott, *Teachers Versus Technocrats* (Eugene: University of Oregon Press, 1977).

26. Apple, *Education and Power*, op. cit.

27. Bloom, op. cit.

28. J. O. Bolvin, "Classroom Organization," in Harold E. Mitzel, ed., *Encyclopedia of Educational Research, 5th Edition*, vol. 1 (New York: Macmillan, 1982).

29. Lee J. Cronbach and Richard E. Snow, *Aptitudes and Instructional Methods* (New York: Irvington, 1977).

30. Steven Lukes, *Individualism* (Oxford: Basil Blackwell, 1973).

31. Fred S. Keller, "Goodbye, Teacher," *Journal of Applied Behavior Analysis* 1, 1 (1968).

32. Skinner, op. cit.

33. Michael Scriven, "Problems and Prospects for Individualization," in Harriet Talmade, ed., *Systems of Individualized Education* (Berkeley, Calif.: McCutchan, 1975).

34. G. M. Boyd, "Four Ways of Providing Computer-Assisted Learning and Their Probable Impacts," *Computers and Education* 6 (1983).

35. Raymond E. Callahan, *Education and the Cult of Efficiency* (Chicago: University of Chicago Press, 1962).

36. Dennis L. Carlson, "'Updating' Individualism and the Work Ethic: Corporate Logic in the Classroom," *Curriculum Inquiry* 12, 2 (1982).

37. Victor Bunderson, "Courseware," in Harold F. O'Neil Jr., ed., *Computer-Based Instruction: A State of the Art Assessment* (New York: Academic Press, 1981).

38. David A. Kolb, *Experiential Learning: Experience as the Source of Learning and Development* (Englewood Cliffs, N.J.: Prentice-Hall, 1984).

39. Dreyfus and Dreyfus, op. cit.

40. Bunderson, op. cit.

41. Elliot W. Eisner, *The Educational Imagination* (New York: Macmillan, 1979).

42. Seymour B. Sarason, *The Culture of the School and the Problem of Change*, 2d ed. (Boston: Allyn and Bacon, 1982).

43. Nunan, op. cit.

44. Wolcott, op. cit.

45. Kenneth D. Benne, "Technology and Community: Conflicting Bases of Educational Authority," in Walter Feinberg and Henry Rosemont, Jr., eds., *Work, Technology, and Education* (Urbana: University of Illinois Press, 1975).

46. Philip W. Jackson, *Life in Classrooms* (New York: Holt, Rinehart, & Winston, 1968).

47. Harold F. O'Neil, Jr., and J. Paris, "Introduction and Overview of Computer-Based Instruction," in O'Neil, op. cit.

48. Alfred Bork, "Interactive Learning," in Robert Taylor, ed., *The Computer in the School* (New York: Teachers College Press, 1980).

49. Paulo Freire, *Education for Critical Consciousness* (New York: Seabury, 1973).

50. Alfred Bork, "Preparing Student-Computer Dialogs: Advice to Teachers," in Taylor, op. cit.

51. Tim O'Shea and John Self, *Learning and Teaching with Computers* (Englewood Cliffs, N.J.: Prentice-Hall, 1983).

52. Richard Nisbett and Lee Ross, *Human Inference: Strategies and Shortcomings of Social Judgment*. (Englewood Cliffs, N.J.: Prentice-Hall, 1980).

53. David Hawkins, *The Informed Vision* (New York: Agathon, 1974).

54. Sherry Turkle, *The Second Self* (New York: Simon and Schuster, 1984).

55. Maxine Greene, *Landscapes of Learning* (New York: Teachers College Press, 1978).

56. Ira Shor, *Critical Teaching and Everyday Life* (Boston: South End, 1980).

57. Ben Shneiderman, *Software Psychology* (Cambridge, Mass.: Winthrop, 1980).

58. Bork, "Preparing Student-Computer Dialogs," op. cit.

59. O'Shea and Self, op. cit.

60. Bork, "Preparing Student-Computer Dialogs," op. cit.

61. Ibid.

62. Shneiderman, op. cit.

63. Jacques Ellul, *The Technological System* (New York: Continuum, 1980).

64. Maxine Greene, "The Literacy That Liberates," Tape No. 612–20312. *Association for Supervision and Curriculum Development* (Alexandria, Va.: 1983).

65. Karl E. Scheibe and Margaret Erwin, "The Computer as Alter," *Journal of Social Psychology* 108 (1979).

66. Joseph Weizenbaum, *Computer Power and Human Reason* (San Francisco: W. H. Freeman, 1976).

67. Kenneth A. Strike, "On the Expressive Potential of Behaviorist Language," *American Educational Research Journal* 11, 2 (1974).

68. Ellul, *The Technological System*, op. cit.

69. Fred Newmann and Donald Oliver, "Education and Community," *Harvard Educational Review* 37, 1 (1967).

70. Hubert L. Dreyfus, *What Computers Can't Do*, 2d ed. (New York: Harper & Row, 1979).

71. Marianne Amarel, "The Classroom: An Instructional Setting for Teachers, Students, and the Computer," in Alex C. Wilkinson, ed., *Classroom Computers and Cognitive Science* (New York: Academic Press, 1983).

72. Michael Polanyi, *The Tacit Dimension* (Garden City, N.J.: Doubleday, 1966).

73. Kolb, op. cit.

74. Myron Krueger, *Artificial Reality* (Reading, Mass.: Addison-Wesley, 1983).

75. Whitehead, op. cit.

76. Greene, *Landscape of Learning*, op. cit.

77. Seymour Papert, *Mindstorms* (New York: Basic, 1980).

78. Margot Critchfield, "Beyond CAI: Computers as Personal Intellectual Tools," *Educational Technology* 19, 10 (1979).

79. Jerome S. Bruner, "Language as an Instrument of Thought," in Alan Davies, ed., *Problems of Language and Learning* (London: Heineman, 1975).

80. K. Iverson, "Notation as a Tool for Thought," *Communications of the ACM* 23 (1980).

81. Zenon W. Pylyshyn, *Computation and Cognition* (Cambridge, Mass.: M.I.T. Press, 1984).

82. Abbe Mowshowitz, *The Conquest of Will* (Reading, Mass.: Addison-Wesley, 1976).

83. Strike, op. cit.

84. James M. Broughton, "Computer Literacy as Political Socialization," presented at the annual meeting of the American Educational Research Association, New Orleans, April, 1984.

85. Polanyi, op. cit.

86. Broughton, op. cit.

87. Arthur Luehrmann, "Computer Literacy: What Should It Be?" *Mathematics Teacher* 74, 9 (1981).

88. Papert, op. cit.

89. R. D. Pea and D. M. Kurland, "On the Cognitive Effects of Learning Computer Programming," *Bank Street Technical Report #18* (New York: Bank Street College, 1983).

90. Marion C. Linn, "The Cognitive Consequences of Programming Instruction in Classrooms," *Educational Researcher* 14, 5 (1985).

91. Luehrmann, op. cit.

92. A. P. Ershov, "Aesthetics and the Human Factor in Programming," *Datamation* 18, 9 (1981).

93. David Grady, "What Every Teacher Should Know about Computer Simulations," *Learning* 11, 8 (1983).

94. John S. Brown and Richard S. Burton, "Diagnostic Model for Procedural Bugs in Basic Mathematical Skills," *Cognitive Science* 2 (1979).

95. Dreyfus and Dreyfus, op. cit.

96. Thomas S. Kuhn, *The Structure of Scientific Revolutions* (Chicago: University of Chicago Press, 1962).

97. A. DiSessa, "Unlearning Aristotelian Physics: A Study of Knowledge-Based Learning," *Cognitive Science* 6, 1 (1982).

98. Jacquetta Megarry, "Thinking, Learning, and Educating: The Role of the Computer," in Jacquetta Megarry et al., *World Yearbook of Education, 1982/83: Computers and Education* (New York: Kogan Page, 1983).

99. Allen Newell and Herbert A. Simon, *Human Problem Solving* (Englewood Cliffs, N.J.: Prentice-Hall, 1972).

100. Douglas D. Noble, "Computer Literacy and Ideology," *Teachers College Record* 85, 4 (1984).

101. Michael J. Streibel, "Beyond Computer Literacy: Analytical Skills, Inquiry Skills, and Personal Empowerment," *T.H.E. Journal* (June 1985).

102. Broughton, op. cit.

103. Ershow, op. cit.

104. Harriet K. Cuffaro, "Microcomputers in the Classroom: Why Is Earlier Better?" *Teachers College Record* 85, 4 (1985).

SIXTEEN

Teaching and Technology: The Hidden Effects of Computers on Teachers and Students

Michael W. Apple

Many of the western industrialized nations are facing extensive structural crises in the economy, in authority relations, in values. The symptoms are visible everywhere—in the very high under- and unemployment rates now plaguing us, in the fear that the United States, for example, is losing its edge in international competition, in the calls for sacrifices by labor and for greater work discipline, and in the seemingly widespread belief that "our" standards are falling. The analyses of these crises have not been limited just to our economic institutions. Commentators and critics have spent a good deal of time focusing on the family and especially on the school. Economically and politically powerful groups have, in fact, been relatively successful in shifting the blame for all of the above-mentioned problems *from* the economy *to* institutions such as schools. That is where the real problem lies or so it is said. Thus, if we could solve the problems of education, we could solve these other problems as well. Change the "competencies" of our teachers and students, and all else will tend to fall into place naturally.

Documents such as *A Nation at Risk* and others have pointed to a crisis in teaching and in education in general. Among the many recommendations these reports make is greater stress on the "new technology." The crisis in schools and teaching, they admit, is complicated and widespread, but one step toward a solution is the rapid introduction of computers into schools. The emphasis on computers is quite strong. It is singled out for special attention in nearly all of the national documents, especially those that are responding to the larger social and economic problems we are now experiencing. This will give our students new skills, skills that are necessary in the international competition for markets and jobs. It will also necessitate and create a more technically knowledgeable teaching force (hence the proposals in many states to mandate computer literacy for all students now in teacher education programs). It will also eliminate much of the drudgery of teaching and make the tasks of teaching more interesting and creative. Will it?

The Politics of Technology

In our society, technology is seen as an autonomous process. It is set apart and viewed as if it had a life of its own, independent of social intentions, power, and privilege. We examine technology as if it was something constantly changing and as something that is constantly altering our lives in schools and elsewhere. This is partly true, of course, and is fine as far as it goes. However, by focusing on what is changing and being changed, we may neglect to ask what relationships are remaining the same. Among the most important of these are the sets of cultural and economic inequalities that dominate even societies like our own.[1]

By thinking of technology in this way, by closely examining whether the changes associated with "technological progress" are really changes in certain relationships after all, we can begin to ask political questions about their causes and especially their multitudinous effects. Whose idea of progress? Progress for what? And fundamentally, who benefits?[2] These questions may seem rather weighty ones to be asking about schools and the curricular and teaching practices that now go on in them or are being proposed. Yet, we are in the midst of one of those many educational bandwagons that governments, industry, and others so like to ride. This wagon is pulled in the direction of a technological workplace, and carries a heavy load of computers as its cargo.

The growth of the new technology in schools is definitely not what one would call a slow movement. In one recent year, a 56 percent increase was reported in the use of computers in schools in the United States and even this may be a conservative estimate. Of the 25,642 schools surveyed, more than 15,000 schools reported some computer usage.[3] In the United States alone, it is estimated that in excess of 350,000 microcomputers have been introduced into the public schools in the past four years.[4] This is a trend that shows no sign of abating. Nor is this phenomenon only limited to the United States. France, Canada, England, Australia, and many other countries have "recognized the future." At its center seems to sit a machine with a keyboard and a screen.

I say "at its center," because in both government agencies and in schools themselves the computer and the new technology have been seen as something of a savior economically and pedagogically. "High tech" will save declining economies and will save our students and teachers in schools. In the latter, it is truly remarkable how wide a path the computer is now cutting.

The expansion of its use, the tendency to see all areas of education as a unified terrain for the growth in use of new technologies, can be seen in a two-day workshop on integrating the microcomputer into the classroom held at my own university, the University of Wisconsin. Among the topics covered were computer applications in writing instruction, in music education, in secondary science and mathematics, in primary language arts, for the handicapped, for teacher recordkeeping and management, in business education, in health occupation training programs, in art, and in social studies. To this is added a series of sessions on the "electronic office," how technology and automation are helping industry, and how we all can "transcend the terror" of technology.[5]

Two things are evident from this list. First, vast areas of school life are now seen to be within the legitimate purview of technological restructuring. Second, a partly hidden but exceptionally close linkage is seen between computers in schools and the needs of management for automated industries, electronic offices, and "skilled" personnel. Thus, recognizing both what is happening inside and outside of schools and the connections between these areas is critical to any understanding of what is likely to happen with the new technologies, especially the computer, in education.

As I have argued elsewhere, all too often educational debates are increasingly limited to technical issues. Questions of "how to" have replaced questions of "why."[6] In this chapter, I want to reverse this tendency. Rather than dealing with what the best way might be to establish closer ties between the technological requirements of the larger society and our formal institutions of education, I want to step back and raise a different set of questions. I want us to consider a number of rather difficult political, economic, and ethical issues about some of the tendencies in schools and the larger society that may make us want to be very cautious about the current technological bandwagon in education. In so doing, a range of areas must be examined: Behind the slogans of technological progress and high-tech industry, what are some of the real effects of the new technology on the future labor market? What may happen to teaching and curriculum if we do not think carefully about the new technology's place in the classroom? Will the growing focus on technological expertise, particularly computer literacy, equalize or further exacerbate the lack of social opportunities for our most disadvantaged students?

At root, my claim will be that the debate about the role of the new technology in society and in schools is not and must not be just about the technical correctness of what computers can and cannot do. These may be the least important kinds of questions, in fact. At the very core of the debate instead are the ideological and ethical issues concerning what schools should be about and whose interests they should serve.[7] The question of interests is very important in contemporary society because, due to the severe problems currently besetting economies like our own, a restructuring of what schools are *for* has reached a rather advanced stage.

Thus, while a relatively close connection has always existed between the two, an even closer relationship now exists between the curriculum in our schools and corporate needs.[8] In a number of countries, educational officials and policy makers, legislators, curriculum workers, and others have been subject to immense pressure to make the "needs" of business and industry the primary goals of the school system. Economic and ideological pressures have become rather intense and often very overt. The language of efficiency, production, standards, cost effectiveness, job skills, work discipline, and so on—all defined by powerful groups and always threatening to become the dominant way we think about schooling[9]—has begun to push aside concerns for a democratic curriculum, teacher autonomy, and class, gender, and race equality. Yet, we cannot fully understand the implications of the new technology in this restructuring unless we gain a more complete idea of what industry is now doing not only in the schools but in the economy as well.

Technological Myths and Economic Realities

Let us look at the larger society first. Some claim that the technological needs of the economy are such that unless we have a technologically literate labor force we will ultimately become outmoded economically. But what will this labor force actually look like?

A helpful way of thinking about this is to use the concepts of increasing *proletarianization* and *deskilling* of jobs. These concepts signify a complex historical process in which the control of labor has altered, one in which the skills workers have developed over many years are broken down and reduced to their atomistic units, automated, and redefined by management to enhance profit levels, efficiency, and control. In the process, the employee's control of timing, over defining the most appropriate way to do a task, and over criteria that establish acceptable performance are slowly taken over as the prerogatives of management personnel who are usually divorced from the place

317

where the actual labor is performed. Loss of control by the worker is almost always the result. Pay is often lowered. And the job itself becomes routinized, boring, and alienating as conception is separated from execution and more and more aspects of jobs are rationalized to bring them into line with management's need for a tighter economic and ideological ship.[10] Finally, and very importantly, many of these jobs may simply disappear.

Undoubtedly, the rapid developments in, say, microelectronics, genetic engineering and associated "biological technologies," and other high-tech areas are in fact partly transforming work in a large number of sectors in the economy. This may lead to economic prosperity in certain sections of our population, but its other effects may be devastating. Thus, as the authors of a recent study that examined the impact of new technologies on the future labor market demonstrate:

> This transformation . . . may stimulate economic growth and competition in the world marketplace, but it will displace thousands of workers and could sustain high unemployment for many years. It may provide increased job opportunities for engineers, computer operators, and robot technicians, but it also promises to generate an even greater number of low level, service jobs such as those of janitors, cashiers, clericals, and food service workers. And while many more workers will be using computers, automated office equipment, and other sophisticated technical devices in their jobs, the increased use of technology may actually reduce the skills and discretion required to perform many jobs.[11]

Let us examine this scenario in greater detail.

Rumberger and Levin make a very useful distinction for this discussion. They differentiate between high-tech industries and high-tech occupations—in essence between what is made and the kinds of jobs these goods require. High-tech industries that manufacture technical devices such as computers, electronic components, and the like currently employ fewer than 15 percent of the paid work force in the United States and other industrialized nations. Just as importantly, a substantial knowledge of technology is required by *fewer than one-fourth* of all occupations within these industries. On the contrary, the largest share of jobs created by high-tech industries are in areas such as clerical and office work or in production and assembly. These actually pay below-average wages.[12] Yet this is not all. High-tech occupations that do require considerable skill—such as computer specialists and engineers—may indeed expand. However, most of these occupations actually "employ relatively few workers compared to many traditional clerical and service fields."[13] Rumberger and Levin summarize a number of these points by stating that "although the percentage growth rate of occupational employment in such high technology fields as engineering and computer programming was higher than the overall growth rate of jobs, far more jobs would be created in low-skilled clerical and service occupations than in high-technology ones."[14]

Some of these claims are supported by the following data. It is estimated that even being generous in one's projections, only 17 percent of new jobs that will be created between now and 1995 will be in high-tech industries. (Less generous and more restrictive projections argue that only 3 to 8 percent of future jobs will be in such industries.)[15] As I noted, though, such jobs will not all be equal. Clerical workers, secretaries, assemblers, warehouse personnel, etc., will comprise the largest percentage of occupations within the industry. If we take the electronic components industry as an example here, this is made much clearer. Engineering, science, and computing occupations constituted approximately 15 percent of all workers in this industry. The majority of the rest of the workers were engaged in low-wage assembly work. Thus, in the late 1970s, nearly two-thirds of all workers in the electronic components industry took home hourly wages "that placed them in the bottom third of the national distribution."[16] If we take the archetypical high-tech industry—computer and data processing—and analyze its labor market, we get similar results. In 1980, technologically oriented and skilled jobs accounted for only 26 percent of the total.[17]

These figures have considerable weight, but they are made even more significant by the fact that many of those 26 percent may themselves experience a deskilling process in the near future. That is, the reduction of jobs to simpler, atomistic components, the separation of conception from execution, and so on—processes that have had such a major impact on the labor process of blue, pink, and white color workers in so many other areas—are now advancing into high-technology jobs as well. Computer programming provides an excellent example. New developments in software packages and machine language and design have meant that a considerable portion of the job of programming now requires little more than performing "standard, routine, machine-like tasks that require little in-depth knowledge."[18]

What does this mean for the activities of schooling and the seemingly widespread belief that the future world of work will require increasing technical competence on the part of all students? Consider the occupations that will contribute the most number of jobs not just in high-tech industries but throughout the society by 1995. Economic forecasts indicate that these will include building custodians, cashiers, secretaries, office clerks, nurses, waiters and waitresses, elementary school teachers, truck drivers, and other health care workers such as nurses aides and orderlies.[19] None of these are directly related to high technology. Excluding teachers and nurses, none of them require any postsecondary education. (Their earnings will be approximately 30 percent below the current average earnings of workers, as well.)[20] If we go further than this and examine an even larger segment of expected new jobs by including the forty job categories that will probably account for about one-half of all the jobs that will be created, only about 25 percent will require people with a college degree.[21]

In many ways, this is strongly related to the effects of the new technology on the job market and the labor process in general. Skill levels will be raised in some areas, but will decline in many others, as will jobs themselves decline. For instance, "a recent study of robotics in the United States suggests that robots will eliminate 100,000 to 200,000 jobs by 1990, while creating 32,000 to 64,000 jobs."[22] My point about declining skill requirements is made nicely by Rumberger and Levin. As they suggest, while it is usually assumed that workers will need computer programming and other sophisticated skills because of the greater use of technology such as computers in their jobs, the ultimate effect of such technology may be somewhat different. "A variety of evidence suggests just the opposite: as machine become more sophisticated, with expanded memories, more computational ability, and sensory capabilities, the knowledge required to use the devices declines."[23] The effect of these trends on the division of labor will be felt for decades. But it will be in the sexual division of labor where it will be even more extreme. Historically, *women's work* has been subject to these processes in very powerful ways; consequently, we will see increased proletarianization and deskilling of women's labor and, undoubtedly, a further increase in the feminization of poverty.[24]

These points clearly have implications for our educational programs. We need to think much more rigorously about what they mean for our transition from school to work programs, especially because many of the "skills" that schools are currently teaching are transitory because the jobs themselves are being transformed (or lost) by new technological developments and new management offensives.

Take office work, for example. In offices, the bulk of the new technology has not been designed to enhance the quality of the job for the largest portion of the employees (usually women clerical workers). Rather, it has usually been designed and implemented in such a way that exactly the opposite will result. Instead of generating work that is stimulating and satisfying, the technology is there to make managers' jobs "easier," to eliminate jobs and cut costs, to divide work into routine and atomized tasks, and to more easily accomplish administrative control.[25] The vision of the future society seen in the microcosm of the office is inherently undemocratic and perhaps increasingly authoritarian. Is this what we wish to prepare our students for? Surely, our task as educators is neither to accept such a future labor market and labor process uncritically nor to have our students accept such practices uncritically as well. To do so is simply to allow the values of a limited but powerful segment of the population to work through us. It may be good business but I have my doubts about whether it is ethically correct educational policy.

In summary, then, what we will witness is the creation of enhanced jobs for a relative few and deskilled and boring work for the majority. Furthermore, even those boring and deskilled jobs will be increasingly hard to find. Take office work, again, an area that is rapidly being transformed by the new technology. It is estimated that between one and five jobs will be lost for every new computer terminal that is introduced.[26] Yet this situation will not be limited to office work. Even those low-paying assembly positions noted earlier will not necessarily be found in the industrialized nations with their increasingly service-oriented economies. Given the international division of labor, and what is called "capital flight," a large portion of these jobs will be moved to countries such as the Philippines and Indonesia.[27]

This is exacerbated considerably by the fact that many governments now find "acceptable" those levels of unemployment that would have been considered a crisis a decade ago. "Full employment" in the United States is now often seen as between 7 and 8 percent *measured* unemployment. (The actual figures are much higher, of course, especially among minority groups and workers who can only get parttime jobs.) This is a figure that is *double* that of previous economic periods. Even higher rates are now seen as "normal" in other countries. The trend is clear. The future will see fewer jobs. Many of those that are created will not be fulfilling, nor will they pay well. Finally, the level of technical skill will continue to be lowered for a large portion of them.[28]

Because of this, we need convincing answers to some very important questions about our future society and the economy before we turn our schools into the "production plants" for creating new workers. *Where* will these new jobs be? *How many* will be created? Will they *equal* the number of positions lost in offices, factories, and service jobs in retailing, banks, telecommunications, and elsewhere? Are the bulk of the jobs that will be created relatively unskilled, less than meaningful, and themselves subject to the inexorable logics of management so that they too will probably be automated out of existence?[29]

These are not inconsequential questions. Before we give the schools over to the requirements of the new technology and the corporation, we must be very certain that it will benefit all of us, not mostly those who already possess economic and cultural power. This requires continued democratic discussion, not a quick decision based on the economic and political pressure now being placed on schools.

Much more could be said about the future labor market. I urge the interested reader to pursue it in greater depth because it will have a profound impact on our school policies and programs, especially in vocational areas, in working-class schools, and among programs for young women. The difficulties with the high-tech vision that permeates the beliefs of the proponents of a technological solution will not remain outside the school door, however. Similar disproportionate benefits and dangers await us inside our educational institutions as well and it is to this that I now turn.

Inequality and The Technological Classroom

Once we go inside the school, a set of questions concerning "who benefits?" also arises. We need to ask about what may be happening to teachers and students given the emphasis now being placed on computers in schools. I will not talk about the individual teacher or student here. Obviously, some teachers will find their jobs enriched by the new technology and some students will find hidden talents and will excell in a computer-oriented classroom. What we need to ask instead (or at least before we deal with the individual) is what may happen to classrooms, teachers, and students differentially. Once again, I seek to raise a set of issues that may not be easy to solve, but cannot be ignored if we are to have a truly democratic educational system in more than name only.

While I have dealt with this in greater detail in *Ideology and Curriculum* and *Education and Power*,[30] let briefly situate the growth of the technologized classroom into what seems to be occurring to teaching and curriculum in general. Currently, considerable pressure is building to have teaching and school curricula be totally prespecified and tightly controlled for the purposes of "efficiency," "cost effectiveness," and "accountability." In many ways, the deskilling that is affecting jobs in general is now having an impact on teachers as more and more decisions are moving out of their hands and as their jobs become even more difficult to do. This is more advanced in some countries than others, but it is clear that the movement to rationalize and control the act of teaching and the content and evaluation of the curriculum is very real.[31] Even in those countries that have made strides away from centralized examination systems, powerful inspectorates and supervisors, and tightly controlled curricula, an identifiable tendency is found to move back toward state control. Many reforms have only a very tenuous hold currently. This is in part due to economic difficulties and partly due as well to the importing of American styles and techniques of educational management, styles and techniques that have their roots in industrial bureaucracies and have almost never had democratic aims.[32] Even though a number of teachers may support computer-oriented curricula, an emphasis on the new technology needs to be seen in this context of the rationalization of teaching and curricula in general.

322

Given these pressures, what will happen to teachers if the new technology is accepted uncritically? One of the major effects of the current (over)emphasis on computers in the classroom may be the deskilling and depowering of a considerable number of teachers. Given the already heavy workload of planning, teaching, participating in meetings, and completing paperwork for most teachers, and given the expense, it is probably wise to assume that the largest proportion of teachers will not be given more than a very small amount of training in computers, their social effects, programming, and so on. This will be the case especially at the primary and elementary school level where most teachers are already teaching a wide array of subject areas. Research indicates, in fact, that few teachers in any district are actually given substantial information before computer curricula are implemented. Often only one or two teachers are the "resident experts."[33] Because of this, most teachers have to rely on prepackaged sets of material, existing software, and specially purchased material from any of the scores of software manufacturing firms that are springing up in a largely unregulated way.

The impact of this can be striking. What is happening is the exacerbation of trends we have begun to see in a number of nations. Rather than teachers having the time and the skill to do their own curriculum planning and deliberation, they become isolated executors of someone else's plans, procedures, and evaluation mechanisms. In industrial terms, this is very close to what I noted in my previous discussion of the labor process, the separation of conception from execution.[34]

The question of time looms larger here, especially in gender terms. Because of the large amount of time it takes to become a "computer expert" and because of the patriarchal relations that still dominate many families, *men teachers* will often be able to use "computer literacy" to advance their own careers while women teachers will tend to remain the recipients of prepackaged units on computers or "canned" programs over which they have little control.

In her excellent ethnographic study of the effects of the introduction of a districtwide computer literacy program on the lives of teachers, Susan Jungck makes exactly this point about what happened in one middle school.

> The condition of time [needs to] be examined in terms of gender differences because it was the women teachers, not the men, in the Math Department who were unprepared to teach about computers and they were the ones most dependent on the availability of the [canned] Unit. Typically, the source of computer literacy for in-service teachers is either college or university courses, school district courses or independent study, all options that take considerable time outside of school. Both [male teachers] had taken a substantial number of university courses on computers in education. Many [of the] women, [because of] child care and household responsibilities . . . , or women who are single parents . . . , have

relatively less out of school time to take additional coursework and prepare new curricula. Therefore, when a new curriculum such as computer literacy is required, women teachers may be more dependent on using the ready-made curriculum materials than most men teachers.[35]

The reliance on prepackaged software can have a number of long-term effects. First, it can cause a decided loss of important skills and dispositions on the part of teachers. When the skills of local curriculum planning, individual evaluation, and so on are not used, they atrophy. The tendency to look outside of one's own or one's colleagues' historical experience about curriculum and teaching is lessened as considerably more of the curriculum, and the teaching and evaluative practices that surround it, are viewed as something one purchases. In the process—and this is very important—the school itself is transformed into a lucrative market. The industrialization of the school I talked of previously is complemented, then, by further opening up the classroom to the mass-produced commodities of industry. In many ways, it will be a publisher's and salesperson's delight. Whether students' educational experiences will markedly improve is open to question.

The issue of the relationship of purchased software and hardware to the possible deskilling and depowering of teachers does not end here, though. The problem is made even more difficult by the rapidity with which software developers have constructed and marketed their products. There is no guarantee that the mass of such material has any major educational value. Exactly the opposite is often the case. One of the most knowledgeable government officials has put it this way. "High-quality educational software is almost nonexistent in our elementary and secondary schools."[36] While perhaps overstating his case to emphasize his points, the director of software evaluation for one of the largest school systems in the United States has concluded that of the more than 10,000 programs available, approximately 200 are educationally significant.[37]

To their credit, the fact that this is a serious problem is recognized by most computer enthusiasts, and reviews and journals have attempted to deal with it. However, the sheer volume of material, the massive amounts of money spent on advertising software in professional publications, at teachers' and administrators' meetings, and so on, the utter "puffery" of the claims made about much of this material, and the constant pressure by industry, government, parents, some school personnel, and others to institute computer programs in schools *immediately*, all of this makes it nearly impossible to do more than make a small dent in the problem. As one educator put it, "There's a lot of junk out there."[38] The situation is not made any easier by the fact that teachers simply do not now have the time to evaluate thoroughly the educational strengths and weaknesses of a considerable portion of the *existing* curricular material and texts before they are used. Adding one more element, and a sizeable one at that, to be evaluated only increases the load. Teachers' work is increasingly becoming what students of the labor process call *intensified*. More and more needs to be done; less and less time is available to do it.[39] Thus, one has little choice but to simply buy ready-made material, in this way continuing a trend in which all of the important curricular elements are not locally produced but purchased from commercial sources whose major aim may be profit, not necessarily educational merit.[40]

There is a key concept found in Jungck's argument above that is essential here, that of gender. As I have demonstrated in considerable detail in *Teachers and Texts*,[41] teaching—especially at the elementary school level—has been defined as "women's work." We cannot ignore the fact that 87 percent of elementary teachers and 67 percent of teachers overall *are* women. Historically, the introduction of prepackaged or standardized curricula and teaching strategies has often been related to the rationalization and attempt to gain external control of the labor process of women workers. Hence, we cannot completely understand what is happening to teachers—the deskilling, the intensification, the separation of conception from execution, the loss of control, and so on—unless we situate these tendencies into this longer history of what has often happened to occupations that primarily comprise women.[42] Needless to say, this is a critically important point, for only by raising the question of *who* is most often doing the teaching in many of these schools now introducing prepackaged software can we see the connections between the effects of the curricula and the gendered composition of the teaching force.

A significant consideration here, besides the loss of skill and control, is expense. This is at least a three-pronged issue. First, we must recognize that we may be dealing with something of a "zero-sum game." While dropping, the cost of computers is still comparatively high, although some manufacturers may keep purchase costs relatively low, knowing that a good deal of their profits may come from the purchase of software later on or through a home/school connection, something I discuss shortly. This money for the new technology *must come from somewhere*. This is an obvious point but one that is very consequential. In a time of fiscal crisis, where funds are already spared too thinly and necessary programs are being starved in many areas, the addition of computer curricula most often means that money must be drained from one area and given to another. What will be sacrificed? If history is any indication, it may be programs that have benefitted the least advantaged. Little serious attention has been paid to this, but it will become an increasingly serious dilemma.

A second issue of expense concerns staffing patterns, for it is not just the content of teachers' work and the growth of purchased materials that are at stake. Teachers' jobs themselves are on the line here. At a secondary school level in many nations, for example, layoffs of teachers have not been unusual as funding for education is cut. Declining enrollment in some regions has meant a loss of positions as well. This has caused intense competition over students within the school itself. Social studies, art, music, and other subjects must fight it out with newer, more "glamorous" subject areas. To lose the student numbers game for too long is to lose a job. The effect of the computer in this situation has been to increase competitiveness among staff, often to replace substance with both gloss and attractive packaging of courses, and to threaten many teachers with the loss of their livelihood.[43] Is it really an educationally or socially wise decision to tacitly eliminate a good deal of the choices in these other fields so that we can support the "glamor" of a computer future? These are not only financial decisions, but are ethical decisions about teachers' lives and what our students are to be educated about. Given the future labor market, do we really want to claim that computers will be more important than further work in humanities and social sciences or, perhaps even more significantly in working-class and ethnically diverse areas, in the students' own cultural, historical, and political heritage and struggles? Such decisions must not be made by only looking at the accountant's bottom line. These too need to be arrived at by the lengthy democratic deliberation of all parties, including the teachers who will be most affected.

Third, given the expense of microcomputers and software in schools, the pressure to introduce such technology may increase the already wide social imbalances that now exist. Private schools to which the affluent send their children and publicly funded schools in more affluent areas will have more ready access to the technology itself.[44] Schools in inner-city, rural, and poor areas will be largely priced out of the market, even if the cost of "hardware" continues to decline. After all, in these poorer areas and in many public school systems in general in a number of countries, it is already difficult to generate enough money to purchase new textbooks and to cover the costs of teachers' salaries. Thus, the computer and literacy debates and resolutions will "naturally" generate further inequalities. Because, by and large, it will be the top 20 percent of the population that will have computers in their homes[45] and many of the jobs and institutions of higher education their children will be applying for will either ask for or assume "computer skills" as keys of entry or advancement, the impact can be enormous in the long run.

The role of the relatively affluent parent in this situation does not go unrecognized by computer manufacturers.

> Computer companies . . . gear much of their advertising to the educational possibilities of computers. The drive to link particular computers to schools is a

frantic competition. Apple, for example, in a highly touted scheme proposed to "donate" an Apple to every school in America. Issues of philanthropy and intent aside, the clear market strategy is to couple particular computer usages to schools where parents—especially middle-class parents with the economic wherewithal and keen motivation [to ensure mobility]—purchase machines compatible with those in schools. The potentially most lucrative part of such a scheme, however, is not in the purchase of hardware (although this is also substantial) but in the sale of proprietary software.[46]

This very coupling of school and home markets, then, cannot fail to further disadvantage large groups of students. Those students who already have computer backgrounds—be it because of their schools or their homes or both—will proceed more rapidly. The social stratification of life chances will increase. These students' original advantage—one *not* due to "natural ability," but to *wealth*—will be heightened.[47]

We should not be surprised by this, nor should we think it odd that many parents, especially middle-class parents, will pursue a computer future. Computer skills and "literacy" are, in part, strategies for the maintenance of middle-class mobility patterns.[48] Having such expertise in a time of fiscal and economic crisis, is similar to having an insurance policy. It partly guarantees that certain doors remain open in a rapidly changing labor market. In a time of credential inflation, more credentials mean less closed doors.[49]

The credential factor here is of considerable moment. In the past, as gains were made by ethnically different people, working-class groups, women, and others in schooling, one of the latent effects was to raise the credentials required by entire sectors of jobs. Thus, class, race, and gender barriers were partly maintained by an ever-increasing credential inflation. Although this was more of a structural than a conscious process, the effect over time has often been to again disqualify entire segments of a population from jobs, resources, and power. This too may be a latent outcome of the computerization of the school curriculum. Even though, as I have shown, the bulk of new jobs will not require "computer literacy," establishing computer requirements and mandated programs in schools will condemn many people to even greater economic disenfranchisement. Because the requirements are, in many ways, artificial—computer knowledge will not be so very necessary and the number of jobs requiring high levels of expertise will be relatively small—we will simply be affixing one more label to these students. "Functional illiteracy" will simply be broadened to include computers.[50]

Thus, rather than blaming an unequal economy and a situation in which meaningful and fulfilling work is not made available, rather than seeing how the new technology for all its benefits is "creating a growing underclass of displaced and marginal workers," the lack is personalized. It becomes the

327

students' or workers' fault for not being computer literate. One significant social and ideological outcome of computer requirements in schools, then, is that they can serve as a means "to justify those lost lives by a process of mass disqualification, which throws the blame for disenfranchisement in education and employment back on the victims themselves."[51]

Of course, this process may not be visible to many parents of individual children. However, the point does not revolve around the question of individual mobility, but large-scale effects. Parents may see such programs as offering important paths to advancement and some will be correct. However, in a time of severe economic problems, parents tend to overestimate what schools can do for their children.[52] As I documented earlier, there simply will not be sufficient jobs and competition will be intense. The uncritical introduction of and investment in hardware and software will, by and large, hide the reality of the transformation of the labor market and will support those who are already advantaged unless thought is given to these implications now.

Let us suppose, however, that it was important that everyone become computer literate and that these large investments in time, money, and personnel were indeed so necessary for our economic and educational future. Given all this, what is currently happening in schools? Is inequality in access and outcome now being produced? While many educators are continually struggling against these effects, we are already seeing signs of this disadvantagement being created.

There is evidence of class, race, and gender-based differences in computer use. In middle-class schools, for example, the number of computers is considerably more than in working-class or inner-city schools populated by children of color. The ratio of computers to children is almost much higher. This in itself is an unfortunate finding. However, something else must be added here. These more economically advantaged schools not only have more contact hours and more technical and teacher support, but the very manner in which the computer is used is often different than what would be generally found in schools in less advantaged areas. Programming skills, generalizability, a sense of the multitudinous things one can do with computers both within and across academic areas, these tend to be stressed more[53] (although simply drill-and-practice uses are still widespread even here).[54] Compare this to the rote, mechanistic, and relatively low-level uses that tend to dominate the working-class school.[55] These differences are not unimportant, for they signify a ratification of class divisions.

Further evidence to support these claims is now becoming more readily available as researchers dig beneath the glowing claims of a computer future for all children. The differential impact is made clearer in the following figures. In the United States, while more than two-thirds of the schools in affluent areas have computers, only approximately 41 percent of the poorer public schools have them. What one does with the machine is just as important as having one, of course, and here the differences are again very real. One study of poorer elementary schools found that White children were four times more likely than Black children to use computers for programming. Another found that the children of professionals employed computers for programming and for other "creative" uses. Children of nonprofessionals were more apt to use them for drill and practice in mathematics and reading, and for "vocational" work. In general, in fact, "programming has been seen as the purview of the gifted and talented" and of those students who are more affluent. Less affluent students seem to find that the computer is only a tool for drill-and-practice sessions.[56]

Gender differences are also very visible. Two out of every three students currently learning about computers are boys. Even here these data are deceptive because girls "tend to be clustered in the general introductory courses," not the more advanced-level ones.[57] One current analyst summarizes the situation in a very clear manner.

> While stories abound about students who will do just about anything to increase their access to computers, most youngsters working with school computers are [economically advantaged,] white, and male. The ever-growing number of private computer camps, after-school and weekend programs serve middle-class white boys. Most minority [and poor] parents just can't afford to send their children to participate in these programs.[58]

This class, race, and gendered impact will also occur because of traditional school practices such as tracking or streaming. Thus, vocational and business tracks will learn operating skills for word processing and will be primarily filled with (working-class) young women.[59] Academic tracks will stress more general programming abilities and uses and will be disproportionately male.[60] Because computer programs usually have their home bases in mathematics and science in most schools, gender differences can be heightened even more given the often differential treatment of girls in these classes and the ways in which mathematics and science curricula already fulfill "the selective function of the school and contribute to the reproduction of gender differences."[61] While many teachers and curriculum workers have devoted considerable time and effort to equalize both the opportunities and outcomes of female students in mathematics and science (and such efforts are important), the problem still remains a substantive one. It can be worsened by the computerization of these subjects in much the same way as it may have a gendered impact on the teachers themselves.

Toward Social Literacy

We have seen some of the possible negative consequences of the new technology in education, including the deskilling and depowering of teachers and the creation of inequalities through expense, credential inflation, and limitations on access. Yet, the issues surrounding the deskilling process are not limited to teachers. They include the very ways students themselves are taught to think about their education, their future roles in society, and the place of technology in that society. Let me explain what I mean by this.

The new technology is not just an assemblage of machines and their accompanying software. It embodies a *form of thinking* that orients a person to approach the world in a particular way. Computers involve ways of thinking that under current educational conditions are primarily *technical*.[62] The more the new technology transforms the classroom into its own image, the more a technical logic will replace critical political and ethical understanding. The discourse of the classroom will center on technique, and less on substance. Once again "how to" will replace "why," but this time at the level of the student. This situation requires what I call *social*, not *technical*, literacy for all students.

Even if computers make sense technically in all curricular areas and even if all students, not mainly affluent White males, become technically proficient in their use, critical questions of politics and ethics remain to be dealt with in the curriculum. Thus, it is crucial that whenever the new technology is introduced into schools students have a serious understanding of the issues surrounding their larger social effects, many of which I raised earlier.

Unfortunately, this is not often the case. When the social and ethical impacts of computers are dealt with, they are usually addressed in a manner that is less than powerful. One example is provided by a recent proposal for a statewide computer curriculum in one of the larger states in the United States. The objectives that dealt with social questions in the curriculum centered around one particular set of issues. The curriculum states that "the student will be aware of some of the major uses of computers in modern society . . . and the student will be aware of career opportunities related to computers."[63] In most curricula, the technical components of the new technology are stressed. Brief glances are given to the history of computers (occasionally mentioning the role of women in their development, which is at least one positive sign). Yet in this history, the close relationship between military use and computer development is largely absent. "Benign" uses are pointed to, coupled with a less than realistic description of the content and possibility of computer careers and what Douglas D. Noble has called "a gee-whiz glance at the marvels of the future." What is almost never mentioned is job loss or social disenfranchisement. The very real destruction of the lives of unemployed autoworkers, assemblers, or clerical workers is marginalized.[64] The ethical dilemmas involved when we choose between, say, "efficiency" and the quality of the work people experience, between profit and someone's job—these too are made invisible.

How would we counterbalance this? By making it clear from the outset that knowledge about the new technology that is necessary for students to know goes well beyond what we now too easily take for granted. A considerable portion of the curriculum would be organized around questions concerned with social literacy. "Where are computers used? What are they used to do? What do people *actually* need to know in order to use them? Does the computer enhance anyone's life? Whose? Does it hurt anyone's life? Whose? Who decides when and where computers will be used?"[65] Unless these are *fully* integrated in a school program at *all* levels, I hesitate advocating the use of the new technology in the curriculum. Raising questions of this type is not just important in our elementary and secondary schools. It is even more essential that they be dealt with in a serious way with teachers both in their own undergraduate teacher education programs where courses in educational computing are more and more being mandated and in the many in-service workshops now springing up throughout the country as school districts frantically seek to keep up with the "computer revolution." To do less makes it much more difficult for teachers and students to think critically and independently about the place the new technology does and should have in the lives of the majority of people in our society. Our jobs as educators involves skilling, not deskilling. Unless teachers and students are able to deal honestly and critically with these complex ethical and social issues, only those now with the power to control technology's uses will have the capacity to act. We cannot afford to let this happen.

Conclusion

I realize that a number of my points in this chapter may prove to be rather contentious. Stressing the negative side, however, can serve to highlight many of the critical issues that are too easy to put off, given the immense amount of work for which school personnel are already responsible. Decisions are often made too quickly, only to be regretted later on when forces are set in motion that could have been avoided if the implications of one's actions had been thought through more fully.

As I noted at the outset of this chapter, there is now something of a mad scramble to employ the computer in every content area. In fact, it is nearly impossible to find a subject that is not being "computerized." Although mathematics and science (and some parts of vocational education) remain the home base for a large portion of proposed computer curricula, other areas are not far behind. If it can be packaged to fit computerized instruction, it will be, even if it is inappropriate, less effective than the methods that teachers have developed after years of hard practical work, or less than sound educationally or economically. Rather than the machine fitting the educational needs and visions of the teacher, students, and community, all too often these needs and visions are made to fit the technology itself.

Yet, as I have shown, the new technology does not stand alone. It is linked to transformations in real groups of people's lives, jobs, hopes, and dreams. For some of these groups, those lives will be enhance. For others, the dreams will be shattered. Wise choices about the appropriate place of the new technology in education, then, are not only educational decisions. They are fundamentally choices about the kind of society we shall have, about the social and ethical responsiveness of our institutions to the majority of our future citizens, and to the teachers who now work in our schools. To understand teaching in this situation requires us to situate it into a more complicated nexus of relationships. Only then can choices be made in an ethically justified way.

In the current difficult social and economic situation, it is exceptionally important that educators not allow powerful groups to export their crisis onto the schools. By redefining the serious dilemmas this society faces as being primarily those of the school, and by then convincing the public that many of these problems can simply be solved by an infusion of computers and computer literacy into our educational institutions, dominant groups may create a climate in which the public continues to blame the already hard-working teachers and administrators for economic conditions over which they may have little control. This would be extremely unfortunate, because as many researchers have shown, the crisis is more widespread, more related to inequalities in the economy and in political representation, than could be accounted for by continually blaming the school.[66]

My discussion here has not been aimed at making us all neo-Luddites, people who go out and smash the machines that threaten our jobs or our children. The new technology is here. It will not go away. Our task as educators is to make sure that when it enters the classroom it is there for politically, economically, and educationally wise reasons, not because powerful groups may be redefining our major educational goals in their own image. We should be very clear about whether the future it promises to our teachers and students is real, not fictitious. We need to be certain that it is a future in which *all* of our students can share, not just a select few. After all, the new technology is expensive and will require a good deal of our time and that of our teachers, administrators, and students. It is more than a little important that we question whether the wagon we have been asked to ride on is going in the right direction. It's a long walk back.

Notes

This article is based on a more extensive analysis in Michael W. Apple, *Teachers and Texts: A Political Economy of Class and Gender Relations in Education* (New York: Routledge and Kegan Paul, 1987).

1. David Noble, *Forces of Production: A Social History of Industrial Automation* (New York: Alfred A. Knopf, 1984), pp. xi–xii. For a more general argument about the relationship between technology and human progress, see Nicholas Rescher, *Unpopular Essays on Technological Progress* (Pittsburgh: University of Pittsburgh Press, 1980).

2. Ibid., p. xv.

3. Paul Olson, "Who Computes? The Politics of Literacy," unpublished paper, Ontario Institute for Studies in Education, Toronto, 1985, p. 6.

4. Patricia B. Campbell, "The Computer Revolution: Guess Who's Left Out?," *Interracial Books for Children Bulletin* 15 3 (1984):3.

5. "Instructional Strategies for Integrating the Microcomputer into the Classroom," The Vocational Studies Center, University of Wisconsin–Madison, 1985.

6. Michael W. Apple, *Ideology and Curriculum* (Boston: Routledge and Kegan Paul, 1979).

7. Olson, op. cit., p. 5.

8. See Michael W. Apple, *Education and Power* (Boston: Routledge and Kegan Paul, 1982).

9. For further discussion of this, see Apple, *Ideology and Curriculum*, op. cit.; Apple, *Education and Power*, op. cit.; and Ira Shor, *Culture Wars* (Boston: Routledge and Kegan Paul, 1986).

10. This is treated in greater detail in Richard Edwards, *Contested Terrain* (New York: Basic, 1979). See also the more extensive discussion of the effect these tendencies are having in education in Apple, *Education and Power*, op. cit.

11. Russell W. Rumberger and Henry M. Levin, "Forecasting the Impact of New Technologies on the Future Job Market," Project Report No. 84–A4, Institute for Research on Educational Finance and Government, School of Education, Stanford University, February 1984, p. 1.

12. Ibid., p. 2.

13. Ibid., p. 3.

14. Ibid., p. 4.

15. Ibid., p. 18.

16. Ibid., p. 18.

17. Ibid., p. 19.

18. Ibid., pp. 19–20.

19. Ibid., p. 31.

20. Ibid., p. 21.

21. Ibid., p. 21.

22. Ibid., p. 25.

23. Ibid., p. 25.

24. The effects of proletarianization and deskilling on women's labor is analyzed in more detail in Michael W. Apple, "Work Gender and Teaching," *Teachers College Record* 84 (Spring 1983):611–28, and Michael W. Apple "Teaching and 'Woman's Work': A Comparative Historical and Ideological Analysis," *Teachers College Record* 86 (Spring 1985). On the history of women's struggles against proletarianization, see Alice Kessler-Harris, *Out to Work* (New York: Oxford University Press, 1982).

25. Ian Reinecke, *Electronic Illusion* (New York: Penguin, 1984), p. 156.

26. See the further discusison of the loss of office jobs and the deskilling of many of those that remain in ibid., pp. 136–58. The very same process could be a threat to middle- and low-level management positions as well. After all, if control is further automated, why does one need as many supervisory positions? The implications of this latter point need to be given much more consideration by many middle-class proponents of technology because their jobs may soon be at risk, too.

27. Peter Dwyer, Bruce Wilson, and Roger Woock, *Confronting School and Work* (Boston: George Allen and Unwin, 1984), pp. 105–106.

28. The paradigm case is given by the fact that three times as many people now work in low-paying positions for MacDonalds as for U.S. Steel. See Martin Carnoy, Derek Shearer, and Russell Rumberger, *A New Social Contract* (New York: Harper and Row, 1983), p. 71. As I have argued at greater length elsewhere, however, it may not be important to our economy if all students and workers are made technically knowledgeable by schools. What is just as important is the production of economically useful knowledge (technical/administrative knowledge) that can be used by corporations to enhance profits, control labor, and increase efficiency. See Apple, *Education and Power*, op cit., especially chapter 2.

29. Reinecke, *Electronic Illusions*, p. 234. For further analysis of the economic data and the effects on education, see W. Norton Grubb, "The Bandwagon Once More: Vocational Preparation for High-Tech Occupations," *Harvard Educational Review* 54 (November 1984):429–51.

30. Apple, *Ideology and Curriculum*, op. cit.; and Apple, *Education and Power*, op. cit. See also Michael W. Apple and Lois Weis, eds., *Ideology and Practice in Schooling* (Philadelphia: Temple University Press, 1983).

31. Ibid. See also Arthur Wise, *Legislated Learning: The Bureaucratization of the American Classroom* (Berkeley: University of California Press, 1979).

32. Apple, *Ideology and Curriculum*, op. cit.; and Apple, *Education and Power*, op. cit. On the general history of the growth of management techniques, see Edwards, op. cit.

33. Douglas D. Noble, "The Underside of Computer Literacy," *Raritan* 3 (Spring 1984):45.

34. See the discussion of this in Apple, *Education and Power*, op. cit., especially chapter 5.

35. Susan Jungck, "Doing Computer Literacy," unpublished Ph.D. dissertation, University of Wisconsin, Madison, 1985, pp. 236–37.

36. Douglas Noble, "Jumping Off the Computer Bandwagon," *Education Week* (October 3, 1984):24.

37. Ibid., p. 24.

38. Ibid. See also, Noble, "The Underside of Computer Literacy," op. cit., p. 45.

39. For further discussion of the intensification of teachers' work, see Apple, "Work, Gender and Teaching," op. cit.

40. Apple, *Education and Power*, op. cit. For further analysis of the textbook publishing industry, see Michael W. Apple, "The Culture and Commerce of the Textbook," *Journal of Curriculum Studies* 17 1 (1985).

41. Michael W. Apple, *Teachers and Texts: A Political Economy of Class and Gender Relations in Education* (New York: Routledge and Kegan Paul, 1987).

42. Ibid.

43. I am indebted to Susan Jungck for this point. See Jungck, "Doing Computer Literacy," op. cit.

44. Reinecke, *Electronic Illusions*, op. cit., p. 176.

45. Ibid., p. 169.

46. Olson, op. cit., p. 23.

47. Ibid., p. 31. Thus, students' familiarity and comfort with computers becomes a form of what has been called the "cultural capital" of advantaged groups. For further analysis of the dynamics of cultural capital, see Apple, *Education and Power*, op. cit.; and Pierre Bourdieu and Jean-Claude Passeron, *Reproduction in Education, Society and Culture* (Beverly Hills, Calif.: Sage, 1977).

48. Ibid., p. 23. See also the discussion of interclass competition over academic qualifications in Pierre Bourdieu, *Distinction* (Cambridge, Mass.: Harvard University Press, 1984), pp. 133–68.

49. Once again, I am indebted to Susan Jungck for this argument.

50. Noble, "The Underside of Computer Literacy," op. cit., p. 54.

51. Douglas D. Noble, "Computer Literacy and Ideology," *Teachers College Record* 85 (Summer 1984):611. This process of "blaming the victim" has a long history in education. See Apple, *Ideology and Curriculum*, op. cit., especially chapter 7.

52. R. W. Connell, *Teachers' Work* (Boston: George Allen and Unwin, 1985), p. 142.

53. Olson, op. cit. p. 22.

54. For an analysis of the emphasis on and pedagogic problems with such limited uses of computers, see Michael J. Streibel, "A Critical Analysis of the Use of Computers in Education," unpublished paper, University of Wisconsin, Madison, 1984, and the chapter by Streibel herein.

55. Olson, op. cit., p. 22.

56. Campbell, op. cit., p. 3. Many computer experts, however, are highly critical of the fact that students are primarily taught to program in BASIC, a less than appropriate language for later advanced computer work. Michael Streibel, personal communication.

57. Ibid.

58. Ibid.

59. An interesting analysis of what happens to young women in such business programs and how they respond to both the curricula and their later work experiences can be found in Linda Valli, "Becoming Clerical Workers: Business Education and the Culture of Femininity," in Apple and Weis, op. cit., pp. 213–34. See also her more extensive treatment in Linda Valli, *Becoming Clerical Workers* (Boston: Routledge and Kegan Paul, 1986).

60. Jane Gaskell in Olson, op. cit., "Who Computes?" p. 33.

61. Feodora Fomin, "The Best and the Brightest: The Selective Function of Mathematics in the School Curriculum," in Lesley Johnson and Deborah Tyler, eds., *Cultural Politics: Papers in Contemporary Australian Education, Culture and Politics* (Melbourne: University of Melbourne, Sociology Research Group in Cultural and Educational Studies, 1984), p. 220.

62. Michael J. Streibel's work on the models of thinking usually incorporated within computers in education is helpful in this regard. See Streibel, "A Critical Analysis of the Use of Computers in Education," op. cit., and his chapter in this volume. The more general issue of the relationship between technology and the control of culture is important here. A useful overview of this can be found in Kathleen Woodward, ed., *The Myths of Information: Technology and Postindustrial Culture* (Madison: Coda, 1980).

63. Quoted in Noble, "The Underside of Computer Literacy," op. cit., p. 56.

64. Ibid., p. 57. An interesting, but little known fact is that the largest proportion of computer programmers actually work for the military. See Joseph Weizenbaum, "Thie Computer in Your Future," *The New York Review of Books* (October 27, 1983):58–62.

65. Noble, "The Underside of Computer Literacy," op. cit., p. 40. For students in vocational curricula especially, these questions would be given more power if they were developed within a larger program that would seek to provide these young women and men with extensive experience in and understanding of *all* aspects of operating an entire industry, not simply those "skills" that reproduce workplace stratification. See Center for Law and Education, "Key Provisions in New Law Reforms Vocational Education: Focus Is on Broader Knowledge and Experience for Students/Workers," *Center for Law and Education, Inc. D.C. Report*, December 28, 1984, 1–6.

66. See, especially, Marcus Raskin, *The Common Good* (New York: Routledge and Kegan Paul, 1987). This does not mean that schools have no place in helping to solve these problems, simply that: (1) it is insufficient and naive to search for mostly educational solutions; and (2) that the solutions must be considerably more democratic in process *and* effects than those being proposed currently.

VI
Curriculum and Evaluation

SEVENTEEN

The Human Problems and Possibilities of Curriculum Evaluation

George Willis

If we are fortunate, at some time in the distant future, historians will be able to look back at the twentieth century and see it clearly as a major turning point in Western educational thought and practice, as an ever chaotic but always interesting period of transition from the major assumptions and ideologies which had guided education until well into the nineteenth century to those which then guided it in the twenty-first century and beyond. If we are to be so fortunate, than the chaos of our century will have proved fertile and the educational practices of the future—including curriculum evaluation—will surely embody a fuller, more comprehensive vision of humanness than those of the present. If so, then the basic problems of curriculum evaluation will come to be seen neither as essentially metaphysical (as they have been seen in the past), nor as essentially technical (as they are usually seen in the present), but as essentially the problems of human possibility they are. Human problems, of course, are subject to multiplicity of perspectives, personal decisions, and inconclusive testing of alternative actions in ways that other kinds of problems are not. How, then, do different orientations to curriculum evaluation embody different presuppositions about how evaluee, evaluator, and audience of evaluation (whether these be different persons or one in the same) actually make decisions or, in a larger sense, actually live their lives?

This chapter will not attempt to provide closure on such broad questions. Its purpose is simply to outline briefly some different possibilities between the messy human approach to curriculum evaluation that may characterize our future and the neater technical approach which now, in the latter half of the twentieth century, dominates curriculum evaluation in the United States. In keeping with this purpose, it will not attempt precisely to define or to delineate the two approaches, for neither can be completely characterized by reference to methodology, procedures, or anything else that is invariant. More properly, therefore, each approach should be seen as a general orientation specifically toward the tasks of curriculum evaluation, but in a broader sense toward life itself. What are the beliefs and intentions of evaluators? Why have they chosen certain procedures? What do they expect to accomplish by casting their findings in certain forms? How do they perceive other people? What do they think about themselves? While orientations differ from one another, they are still broad and flexible enough to admit of some change and some overlap. Thus, although statistically derived generalizations are commonly used in the technical approach, a humanly oriented evaluator may sometimes find ways of using such generalizations to inform the autonomous actions of students and teachers. Although case studies of specific individuals and situations are commonly used in the human approach, a technically oriented evaluator may believe such studies represent universal truths from which desirable courses of action for all students and teachers can always be derived and warranted. Rather than provide definitions, this chapter will attempt to gradually build up portraits of the two approaches.

What Is Being Evaluated?

In general, a curriculum can be considered in one of two ways. Perhaps the more common way is to define a curriculum as a course of study, an arrangement of subject matter, or a plan of what is to happen in school. The technical approach to curriculum evaluation usually views curricula in this way and is based on the assumption that a curriculum can best be evaluated by determining its results. For instance, one assumes that if students learn more when subject matter is arranged the first way than the second way, then the first arrangement is a more desirable curriculum than the second. Evaluation becomes the search—usually "objective" or "scientific"—for results, usually those prespecified as "goals." On its surface this assumption is straightforward and commonsensical; evidence of success is hard to argue with, especially if it is gathered in an open and aboveboard way. At the very least, however, the technical approach leaves the term *curriculum evaluation* as a misnomer.

In the first place, this approach begs the question of the desirability of the curriculum; hence, it is not really evaluation at all. Because students learned the chosen subject matter does not mean that subject matter was worth learning. Why was that subject matter chosen? Why is it more worthwhile than some other subject matter? Any complete vision of curriculum evaluation must include the human application of values to competing states of affairs (i.e., proposed curricula) in order to determine their desirability. Questions of value require direct analysis of the curriculum itself and cannot be answered simply by appeal to results. Direct analysis begins with such fundamental questions as: How adequately does proposed subject matter represent reality? How logically is subject matter arranged? These questions are essentially metaphysical, and the evaluator may believe that the most desirable state of affairs is the one which most accurately reflects the underlying reality of the universe. Surely a course of study that accurately and coherently reflects reality is more intrinsically worthwhile than one that does not and is also more likely—even if incidentally—to yield desirable utilitarian results. Beginning with metaphysical questions precludes consideration of neither human problems nor utilitarian ends. However, it is a reminder that when curriculum is considered as the course of study, curriculum evaluation must include direct analysis of the subject matter itself and some search for how its intrinsic characteristics can be valued in human terms. In general, the technical approach fails to undertake these tasks, for in reducing its focus to the search for specific results, it assumes that subject matter has no intrinsic value, that it can be valued only as it contributes to certain extrinsic goals, that, in effect, curricular means are justified only by their utilitarian ends. This is not to evaluate the curriculum itself.

In the second place, the technical approach always involves a leap of faith: the evaluator assumes, but can never be sure, that any results discerned are actually the results of the course of study. Hence, what the evaluator investigates may have nothing to do with the curriculum at all. In the natural sciences, which the technical approach takes as its model, the search is for unambiguous causal relationships. When these always apply under the same conditions they can be stated as causal laws; thus, in the natural sciences leaps of faith are minimized or avoided altogether. But the human sciences are different. Human sciences deal with individual human beings as autonomous moral agents living under a myriad of constantly changing circumstances that can never be exactly repeated. Although influenced by their environments, autonomous human beings work out their own values and take their own actions. Therefore, in human affairs causal laws never apply. What the technical approach offers as the results of the curriculum are only a few of the many things that may be influenced by it, but even these have been highly mediated by numerous intervening human decisions (mostly by teachers and students) and by the complex social context in which they take place. Such considerations are what make the study of schooling at once immensely complicated and immensely fascinating. The technical approach usually attempts to deal with these difficulties by focusing only on prespecified goals and by using statistical procedures to derive generalizations about the fit between goals and selected evidence. While such generalizations are sometimes useful, they reduce live human beings and their problems to abstractions and illicitly suggest that causal relationships can be established in human affairs. Evidence of presumed results of a course of study can never avoid the leap of faith and can never settle questions of value. In education, as in all human affairs, good means can exist simultaneously with bad ends and vice versa, and causal connections are at best tenuous. The notorious truth about schooling is that what students learn depends on a lot more than the formal course of study.

A curriculum can be considered in a second general way, however: not as the course of study or a plan, but as what actually happens to the student. The technical approach seldom views a curriculum in this way (and when it does so it begins to blend off into the human approach to curriculum evaluation). This second view obviates some major difficulties of the first but opens up some new complexities. Because evidence of "what actually happens" is considered a manifestation of a curriculum itself, the evaluator need not attempt to establish connections between evidence and something more remote. Classroom life itself is thrust to the forefront of evaluation, becoming both means and ends simultaneously; therefore, a leap of faith is unnecessary. Furthermore, although the central task of evaluating can still be evaded by whoever refuses to apply values and insists on collecting evidence only (leaving the term *curriculum evaluation* a misnomer), this evasion becomes less likely. Because the curriculum is viewed as immediate instead of remote, it can also be analyzed and valued immediately, in terms of both its intrinsic and extrinsic characteristics. No longer bound by prespecified goals, the evaluator is free to ponder the desirability of what happens in a variety of ways, both before and after the fact. For instance, the evaluator may decide that what happened was different from but more desirable than what was anticipated.

In this second view of curriculum, the "what actually happens" can itself be considered in a variety of ways ranging from the narrow notion that what happens to the student is the same as what the student is exposed to (leaving this view little different from the first view), to the broader notion that what happens is what the student does, to the broadest possible notion that what happens is what the student experiences. The idea of experiencing is itself subject to a variety of interpretations. In general, the human approach to curriculum evaluation considers the curriculum as experience in the broadest possible sense, as the complex array of thoughts, feelings, and actions that individual students undergo and undertake in living their lives in schools. In this sense, evaluating the curriculum is not much different from evaluating living in general. The same problems of human possibility obtrude whenever one attempts to assess the quality of experiencing or living. In weighing alternative values and alternative courses of action, the same complexity obtains. In the human approach, the course of study is viewed as one of many things that influences the curriculum, the experience of individual students, but investigation focuses on the quality of experiencing itself. Thus, the second general view of curriculum, as what actually happens to students (unless the "what actually happens" is itself defined extremely narrowly), opens up a wide variety of tasks to the evaluator. These may include analysis of the course of study and investigation of how parts of the environment influence students, but they also include the weighing of how autonomous individuals choose to live their lives.

A Little History

Until well into and perhaps even throughout the nineteenth century, the course of study in most American schools was more classical than utilitarian. American schools largely embodied the time-honored Western belief that a relatively few, well-ordered, academic subjects were repositories of the highest knowledge and led to understanding, virtue, and godliness, the proper condition of cultivated human beings. There were a few protests, such as Benjamin Franklin's proposal for a practical course of study for the youth of Pennsylvania, and, of course, the study of such classical subjects as mathematics did yield utilitarian benefits. But in a sparsely settled, agrarian country, few Americans received more than a rudimentary formal education, and practical pursuits were learned in the home, through apprenticeships, and through the activities of daily living.

The prevailing ideology was culturally conservative. The aim of schooling was to preserve the culture by immersing students in it. The mass of students whose brief immersion led to little more than basic skills in reading, writing, and mathematics could at least take their appropriate places in the American social order. The few who were cultivated by any higher knowledge could become the leaders of society. The major difference between American ideology and that which usually prevailed elsewhere in Western civilization lay in the growing American impulse toward egalitarianism and democracy. This impulse provided the ethical basis for the expanded schooling made available to increasing numbers of students, though expanded schooling soon became justified in utilitarian terms. At the beginning of the nineteenth century, most Americans probably believed that everyone deserved a little formal education but only a few people would actually benefit from a lot; by the beginning of the twentieth century, most seemed to believe that almost everyone could benefit materially from extended formal education.

As long as the older order prevailed, however, curriculum evaluation was divorced from a search for practical results. The course of study was viewed as the curriculum, and asking about its metaphysical character was primary: How well did the time-honored academic subjects embody the underlying truths and order of the universe? Curriculum evaluation *was* this kind of analysis of subject matter. Although different arrangements of subject matter were advocated, few evaluators saw any reason to question the assumptions that the basic purpose of the curriculum was to reflect the metaphysical order and that classical subjects did so more directly than did utilitarian subjects. And if students failed to learn, these deficiencies were not attributable to the curriculum, but to deficiencies in the students themselves or in how they were instructed.

By the twentieth century, the older order was crumbling. Shifts from a rural-agrarian society to an urban-industrial one, massive waves of immigrants, the gradual expansion of schooling, and numerous other changes in American life helped create conditions under which the prevailing educational ideology in the United States had become essentially utilitarian. Although resisted by conservatives, emphasis increasingly fell on the practical and social ends of schooling. With the rise of progressive education, many educators came to believe that society itself could be improved either through the direct efforts of the school or as an indirect consequence of the individual development of large numbers of students. Education could begin with the individual interests of students, and the course of study could largely be determined by those activities which led to good consequences. As the leading spokesman for progressive education, John Dewey made clear that this kind of utilitarianism must not be construed too narrowly, that the enrichment of individual experience began in the cultivation of the student's intelligence and led to the individual's autonomous and humane participation in a democratic social order. However, despite Dewey's warnings, on a mass scale the utilitarian ideology was construed narrowly: many educators focused not on the development of intelligence but on the development of specific skills, not on autonomous participation in a democratically evolving society but on fitting into the existing society. The ethical basis for the ideology, fostering the fullest development of all students by treating them in individually appropriate ways, could be subverted when ends were chosen for students, conceived narrowly, or otherwise constrained.

Given the new ideology, how it was commonly interpreted, and the growing number and kinds of courses taught in American schools, the cur-

344

riculum came to be regarded as something that should be evaluated primarily by its results. No longer could classical, academic, or any other subjects be regarded as intrinsically valuable; their value had to be demonstrated in terms of their usefulness. Further compounding the problem was the fact that the same subject could have different degrees of usefulness for different students or simply because of differences in how it was arranged or taught. Dewey in his own writings identified the curriculum with experience, but progressive education in general tended to emphasize the social side of experience more than the personal side. This emphasis tended to thrust back toward the older view of curriculum as subject matter, which was held by most socially conservative educators, whether they were old-line advocates of a classical, academic curriculum or newer advocates of a functional, well-ordered, efficient society. During the first half of the twentieth century the main educational and social currents in the United States were, therefore, more conducive to the development of the technical approach to curriculum evaluation than the human approach.

Illustrating the conflicting forces in curriculum evaluation during the first half of the century is the Eight-Year Study.[1] This study in some ways still represents the single most significant piece of curriculum research and evaluation ever undertaken. It compared students who attended progressive, experimental secondary schools with those who attended traditional schools, following them from 1932 to 1940, their eight high school and college years. Students from each of the two types of secondary schools were placed in 1,475 matched pairs on the basis of their background, academic aptitude, and other personal characteristics. Comparisons were made not only on their academic achievement, but also on such things as their intellectual and personal resourcefulness, particularly their ability to solve problems, meet new situations, and participate in a variety of activities. What the study seemed to demonstrate was that in general students from the experimental secondary schools did slightly better in college academically but were decidedly better off in their personal and social lives. It was widely interpreted as indicating the superiority of a progressive over a traditional arrangement of subject matter, especially one which left choices open to students.

As an outgrowth of progressive education, the Eight-Year Study accepted the utilitarian ideology but interpreted it more broadly and generously than any other large-scale evaluation study of the time. It served as an example in which what was seen as useful was not just academic achievement or specific skills, but a whole host of things that helped students live their lives well. Long-range, relatively intangible forms of growth were carefully considered. Particularly impressive were the many new techniques that the study pioneered for collecting information about thinking, interests, social adjustment, and so on. In thus evincing concern for the overall experience of students and how they managed their own development, it was consistent with the human approach to curriculum evaluation and can appropriately be seen as a forerunner of this approach. On the other hand, the study hinged on comparing two alternative forms of education (largely defined by alternative arrangements of subject matter and their implementation) in terms of discernible results. In so doing it treated generalized results as more important in determining desirability than the immediate and specific qualities of classroom experience. What, for instance, did the study mean for those specific students in matched pairs in which results were mixed or the student from the traditional school seemed to develop more fully? Generalized results were not very helpful in understanding their specific situations. In creating new techniques for collecting information about developmental growth, the study also seemed to suggest that desirable experiencing could be inferred directly from evidence of growth and that all useful evidence could be somehow discerned objectively, without painstakingly sifting the divergent—and perhaps equally valuable—perspectives of different participants for their own insights. In so embodying a less than full notion of experiencing and a utilitarian means-ends rationale implicit in its search for objective results, the Eight-Year Study was thereby also consistent with the technical approach to curriculum evaluation. Certainly, it ran against the main currents of the time, proved instructive, and advanced some forms of progressive education that tended to open up human possibilities, but in the last analysis it embodied a mixed approach to evaluation that was perhaps as much technical as human.

Despite its example, in the second half of the century, educational and social currents have become even more conducive to the technical approach and the Eight-Year Study has been largely forgotten or ignored by curriculum evaluators. The prevailing educational ideology in the United States has become increasingly homogenized and more pointedly utilitarian, not in the relatively grotesque ways of the earlier social efficiency movements, which were easy to burlesque, but in more subtle and seductive ways. For example, the ethical impulse behind the national push toward egalitarianism and democracy was originally based on Enlightenment ideas about the value and the rights of individuals. It led in the nineteenth century toward the breakup of the old, culturally conservative educational ideology and the demand for universal education, and in the first half of the twentieth century toward the development of a utilitarian ideology that could accommodate cultural change and the concomitant demand for education of sufficient quality and appropriateness to actualize the diverse individual potentials of all students. In the second half of the century, however, the ethical impulse has been transmuted as the utilitarian ideology has been interpreted more and more in strictly materialistic terms. Egalitarianism and democracy may no longer mean to most Americans that all individuals should have the same rights and opportunities to participate in a pluralistic society, but that all should receive the same tangible benefits from their participation. Therefore, schools have been seen as placed that should homogenize society by guaranteeing that all students learn the same things. After all, countless students have been economically handicapped throughout their lives because they have not learned to read, or write, or perform simple mathematical calculations as well as their peers. Thoughtful critics have pointed out how schools, at times, have served to maintain social stratification. For these and many other reasons, schools have been seen increasingly as places that fulfill their ethical obligations primarily by bestowing the same tangible benefits and only secondarily by releasing diverse human potential. The egalitarian push has shifted in the direction of educational and social sameness; hence, the new utilitarian ideology has become culturally conservative once more. Under these circumstances, curriculum evaluation is itself pushed toward the search for discernible evidence of those useful results that society believes the schools should be achieving, and, particularly during the 1980s, usefulness has been seen by American society primarily in terms of specific skills and financial rewards.

This narrowing of America's ethical impulse and its collective interpretation of utilitarianism has been channelled by numerous cultural, economic, and political currents in the social mainstream. Among those most powerful in carrying forward the technical approach to curriculum evaluation have been certain well-intentioned actions of the federal government. Focused by the *Brown v. Board of Education of Topeka* decision of the Supreme Court in 1954, the federal government became increasingly concerned with the problem the Court called "equality of educational opportunity." Efforts to end segregation met opposition, of course, but left the government with no great psychic dilemma. But should the government attempt more directly to promote educational equality? And if so, on ethical or economic grounds? In *Brown*, the Court had held that both grounds are important, ruling that segregated education deprives students of constitutional rights *and* impedes learning. In the 1960s, the government answered these questions with the Great Society programs of the Johnson Administration, which stressed the economic value of education, particularly to poor or potentially poor people who, it claimed, could use education to lift themselves out of poverty. Clearly, however, the quality of education in the diverse public schools across the nation was highly uneven. The United States had achieved universal education, but not all schools achieved the same universally good results. The programs of the Johnson administration dealt with this problem by infusing into local schools large amounts of federal financial aid on an unprecedented scale. These programs did not equalize the quality of education across the country (though they did serve to distribute more equally some of its benefits), but they helped create a new set of national expectations and certainly created a new breed of educational evaluator.

Although the intentions of the Johnson Administration were in part shaped by ethical concerns for the individual, the effects of its programs were to help foster the beliefs that education can be judged by its tangible results and that tangible results should be equalized for all students, closely related to economic benefits, and created on a mass scale by appropriate strategies and actions. Such beliefs, of course, were instrumental in shifting educators' efforts from attempting to maximize each individual's development to attempting to equalize what each individual learned. Furthermore, in order to ensure that aid was being used in intended programs and to bring about intended results, most federal legislation soon required that 10 percent of the aid be used for "objective" evaluation of the programs. Prior to this period, most educational evaluation had been relatively small and informal. Districts or individual schools worked out their own principles and procedures. Where there was formal evaluation, it was often tied to classroom observations of supervisors aimed at helping teachers improve or to the districtwide administration of standardized achievement tests. It was obvious that across the nation few districts were prepared to provide the kind of evaluations that the federal government now demanded and that even those who could do so should not be entrusted with evaluating themselves. A lot was at stake. The curriculum to be evaluated was no longer just the course of study, it was the whole host of new, federally funded programs intended to solve the nation's most intractable educational and social problems. Determining results (and, by the 1970s, cost effectiveness) became a national priority. A vague, human approach would not satisfy the federal government, which now paid the evaluation piper; the technical approach quickly became the only called-for tune in town.

Drawn into this vacuum created by federal expectations and money was the new breed of educational evaluator, which included people who could most convincingly lay claim to objectivity and technical expertise. With few exceptions, they were neither school people nor familiar with the Eight-Year Study; they were trained in the then-emerging techniques of social science research—measurement, statistical analysis, experimental design—which largely emulated the natural sciences. Many came from specialties outside of education, such as psychology and sociology, because familiarity with techniques was seen as necessary for evaluators, not familiarity with educational issues and settings. Use of social science techniques itself seemed important, whereas insight into education did not. Ability to distance oneself from the situation and to abstract data seemed to provide objectivity, whereas ability to immerse oneself in the situation and to interpret data in context did not. Perhaps drawn into this vacuum also was the nation at large, for it seemed willing to accept the specific assumptions and the overall ethos of the technical approach. Over the last two decades the new breed of evaluator has gradually learned some of the inherent limitations and difficulties of attempting to provide a warrant of success or failure for programs by abstracting selected evidence. For at least the first of these two decades, however, the technical approach completely dominated educational evaluation in the United States. Only since the late 1970s and early 1980s has the evaluation community formed by the vacuum of the 1960s grudgingly afforded any real legitimacy to procedures associated with the human approach (for example, use of participant observation and the case-study format), and it still collectively persists in forcing even these into a technical framework. Progress toward a broadened view of evaluation has been exceedingly slow.

These developments, however, merely illustrate what is at the heart of the matter, the twentieth-century shift in America's utilitarian educational ideology and in what the nation collectively believes the schools can and should accomplish. If usefulness is interpreted in the most narrowly practical way, then schools will have little more to do than teach specific skills useful in maintaining the existing society. If America's democratic impulses are continually compressed into a materialistic egalitarianism, then schools will not be encouraged to aim at maximizing diverse human potential but at teaching minimum competencies. There is a twofold problem with education that aims at providing everyone with similar results, particularly in a narrowly utilitarian, materialistic sense. First, as a practical matter, the aims cannot be realized. Individual people and their interests, aspirations, ideas, and skills are too diverse. Then, too, the health of a democracy and the enrichment of individual lives depend on this diversity. Second, as an ethical matter the aims themselves become a source of error, both because they encourage educators to claim they can produce results that they cannot (inevitably lacking certain knowledge of the relationship between means and ends, B. F. Skinner notwithstanding) and because they encourage educators to try in ways that treat students as less than fully human (not, for instance, as autonomous). The basic problem with the technical approach to curriculum evaluation is the same. In accepting the task of providing warrant for education defined in terms of results, it accepts a distorted and stereotypical vision of education, of human beings, and of the real human problems and possibilities in ethical living.

A Potential Ideology

What this chapter has thus far suggested is that under the twentieth-century press toward social efficiency in the United States, the nation's educational ideology and ethical impulses have become unduly narrow, focusing

349

less on individual development and democratic social change and more on specific functioning within the prevailing social framework. As education has become more narrowly utilitarian it has tended to treat individuals in technical, less than fully human terms. Therefore, what is needed is a new ideology within which the development of individual potential can be highly valued and a complete vision of humanness can emerge, one in which the individual is seen as an autonomous perceiver, meaning maker, and world builder. Within such an ideology the curriculum might come to be valued more for how it helps people become fully human and less for its purported technical results; hence, curriculum evaluation would itself be seen in light of human problems and possibilities. The precise form of such an ideology that might actually emerge in the twenty-first century is, of course, impossible to foresee, but James B. Macdonald has sketched a possible prototype in his essay "A Transcendental Developmental Ideology of Education."[2]

According to Macdonald, an ideology must account for the dialectic between the inner experience of individuals and the outer world in which they live. In his view, the four specific ideologies that have recently vied for currency in the United States do not adequately account for the dialectic. These are the romantic, developmental, cultural transmission, and radical ideologies. The romantic ideology deals with only one side of the dialectic. It locates knowledge and value solely in inner experience. Truth is self-knowledge, and value is derived from the unfolding or maturation of the individual. As long as individuals are free, they are essentially good unless somehow corrupted by society. The cultural transmission ideology deals only with the opposite side of the dialectic. It locates knowledge and value solely in the outer world. The individual is to learn about and to be shaped by the "objective" world and its truths, or at least by those cultural values for which there is a consensus. The developmental ideology locates knowledge and value in transactions between the inner self and the outer world. Truth is pragmatic in that it is what is useful in resolving relationships between the inner and the outer, but, as this ideology is interpreted by most adherents, values are based upon ethical universals that are derived rationally and serve developmental means and ends. Although the developmental ideology deals with both sides of the dialectic, it is weighted toward the side of inner experience in assuming that transactions can best be carried out only by individuals who have developed in terms of universal cognitive and moral structures, and it therefore assumes that inner experience should be fundamentally the same for all individuals. The radical ideology is similar to the developmental in locating knowledge and value in transactions, and viewing truth as pragmatic and values as rationally derived. Historically, however, radical ideology has so heavily emphasized the analysis of shortcomings in social reality that it is weighted toward the side of the outer world in assuming that analysis must be carried out in terms of external, environmental structures, and it therefore assumes that the outer world affects all individuals in fundamentally the same way.

The major shifts in America's educational ideology exemplify Macdonald's analysis. The prevailing ideology in the nineteenth century was that of cultural transmission, which emphasized the structures of the outer world and a pedagogy of efficient transmission. The twentieth-century shifts to a predominantly utilitarian ideology at first opened the possibility of a balanced dialectic between inner experience and outer world, but as even progressive education came to encourage socialization more than personal development, emphasis again fell on the outer world. Social adjustment could be facilitated by using principles from behavioral psychology, and even personal development came to be seen in terms of universal structures that could be sought out scientifically, encouraged efficiently, and evaluated technically. As utilitarianism became interpreted in more narrow and materialistic ways, the split between inner experience and outer world deepened and technical, socially efficient approaches to education, such as behaviorism, became thoroughly engrained. Radicalism might emphasize why democratic ideals have not been fully realized in American society, and romanticism the value of unrestrained personal development, but neither could establish a balanced dialectic. For instance, Macdonald sees considerable value in the radical critique of society but believes the radical ideology accepts too many of the same assumptions about the external world and rationality as do the cultural transmission and development ideologies to undermine the current utilitarianism.

The transcendental developmental ideology Macdonald advocates strikes a balance between inner experience and outer world and is meant to overcome misguided efforts to provide empirical grounding of developmental norms and benign control of developmental growth. Both efforts place undue limits on human potential and distort the nature of inner experience. The transcendental developmental ideology is based on a dual dialectical process. One dialectic exists between individuals and their outer worlds; another, within individuals themselves. The outer world consists not only of the immediate environment, situations, decisions, and acts of which the individual is aware, but also of all larger environmental structures that impinge on each situation. The outer dialectic exists as a reflective transaction between the outer world and the explicit awareness of the individual (the individual's explicit knowledge, beliefs, ideas, and wishes). The inner dialectic exists as an aesthetic transaction between explicit beliefs, ideas, and wishes and the individual's preconscious and unconscious functioning (the tacit knowledge, values, needs, and potentials that are the source and grounding of explicit beliefs). The outer dialectic is the source of utilitarian values as the individual intelligently reflects upon the consequences of human activities within objective and historical situational contexts. The inner dialectic is the source both

351

of values beyond the utilitarian (such as personal and aesthetic) and of the validation of values as the individual encounters what it means to be a human being. For instance, one could not *decide* to act rationally without grounding this decision in the tacit self. Thus, one literally feels one's way to being fully human by living values in addition to the utilitarian. The outer dialectic puts us in touch with the human problems and possibilities of acting rationally in the outer world; the inner dialectic, with the human problems and possibilities of being fully human. As Macdonald states:

> Values, I believe, are articulated in the lives of people by the dual dialectic of reflecting upon the consequences of an action and sounding the depths of our inner selves. Only a process something like this can explain why "what works is not always good." Some dual dialectic is also needed to explain the existence of reason, or aesthetic rationality, to counterbalance purely technological rationality.[3]

Given the dual dialectic, which balances outer worlds and inner experience, the general aim of education consistent with the transcendental developmental ideology is what Macdonald calls *centering*. Centering cannot be defined in specific terms. It is a search that is facilitated by a spiritual attitude, utilizes the full potential of each individual, and leads toward the creation of meaning and the awareness of wholeness as a person. It depends on knowledge of the outer world waiting to be discovered, but this knowledge must be personalized and validated within the idiosyncratic inner experience of each individual. But personal knowledge thrusts back toward the outer world because culture is created by the common set of personal constructs that individuals use to share their perceptions of what it means to be human, therefore, within this ideology, education may be culturally conservative yet still promote cultural change as centering grounds knowledge in the human base from which it grows.

Centering can be seen as the developmental goal of education, but being a process of releasing an almost infinite variety of human potential, it transcends the ordinary developmental goals that are empirically grounded in the outer world and that can, thus, be as limiting as liberating. The curriculum should not be seen, therefore, as a series of goals or results justified by their utility in the outer world but as a series of processes that include activities consonant with the process of centering itself, hence innately valuable in releasing potential. Macdonald suggests that many processes facilitate centering, among which are pattern making, playing, meditative thinking, imagining, educating awareness of aesthetic principles, educating awareness of the body and our biology, and educating perception. Clearly, activities embodying such processes traditionally have been absent or neglected within the curricula of American schools or rendered inconsonant with the aim of centering under the utilitarian press of the twentieth century. Macdonald also suggests the kinds of questions that can be asked about curricula in light of the transcendental developmental aim of centering.

1. What kinds of activity are encouraged that provide for opening up perceptual experiences?
2. What kinds of activity facilitate the process of sensitizing people to others, to inner vibrations?
3. What kinds of activity provide experiences for developing closeknit community relationships?
4. What kinds of activity encourage and facilitate religious experiences?
5. What kinds of activity facilitate the development of patterned meaning structures?
6. What ways can we organize knowledge to enlarge human potential through meaning?
7. How can we facilitate the development of inner strength and power in human beings?[4]

This list of questions is far from exhaustive of those that could be asked about curricula within a new and human ideology of the type Macdonald describes and that could guide American education in the twenty-first century. For the purposes of this chapter, it illustrates the kinds of questions about curricula that the technical approach to evaluation does not ask and the human approach does. Curriculum evaluation *can* focus on such human questions concerning centering and not merely on questions about utilitarian results. Even more important for the purposes of this chapter, the list illustrates the kinds of questions that can be asked about curriculum evaluation itself. Curriculum evaluation can be evaluated in terms of whether its assumptions and activities promote centering, for curriculum evaluators cannot suppress their inner dialectics and still hope to carry on adequate dialectics with the outer world.

The Perceptive and Reflective Evaluator

To be fully human, all people must engage in the dual dialectic. Hence, centering is the general transcendental aim of all education and all living, regardless of whatever smaller, more narrowly utilitarian goals may obtrude along the way. The point is not that such goals never serve certain limited developmental outcomes, but that they may interfere with the process of being fully human. At the close of his essay, Macdonald points out that in the ordinary developmental ideology the teacher stands back from the student in a judgmental stance. The teacher's knowledge of the student, the student's developmental status, and long-range developmental goals are explicitly cognitive. Despite any humane intentions, the teacher's predominant rationality is technical: planning, manipulating, calculating. In contrast, when teachers and students immerse themselves in the mutual process of centering, the predominant rationality becomes aesthetic, intuitive, and spontaneous. They become willing to "let go" of externally defined roles, to undertake a joint pilgrimage in creative human living, having faith that they themselves, others, and the culture in which they exist will become a medium for developing centering.

The same relationships can exist between evaluators and evaluees. Evaluators may distance themselves from specific situations, adopt a technical rationality, attempt to obtain objectified evidence, and make judgments in terms of utilitarian goals for "the good of" evaluees or the external society. In contrast, they may immerse themselves in specific situations with evaluees, carry on a dual dialectic, respond aesthetically and intuitively to the lived situations, and make judgments in terms of how this joint living contributes to the mutual aim of centering. In the former case, good evaluation is seen as skillful use of techniques that reify the situation, the evaluator's dialectic is solely outer, and the value system on which judgments are based is some kind of rationalistic calculus about utility in the outer world. Whether the curriculum is considered as subject matter, activities, or experience, emphasis falls on efficiency and control. How well does the curriculum contribute to the prescribed utility? How can its utility be demonstrated? In the latter case, good evaluation is seen as perceptive and reflective apprehension of the human complexities of the entire situation, the evaluator's dialectic is both outer and inner, and the value system on which judgments are based originates in this dual dialectic and balances personal, aesthetic, and utilitarian concerns. Regardless of how the curriculum is considered, emphasis falls on ethical living. How does the curriculum free the potentials of all participants in the situation? How can such liberation be communicated to and lived by other people?

If centering is to become the general transcendental aim of curriculum evaluation, then evaluators will gradually relinquish the technical approach to evaluation and adopt the human approach as their own orientations shift toward the human problems and possibilities at the heart of ethical living. They will gradually become aware of their inner dialectics and will enhance their perceptiveness, which makes accessible the ever-present, but often overlooked, qualities of the outer world and which puts explicit consciousness in touch with the tacit self. In developing perceptiveness they will expand the basis upon which they carry on reflective transactions through the outer dialectic with the outer world. They will become increasingly aware that good evaluation depends on refining both perceptiveness and reflectiveness and that these processes reinforce each other. Perceptiveness is a way of encountering an ever-richer variety of multiple and ambiguous data from the outer world and the tacit self. Reflectiveness is the dialogue within explicit consciousness in which the self attempts to make sense of varied perceptual data and to decide which always ambiguous actions should be taken in the always imperfect and imperfectly perceived outside world. Evaluators will come to realize there are neither complete perceptions nor perfect actions, but, lacking final answers, it is still better to try than not to try. This is perhaps the fundamental human problem of curriculum evaluation: to struggle to perceive clearly and completely, to value wisely, and to act ethically, all the while knowing that in terms of achieving all that we can hope, the struggle will ultimately fail. There are no unequivocally good actions, whatever our intentions. But the struggle is the essence of being human, for the struggle itself becomes the "curriculum" that releases potential. There is no centering without this course of study. It always has intrinsic value, although not necessarily utilitarian value. Once evaluators perceive this truth about the world, they will value their own activities by the same criteria they evaluate the curriculum. They will not look for specific results but will look to activities such as pattern making and educating perception that are consonant with and facilitate centering.

The basic differences between the technical approach and the human approach to curriculum evaluation therefore depend primarily on the perceptiveness and the reflectiveness of the evaluator. The evaluator who pursues the goal of centering acts in general as fully human and perceives evaluees as fully human. Specific actions intended to release potential thus embody the evaluator's reflective assumptions about the centrality of autonomy in human life. The evaluator who pursues the goal of utilitarian results acts in general as less than fully human and perceives evaluees as less than fully human. Specific actions intended to warrant results thus embody the evaluator's reflective assumptions about the lack of autonomy in human life. Although certain actions or techniques are more closely associated with one approach to evaluation or the other, they do not embody that approach in and of themselves but—more accurately—reflect the orientation and assumptions of the evaluator. For instance, ethnography, the case-study format, and qualitative data are usually associated with the human approach, but efforts to treat ethnographies as a science of invariant cultural structures, to use case studies to portray universals, or to analyze or interpret qualitative data as unambiguous are consistent with a technological rationality and embody assumptions about the lack of human autonomy. In contrast, behavioral goals are usually associated with the technological approach to evaluation but may under some circumstances (such as use by someone learning meditation through biofeedback) serve the larger goal of centering and embody assumptions about the centrality of human autonomy. To be sure, the perceptive and reflective evaluator is not likely to undertake many of the same actions that the nonperceptive and non-reflective evaluator is, but some specific actions overlap both approaches to evaluation.

Because the basic differences between the two approaches depend on the perceptiveness and reflectiveness of the evaluator, this chapter will conclude by noting some salient differences within evaluators themselves. The technically oriented evaluator accepts limits on human potential and relies only on the outer dialectic (and this, unfortunately, sometimes only in attenuated form). Standing before the real mysteries of the universe, this evaluator insists they are not there, for they are of no account within a rationalistic-materialistic calculus. Thus, in general, the perceptiveness and reflectiveness of the technically oriented evaluator are less fully developed than those of the humanly oriented evaluator, who accepts no limits on human potential, relies on both the outer and the inner dialectics, and, standing in awe of the real mysteries of the universe, attempts to embrace them. The development of perceptiveness and reflectiveness helps to orient this evaluator to the fullness of human potential; in turn, this orientation expands perceptions and reflections. Both contribute to centering. In contrast to the developed perceptiveness and reflectiveness of the humanly oriented evaluator, the technically oriented evaluator tends to look but not to see, to hypothesize but not to realize, to find facts but not to make meanings, to participate but not to create, and to evaluate but not to value.

In the final analysis, then, human beings seem to consider evaluation in two different but related ways. The ordinary way views evaluation as appraisal, the determining of the worth of something. There is value in carefully and coolly calculating worth. Doing so helps us know how to live, and we should avoid all the mistakes we can. Both the technical and the human approaches to curriculum evaluation eventually get around to deciding on a value system against which appraisals can be made, although the technical often seems all too ready to accept uncritically given values, and its nominal evaluators themselves seldom actually weigh alternative value systems. Still, both approaches consider evaluation as a process of determining worth, however different they may be on how evaluation should be carried out.

The human approach, however, is more attuned to a second way of considering evaluation. This less ordinary way views evaluation as the valuing of something in the sense of celebrating it. What can always be celebrated is intrinsic worth. Intrinsic worth does not need to be calculated against some external standard, for it radiates its own warmth. For the humanly oriented evaluator, there is intrinsic worth in centering; in viewing human beings as free, autonomous meaning makers and world builders; in helping them perceptively and reflectively value their own inner experiences and the outer world. Instead of turning away from the problems and possibilities of human living, the curriculum evaluator can celebrate them. The humanly oriented evaluator has found there indeed is value in both seeing and joining in the celebration.

Notes

1. The Eight-Year Study was reported in five volumes, the first of which summarizes the entire study. See Wilford M. Aikin, *The Story of the Eight-Year Study* (New York: Harper & Bros., 1942).

2. James B. Macdonald, "A Transcendental Developmental Ideology of Education," in *Heightened Consciousness, Cultural Revolution, and Curriculum Theory*, William F. Pinar, ed. (Berkely, Calif.: McCutchan, 1974).

3. Ibid., p. 96.

4. Ibid., pp. 105–106.

EIGHTEEN

Developing Curriculum through School Self-Evaluation

Helen Simons

In the current context there is tremendous pressure on schools to adopt external initiatives in order to improve: to adhere to national curriculum frameworks, for instance, to align school curricula with state guidelines or texts, to direct curriculum and pedagogy to ensure successful test outcomes. It has always been the case, perhaps, that those outside schools, particularly at local or central government level, have believed that they can prescribe curricula that will lead to improved outcomes in schools, but it is the extent of the prescription that is currently the cause for concern.

The fallacy of this position has been pointed out many times over, no more pointedly so than by Madeleine Grumet when she commented that curriculum devised in the abstract—whether by state education departments, superintendents, or book publishers, for instance—"rarely rests upon a thorough or even a casual acquaintance with the children for whom it is intended." Rather they are designed with "other people's children" in mind, guided, she goes on to say, by "the rules we use to tell us how to treat people we don't know."[1] If we devised curricula in relation to children we know and care about, she argues, the curricula we propose for schools would look very different indeed.

Similar arguments, less poignantly stated, have been made by other curriculum theorists who have advocated more attention to process values in the curriculum, cultural and social values in particular contexts, and to professional values of teachers in granting them some ownership of curriculum ideas and the pedagogies through which they are realized.

The force of such arguments is evident to educators but for social, political, and economic reasons that other authors in this volume have pointed out, such perspectives have not been embraced, or indeed even welcomed, by agencies concerned with generating curriculum prescriptions for the 1990s for "other people's children." The strongest example of this can be seen in the case of the National Curriculum in the United Kingdom which, even though slimmed down from its initial conception, has left little room for social and human values. Driven by a concern for outcomes, standards, and assessment, the dominant language of reform is one of delivery of that which is prespecified rather than exploration of that which is educational.

This chapter focuses on examining the value of curriculum programs and policies from a perspective that is in harmony with Grumet's advocacy for curriculum practices that reflect individuals we know. It argues that one of the best ways to develop effective curriculum practices is to grant schools the authority to formally evaluate the curriculum and in so doing give teachers and students the opportunity to analyze the value of the curriculum they experience, as well as the one external agencies prescribe for them. By placing teachers and schools at the center of the evaluation process, evaluation can document and analyze particular curriculum effects in context, and provide relevant feedback to inform curriculum development at a point of need and in precise recognition of the needs and interests of the particular clientele in the school.

It is important to say at the outset that the form of evaluation advocated in this chapter is not the only evaluation of schools that may be needed in any state or nationwide evaluation system. In a discussion of evaluation related to governance of education House has indicated that "a dual evaluation system, or one with several different levels, is a necessity,"[2] especially in the accountability climate facing many Western democracies. Evaluation is needed by state and central governments, he argues, for legitimation purposes. A professional view alone will not suffice. The form of school evaluation advocated in this chapter is one that has the development of the curriculum and the professional growth of individuals and the school at its core. As such it is an educative process that is integrated into the ongoing functioning of the school. In the sharing of the process and results with parents and the community, it is

359

also responsive and accountable at that level. What it does not do necessarily (though this element could be built into a school self-evaluation) is to provide detailed comparative outcome data for state or national purposes. Such an evaluation aim would be met by a different process.

The chapter is organized in a number of sections. Evaluation models and processes do not arise in a vacuum. The first section indicates how the concept of school self-evaluation arose and where it is located within the field of evaluation theory and the political context in which evaluations are conducted. The next section outlines what the process entails and in so doing further distinguishes its characteristics. The third and final section indicates how the model could be strengthened as a process to become more widely embedded in state and local communities.

Evolution of School Evaluation: Historical Location in Evaluation Theory

The process of school self-evaluation described in this chapter had its origins in an analysis of the curriculum reform movement of the late sixties and seventies in the United Kingdom. It was through external evaluation of center-periphery curriculum reform that I came to formulate the model and process of school self-evaluation articulated in School Self-Evaluation, below. The external evaluation focus is important in three particular respects. The first is the potential the alternative methodologies developed at that time had for adaptation to the school level. The second is the recognition of the political dimension of evaluation. The third is the failure of many external reform efforts to impact upon the system.

Case-Study Evaluation

Development of the case-study approach to evaluation in the United Kingdom had its origins in the external evaluation of center-periphery curriculum reform and one project in particular, the Humanities Curriculum Project. This was a broad-aims program that aspired to "develop an understanding of social situations, human acts and the controversial value issues which they raise."[3] Such a broad aim did not lend itself to evaluation by commonly accepted methods of evaluation at that time such as the objectives model of curriculum planning and evaluation. Indeed the project did not have objectives and the project team did not wish to formulate any as objectives were considered inappropriate for the educational purpose they had in mind. The project had its educational rationale in a view of education that had little to do with prespecified objectives or intended learning outcomes. On the contrary, as written at the time, "Education as induction into knowledge is successful to the extent that it makes the behavioral outcomes of the students unpredictable."[4] Such a view of education may seem like heresy in the 1990s context of high-stakes testing, prespecification of content, and pressure for evidence of outcomes. But as a rationale for education it is as valid now as it was then, even if not valued by those who have statutory responsibility for prescribing curriculum. The important point for this chapter however is the alternative approach to evaluation that evolved in this context.

Faced with trying to understand the effects of a broad-aims program that respected the autonomy of students and the unpredictability of learning outcomes, the evaluators had no choice but to develop a different approach if they were to provide useful information for decision makers, which was the aspiration of the evaluation. Early field observations of the program in action confirmed this view as the reactions differed so markedly from one context to another.[5] What it offered was an opportunity to study in depth the culture of the context in which the innovative curriculum was implemented; to understand how the curriculum was experienced from the perspectives of the different actors involved; and to document the complex interactions and dynamics of change over time. Interviewing, observation, and documentary analysis were the primary methods that allowed an exploration of these issues in case studies of specific institutions implementing the innovation. It is important to record also, however, that another facet of the evaluation of this project was a large-scale testing program. This was used not to test prespecified outcomes but in an exploratory way to see what, if anything, in the dimensions recorded by the tests was significant in this project. These were then analyzed in relation to the effects documented within the school case studies.

Thirty years later the case-study approach to evaluation is now well accepted and legitimated in the evaluation literature and is widely used in evaluation designs either as the primary approach to data gathering and reporting or as an element in a multifaceted, multimethod design.[6] The case-study approach shares a number of attributes with other pluralistic approaches to evaluation that evolved at a similar time. These include responsive evaluation,[7] portrayal evaluation, transactional evaluation,[8] illuminative evaluation,[9] and holistic evaluation. Significant features of these approaches were summarized at the time by Hamilton:

> Compared with the classical models, they tend to be more extensive (not necessarily centered on numerical data), more naturalistic (based upon program activity rather than program intent), and more adaptable (not constrained by experimental or preordinate designs). In turn they are likely to be sensitive to the different values of program participants, to endorse empirical methods which incorporate ethnographic fieldwork, to develop feedback materials which are

couched in the natural language of the recipients, and to shift the locus of formal judgement from the evaluator to participants.[10]

While the case-study approach to evaluation evolved in a context of external evaluation of curriculum programmed, it was easily adaptable to school self-evaluation. The focus on accessible methods of data collection and analysis and accessible language in reporting matched, at a slightly different level and with a different purpose in mind, skills teachers already used in the context of teaching. While these skills did not necessarily automatically translate to an evaluation context without further training, the potential was clearly there.[11]

The Political Dimension of Evaluation

The concept of school self-evaluation is also an extension of a democratic stance to evaluation. At the same time as these new approaches to evaluation were evolving in response to the deficiencies of earlier classical models, there was a growing recognition of the inherent political dimension of evaluation.[12] In the UK in his 1974 paper "Evaluation and the Control of Education," MacDonald offered a political classification of evaluation models in outlining three ideal types—autocratic, bureaucratic, and democratic. Classifying evaluation in this way emphasized that evaluation was much more than a technical methodological exercise. Choices evaluators make about methodologies have political implications for the distribution of power. There were two main reasons for the sharp focus on political stances at this time. One was a consequence of moving to the new methodological approaches described above; as evaluators moved 'beyond the numbers game' to study people, institutions, and policies, they could not avoid confronting their political role. The methods they chose, the data they selected, the way they represented people, institutions, and policies in evaluation reports and when, to whom, and how they were distributed, had ethical and political implications for the way people were treated and how knowledge was created and distributed. The second reason was the growing awareness in the early seventies of the increasing centralizing tendency to control and prescribe curriculum change. The concept of democratic evaluation introduced by MacDonald in 1974 was a response to this growing unease about the role of the evaluator in the distribution of power. What it proposed was that evaluation become more consistent with the professed values of the liberal democratic state. His central proposal was that the evaluator adopt an impartial role in the sharing of information between the powerful and the powerless, placing a responsibility on the evaluator to adopt methods of generating and reporting information that were easily understood and widely accessible.

Briefly stated, the concept of democratic evaluation has as its central aspiration how to find an appropriate balance between the public's right to know and the individual's right to privacy in the conduct and dissemination of evaluation. The concept derives from the rhetoric of liberal democracy, a rhetoric that is morally and politically acceptable to those exercising delegated power. From this rhetoric is derived a set of power-equalizing procedures that cut into the customary relationships embedded in organizations, holding participants at all levels accountable to criteria endorsed by them. Central precepts in the procedures include confidentiality, negotiation, and accessibility. Such procedures cannot, of course, change the power relationships, but what they can do is to accord equal treatment to individuals and ideas, establish a flow of information that is independent of hierarchical or powerful interests, and ensure that no one group or person has the power of veto. In such a context all relevant perspectives can be represented, information fairly and equitably exchanged, and deliberation encouraged.

Theory of Change

The development of alternative methodologies and recognition of the political dimension of evaluation were useful for the development of school self-evaluation. But the most significant legacy from external evaluation of the curriculum reform movement was what we learned about the failure of center-periphery curriculum reform to impact the system. For it was from this that it was possible to generate a theory of change to underpin future school development. There were many reasons for the failure of center-periphery curriculum reforms. The first and most obvious was that they failed to engage teachers—the central agents in curriculum transactions—in developing changes they were expected to adopt. Second, they frequently did not take account of the specific culture of the school. Third, they did not recognize that fundamental changes in the structure and management of schools would be necessary if anything else was to change within them.

These were early observations. Similar observations in many different settings have confirmed time and time again the deficiencies of central reform efforts such that it is now possible to summarize the main tenets of a theory of change that does have the potential to improve curriculum practice in schools.

Theory of Change Underpinning School Development

1. The school is the basic unit of change. Notwithstanding the good ideas that come from outside the school to influence teachers and

classroom curricula, it is now widely recognized that we need to pay attention to the institution as the site of change if we wish to have an influence on curriculum practice in classrooms.

2. There can be no curriculum development without teacher development. This phrase was first coined by Lawrence Stenhouse to emphasize the fact that it is teachers—not curriculum packages—who actually develop curricula and that if the curriculum is to change, teachers need to experiment with their teaching and evaluate the processes and outcomes.[13] It was from this idea that the now familiar notion of "the teacher as researcher" evolved and the action research movement was subsequently developed.[14]

3. There can be no significant teacher development, and therefore no curriculum development, without institutional development. This extension of the above concept is a conclusion drawn from my own research to take into account the fact that institutional values can be a powerful force in limiting or containing teacher development.[15] Changing the curriculum means not only a professional change for teachers but changing the culture of the school to provide the conditions in which teachers can research their teaching. This is a very large task, of course, requiring commitment at a philosophical and structural level which I have no time to explore in this chapter. But elsewhere I have indicated what value shifts are needed in the culture of schools if they are to support teacher and curriculum development.[16]

4. Schools need to have some ownership of the change process. For many years change theorists have acknowledged the centrality of this point.[17] Many current reform efforts, however, still fail to take this into account.

5. Evaluators and curriculum theorists are not the only people who generate theory about curriculum and school development. Teachers have a major role to play in the process of theorizing in their own context. Such a role can be enhanced through a self-evaluation process in a collaborative framework. We need to build a community of theorizers within the school—that is, teachers who collectively analyze and theorize about their progress and policies to provide a sound basis for curriculum and school development—if we are to systematically develop curriculum policies and practices from within.

6. Teachers cannot break through and sustain new practice without support at the institutional and local advisory level. This is obvious now, perhaps, but many curriculum projects had assumed that they could work directly and exclusively with individual classroom teachers. Change is a professional community activity.

7. Power-coercive strategies of change gain surface adoption but fail to affect basic attitudes. They are, moreover, likely to fuel resistance to change. Innovations that are not challenging are easily adopted; those that embody fundamental change are difficult to implement and are frequently rejected.
8. Schools, as Whitehead observed long ago, need to be understood in their particular circumstances and with regard to their local clientele.[18] Prescriptions for curricular action should not supplant the judgment of those who have to implement it.
9. Neither the free-market strategy (the rationale of curriculum development in the 1960s) nor command/compliance (the rationale of curriculum development more characteristic of the 1970s and 1980s) appear to yield the kind of curriculum change sought. We should think, rather, in terms of educational communities of professionals and their constituencies working together in a spirit of shared responsibility and mutual accountability.[19]

It is these tenets of change theory that underpin the process of school self-evaluation outlined in the next segment and which, I argue, provide a stronger basis for effective curriculum development than external prescriptions of curriculum intent.

School Self-Evaluation: Purpose and Process

School self-evaluation is a process of conceiving, collecting, and communicating information and evidence for the purpose of informing decision making, ascribing value to a program and establishing public confidence in the school. The key words here are *evidence, value, communication,* and *purpose. Evidence* is important to indicate the research focus of the process; unsubstantiated assertion or opinion is not acceptable. *Value* is important to remind us that evaluation is, essentially, establishing the worth of something, and that ascribing of value is a process done by people—it is not embedded in evaluation instruments such as tests or questionnaires. *Communication* is crucial if the process is to feed into policy making within the school and serve the purpose of establishing public confidence in the school. External evaluations often serve a limited audience and a one-off purpose. But school self-evaluation as I am outlining it here is an ongoing process that has implications for development and action. As such it needs to be accompanied by an internal strategy for communicating and discussing the findings, first among staff and then with parents and the wider community.

The last point I have emphasized is *purpose*. Any evaluation needs to be related to purpose. This may seem an obvious point to make but I think it is worth reiterating (at a time when evaluation is so widespread and means different things to different people) that evaluation can be undertaken for many purposes. It is important to be clear what kind of process serves which purpose. School self-evaluation in my view has three purposes:

- informing decision making within the school (i.e., to help a school's individual development);
- ascribing value to a program—to emphasize that the process is one of actively placing a value on something in the light of evidence; and
- establishing public confidence in the school.

This last purpose is very important at any time but it is particularly important when the political climate is uncertain and schools are the subject of much reform and change. This purpose also underlines the fact that school self-evaluation, while conducted by the school for its own internal development, also has a broader purpose, which is to demonstrate and communicate the schools' achievements to the broader community so they will understand the work of the school and be better able to support its development.

There are three other points that I wish to highlight about the process. The first is clearly that the notion of self is not individual. The concept of self is extended to mean that the whole school as a community is engaged in the process of evaluating the school's policies and practices (though not all of course at the same time). To this end teams of teachers (which could be extended to parents and pupils) evaluate different aspects of school policy or practice on behalf of the whole school.

The second point is that the control of the process is within the school. This is very important if school self-evaluation is to be a process of teacher and curriculum development. Teachers need to be able to take risks in interpretation, in understanding and in examining implications for action. They cannot do this if they are constantly under scrutiny from outsiders external to the school. To say that control of the process should lie within the school does not mean, however, that the school should not pay attention to issues that audiences outside the school think need evaluating. Neither does it imply that the school should not communicate its results to outsiders. This may be an important purpose, as I have said. But controlling the process and the timing of the release of findings to other audiences is a necessary procedure to enable teachers to gain confidence in the process and have that ownership over the process of change that has been lacking in previous reform efforts.

The third point is that in order for the process to influence teacher development and curriculum development, it needs to be an ongoing process built into the structure and functioning of the school. If it is to be valued as such the process needs to be underpinned by giving it some time on the timetable.

The process in practice has the following features:

- the institution, not the individual teacher or student, is the major unit of change: teacher development and pupil performance are considered in the context of whole-school policies;
- the focus of evaluation is curricular policies—policies which affect all pupils and to which all teachers are committed;
- the utilization of "low-technology" techniques and methods such as interviewing, observation, documentary analysis, questionnaires—techniques that are familiar to teachers in the context of teaching and can be adapted for the purpose of evaluating;
- the adoption of a collaborative and participatory ethic involving as many teachers as possible in the process, though not all at the same time; and
- the implementation of forms of organization that ensure the process is built into the working structure of the school.

What is being suggested here, in summary, is that teams of teachers (and different teams at different times) evaluate, on behalf of the school, an aspect of the curriculum or a cross-curricular issue in depth. The team would aspire to engage a range of teachers, students, and possibly parents in the exercise, collect evidence relevant to issues identified within the focus chosen, analyze the data, and communicate the findings in written and oral form to forums organized within the school to discuss implications for action.

Focus on Curriculum

The focus on curriculum is essential for a number of reasons. The curriculum is the core of the intellectual life of the school. It is through the curriculum that teaching and learning opportunities are created by teachers and students. And it is through the curriculum that knowledge is mediated, attitudes formed, and values discussed.

Curriculum is not an abstract entity but a lived experience that has relevance for particular students and particular teachers in a particular context. While it is possible, of course, for external evaluators to reflect this "lived experience," those closer to the setting have a more immediate understanding and intimate knowledge of the students. This makes a difference (1) to how the issues for evaluation are conceptualized (frequently generated from observations in practice); (2) to the analysis, where outcomes can be related to specific processes and particular students; and (3) to the implications to be drawn for further curriculum development in the specific context.

As active agents in the mediation of knowledge, teachers are closer to understanding the formal and informal curriculum experience of all students and how to access it. Since many of the creative opportunities for learning take place in unexpected ways and at unexpected times, teachers and students are often in a better position than external evaluators to document and evaluate the rich experience of learning, just as they may be closer to uncovering the specific elements, themes, and topics that will engage the hitherto reluctant learner, the underachiever, or the gifted. They "know" the students in a concrete, personal, individualized way.

Political Framework

In terms of the overall political structure in which evaluation has to be considered, the form of school self-evaluation advocated here has a place primarily at the local level, although it could also be an element in a state, regional, or nationwide system of evaluation. House has proposed a model of idealized evaluation procedures based on Lundgren's models for the governance of education, which enables us to examine this more closely.[20] One axis is the central-local dimension; the other the political-professional.

In each of the four resulting cells, House has suggested ideal evaluation procedures; he cites the teacher-researcher evaluation of classroom practice, for example, in the *local-professional cell*; case studies of schools involving parents and communities in the *local-political cell*; national evaluations and national testing in the *central-political cell*; and the contribution of national subject associations and teacher associations in the *central-professional cell*. These ideal evaluation procedures, according to House, are based on two assumptions worth emphasizing, given the implications they have for the location of the value of the model of school self-evaluation advocated in this chapter.[21] The first is that the primary causal factors of classroom learning are under the direct control of local teachers who essentially determine classroom processes, whatever mandates or restrictions are imposed by political authorities. The second assumption is that other groups—politicians, parents, the local community—have a right to public knowledge about what goes on in schools.[22]

Two further points can be made about evaluation procedures. The first is that there is an evaluation role and responsibility for different groups at every level in the system in relation to particular purposes. Different groups have different information needs that may be legitimate for a particular purpose but should not be assumed to cover all purposes of education. State and local administrations have quite legitimate demands for certain information about schools but they do not need to know everything that a school does in carrying out its responsibilities. A school needs a certain degree of autonomy, free from outside scrutiny, to experiment and take risks in order to develop. A nation may well need broad indicators, obtained through a national testing program, in order to indicate the state of the nation's health in particular areas of schooling and/or an evaluation of the "state of the art" in certain curriculum areas, but the results of a national testing program should not serve as the sole indicator of a particular school's achievements. More recognition of the precise purposes different evaluation procedures serve could help avoid some of the misuses or abuses of evaluation frequently encountered in which an evaluation procedure designed for one purpose is misused for another or, alternatively, denigrated because it has not fulfilled a purpose it was not designed to serve.

The second point is that there are far more resources being spent on evaluation in the political dimension, of which national testing forms an important part, and far fewer in the professional dimension. Resource support is sometimes given at a local level indirectly through association with centrally funded projects and sometimes through local administrations. But this is minimal compared with funding for national testing programs and is disproportionate to what is needed at the site of practice if evaluation is to be closely related to school development.

The political stance underpinning the process of school evaluation is essentially democratic in its "respect for persons" (the autonomy of individuals and their judgment and reason) and "respect for society" (in the intention to communicate the process and findings to legitimate audiences beyond the school). It is within this framework that I find the potential for evaluation to be educative both in the immediate sense for those involved and more broadly to those who receive the findings of evaluation. This is more than a rhetorical statement. It is embodied in the ethical procedures that underpin the process of democratic evaluation. These acknowledge the importance of establishing and sustaining educative relationships if we aspire to make a difference through the knowledge we create and disseminate through evaluations. It is in this social dynamic that the political import of findings can be sensitively and effectively used. To be educative in this sense, for me, means that knowledge must be created and shared in ways that add to the self-knowledge of individuals and contribute to the political knowledge of social groups.

Self-Accountable Professionals

School self-evaluation has often been introduced into schools or local districts in response to external demands or pressures for accountability of schools. While external accountability can indeed be one of its purposes, it is not the main purpose, if curriculum and school development is the aim. This was especially the case when the process was first devised in the late seventies, although it has been developed and extended since then to take account of the need for professionals to be self-accountable not only to each other but to constituencies outside the school. Compared with traditional models of evaluation available at that time and the dominant model of evaluation practice, which was to determine the worth of a program at the end of a chain of development and diffusion of central curriculum initiatives, this process was a radical departure. What I argued then was that the process be reversed, that evaluation precede curriculum development rather than follow in its wake.[23] I also suggested that the style of evaluation should more closely reflect the ways in which schools do evaluate the quality of the education they provide (that is, formal evaluation should build upon the natural processes schools already adopt in demonstrating the worth of what they do). Placing evaluation at the center of attempts to improve schools would lead, I concluded, to more relevant curriculum development related to particular client needs and avoid wasted effort and time on expensive, possibly irrelevant imported alternatives.

The process has come to be refined over time, as I have said, to include a stronger connection with professional and social accountability. This was an inevitable and welcome step in strengthening the utility and credibility of the process. In outlining the process in the late seventies[24] I suggested that in the short term, to give teachers the opportunity to gain confidence in professional evaluation, development of the process needed to be insulated from accountability demands, but I also argued that in the long term, such evaluation would provide an effective and constructive model of accountability.[25]

What I did not anticipate is quite how rapidly the process would have to incorporate a public professional accountable dimension. In 1988 and 1989 I reformulated the process within a concept of self-accountable professionalism. What I argued then was that, while the process of school self-evaluation has as its major purpose the enhancement of teacher professionalism and the development of professional schools, this is not incompatible with a commitment to accountability if the aspiration to be accountable stems from within and is responsive to the local community and local administration as well as colleagues within the profession. Indeed one could argue, following Reid, that it is this very responsiveness to local constituencies that actually confers on schools the professionalism they frequently claim:

> We should remind ourselves of the importance for professional practice of the support of publics outside the professions and beyond institutions . . . the theory on which professions act gets its essential meaning and significance from the outside world, not simply from the consensus of those within a profession. It is therefore essential that they address themselves to these wider publics to implant in their minds the image of the profession which those within it would like to own.[26]

Strengthening the Process

The process of school self-evaluation I have outlined above has been criticized on a number of grounds that I wish to acknowledge before indicating how the process can be strengthened.

The first and perhaps most obvious criticism, given the political democratic stance advocated for the model, is that it does not go very far in the direction of democracy. Where are the students, parents, and governors in this process? Other schools and the wider community? Some have likened it to a "teachers charter," even a protectionist one, as through this process, teachers can justify that they are evaluating their work and therefore do not need scrutiny from outsiders.

The point about democracy is fair but it needs to be placed in context. There are three specific points. First it is important to remember that evaluation is a difficult task to accomplish well. When the process was first introduced, teachers experienced the same initial deskilling that accompanies many a curriculum innovative effort. While they had the skills required, they had not at that point had any training or practice in using them in an evaluation framework. They needed time to build up their confidence in the process before sharing the results with others.

Secondly, the focus will always be on teachers as they are the main protagonists in creating effective schools, but this should not be taken to mean that only teachers are involved. Even in the early days of using a school self-evaluation process, many schools involved students and parents as a data source, though few included them as members of the evaluation team. In one context, where parents were involved at the outset in setting the agenda for the evaluation, the process ran into difficulties creating undue anxiety for teachers who, at that stage, were unfamiliar with the process of evaluation and lacked confidence. This gives weight to the point that teachers need time and training in the process before going public. There are two ways to resolve this for the future. The first is to regard the process as two staged, the first stage being the school's development of the process with appropriate support and training, the second the sharing of the process and results with the wider community. Alternatively, the process could be set up to be inclusive of all constituencies right at the beginning. In the current context, it is this second approach that I will argue later *is* the way forward provided appropriate training development and ongoing support is built in to facilitate the process.

The third point I have already made clear in the course of this chapter. In locating the process of school self-evaluation within a framework of self-accountable professionalism, I accept that schools do need to be accountable, that they should evaluate and document their work and share the results with the constituencies they serve. This is being "open to scrutiny," on criteria and in ways defined by schools themselves.

A second criticism that has been made of the school self-evaluation process described above is that it does not focus enough on student outcomes. How can we be sure, the critic's argument runs, that the process improves student outcomes? The short answer to that is we can't, just as we cannot be certain that other educative processes we engage in lead directly to improved student outcomes. There are so many factors involved. The process of school self-evaluation may facilitate teachers to improve their practice, to reorganize, regroup, or restructure the curriculum, for example, to treat students differently, and/or manage school resources more effectively, and so on. Indirectly this has an effect on the opportunities students have to learn but the direct link with improved student outcomes may be difficult to track.

The other point to be made about this criticism is more major. It is a case of asking the wrong question, of attributing to the process a purpose it was never designed to serve. What schools gain from adopting a process of school self-evaluation such as the one outlined in this chapter is of a different order from the one presumed in the question. The benefits are many but may be summarized in the three broad categories covered below.[27]

First is the growth in teacher development, self-esteem, and confidence. This has been expressed by numerous teachers who have been through a training program and conducted school self-evaluations. Second, there is the advantage that accrues to the school as a whole through teachers collectively examining their policies and practices, especially if in collaboration with parents and governors. The third and most important advantage is that schools who have instituted self-evaluation as an ongoing process, built into the structure of the school, are in a strong position to cope with any future changes. They can quickly, flexibly, and sensitively respond to external changes on the basis of an evaluation of the relevance of such initiatives for their particular context and clientele, and they will be more alert to the internal changes necessary to facilitate new developments. While school self-evaluation of particular curriculum issues will address outcomes and will indicate not only which were achieved but what factors contributed to those achievements, the overall value of the model is the process and strategy of change that it provides for the school in the short as well as in the long term.

Future Development

Evaluation of this model of school self-evaluation over fifteen years indicates a number of ways in which it can be strengthened as a form of school improvement that is also a form of school accountability. These suggestions do not depend on the school alone. School self-evaluation, as I

372

have argued previously, is a system responsibility.[28] For the process to be effective, professionals at all levels in the system need to adopt a specific supportive role.

Creating an Effective Policy Context

The first and perhaps most difficult development to achieve is creating the appropriate relationships at the policy level for school self-evaluation to have credibility. Effective evaluation systems do not depend only upon adequate conception and purpose but, crucially, upon creating appropriate relationships between all those in the school system with a responsibility for creating effective schools. For this to happen two changes are necessary.

First we need to have a clearer conceptualization of the different roles and responsibilities of each partner in the system. I use the word *partner* deliberately to reinforce the point that school evaluation is a system responsibility, not merely a task for schools alone. In this context it needs to be clearly recognized that there are legitimate different information needs at different levels in the system for different purposes and audiences and these need to be clearly stated and understood. The regular, systematic collection of information for monitoring resources and gaining an indication of broad standards of achievement needs to be separated, for instance, from evaluation of local schools for development purposes. Failure to be clear about these differences often leads to evaluating for one purpose, becoming conflated or confused with evaluation for another purpose, and to a conflict developing between the center and the local region and schools.

Second, we need a new conceptualization of the appropriate relationships to create between the different agencies who have a responsibility for education. In responding to a presentation at AERA in San Francisco, in 1992, by Granheim and Lundgren[29] on the model of steering and evaluation through goals, David Cohen offered a way forward. Cohen said that we need to examine the processes by which evaluation instruments are put into place and the values underlying those processes and that if we want to improve teaching and learning in our schools, we must find policy processes that are consistent with the educational aims we espouse for education. We need, he said, to create "pedagogies of policies" that support development of the kind of relationship we would like to see enacted in our schools—in other words, that we mirror in our policy deliberations and procedures the kind of educational processes we would like to see taking place in schools. This suggests a relationship between central agencies and schools quite different from the one we have at the current time. There can be little doubt that such redefining of these relationships is required if evaluation systems are to be successfully introduced and credibly received and enacted by all involved.

Earlier in the chapter, commenting on previous curriculum reform efforts, it was noted that traditional top-down models of curriculum change—where power is concentrated at the center and relationships hierarchically organized—are not effective for generating change. Nor are they likely to be effective in introducing evaluation systems with potential to improve schools. The alternative proposed below places curriculum and teaching and learning at the center of concern.

This alternative model[30] suggests that, instead of drawing direct, linear lines of accountability as is common in many descriptions of relationships between partners/levels in education systems, relationships be formulated with greater potential for interaction between different partners and held in a state of creative tension. For this to be a healthy state of tension and consistent with what I have said above about information needs, the roles and responsibilities of each partner in the system need to be clear. It also needs to be acknowledged that power relationships, whatever the formal structure, shift and change in political systems. The politics of education is rarely in a static state; the political climate changes, the function of agencies in different parts of the system changes, and individuals in key positions change or new agencies are created with new functions, new roles, and new personnel. The springlike linkages in this model allow for local variations according to local needs and for movement between any and all of them. The point is that, where there is an imbalance in the system, actions and reactions occur, the system will oscillate, and new alliances may form. If pushed too far in any one direction, the spring will snap and relationships will have broken down. But if adjustments are sensitively made in other parts of the system, then temporary wobbles can be accommodated and equilibrium restored, albeit with different partners then playing a key role. The implications of this model for how we think about roles and responsibilities of different groups in the system has yet to be fully explored but it holds promise for understanding the dynamics of change in volatile political systems. The model depends on the appropriate relationships indicated above, respect for the agency and political rights of individuals, and a degree of trust. It is not the model of relationships and responsibilities that we currently have in many Western democracies but, as an alternative scenario, it is something to which we can aspire and maybe even accomplish at a local level. More extensive development may have to await more propitious times.

National Goals—Local Development

A second aspiration for the future is to work to establish a more adequate balance between the different professional and political evaluation procedures outlined in House's models of evaluation.[31] These should take into account the research evidence that suggests that, compared with external attempts to reform schools, school-based evaluation (provided it is supported with adequate resources and political commitment) offers more potential for school development long term than mandated central reform.

Whatever national curriculum frameworks or guidelines are established by central governments, education takes place locally, in local classrooms, local communities, local schools, and local regions. In order to maximize educational development at the local level it is important to have systems of evaluation that take into account local difference at the point of need for local schools and their communities. It may always be the case, as House indicates, that dual systems of evaluation are needed.[32] There is a quite legitimate need for central governments to have some kind of national indicators of school performance and, from time to time, systematic reviews of certain issues across the nation. But if school development and the improvement of teaching and learning is a major aspiration, there is also an important need for self-evaluation at the local level by schools and their communities. In this context, while I would wish to retain some scope for schools to experiment at the local professional level in House's model of idealized evaluation procedures, I think it is imperative for the future to strengthen the local political accountability dimension. In the current political climate it will continue to be important for teachers and schools to demonstrate the worth of what they are doing, and it will be increasingly important for them to develop alliances with parents, governors, and local communities in efforts to improve schools.

Whatever national systems are set in place should be consonant with and not counterproductive to forms of school evaluation and development that are in the control of teachers, who are the mediators and interpreters of national goals and guidelines into local curricula. In this context it is absolutely crucial that teachers individually and collectively be supported professionally and personally. Many of the externally generated systems of evaluation focusing on the management and organization of schools over the past twenty years have neglected the personal needs of teachers, not only in terms of their major professional role but also in terms of the quality of their lives as people. Quality of learning does not depend only on quality of curriculum and teachers' knowledge but also on their quality of life. As Hargreaves and Fullan have acknowledged, "balancing work and life is an important protection against burnout. It also leads to more interested teachers and more interested teaching."[33]

Extending Local Boundaries

In relation to the process itself, there are several developments that will strengthen its acceptability as a form of curriculum and school development and give schools confidence in the process. The first is to introduce a system of school evaluation within a local district where schools are paired or consortia of schools form a cluster. This has several advantages. First, the local district is seen to take the process seriously. This is important for credibility. Second, a peer external element can be built into the process where teachers from one school can act as consultants or "critical friends" to facilitate development in each other's context. This is important to facilitate confidence in the process, and to develop a culture of mutual understanding of problems encountered and sensitive reception of results. Third, schools, or schools and the local district, can decide to focus on evaluating specific parts of the curriculum or cross-curricula issues at the same time. This would give the local administration both an indepth profile of how schools value particular areas of work and provide a cumulative knowledge base across schools that could inform future policy making.

With these three developments the process of school self-evaluation has moved firmly beyond the voluntary investigation of one school for its own internal purposes (which has its own specific advantages as a local professional evaluation) to acknowledge the process as one that is valuable for all schools, and to acknowledging teachers as important contributors to the theory of curriculum change. If the strategy indicated here were also to embrace the extension of democracy advocated in the previous section to include students, parents, and governors, then the process will clearly have become a form of local political accountability as well.

If such a system were to be introduced across a district, three further developments would be required to maintain and protect the professional growth and teacher development that is an inherent and essential part of the model, at the same time establishing the credibility and accountability of the process to local constituencies. The first would be to develop a set of ethical guidelines for practice. These would need to include who has responsibility for deciding the focus of any evaluation, the length of time devoted to it, the kind of data that is appropriate for external release and that which is not, the format and style of external reporting, and the timing of release of data to other schools and the district office.

The second would be to ensure that a system of evaluation training and ongoing support was provided by the local administration. This would need to include resources for schools for production and dissemination of evaluation reports, specific training in evaluation skills and processes, and the availability of, and resources for, specific consultant support at a point of need from a range of individuals including local advisers, academics, or members of the local community.[34]

The third would be to establish a broad framework for the operation of the scheme. This would include an outline of the different responsibilities of each partner, the expectations that are reasonable for each, the purposes that the scheme could and could not meet, and the results that could reasonably be expected. In this context the issue of outcomes and its relative status in the evaluation could be addressed as well as other contentious issues that might be driving curriculum reform. The framework would need to be endorsed by all parties.

There are some who may argue that extending the process of school self-evaluation to the district level in this way gives it a mandate that will not ensure its success but rather the opposite. If we were to take Fullan's point that "you cannot mandate what matters," then such a policy is doomed to failure like any other mandated reform.[35] What would be missing in such a judgment, however, would be the intention and principles that underpin the process. The intention in what I have outlined here is to strengthen the potential for professional growth and teacher development within and by schools by underpinning a process at the school level with administrative commitment to resource and training support. The principles underlying the extension of this process are respect for persons at whatever level in the system they have a responsibility for education and their personal development, mutual reciprocity and accountability, and growth of community, whether that community is within the school, between schools, or between schools and their local administration. If these principles are upheld in the implementation of a districtwide scheme, teacher morale might be greatly enhanced as teachers engage collectively in understanding curriculum practice and see that the results of their evaluations are valued by the local administration and the local community. The local administration and local community could rest assured that they were supporting the development of professional schools and, moreover, gaining knowledge about their schools that could be useful for future policy development.

Notes

1. Madeleine Grumet, *Bitter Milk* (Amherst: University of Massachusetts Press, 1988), p. 164.

2. Ernest R. House, "Future Policy for School-based Evaluation," in *The Theory and Practice of School-based Evaluation: A Research Perspective*, T. Alvik, A. Indrebo, and L. Monsen, eds. (Lillehammer, Norway: Oppland College, 1992), pp. 113–19.

3. *The Humanities Curriculum Project: An Introduction* (London: Heinemann Educational Books, 1971).

4. Lawrence Stenhouse, *An Introduction to Curriculum Research and Development* (London: Heinemann Educational Books, 1975), p. 82.

5. The precise way in which the case-study approach developed is detailed in Helen Simons, *Getting to Know Schools in a Democracy: The Politics and Process of Evaluation* (Lewes: Falmer, 1987).

6. See, for example, Robert E. Stake "The Case-Study Method in Social Inquiry," *Educational Researcher* (1978); and Helen Simons, *Toward a Science of the Singular: Essays about Case Study in Educational Research and Evaluation*, CARE Occasional Publications No. 10 (Norwich: Center for Applied Research in Education, University of East Anglia, 1980).

7. See Stake, ibid.

8. See Robert M. Rippey, *Studies in Transactional Evaluation* (Berkeley: McCutchan, 1973).

9. See Malcolm Parlett and David Hamilton, "Evaluation as Illumination: A New Approach to the Study of Innovatory Programs," in *Evaluation Studies Review Annual*, Gene Glass, ed. (Beverly Hills, Calif.: Sage, 1976).

10. David Hamilton, "Making Sense of Curriculum Evaluation: Continuities and Discontinuities in an Educational Idea," in *Review of Research in Education*, vol. 5, Lee Shulman, ed. (Itasca, Ill.: Peacock Press, 1977).

11. See Helen Simons, "Process Evaluation in Schools," in *Issues in Accountability and Evaluation*, Colin Lacey and Denis Lawton, eds. (London: Methuen, 1981); and "Evaluation and the Reform of Schools," in *The Evaluation of Educational Programs, Methods, Uses and Benefits: A Report of the Educational Research Workshop Held in North Berwick, Scotland* (Amsterdam/Lisse: Swets and Zeitlinger, 1989).

12. See Ernest R. House, "The Conscience of Educational Evaluation," *Teachers College Record* 73, 3 (1972); Barry MacDonald, "Evaluation and the Control of Education," in *Innovation, Evaluation, Research and the Problem of Control*, Barry MacDonald and R. Walker, eds. (Norwich: Center for Applied Research in Education, 1974); and Michael W. Apple, "The Process and Ideology of Valuing in Educational Settings," in *Educational Evaluation: Analysis and Responsibility*, Michael W. Apple, Michael G. Subkoviak, and Henry A. Lufler, eds. (Berkeley: McCutchan, 1974).

13. See Stenhouse, op. cit.

14. See, for example, John Elliott, *The Teacher as Researcher: Implications for the Supervision of Teachers*, invited address to the Annual Meeting of the American Educational Research Association, New Orleans, 1988.

15. Helen Simons, "Against the Rules: Procedural Problems in School Self-Evaluation," *Curriculum Perspectives* 5, 2, (1985).

16. See Simons, *The Evaluation of Educational Programs, Methods, Uses and Benefits*, op. cit., and *Getting to Know Schools in a Democracy*, op. cit.

17. See, for example, Michael Fullan, *Change Forces: Probing the Depth of Educational Reform* (New York: Falmer, 1993); and Barry MacDonald, "Critical Introduction: From Innovation to Reform—A Framework for Analyzing Change," in *Innovation and Change*, Jean Rudduck, ed. (Milton Keynes: Open University Press, 1991).

18. Alfred North Whitehead, *The Aims of Education and Other Essays* (London: Ernest Benn, 1932).

19. See MacDonald, "Critical Introduction: From Innovation to Reform," op. cit.

20. See Ernest R. House, "Decentralized Evaluation for Norway," in *Evaluation as Policymaking*, M. Granheim, M. Kogan, and Ulf Lundgren, eds. (London: Jessica Kingsley, 1991).

21. Ibid.

22. Ibid.

23. See Simons, "Process Evaluation in Schools," op. cit.

24. Ibid.

25. Simons, *Getting to Know Schools in a Democracy*, op. cit., p. 198.

26. William A. Reid, "Institutions and Practices: Professional Education Reports and the Language of Reform," *Educational Researcher* (November 1987):14.

27. For an extensive evaluation of participants' experience of the school self-evaluation process and training, see V. Klenowski, *Professional Development for Self-Evaluation: A Self-Sustaining Process?* Paper presented at the Annual Meeting of the American Educational Research Association, San Francisco, April 1992.

28. See Helen Simons, "Toward Professional Schools: The State of the Art," in *The Theory and Practice of School-based Evaluation: A Research Perspective*, T. Alvik, A. Indrebo, and L. Monsen, eds. (Lillehammer, Norway: Oppland College, 1992).

29. M. K. Granheim and Ulf P. Lundgren, "Steering by Goals and Evaluation in the Norwegian Education System: A Report from the Emk Project," *Journal of Curriculum Studies* 23, 6 (1991).

30. See B. J. Wiggins, "Curriculum Development," mimeographed paper, University of Southampton, 1992.

31. See House, "Future Policy for School-based Evaluation," op. cit.

32. Ibid.

33. Andy Hargreaves and Michael Fullan *What's Worth Fighting For? Working Together for your School* (Ontario, Canada: Ontario Institute for Studies in Education, 1991).

34. For an example of one such program for specific training and on-going support, see Helen Simons, "School Self-Evaluation as a Process of Teacher Development: In Support of Democratic Schools," in *Volver a Pensar La Educacion* (Spain: Morata Press, 1995).

35. See Michael Fullan, *Change Forces*, op. cit.

NINETEEN

Democratic Evaluation:
Aesthetic, Ethical Stories in Schools

Landon E. Beyer and *Jo Anne Pagano*

Educational evaluations serve a variety of purposes. For example, they enable judgments concerning teaching effectiveness for the purpose of decisions regarding promotion or salary level; they determine whether a particular curriculum ought to be continued or revised; and they gauge new policies against certain stated educational purposes. Often, and perhaps characteristically in the public schools, evaluation is thought of as something *done to* teachers or students or administrators, an activity over which those undergoing evaluation have little control and the practices and principles of which they may have slight understanding. However slight their control, however, evaluation has significant personal and professional consequences for those evaluated. In many cases, evaluative activities will rightly be seen as punitive, and often, unjust or unjustifiable. The dynamics of interpersonal and institutional power are central here, as these take place within particular settings with their own norms and traditions. In schools where technical-industrial forms of control continue to dominate, and where hierarchical, linear modes of communication persist, we should not be surprised to discover that evaluation is not only unwelcome, but is seen as invasive.[1]

Industrial models of evaluation are appropriate to industrial models of education. But such models of education have been thoroughly criticized over the last three decades, and teachers, curriculum designers, and principals have increasingly eschewed such models—at least in theory. When evaluative activities are conceptualized and implemented along early industrial lines, we might well ask if they are worth undertaking in the first place. One common response is that they provide useful information for those whose role it is to make decisions or formulate policies—about people or programs or what to do in the future. Summative evaluations of this kind are commonplace in schools as well as in colleges and universities, and in some form or other must be undertaken. They must be undertaken if only because of the current public lust for "accountability" in education. But evaluation cannot serve only a legal or regulatory master. Evaluation, of schools, of programs, of teaching, must, like classroom evaluation practices, be embedded in an educative project.

We make the bold assertion that the prior and overriding claim on our attention is the education of those who work in schools and of the communities in which they are located. Evaluation should enable those who work in schools, along with their constituents in their communities, to examine critically their educational assumptions and commitments and to examine the extent of their instantiation through practice. We assume that the relationship between evaluators and teachers is similar to that between teachers and students, and that the activities in which both engage grow out of mutual concern. Our central aim is to increase the legitimacy of evaluation as a way of moving schools as social and political institutions toward more democratic, ethical, inclusive, aesthetic environments that in turn help provide avenues for increasing social justice within the activities of classrooms and schools themselves. In essence, we argue that not only should curricular and pedagogical initiatives become more sensitive to the ideological, political, and value-laden nature of schools and their social contexts, but so too should the process of evaluation.[2] We claim that evaluation, if it is to be effective in improving schools, developing the talents of teachers, and opening the world to students, must enlarge the awareness of the virtues and vicissitudes of school practice. Evaluation must disclose the complex realities of classroom life and the varied understandings of that life that secure the evolving relationships between members of the community and their forms of knowledge. This is the job of education, and it is the job of evaluation. Because we conceive of evaluation as education, we necessarily believe that the purpose of evaluation is to aid in forming, strengthening, and sustaining democratic communities that are educative sites of moral discourses and actions. Clearly we bring to our understanding of both evaluation and education a particular set of assumptions and commitments, but a set of assumptions and commitments that have long been promoted in educational discourse.

381

Education for Democratic Living

The public schools are commonly championed as promoting democratic values and ideas and as providing opportunities for students' subsequent democratic participation in adult civic life. Yet the meaning of democracy, not to mention its practical import in classroom life, remains one of the most contested concepts in education. For democratic ideals are claimed by parties taking widely divergent, and often opposing, perspectives and promoting quite different agendas.

Educational reforms have been promoted as democratic when it is claimed that they will raise those standards that will enable future generations to maintain a competitive edge in the global marketplace. Reforms that emphasize the importance of civic participation through service learning are embedded in a significantly different perspective. Some reforms promoted in the name of democracy call for a curriculum emphasizing a common cultural heritage of historically important ideas, events, texts, and people to provide the cultural glue that holds Americans together. Still others contest the common curriculum in the name of a democratic politics of identity that highlights the varieties of texture out of which a common culture of difference will emerge. From the call by members of the Republican Revolution to scale back, if not abandon, the "Welfare State" in order to hold individuals more accountable, to the conservative and liberal embrace of the "new technology" and "post-capitalist" economic arrangements, to the national obsession with female teenage pregnancy, we mistakenly use the term *democracy* as if we were agreed on a single and unambiguous meaning, universalizable in practice.

Democracy is commonly associated with certain "founding documents" of our country, such as the Constitution and Bill of Rights, and with the freedoms and rights that these and other documents and institutions were established to protect. Regulated activities, such as electoral participation, are also frequently pointed to as crucial in maintaining democratic traditions and processes. Such documents and activities are central to what we might call the political-structural domain of U.S. society. Yet democracy as a set of possibilities—even as a vision that corresponds to particular principles, values, and beliefs—has a more encompassing purview than that of documents and electoral processes.

Democracy, as does any organizing political concept, refers to the way we make decisions and enter into communal life with others, to the ways that we identify and respond to those with whom we have interests in common and to those with whom we have not. It refers to the ways that we understand ourselves and our relationships to others and to the vision of the kind of world we aspire to construct out of those understandings. It refers, that is, to the way we live our lives each day and to our chosen obligations to others and the worlds we make with them. In this sense, the concept of democracy serves as a moral call for action in and on the world that extends beyond civic participation in the political-structural domain.

From democratic values and practices, we construct, in part, our personal and professional identities within a nexus of moral, political, social, cultural, economic, and aesthetic practices. Or at least, we ought to. At this level, we may think of democracy not as a subscribed set of practices, but as a set of normative parameters that help us to define and organize our practices and our lives. It is a live and constitutive concept having repercussions for social, cultural, political, and economic life. Thus democracy entails a set of moral imperatives that must undergo continual scrutiny in the world of practice.

These moral imperatives are often difficult to grasp and act upon because of an entrenched egoistic individualism that is a central part of our "common" cultural heritage. This perspective fosters a view of persons as "naturally" independent and autonomous, self-serving and individually motivated, concerned only for their own welfare, and perhaps that of their immediate families. This, as de Tocqueville noted, is the peculiar mark of American citizenship.[3] This perspective depicts humans as born with innate interests and desires, the expression of which often leads to conflicts the state or government must prevent or somehow harmonize. This popular view is now receiving scientific support from the research in evolutionary psychology reported by Robert Wright.[4] Wright summarizes a body of research that relies on Darwinian natural selection to support the view that all of our psychological, moral, aesthetic, political, and affectional dispositions exist because of their survival value, and it is the struggle to survive and to maximize the presence of our own genes in the gene pool that drives us to select certain social, familial, and political arrangements. Therefore, we cannot but have chosen democracy. At the same time, Wright realizes that he is compelled to make a curious argument. That is, we *ought* to choose liberal democratic structures over others because we are *genetically programmed* to do so. In other words, we ought to choose what nature determines we must choose. This naturalistic view of humans and their social and political structures presents all kinds of problems, and they are not all problems in logic.

Given the primacy of the individual, and the construction of humans as "naturally" (and not just incidentally) self-interested and -defined, we are to be allowed a freedom of expression and action circumscribed only when its exercise may infringe on those same freedoms of others. Consistent with this individualistic orientation is the embrace of a "negative freedom" to "be left alone," which seems central to a conventional understanding of democratic life. Governed by constitutional and other guarantees that protect individual rights, striving to maximize our individual happiness and sense of worth, not to mention the dispersal and survival of our genes, we form associations, in large part, because we believe these will protect our private interests.

In rejecting this emphasis on self-serving individuals who utilize freedoms only to further their private interests, we offer an alternative that draws on a different understanding of democracy and its moral contours. In this view, freedom means more than allowing individuals to undertake whatever actions they believe will serve their independently calculated private interests. To say that we are committed to "freedom of action," say, while such a commitment is in many situations obviously indispensable, is to say nothing about what *sort* of action we ought to commit ourselves to. As Benjamin Barber insightfully points out:

> Although we may use the imagery of laissez faire as the key to our liberty, most people simply do not conceive of liberty in practice as being tied up with solitude, and endless choice. People feel free concretely not simply when they have choices, but *when their choices feel meaningful*; not when there is chaos and disorder in which anything is possible, but when what is possible is a set of choices *ordered by ethical or religious values* they have chosen for themselves; not when they are left alone, but when they *participate in the free communities that permit them to define common lives autonomously and establish common identities freely.*[5]

Contrary to the emphases on individualism and negative freedom associated with some conceptions of democracy, we claim that any social group must structure its activities around one set of values or another in furthering the development of its members' identities and in the pursuit of its own continuity. All social groups are dedicated to creating principles that govern their interactions and their organization of decision making in accordance with which its members will live. It is through the continual evolution of such principles and activities that we become human—that is, through which we become a people—and attain the sort of communal identity necessary for the development and exercise of individuality and collective freedom. We are human beings, in short, not by virtue of an ability to express pre-given interests that are inherent in self-serving, isolated individuals built of selfish genes, but by virtue of those social and cultural contexts and interactions that help us to *become* human. In and through engagement with others within institutional structures, cultural practices, and political situations, we become who we are, and other than we used to be, for these contexts and interactions change us, even as we change them. Character is more than a matter of individual orientation and action. It is related to the ways of life, cultural values and goods, economic patterns, and so on, that we are invited to participate in. It is the *social* quality of experience and the values we acquire through it that shapes, in important ways, who we

384

are and who we might become. The quality of experience is tempered through the enactment of democratic values and principles.

In *Democracy on Trial,* Jean Bethke Elshtain recognizes and understands the mistrust contemporary Americans have expressed in their elected leaders, in governmental institutions, and indeed, in current practices alleged to embody democratic ideals. She suggests as a response to this prevailing cynicism that we undertake to construct "a new covenant." The terms of this covenant recognize the need simultaneously for a commitment to a common good and a commitment to divergence and diversity. As Elshtain puts it:

> Unless Americans, or the citizens of any faltering democracy, can once again be shown that they are all in it together; unless democratic citizens remember that being a citizen is a *civic* identity, not primarily a private sinecure; unless government can find a way to respond to people's deepest concerns, a new democratic social covenant has precious little chance of taking hold. . . . The social covenant is not a dream of unanimity or harmony, but the name given to a hope that we can draw on what we hold in common even as we disagree.[6]

The moral choices we make must help rejuvenate social and communal bonds around processes through which a common good may be articulated and pursued. Such communities cannot flourish in societies in which disparities of power, influence, wealth, and general well being are as large—and growing—as they are in the United States.[7] Such disparities stifle or prevent the sort of interactions required if public debate and analysis are to flourish in a climate of reason. If we are to participate as equals in the public arena to make collective, morally informed decisions about policies and practices that operate genuinely in the public interest, we must create opportunities for equal access to that space, recognize the importance of cultural values and ideas as these shape our consciousness, and consider the values by which we should choose to be governed. Equally important is the need to develop aptitudes for empathy, nurturance, caring, and concern as these are delineated by certain feminists and cultural critics.[8]

Democracy, considered as a way of life governed by moral values that generate particular kinds of interactions and practices, relies for its expression on the development of communities devoted to a public good, collectively articulated and enacted. In arguing that education has a crucial role in the development of a genuinely participatory democracy aimed at creating a common good, we recognize the importance of reestablishing a sense of community within schools. Yet the values crucial to the task of reestablishing participation and the sort of community demanded of a participatory democracy are often defied in classrooms—notably by hierarchical, reductive, and demeaning evaluation practices that emerged from industrial educational

385

models. It is important that teachers seeking to rekindle democratic values in their classrooms understand both how school practices currently contravene those values, and the means by which they can be reasserted in classroom practice.

Democracy as a way of life outlines the form of our regard for and treatment of others, indicates certain choices rather than others, and suggests means for enabling more widely shared decision making. Democratic practice diminishes inequalities of power and status and helps to arrive at a sense of the common good and an interest that is truly common and public. Democratic practice thrives in an atmosphere of conflict seasoned by attitudes of empathy, nurturance, caring, and concern. As Elshtain puts it, democracy "is not simply a set of procedures or a constitution, but an ethos, a spirit, a way of responding, and a way of conducting oneself."[9]

We are proposing a broadly based cultural vision for democratic practice in which daily activities and interactions are played out in a context of commitment to a search for a common good, to the reinvigoration of community out of an attitude of openness to dissent and difference toward new forms of social life, and to a dismantling of inequalities. A democratic community must educate its members to develop values and ideas for alternative practices, practices that enact the moral visions of democracy. Teaching and evaluating, as analogous practices, might be seen as involving deliberative processes that attempt to help others to balance and integrate rich understandings of and skillful accomplishments in a world along with awareness of the larger social dynamics and life contexts within which these understandings and accomplishments are enacted.

In working toward an education cognizant of the impediments to participatory possibilities for democratic life, we must engage students, teachers, and evaluators in meaningful and challenging conversations. This means an education that recognizes who students are, and helps them to develop forms of knowledge and understanding that will lead them to become human beings fully engaged with democratic forms of life. It implies an arena wherein teachers are participants in the construction of educational realities and a forum in which deliberation is ongoing, open, and communal. It requires an understanding of professionalism, pedagogy, and classroom culture based on a commitment to the common good rather than to the maintenance of hierarchy and conventional social and professional roles.

Educative Evaluation

Evaluative activities must themselves be part of an ensemble of educative practices that are democratic in character. Such practices employ, among other methods, a method of democratic conversation, a method intelligible against certain principles or paradigmatic propositions. Among other things, this conversation concerns the proper aims of education and the means appropriate to those aims. Here we investigate the moral paradigms that currently guide many evaluation practices, and we argue that they are subversive of the democratic ideals outlined above.

We take our notion of practices from Alasdair MacIntyre who defines a practice as

> any coherent and complex form of socially established co-operative human activity through which goods internal to that form of activity are realised in the course of trying to achieve those standards of excellence which are appropriate to, and partially definitive of, that form of activity, with the result that human powers to achieve excellence, and human conceptions of the ends and goods involved are systematically extended.[10]

Important to MacIntyre's sense of a "practice" is that it be directed toward realizing "goods internal to [a] form of activity." The first step in any educative evaluation, then, is to discover the goods internal to whatever practice is under evaluation. This is the first step, of course, only assuming that we have a clear sense of those goods internal to the practice of educative evaluation. In order to make this determination, evaluative and school practices both must be embedded within the framework of general educative practices consistent with democracy as a way of life.

The principles that structure educative evaluation practices are neither universal nor immutable; they are connected to the context for the preparation of persons for democratic living. Such preparation carries with it particular practices that enable members of communities to recognize themselves and others as members of the same communities. They are principles-in-context, and they are articulated within the practices of discursive communities. They are neither ethically nor politically neutral, and they have considerable psychological force since we are talking about questions of individual identity within cultural contexts.

While the ideal of the detached, disinterested observer who provides feedback, or the mediator who simply "elicits needs statements," has often been advocated or assumed in evaluative practice, the posture of detachment yields impoverished understanding and defies a democratic agenda. The activity of evaluation must include an analysis of the values, beliefs, and perspectives that guide community members and the practices being evaluated. Because analysis is itself guided by values, beliefs, and perspectives, the analysis itself must be subject to similar scrutiny. There must be, in effect, a conversation between the analysis and its object. But conversation is possible only in an open, inclusive, and democratic setting. Because "placing value on" an activity or object is central to the practice of evaluation, evaluators must be critically aware of the particular values that accompany perceptions as well as judgments.[11] And they must be aware of the nature of their involvement in the conversation.

In her elaboration of Wittgenstein's claim that knowledge is a form of acknowledgment, Lorraine Code reminds us that knowledge is political and moral as well as epistemic. Her project is to "rethink women's capacity for thinking" against the background of mainstream epistemological theory. She argues that the sex of the knower makes a difference, notably a political difference. Her aim is to employ feminist epistemological theory toward the end of increasing social justice. In order to do so, she says, we must move into a conversational mode. She maintains that thinking is itself conversational and that conversations bring forward a diversity of meanings. In mainstream philosophy the aim of theory building is to find a resolution to diversity and bring closure. In a conversational model, the aim is to maintain "a creative tension within this diversity of meanings."[12] Elizabeth Young-Bruehl also urges us to adopt a conversational model in thinking about knowledge and education. She says that traditional epistemologies are funded in a drive toward assimilation and unification of elements of the psyche under the domination of the rational, and a rationality very narrowly conceived at that. Such models of mind and knowledge shore up authoritarian power and serve authoritarian governments well. Her argument for a conversational model, one in which all elements of the psyche are heard equally, rests on the belief that democracy is the best form of social and political life and that our models of social and political life mirror our models of knowledge. If we choose democracy in the social world, then we must choose democracy in the psychological world.[13]

Code describes conversation in the following way:

> Productive conversations have to be open, moving, and resistant to arbitrary closure; sensitive to revisions of judgment; prepared to leave gaps where no obvious consensus is possible. They will be characterized by . . . "productive ambiguity"—an idea rich in possibilities, and anathema to the philosophical tradition. The emphasis on ambiguity signals the thoroughly interpretive tenor of such conversations: a hermeneutic dimension committed not to seeking a single, privileged *Urtext* beneath conversational variants, nor aiming primarily at a fusion of horizons in which differences would be dissolved, but to working dialogically to preserve the best features of the consciousness raising that participated at the birth of the women's movement. No assumptions can be made, from the outset, about the commensurability of languages spoken or

the experiences spoken about, even when the participants ostensibly speak "the same" language.[14]

The notion that evaluations can, or ought to be, conducted by "outsiders," is fundamentally opposed to our conversational approach. Evaluators must perceive themselves as having a stake in the evaluation, for nothing less is at stake than the education of the young, and this must be of concern to us all. Evaluators must understand that they are implicated in the communities they enter. We do not mean, as others seem to suggest, that evaluators should simply make known their positions and allow practitioners to respond. An evaluation, whether one is aware of it or not, becomes a part of the community it enters; it changes the conversation among those who are already members of that community. Evaluators must acknowledge their entry into communities *as actors and practitioners themselves.* To so acknowledge their positions implicates them in the nurture and growth of that community. They become, in a serious sense, stakeholders in that community.

Virginia Woolf once said that the crucial educational question to be resolved is, What kind of human being do we wish our young people to become? The corollary question, of course, is, What sort of world do we wish them to produce and sustain?[15] Were we to settle these questions once and for all time, educative evaluation would be a relatively simple matter. But there are at least two problems plaguing this practice. The first—one we have dealt with already—concerns the central propositions around which a genuinely democratic community and society may function. The second and more immediate problem concerns what evaluative practices are in accord with the requirements for a democratic way of life. One problem here is that democracy is often assumed to be an accomplished fact rather than an ongoing inquiry into normative and political possibilities, as well as an accompanying set of practices that diverge from contemporary social and cultural ways of life.

What sort of human beings do we want our young to become, and what sort of world do we want them to support? We want them to become like ourselves, and we want them to perfect the world that we envision. Stanley Cavell, among many others, writes that all education is political, because through education we attempt to form our communities. We attempt to do so by posing ourselves as representative[s] of our cultures and by providing the resources that will enable the young to represent us, to become representative[s] of our communities, *to speak as one of us.*[16] In its dangerous form, the activities that guide the practice of education are, according to Madeleine Grumet, deeply embedded in mimetic engagement. That is, as teachers and as students, we understand and judge the object at hand according to the degree to which it feels like home. We identify and are identified within a certain relation. That is typically what we mean when we talk about education or evaluation as an art. We attempt to mimic, to enact a relation, and to encourage in our students the reinscription in their lives of our enacted relations. But Grumet argues that educative practices must move from mimesis to transformation of those relations, from transformation to mimesis and back to transformation.[17] A democratic world cannot be a world identical to ourselves. And here is the trick that must be untricked: education is about finding and forming identity within a community that is not simply my identity nor the sum of identities within which my relationships are formed. This is another form of conversation. Grumet says:

> If it is as a teacher that I engage in inquiry into teaching, then I do not deny or disguise my relation to the object of that inquiry but make that relation the object of the inquiry itself. If teaching requires that we bring to consciousness our relation to the object both so that the relation may be extended to the student through mimesis and so that the relationship of both student and teacher to the object may be reconsidered and perhaps transformed, then research into teaching demands the most rigorous attention to these relations.[18]

Evaluation practices are implicated in questions of identity just as are pedagogical and curricular practices. They are enactments of the evaluator's relation to the objects of evaluation. However much certain so-called scientific practices enjoin on us distance, that distance is a fantasy, an enactment of a fantasy of control in which we are all presumed to be, nonetheless, one of us. There is irony in asserting a distance that merely presumes identity within and identification with a particular discursive community.

We do not mean to exclude certain commonplaces of evaluation from our conversational model. Testing, counting, observing and recording, doing case studies—all of these should be a part of any evaluation. But these do not in themselves tell a story. And evaluation finally is a story we tell about the results of our tests, our surveys, our records, and our observations. Too often this story is not told directly, and we miss its human implications. In talking about storytelling, Oliver Sacks says:

> My work, my life, is all with the sick—but the sick and their sickness drives me to thoughts which, perhaps, I might otherwise not have. Constantly my patients drive me to question, and constantly my questions drive me to patients— thus in the stories or studies which follow there is a continual movement from one to the other. Studies, yes; why stories, or cases? To restore the human subject at its centre—the suffering, afflicted, fighting, human subject—we must deepen a case history to a narrative or tale; only then do we have a "who" as well

as a "what," a real person, a patient, in relation to disease—in relation to the physical.[19]

Sacks knows that professional practice always implicates the practitioner because it is in relationship to his patients that the practitioner locates his own thoughts and questions. He finds himself inflected toward the patient, and it is out of his inflection that the story emerges. Similarly in educating and evaluating, we are inflected toward those who participate with us in a relationship out of which a story emerges. The conversational model that we adopt for educative evaluative practice must end in a story, but always a provisional story. The stories we tell must sustain the creative tensions among the diversity of perspectives and experiences observed and reported, seeing in this diversity a productive ambiguity that the evaluator may then employ in fashioning a story productive of still other stories.

Evaluation should be educative in at least two ways—in its ability to heighten the sensibilities of those involved, and in its ability to disclose something to those engaged in the evaluation process. On the one hand, an evaluator who observes a variety of situations may be able to notice or interpret events differently from someone who is caught up in the daily ebb and flow of activities, and thus communicate other ways of seeing the situation—helping to create new forms of awareness that the teacher will find helpful and even reinvigorating. On the other hand, the teacher may equally be able to enlighten evaluators in a way that not only provides new perspective on the situation, but provides a different evaluative framework or emphasis. In both of these cases, evaluations will become more meaningful when attention is paid to the stories constructed out of the conversations of classroom life and the artistic qualities of evaluation seen as a narrative form.

Stories, Democracy, and Community

Democracy is a story, or a set of stories, we tell ourselves. Stories of democracy have moral, aesthetic, and psychological as well as political resonances. With the emergence of literatures critical of the cultural, racial, sexual, and gender politics of our inherited stories of democracy have come contesting histories and conflicting stories. Contemporary critics of education who dominate the popular press lament the loss of a unifying story fearing that its loss presages the abdication of community and democracy both. The response to this fear is an attempt to reassert in schools our inherited stories through the regime of a strictly defined canon enforced by discipline, standardized testing, dress codes, and other instruments of unification. And the "suffering, afflicted, fighting human subject" is lost from the center of our stories of democracy and education.

Critics from the right are correct in their observation that we need common stories toward which to orient ourselves as acting, knowing, feeling human subjects. We need to share stories that inflect us toward one another in deeply caring ways. Those stories mediate our understanding of ourselves, of what we owe to others, and what they owe to us. They are the place we stand when we judge the world and make our choices about the lives we choose to lead. But stories of democracy cannot be enforced; by their nature they are in a constant state of revision. We may say that democracy is not a foundational state, but a regulative ideal whose stories should enable multiple conversations that lead to new stories.

Richard Rorty argues that our problem is that the metaphysical vocabulary we have inherited from Enlightenment rationalism no longer serves us well. Disputes between liberals and conservatives, for example, "are a contest between an entrenched vocabulary which has become a nuisance, and a half-formed new vocabulary which vaguely promises great things." He recommends a new method for doing philosophy which,

> is to redescribe lots and lots of things in new ways, until you have created a pattern of linguistic behavior which will tempt the rising generation to adopt it, thereby causing them to look for new forms of nonlinguistic behavior, for example, the adoption of new scientific equipment or new social institutions. . . . [This philosophy] works holistically and pragmatically. . . . It does not pretend to have a better candidate for doing the same old things which we did when we spoke in the old way. Rather, it suggests that we might want to stop doing those things and do something else.[20]

The new vocabulary Rorty urges philosophers to adopt is a vocabulary of self-creation and metaphor. This is a vocabulary we urge educators and evaluators to adopt as they seek to "do something else" within the necessary work of evaluation.

According to Charles Taylor, self-interpretation is the defining mark of human beings. Human beings are creatures who interpret themselves and reinterpret themselves. We may say that we never just are what we are, for what we are, that is what we take ourselves to be, is in a constant state of revision. For Taylor, self-interpretation occurs within a context of encounter within which our sense of our own identity is constituted partially from our sense of others, objects, and situations; there exists a conversation between self and other out of which meaning is constituted. This conversation develops only within the context of community, and helps build the culture for democracy. Access to self entails access to a common vocabulary, which is access to a language community.[21]

In schools we come to our self-interpretations through the stories that guide our conversations with others. These stories provide the vocabulary out of which we glean significance and from which we learn to judge and act. Too often these are stories of absolutes and universals that derogate the specificity of experience and desire, wiping our names off the page—not even a footnote to history. Democratic stories require a new vocabulary that provides us with metaphors for our self-creation. And self-creation is not just moral and psychological; it is political, and it is an aesthetic act.

Educative, democratic evaluation is an activity through which we render the multiple metaphors of self-creation in the vocabularies within which they are inscribed. The purpose is not to harmonize vocabularies, but to discover new ones that enable us to act in new ways, ways that will enlarge the possibilities of self creation for all.

Educative Evaluation, Aesthetics, and Stories

Aesthetics can help us to enlarge those possibilities of self-creation by providing us with vocabularies that place the human subject at the center of our stories and help us to see it as he or she perceives it as well as how we perceive it. Of course, in education and evaluation, there will be multiple stories to read and write.

The arts have been valued for a number of reasons, and highlighted for their ability to serve a number of personal and social aims. As cultural creations often said to be among the most fulfilling of human achievements, the arts have been touted as a civilizing feature of human existence. Beyond other characteristics, the arts, and individual works of art, are characterized by the use of symbols—whether these are words, musical notations that elicit certain kinds of performance, the patterns of dark and shadow on canvas, or the pattern and grace of human movement. But the arts are more than just the surface qualities of which they are partially comprised—they generate meanings and values that cannot be conveyed in the same way or to the same end through more didactic forms of exposition. The arts do not duplicate what other ways of communicating express, and cannot be reduced to experiences which they make more vivid or significant. As opposed to more utilitarian, pragmatically generated claims or expressions, the arts offer liberating possibilities. While portraying realities or ways of seeing and making sense of situations that diverge from conventional ones, the arts make clearer the worlds we inhabit, helping us see them from a different perspective. As symbolic creations that are *in* but not exactly *of* the day-to-day worlds in which we live, they make possible imaginative renderings that both connect us to the world and make it possible for us to imagine better ones we can, as a result, work toward.[22] Works of art represent a kind of wholeness in which the patterns composing it provide a unity within which the elements of its composition direct our attention. This is not just the unity of formal elements with which a painting or song is formed, but a unity of experience, feeling, and reflection prompted by the work of art that can affect the ideas, perceptions, and identity of the person interacting with it. It is important to note that this is not an enforced unity, but one that emerges out of conversation within a shared story.

The domain of the arts can be conceptualized as the appreciative interaction with artifacts that have symbolic significance and meaning. Yet there are a number of nonartifactual experiences possible that also have aesthetic significance—for example, appreciative activities involving nature. While not created by human beings, such experiences evoke meanings with participants not unlike those provided by works of art. If we regard "the aesthetic" as a more encompassing domain—one that includes artifacts, acts, and natural phenomena—we could say that a variety of experiences, objects, and actions can be perceived so as to allow for new insights into experiences and possibilities for new actions and interactions, in a way that contributes to some notion of individual and social well being. Just as reading a poem or contemplating the pattern of light, shadow, and color in a forest can convey something that affects how we perceive and live in the world, evaluation as an aesthetic activity can convey something that would otherwise be missed about classroom activities through the telling and retelling of stories generated by communities framed by democratic discourses and practices.

Yet typical forms of evaluation are concerned with such things as standardized test scores, various quantitative measures of teacher effectiveness or student success, and numerical rankings of a person's productivity. These are felt to summarize—perhaps *essentialize* would be a more appropriate term—a person's efforts or degree of success. They attempt to offer comparative data according to which a person can be judged. In providing such summary data, however, they necessarily overlook the complexity of actual situations and human dynamics, reducing elaborate situations to their supposed numerical equivalents. Even more qualitative analyses offer a form of inquiry and analysis that favors some aspects over others, or explains phenomena in ways that may not capture their most important aspects. While these analyses provide a richer, more subtle rendering of experience than quantitative data, they do not necessarily provide an understanding that reflects the deep meanings generated from the experiences of those involved.

We propose, therefore, an alternative to more conventional evaluation efforts that highlights the actual lived experience of teachers through a narrative form that allows them to harness the symbolic and creative features of the arts with the aim of making evaluation more comprehensive, fair, and educative. Through narratives that can more fully reveal the qualities of lived experience, utilizing symbolic domains that capture meanings not possible through quantitative, "bottom line" results, teachers can disclose something of their worlds not achievable by other means. Teachers can engage in acts of self-creation that help to focus their critical attention on the metaphors through which they shape the stories that provide the vocabulary for classroom conversation.

The use of metaphor in narrative depictions of lived experience can tell a story that is more understandable and revealing for those charged with providing evaluative feedback. The use of metaphor also provides a method for critical analysis, for metaphor reveals our deeper purposes and desires. While conventional evaluation studies may be filled with less than graceful prose, something other than the captivating metaphor, and imagery that is less than artistic, narratives of school life done with insight and care, penetrating images and forceful depictions, are of central value to those responsible for understanding and evaluating school practice.

This is related to something we suggested earlier that characterizes educative forms of evaluation—the articulation of principles that ground choices in schools and an understanding of the normative beliefs and structures that are related to those principles. Moreover, aesthetically sensitive narrations that capture the meaning of lived experience are far more likely to disclose something about the setting involved; it is precisely this disclosure potential of the story that makes this kind of evaluative activity more likely to be educative than more usual quantitative and qualitative kinds.

Educative evaluation is an act and not a summary. Educative evaluation can stop us from doing the same old things. It aims to change educational practice by helping to develop new vocabularies. These new vocabularies provide metaphors which enable us to reinscribe ourselves within new relationships and new commitments. Finally, education itself is about the reinscription of the self through the vocabularies through which we encounter ourselves in relation to texts and others. It is about ways to forge democratic practices that may be only hinted at in current language patterns and social practices.

Notes

1. For a critique of the patterns of discourse commonly used in administrative relationships in schools, and an outline for a different pattern, see Landon E. Beyer, "Communication, Power, and Emancipation: A Contextual View of Educational Administration," *Journal of Management Systems* 5, 2 (1993).

2. See Michael W. Apple and Landon E. Beyer, "Social Evaluation of Curriculum," *Educational Evaluation and Policy Analysis* 5, 4 (Winter 1983).

3. Alexis de Tocqueville, *Democracy in America* (New York: Collier, 1900).

4. Robert Wright, *The Moral Animal: The New Science of Evolutionary Psychology* (New York: Pantheon, 1994).

5. Benjamin R. Barber, *An Aristocracy of Everyone: The Politics of Education and the Future of America* (New York: Ballantine, 1992), p. 25, emphasis added.

6. Jean Bethke Elshtain, *Democracy on Trial* (New York: Basic, 1995), pp. 30–31, italics in original.

7. See "Workers' pay drops sharply despite rise in firms' profits," *Chicago Tribune*, Friday, June 23, 1995, section 1, p. 11; and Benjamin M. Friedman, *Day of Reckoning: The Consequences of American Economic Policy* (New York: Vintage, 1989).

8. See Jane Roland Martin, *The Schoolhome* (Cambridge: Harvard University Press, 1992); Nel Noddings, *Caring: A Feminist Approach to Ethics and Moral Education* (Berkeley: University of California Press, 1984); Mary Jeanne Larrabee, *An Ethic of Care: Feminist and Interdisciplinary Perspectives* (New York: Routledge, 1993); Cornel West, *Race Matters* (Boston: Beacon, 1983); and bell hooks, *Talking Back* (Boston: South End, 1989); and *Outlaw Culture* (New York: Routledge, 1994).

9. Elshtain, op. cit., p. 80.

10. Alasdair MacIntyre, *After Virtue* (London: Duckworth, 1981), p. 175.

11. See Apple and Beyer, op. cit., and Michael W. Apple, Michael J. Subkoviak, and Henry S. Lufler, eds., *Educational Evaluation: Analysis and Responsibility* (Berkeley: McCutchan, 1974).

12. Lorraine Code, *What Can She Know? Feminist Theory and the Construction of Knowledge* (Ithaca, N.Y.: Cornell University Press, 1991), p. 306.

13. Elizabeth Young-Bruehl, "The Education of Women as Philosophers," *Signs* 12, 12 (Winter 1987).

14. Cade, op. cit., p. 308.

15. Virginia Woolf, *Three Guineas* (New York: Harcourt Brace Jovanovich, 1938).

16. Stanley Cavell, *The Claim of Reason* (New York: Oxford University Press, 1979).

17. Madeleine R. Grumet, "On Daffodils That Come before the Swallow Dares," in E. W. Eisner and A. Peshkin, eds., *Qualitative Inquiry: The Continuing Debate* (New York: Teachers College Press, 1990).

18. Ibid., p. 105.

19. Oliver Sacks, *The Man Who Mistook His Wife for a Hat and Other Clinical Tales* (New York: Summit Books, 1985).

20. Richard Rorty, *Contingency, Irony, and Solidarity* (New York: Cambridge University Press, 1989), p. 9.

21. Charles Taylor, *Sources of the Self* (Cambridge: Cambridge University Press, 1990).

22. See Landon E. Beyer, "The Arts as Personal and Social Communication: Popular/Ethical Culture in Schools," *Discourse: Studies in the Cultural Politics of Education*, 17, 2 (1996).

CONTRIBUTORS

MICHAEL W. APPLE is the John Bascom Professor of Curriculum and Instruction and Educational Policy Studies at the University of Wisconsin–Madison. He has written extensively on the relationship between knowledge and power. Among his many books are *Ideology and Curriculum* (second edition 1990), *Teachers and Texts* (1986), *Education and Power* (second edition 1995), *Official Knowledge* (1993), *Democratic Schools* (1995), and *Cultural Politics and Education* (1996).

THOMAS E. BARONE is Professor of Curriculum and Instruction and of Educational Leadership and Policy Studies at Arizona State University. His writings reveal an interest in curriculum as aesthetic, political, and institutional text. He has also theorized about and experimented with a variety of literary-style modes of educational inquiry, including literary journalism, critical biography, and novelistic storytelling.

JAMES A. BEANE is a professor in the National College of Education at National-Louis University. He is the author of *Curriculum Integration, Affect in the Curriculum: Toward Democracy, Dignity and Diversity* and *A Middle School Curriculum: From Rhetoric to Reality* and co-author or editor of several other works.

LANDON E. BEYER is Associate Dean for Teacher Education at Indiana University, Bloomington. His publications include *Knowing and Acting: In-*

quiry, Ideology, and Educational Studies (1988), *Preparing Teachers as Professionals: The Role of Educational Studies and Other Liberal Disciplines* (1989, co-authored with Walter Feinberg, Jo Anne Pagano, and James Anthony Whitson), *Creating Democratic Classrooms: The Struggle to Integrate Theory and Practice* (1996), and *Curriculum in Conflict: Social Visions, Educational Agendas, and Progressive School Reform* (1996, with Daniel P. Liston).

GLORIA LADSON-BILLINGS is Associate Professor in the Department of Curriculum and Instruction at the University of Wisconsin–Madison. Her specializations are multicultural education and social studies. She is co-editor (with Carl A. Grant) of the *Dictionary of Multicultural Education* (1997), and author of *The Dreamkeepers: Successful Teachers of African-American children (1994).*

DONALD S. BLUMENFELD-JONES is an Assistant Professor of Curriculum and Instruction at Arizona State University. He recently received the James B. Macdonald Prize in Curriculum Theory for his paper, " 'Teacher as Authority': A Model for Curriculum and Pedagogy." He has published articles in *The Journal of Curriculum Theorizing*, the *International Journal of Qualitative Studies in Education*, and *Teachers and Teaching: Theory and Practice*. His areas of research include classroom discipline, teacher beliefs, and issues of qualitative research. He is also the director for the Teaching for a Diverse Future teacher preparation program.

BARBARA BRODHAGEN is a middle school teacher in the Madison, Wisconsin, Metropolitan Schools and a doctoral student in Curriculum and Instruction at the University of Wisconsin–Madison. Her work on developing an integrative curriculum and teacher-student planning has been cited in several books and journals on curriculum integration and democratic education.

DOUGLAS D. NOBLE is the author of *The Classroom Arsenal: Military Research, Information Technology, and Public Education* (1991), and numerous articles on the history and politics of educational technology. He is co-founder and currently Teacher Coordinator at Cobblestone School in Rochester, New York, and Learning Specialist at the Rochester Institute of Technology.

SARA E. FREEDMAN is Assistant Professor of Education at Boston College, where she teaches courses in the social contexts of education and curriculum and instruction. Her research interests include the politics of gender, race, and class in urban schools, the role of private funding in the movement to privatize public education, and the political economy of schooling within the broader context of postindustrial capitalism. She was a founding member of the Boston Women's Teacher's Group and is on the editorial board of *Radical Teacher*. She presently coordinates the Donovan Teaching Scholars program at Boston College, which recruits and prepares teachers to work in urban schools.

HERBERT M. KLIEBARD is currently a Professor of Curriculum and Instruction and Educational Policy Studies at the University of Wisconsin–Madison. His most recent books are *The Struggle for the American Curriculum* (second edition, 1996), and *The Forging of the American Curriculum* (1993). A new volume, *The Vocationalizing of the American Curriculum*, is now in preparation.

SUSAN E. NOFFKE was a teacher of elementary and middle school aged children in Wisconsin for ten years. She is currently Assistant Professor of Curriculum and Instruction at the University of Illinois at Urbana–Champaign, where she works with preservice elementary teachers as well as graduate students. Her scholarly work, focusing on curriculum history, action research, and collaboration across difference, has been published in *Teaching and Teacher Education, Curriculum Perspectives, Theory into Practice*, and *Review of Research in Education*. She is co-editor (with Robert Stevenson) of *Educational Action Research* (1995).

JO ANNE PAGANO is Professor of Education at Colgate University. She is the author of *Exiles and Communities: Teaching in the Patriarchal Wilderness*, and with Landon E. Beyer, Walter Feinberg, and James Anthony Whitson, *Preparing Teachers as Professionals*. Her work has also appeared in *Educational Theory, Curriculum Inquiry*, the *Journal of Moral Education, Educational Studies, JCT: An Interdisciplinary Journal of Curriculum Studies*, and in numerous anthologies.

GEORGE J. POSNER is Professor of Education at Cornell University in Ithaca, New York. He is the author of *Course Design: A Guide to Curriculum Development for Teachers*, fifth edition (with Alan Rudnitsky), *Field Experience: A Guide to Reflective Teaching*, fourth edition, and *Analyzing the Curriculum*, second edition, as well as numerous articles in curriculum development and science education. While on the faculty at Cornell he served as a school board member for the Ithaca City School District (1987–90) and as a science teacher in the seventh grade (1992). He also serves as an independent educational consultant working for families looking for educational and treatment options outside the public schools.

HELEN SIMONS is Professor of Curriculum Policy and Evaluation at the University of Southampton, United Kingdom, where she specializes in program, policy, and institutional evaluation, school development, and the politics of change. Her main research interests and publications center on evaluation, case-study methodology, and the ethics of research. During the past twenty years, she has conducted numerous evaluations and evaluation training activities in the UK and overseas, and has acted as consultant to many ministries and local agencies in helping establish evaluation systems.

MICHAEL J. STREIBEL is Associate Professor in the Education Technology Program of the Department of Curriculum and Instruction at the University of Wisconsin–Madison. His current line of inquiry includes both a critical analysis of how computers are used in education and an investigation into the design of intelligent tutoring software for undergraduate science education. He also teaches a number of graduate courses in educational media, instructional design, and educational research with and about computers.

KENNETH A. SIROTNIK is Professor and Chair of Educational Leadership and Policy Studies in the College of Education at the University of Washington. His research, teaching, and other professional activities range widely over many issues, including measurement, statistics, evaluation, technology, educational policy, organizational change, and school improvement. Among his latest books are *The Moral Dimensions of Teaching* (co-edited with John Goodlad and Roger Soder) and *Understanding Educational Statistics* (co-authored with James Popham).

KENNETH N. TEITELBAUM is an Associate Professor in the School of Education and Human Development at Binghamton University. His scholarly interests focus on schooling and issues of power, equality and justice; school knowledge within current and historical contexts; and critical reflection in teacher education and teachers' work. He has published on these and related issues in scholarly journals and books, and is the author of *Schooling for "Good Rebels": Socialism, American Education, and The Search for Radical Curriculum* (1995).

GARY WEILBACHER is a seventh-grade teacher at Sherman Middle School in Madison, Wisconsin. He is presently working on his doctoral dissertation in the Department of Curriculum and Instruction at the University of Wisconsin–Madison. In addition to working for six years in the middle school setting, his teaching experiences include four years in a juvenile correctional institution and involvement with an alternative school.

400

GEORGE WILLIS is Professor of Education at the University of Rhode Island. He is editor of *Qualitative Education: Concepts and Cases in Curriculum Criticism* (1978), co-editor of *Reflections from the Heart of Educational Inquiry: Understanding Curriculum and Teaching Through the Arts* (1991), and *The American Curriculum: A Documentary History* (1993), and co-author of *Curriculum: Alternative Approaches, Ongoing Issues* (1995). He is a founding member and former president of the Society for the Study of Curriculum History.

GEORGE H. WOOD is Principal of Federal Hocking High School in Stewart, Ohio, and Professor of Educational Administration at Ohio University. He is also the founder of the Institute for Democracy in Education and co-editor of its journal, *Democracy and Education*. George spends his time away from work writing about schools (his most recent book is *Schools That Work*, and he will have a new book out about high school reform, from Dutton, in early 1998), admiring his wife's (Marcia Burchby) ability as a Kindergarten teacher, camping and hiking with his sons (Michael and John), and planting trees to replace the ones used up by the pages on which his ideas are printed.

SUNY Series: Frontiers in Education
Philip G. Altbach, editor

List of Titles

Class, Race, and Gender in American Education—Lois Weis (ed.)

Excellence and Equality: A Qualitatively Different Perspective on Gifted and Talented Education—David M. Fetterman

Change and Effectiveness in Schools: A Cultural Perspective—Gretchen B. Rossman, H. Dickson Corbett, and William A. Firestone

The Curriculum: Problems, Politics, and Possibilities—Landon E. Beyer and Michael W. Apple (eds.)

The Character of American Higher Education and Intercollegiate Sport—Donald Chu

Crisis in Teaching: Perspectives on Current Reforms—Lois Weis, Philip G. Altbach, Gail P. Kelly, Hugh G. Petrie, and Sheila Slaughter (eds.)

The High Status Track: Studies of Elite Schools and Stratification—Paul William Kingston and Lionel S. Lewis (eds.)

The Economics of American Universities: Management, Operations, and Fiscal Environment—Stephen A. Hoenack and Eileen L. Collins (eds.)

The Higher Learning and High Technology: Dynamics of Higher Education and Policy Formation—Sheila Slaughter

Dropouts from Schools: Issues, Dilemmas and Solutions—Lois Weis, Eleanor Farrar, and Hugh G. Petrie (eds.)

Religious Fundamentalism and American Education: The Battle for the Public Schools—Eugene F. Provenzo, Jr.

Going to School: The African-American Experience—Kofi Lomotey (ed.)

Curriculum Differentiation: Interpretive Studies in U.S. Secondary Schools—Reba Page and Linda Valli (eds.)

The Racial Crisis in American Higher Education—Philip G. Altbach and Kofi Lomotey (eds.)

The Great Transformation in Higher Education, 1960–1980—Clark Kerr

College in Black and White: African-American Students in Predominantly White and in Historically Black Public Universities—Walter R. Allen, Edgar G. Epps, and Nesha Z. Haniff (eds.)

Textbooks in American Society: Politics, Policy, and Pedagogy—Philip G. Altbach, Gail P. Kelly, Hugh G. Petrie, and Lois Weis (eds.)

Critical Perspectives on Early Childhood Education—Lois Weis, Philip G. Altbach, Gail P. Kelly, and Hugh G. Petrie (eds.)

Black Resistance in High School: Forging a Separatist Culture—R. Patrick Solomon

Emergent Issues in Education: Comparative Perspectives—Robert F. Arnove, Philip G. Altbach, and Gail P. Kelly (eds.)

Creating Community on College Campuses—Irving J. Spitzberg and Virginia V. Thorndike

Teacher Education Policy: Narratives, Stories, and Cases—Hendrick D. Gideonse (ed.)

Beyond Silenced Voices: Class, Race, and Gender in the United States Schools—Lois Weis and Michelle Fine (eds.)

Troubled Times for American Higher Education: The 1990s and Beyond—Clark Kerr (ed.)

Higher Education Cannot Escape History: Issues for the Twenty-first Century—Clark Kerr (ed.)

The Cold War and Academic Governance: The Lattimore Case at Johns Hopkins—Lionel S. Lewis (ed.)

Multiculturalism and Education: Diversity and Its Impact on Schools and Society—Thomas J. LaBelle and Christopher R. Ward (eds.)

The Contradictory College: The Conflicting Origins, Impacts, and Futures of the Community College—Kevin J. Dougherty (ed.)

Race and Educational Reform in the American Metropolis: A Study of School Decentralization—Dan A. Lewis (ed.)

Professionalization, Partnership, and Power: Building Professional Development Schools—Hugh Petrie (ed.)

Ethnic Studies and Multiculturalism—Thomas J. LaBelle and Christopher R. Ward

Promotion and Tenure: Community and Socialization in Academe—William G. Tierney and Estela Mara Bensimon (eds.)

Sailing Against the Wind: African Americans and Women in U.S. Education—Kofi Lomotey (ed.)

The Challenge of Eastern Asian Education: Implications for America—William K. Cummings and Philip G. Altbach (eds.)

Conversations with Educational Leaders: Contemporary Viewpoints on Education in America—Anne Tumbau-Lockwood

Managed Professionals: Unionized Faculty and Restructuring Academic Labor—Gary Rhoades

Education/Technology/Power: Educational Computing as a Social Practice—Hank Bromley and Michael W. Apple

INDEX

Accountability, 6, 276, 382; for action, 254; in evaluation, 369–370; personal, 207, 210–211

Action: accountability for, 254; based on critical reflection, 93; collaborative, 258; conceptions of, 253; curricular, 182; experimental, 67; freedom of, 383; future, 141; human, 141; individual, 144; made meaningful, 140, 143, 144; moral, 247; as narrative expression, 140; past, 141; political, 93, 181; practical, 255; proactive, 210; on reality, 93; research, 107; significance of, 143; social, 257; valorized, 141

Adler, Mortimer, 188

"Adopt-a-School" program, 53

AESA. *See* American Educational Studies Association

African American Infusion Project, 101

African Americans, 101–113, 201–221

Afrocentrism, 101

Akers, John, 276

Alexander, Lamar, 273

Amalgamated Clothing Workers of America, 37

American Educational Research Association, 101, 272

American Educational Studies Association, 186

American Herbartian movement, 28

Americans All, 108, 109

America 2000 Plan, 277

Analysis: activity, 27, 103; of issues, 111; policy, 112

Anderson, Richard C., 272

Anthony, Susan B., 47

Apple, Michael W., 3–15, 13, 14, 44, 157–172, 314–333

Apple Classrooms of Tomorrow, 273, 274, 279

Apple Computer Company, 273, 276, 281

Appy, Nellie, 109

Argueta, Manlio, 146

Aristotle, 21, 141

Arm and Torch League, 55*n30*

Artificial intelligence, 271, 274

Assertive Discipline, 192

Assessment. *See also* Evaluation; "authentic," 9; language of, 7; multifaceted, 218; needs, 67; strategies, 219

Association for the Study of Negro Life and History, 103

Auerbach, Erich, 148

Augustine, Norman, 280

Barber, Benjamin R., 254, 383

Barnes, Douglas, 81

Barone, Thomas E., 13, 137–154, 145

Beane, James, 12, 117–132

Beecher, Catherine, 234

Behaviorism, 6

Behavior modification, 192
Belsey, Catherine, 145
Bennett, William, 248, 249, 250
Bernstein, Basil, 158
Beyer, Landon E., 3–15, 14, 15, 245–261, 380–395
Blumenfeld-Jones, Donald S., 13, 137–154
Bobbitt, Franklin, 27, 81
Bond, Horace Mann, 103, 104, 109
Boston Women's Teachers' Group, 13
Bourdieu, Pierre, 158, 161
Boyer, Ernest, 188
Boyte, Harry, 191
Brave Bird, Mary, 146
Brodhagen, Barbara, 12, 117–132
Brooks, Peter, 140
Brown, John Seeley, 272, 274
Brown v. Board of Education of Topeka, 347
Bruner, Jerome, 147
Bunderson, Victor, 291, 292, 293, 294
Bureaucratization, 35, 182, 186, 242
Bush, George, 273, 276, 277
Business Roundtable's Education Task Force, 276
Butchart, Ronald E., 107

Callahan, Raymond, 184
Calvert, Bruce, 39
Capital: accumulation, 34, 161, 262n7; cultural, 159, 171, 190–191, 227n62, 335n47; financial, 161, 165, 169; flight, 321; human, 278, 280, 281; investment, 280; production, 34; symbolic, 161, 165
Capitalism, 34, 40, 41, 42, 46, 47, 48, 49, 158; culture of, 256; deficiencies of, 30; economic prerogatives of, 252; expansion of, 248; industrial, 35; nature of, 35; and public school, 36–37
Carr, Davis, 140
Cavell, Stanley, 389
Centering, 352–353, 354–357
Change: classroom, 62; cultural, 35; economic, 104; gender role, 31; institutional, 25; power-coercive strate-

gies, 365; response to, 22; social, 22, 25, 26–27, 30, 39, 52, 104; structural, 258; theory, 363–365
Charters, W.W., 27
Children's Socialist Lyceum, 55n30
Clark, Septima, 102
Class: compromise, 45; cultural reproduction of, 159; differences in computer use, 328–329; distinctions, 30; dominant, 36, 159; dynamics, 158, 159; inequities, 5, 253, 268; oppression, 145, 146; pride, 44, 52; social, 27, 52; solidarity, 42; structure, 163; struggle, 35, 45, 48; working, 40, 41, 42, 43, 44, 45, 52
Classrooms: changes in, 62; consistency in, 62; control of, 192; current situations in, 58–76; democratic, 117–132; interactions, 60–64; management of, 192; materials, 110; open, 62; sociology of, 86; technological, 322–329; time spent in, 61, 62, 63, 64, 71n19
Clinton, Bill, 276
Cobb, Stanwood, 30
Code, Lorraine, 205, 388–389
Cohen, David, 184, 373
Cole, G.D.H., 180, 181
Collins, Allan, 272, 273, 274, 279
Collins, Patricia Hill, 207, 208, 210
Comer, James, 269
Commission of Interracial Cooperation, 103
Communication, 67
Community, 25; autonomy within, 197n32; creation of, 247, 255; defining, 22; involvement, 256; issues of, 193; revitalizing, 257; school boards, 34; welfare of, 210
Computer Curriculum Corporation, 277
Computers, 14, 284–308. *See also* Technology; control of performance by, 277; corporate interests, 317; criticisms of uses of, 14; differential uses of, 328–329; drill-and-practice programs, 284, 285, 287–294; in education, 284–308; effects on teachers/

Computers (*continued*), students, 314–333; gender differences in use of, 323–324; growth of, 267–281; and human interaction, 297–301; as intellectual tools, 301–308; and interactive proofs, 297; prepackaged software, 323, 324; programming, 284, 303–308; remedial dialogues on, 296–297; replacing teachers, 279; simulations, 284, 303–308; teacher training in, 323; and tracking, 329; tutorial programs, 284, 285, 295–301

Consciousness: coming to, 146; critical, 93, 95, 216, 220; of existence, 140; stream of, 139

Consumerism, 256

Cook, Lloyd A., 107

Cooperative Commonwealth, 49

Counts, George S., 30, 31, 258, 259

The Crisis, 107

Cubberly, Ellwood P., 184

Cultural: appropriateness, 203; awareness, 190–191; capital, 159, 171, 190–191, 227*n62*, 335*n47*; compatibility, 202, 203; competence, 212–213, 216, 220, 227*n62*; congruence, 202, 203; critique, 213–214, 227*n63*; deficit, 204, 224*n23*; disadvantage, 204; formations, 144; goals and objectives, 74; heritage, 383; identity, 106, 204, 212; institutions, 4; integrity, 212; isolation, 185; literacy, 249, 252; mores, 204; production, 157, 158, 160; reproduction, 5, 52; responsiveness, 202, 203; self-awareness, 111; synchronization, 204; transmission, 158, 350, 351; values, 254

Culture: African American, 101; of capitalism, 256; changes in, 35; circles, 93; as commodity, 157; as constitutive social process, 157; devaluation of, 227*n62*; of difference, 382; distribution of, 158; dual nature of, 157; economic control of, 172; elite, 162; Euro-American, 110; hegemonic, 42; irrationalities in, 154; as lived process, 157; mainstream, 203; and narrative, 141–142; organization of, 158; political economy of, 13, 158, 162; popular, 162; relation to, 148; student, 217, 220; teacher-centered, 292; and teaching, 202–204

Current Events (newspaper), 38, 39

Curriculum, 59; activity, 29; alternative, 112; appropriate, 21; "areas of living," 32; centralization of, 182, 185; child-centered, 28–29, 270; and child study, 28–29; conceptual system, 68, 79, 90–91; conscience, 96; construction, 89; content areas, 3, 11, 24, 108; content issues, 158; content selection, 13, 177–195; control of, 11, 26, 35, 182, 185; critical thinking in, 65; current situations in, 58–76; decentering, 110–111; decisionmaking in, 79, 104; defining, 69*n1*, 82, 95, 231, 232, 340; deliberative nature of, 6, 84–85, 87, 88, 137; and democracy, 177–195; design, 8, 13, 87, 88*fig*, 258; development, 11, 15, 24, 27, 52, 90, 96, 108, 109, 112, 138, 358–377, 364; differentiation, 27, 40; domains of, 59, 60, 69*n5*; equivalence of subjects in, 26; evaluation, 3, 11, 15, 90, 125, 339–357; exclusionary, 23–24; expectations *vs.* reality, 58–76; experience, 29; formal, 58, 60, 61; frameworks for, 108, 109; guides, 58; hidden, 5; history of, 11, 12, 21–32, 34–53; humanist, 32; implementation, 8; integrated approach, 12, 117–132; issues in, 5–6; knowledge in, 101–113; liberal arts, 22, 26, 59, 186, 187; making, 29; marketing, 13; multicultural, 12, 101–113; national, 358; naturalistic, 88*fig*, 79, 88, 138; nature of, 11; and nonmainstream groups, 34–53; organization issues, 11, 158; pendulum swings in, 59; planning, 12, 79–96, 324; platforms, 87, 88*fig*, 90, 137–154; political

Curriculum (*continued*), nature of, 3–15, 159; practice, 3; prepackaged, 112, 323, 325; problems, 127–129; project model, 28–29; and publishing industry, 13; "purposing" in, 29; rationality, 95; recentering, 110–111; reconstruction of, 21–32; reform, 6, 23, 24, 26, 28, 31–32

Darwin, Charles, 23, 24, 25, 28
Debs, Eugene, 47
Decisionmaking: control of, 188; curriculum, 79, 104; democratic, 8, 382; educational, 8; and evaluation, 366; experience in, 191; knowledge for, 92; political, 179, 180, 181; in publishing, 166, 170–172; rational, 82; student involvement in, 29, 187, 191–192; value-based, 141
Delpit, Lisa, 260, 261
Democracy, 4; conceptions of, 181, 248; and curriculum, 177–195; defining, 179; education for, 14; empowerment in, 186–195; in evaluation, 380–395; expression of, 383–384; meaning of, 14, 178, 179–182, 382; participatory, 180, 181; protectionist, 180, 182–186; pursuit of, 15; schooling for, 178, 245–261; theories of, 179; workplace, 181
Democratic Human Relations, 107–108, 109
Denzin, Norman, 153
Deskilling, 4, 14, 172, 317, 319, 322, 323, 325, 330, 334*n26*
Development, 137; child, 28–29; cognitive, 86; of critical consciousness, 95; of critical literacy, 189, 190; of critical thinking, 111; curriculum, 11, 15, 24, 27, 52, 90, 96, 108, 109, 112, 138, 358–377, 364; human relations skills, 111; institutional, 364; intellectual, 73; natural order of, 28; political, 104; process, 137; social, 104; teacher, 364; technological, 267, 269, 274; theory, 112

Dewey, John, 8, 25, 26, 30, 32, 62, 105, 139, 143, 180, 253, 257, 258, 259, 269, 344
Dewey School, 106
Dezell, James, 278
Dilthey, Wilhelm, 142
Discourse: alternative forms, 256; competent, 65, 67; democratic, 247; dominant, 7; educational, 7; everyday, 171; home, 260; informed, 67; moral, 247, 255, 256, 257; school, 260; stacking, 260; structures, 141; sustained, 67; technical, 330
Diversity, 103, 105, 107
Dole, Bob, 248
Dopp, Katherine, 43
Doyle, Denis, 278–279
Dreier, Peter, 193
DuBois, W.E.B., 104

EAI. *See* Education Alternatives, Inc.
Economic: change, 104; cooperation, 45; depression, 30; equality, 49; exchange, 251; inequalities, 37, 255; institutions, 5; justice, 104; laissez faire, 24; power, 5; radicalism, 35; reductionism, 158; reform, 35; reproduction, 52; stratification, 59
Edison Project, 277
Education: alternative models, 12, 40–51; automated, 279; "back to basics," 9, 59, 64, 183, 189; "banking" concept, 92, 93, 94; character, 250; compulsory, 24; conservatism in, 10, 34, 343, 382; corporate agendas, 275–281; critical inquiry in, 66–68; cult of efficiency in, 184; cultural transmission ideology, 350, 351; current state of, 58; decisionmaking in, 8; defining, 183; delivery of, 268; and democracy, 4, 14; for democratic living, 382–386; developmental, 350, 351, 353; discourse of, 7; equality of opportunity in, 347; expansion of, 35; expectations *vs.* reality, 58–76; "Factory System," 184; federal funding,

Education (*continued*): 274, 347–348; goals in, 10; historical perspective, 343–349; and industrial/economic needs, 6, 34; intercultural, 102, 107, 108, 109; materialistic ends of, 346–347; multicultural, 101–113; and New Right, 4; policy, 268, 275, 276; as political activity, 67; potential of democratic participation in, 245–261; process of, 6; as production system, 82; progressive, 103, 104, 117, 247, 344, 345; public, 4, 178, 268, 269; purposes of, 4; radical ideology, 350, 351; rationale for, 178; reform, 274, 275, 276; "reinventing," 273; remedial, 249; restructuring of, 269; rhetoric in, 67, 68; romantic ideology, 350; scientific control of, 184, 185; social ends of, 344; and social inequalities, 7; socialist, 40–51; as social predestination, 27; state/federal departments of, 6, 34, 246, 347, 358; Sunday School movement, 12, 40–51, 55*n30*; technology in, 267–281, 284–308; traditional, 24; universal, 347; utilitarian ideology of, 344, 346; vocational, 73–74

Educational Leadership, 110

Educational Technology, 273

Education Alternatives, Inc., 277

Education Commission of the States, 196*n11*

Education Policy Advisory Committee, 276

Educators for Social Responsibility, 190

EduQuest, 278

Eight-Year Study, 345, 348

Eisenhower Leadership Group, 247

Eisner, Elliott, 6, 81

Eliot, Charles W., 26

Elshtain, Jean Bethke, 255, 385, 386

Empathy, 142–144, 146

Empowerment, 15, 67, 112, 144, 178, 186–195, 269

Environment, 6

Erickson, Frederick, 203

Ethics: of caring, 207, 209–210; of developing a platform, 144; obligations of, 7; of personal accountability, 207, 210–211

Ethnicity, 7

Evaluation, 3, 69*n1*, 108; accountability in, 369–370; case-study, 360–362; communication in, 365; content of, 340–343; curriculum, 11, 15, 90, 125, 339–357; decisionmaking in, 366; democratic, 380–395; dual system, 353–357, 359; of educational software, 324–325; educative, 386–391; embedded, 381; evidence in, 365; evolution of, 360–365; expertise in, 348–349; goals, 340, 342; historical perspective, 343–349; individual, 324; instructional, 90; invasive, 380–381; legitimacy, 381; objective, 81, 348; political dimension of, 362–363; possibilities for, 358–377; presuppositions on objects of, 339–357; problems of, 15, 339–357; procedures, 368–369; process of, 15, 371–377; provision for, 81; purpose, 365, 366, 380; relationship to curriculum, 358–377; results of, 341–342; self, 15, 358–377; standardized, 65; of storied selves, 144; strategies, 111; strong, 144, 145, 146, 148; of student work, 125; subjects of, 15; summative, 381; of teaching, 3; technical, 91, 91*tab*, 340–342, 355; theory, 360–365; value in, 365; weak, 144–145, 146

Evans, Sara, 191

"Excellence," 9, 10, 59, 183

Experience(s): aesthetic, 15; Black, 104, 106; building, 139; communicated, 257; concepts of, 139; concrete, 207, 208–209; conjoint, 257; cumulative effects of, 80; of decisionmaking, 191; educational, 80; environmental, 13; everyday, 139; learning, 83; meaning in, 139; and memory, 139; organization of, 80, 81; part and whole, 139; provision of, 80; school, 107; selection

Experience(s) (*continued*): of, 81; sequence of, 81; social quality of, 253; stream of consciousness, 139

Federated Trades Council, 38
Finn, Chester, 248
Franklin, Benjamin, 343
Fraser, Bertha, 45
Freedman, Sara E., 13, 230–243
Freire, Paulo, 92, 94, 95, 213–214, 257
Fullan, Michael, 375

Gadamer, Hans-Georg, 143
Gagne, Robert, 272
Garrison, William Lloyd, 47
Geertz, Clifford, 143
Gender: changing roles, 31; cultural reproduction of, 159; differences in computer use, 328–329; distinctions, 30; dynamics of, 158, 159; inequities, 5, 7, 48, 253; and publishing, 165; in teaching, 230–243
Gill, Frances, 42
Giroux, Henry, 95–96
Glaser, Robert, 272
Goals and objectives, 69*n1*; academic, 73; achievement of, 27; articulation of, 61; behavioral, 270; and business/industry, 10, 317; centering, 352–353, 354–357; civic, 74; conflicts over, 34; critical thinking, 65; cultural, 74; educational, 81–82; efficiency in, 27; enculturation, 70*n11*; of evaluation, 340, 342; formulation of, 84; general, 90; influences on, 34, 35; intended roles of, 65; learning, 83, 84; of multicultural education, 112; national, 374–375; personal, 75–76; redefining, 10; scientific method in, 81; selection of, 81, 84, 90; setting, 91, 91*tab;* social, 74; statements of, 59; typical, 73–76; vocational, 70*n11*, 73–74
Good: common, 7, 8, 118, 192, 251, 256, 257; public, 4; social, 193, 250, 251

Goodlad, John, 59, 60, 79, 82, 89, 90, 91, 92, 188
Gramsci, Antonio, 170
Granheim, M.K., 373
Greenberg, David S., 46
Greene, Maxine, 6
Griswold, Wendy, 162
Grumet, Madeleine, 358, 359, 389, 390

Haberman, Martin, 220
Haley, Margaret, 184
Hall, G. Stanley, 28
Hargreaves, Andy, 375
Harris, Violet, 101, 107
Harris, William Torrey, 26
Heidegger, Martin, 140–141, 144
Hirsch, E. D., 249
hooks, bell, 145
House, Ernest, 359, 368, 374–375
Huebner, Dwayne, 6, 14
Humanities Curriculum Project, 360–361
Hurston, Nora Zeale, 146
Huxley, Thomas Henry, 23, 25

IBM Corporation, 273, 276, 277
Identity: and commodities, 256; cultural, 106, 204, 212; personal, 383; politics of, 382; professional, 383; self, 138, 145
Immigration, 35
Individualism, 24, 44, 163, 251, 252, 253, 255, 256, 383
Industrialization, 22, 30, 35, 270, 344
Institute for Learning Sciences, 279
Institute for Research on Learning, 272, 276
Institutions: changes in, 25; cultural, 4; economic, 5; inequalities in, 5; political, 5; social, 22, 25, 30, 196*n10*, 252, 253, 257
Instruction: automated, 271, 279; behavioral objectives in, 270; command-and-control of, 273–274; competency-based, 6; computer-based, 271; drill-and-practice, 284,

Instruction (*continued*): 285, 287–294, 291; individualized, 290–291; intensified, 276; programmed, 270, 271
Internationalism, 46
International Ladies' Garment Workers' Union, 37
Irvine, Jacqueline Jordan, 204

Jackson, Philip W., 235
Jacobson, Abraham, 47
Jefferson, Thomas, 178, 247
Johnson, Lyndon, 347, 348
Johnson, Marietta, 30
Johnson, Mauritz, 79, 89, 90, 91, 92, 95
Johnson, Richard, 52
Johnston, Basil, 146
Journal of Negro Education, 103
Jungck, Susan, 323, 325

Karp, Walter, 186
Kearns, David, 276, 278
Kemp, Jack, 248
Kerby, Anthony P., 145
Kermode, Frank, 147
Kerr, Donna, 68
Kilpatrick, William Heard, 28, 29, 32, 106
Kliebard, Herbert M., 11, 21–32, 53, 59
Knowledge: accessibility of, 14; acquisition, 188; assessing, 207, 209, 218; classroom transformation of, 232; conceptions of, 215, 218–219; construction of, 218; content, 102; control of, 188; for decisionmaking, 92; differentiated, 188; distribution of, 25, 30; exposure to, 43; genesis of, 24; integration of, 81, 106; legitimate, 3, 159; nature of, 102, 112; official, 165; organization of, 106; and power, 13; production of, 173*n*5, 231; professional, 241; questions of, 110; of reality, 285; relationship to learner, 12, 102; sanctioned, 13; school, 52, 159; scientific, 23, 24; selection, 13, 106, 177–195; self, 350; status of, 158; student's relationships to, 12;

test, 129; translinguistic, 249; transmission of, 173*n*5; useful, 52; uses of, 117, 131; "whose?," 101–113, 115*n*44; worthwhile, 3, 183
Kohl, Herbert, 193
Kozol, Jonathan, 145
Kruse, William F., 44

Labor: child, 48; contributions of, 37; control of, 325; dignity of, 44; downsizing, 280; exploitation of, 45; gender division of, 165, 172, 233–235, 320, 325; hierarchical division of, 37; hostility to, 37, 39; human, 157; impact of technology on, 318–322; intensified, 325; international division of, 321; loss of control by, 318; manual, 37; mental, 37; organized, 37, 38; products of, 157; sacrifices by, 314; unions, 37
Ladson-Billings, Gloria, 13, 201–221
Language: alternative forms of, 8; arts, 118; of assessment, 7; classical, 22, 23; of competency, 7; computer, 301; as decoding device, 189; of democratic imagery, 146; of efficiency, 7, 8, 317; of empowerment, 67; of equity, 7; interactions, 202, 203, 204; making, 285; "of lacking," 215; patterns, 203; of possibility, 36; practical, 85; of reform, 359; of sharing, 7
Learning: accommodation in, 286; accretion, 296; activities, 69*n*1, 108; assimilation in, 286; collaborative, 217–218; cooperative, 216, 218; cross-aged, 216; experiences, 83; facilitation of, 218; "how to learn," 29; integrated systems, 274; mastery, 270, 288–290; maximization of, 204; multi-aged, 216; nature of, 52; opportunities for, 90; organizing centers for, 90; outcomes, 82, 83–84, 90; process of, 29; production of, 81; psychology of, 80; rates of, 288; rote, 185; science, 272; service, 382; technical control of, 291; theories, 84, 270

Levin, Henry, 269
Licklider, J.C.R., 280
Lindenberg, Sadie, 51
Literacy: critical, 189–190; cultural, 249, 252; social, 330–331; technical, 330
Lowy, Helen, 42
Lundgren, Ulf, 368, 373

MacDonald, Barry, 362
Macdonald, James B., 6, 350, 351, 352, 353
MacIntyre, Alasdair, 141, 387
Mailly, Bertha, 44
Management: and automation, 334n26; classroom, 192; educational, 322; efficient, 10; scientific, 27, 184, 185; systems, 6
Mann, Horace, 247
Marcuse, Herbert, 96
Marketing, 13
Marx, Karl, 47, 144, 157
Mead, George Herbert, 140, 142
Meaning: of actions, 143; construction of, 107, 110; creation of, 286; criterion of, 207, 208–209; of democracy, 14, 178, 179–182, 382; of difference, 107; in experiences, 139; expression of, 286; making, 285, 350; and narrative, 140–141; restoration of, 143; securing, 140; social, 118
Meier, Deborah, 269
Meritocracy, 203
Militarism, 31, 37, 38, 41, 46
Mill, John Stuart, 180, 181
Mills, Walter Thomas, 43
Models: alternative, 12; child-centered, 28–29, 270; curriculum development, 83–84; curriculum integration, 117–132; curriculum planning, 79–96; ideologically neutral, 95; integrated, 12; multicultural, 101–113; naturalistic, 79, 88fig, 138; P-I-E, 90, 91; planning, 94; procedural, 94; top-down, 6; unit plan, 111
Mohatt, Gerald, 203
Montessori Method, 104

Moral, 26; agency, 144, 145, 146; character, 252; choices, 256, 383; concepts, 250; conservatism, 253; decay, 250, 254; discourse, 255, 256, 257; individual, 39; neutrality, 253; social, 39; spaces, 141; stories, 137–154; visions, 257–258
Morris, William, 47
Morrison, Toni, 146
Multiculturalism, 12, 101–113

Narrative(s): aesthetic, 150; authoritative, 145; of community, 391–393; creation of, 153; cultural, 141–142, 145; declarative, 145; defining, 140; of the disenfranchised, 144; and empathy, 142–144; engaged literature, 145–146; expression, 140–141; and imagination, 146–148; inherited scripts in, 144–146, 151; life, 147; life-altering events, 148–153; moral, 144–148; of people, 143; personal, 13, 137–154; and reality, 140; resistance in, 146; self, 140; socially committed, 145–146; of struggle, 145, 146; of teaching, 13, 137–154; and virtue, 141–142
NASDC. See New American Schools Development Corporation
National Academy of Education, 272
National Center on Education and the Economy, 273, 276, 281
National Commission on Excellence in Education, 183, 196n11, 224n23, 247
National Council for the Social Studies, 102, 107
National Council of Teachers of English, 108
National Education Association, 102, 108
National Science Board, 183
National Science Foundation, 196n11
A Nation at Risk, 66, 183, 184, 186, 196n11, 314
Native Americans, 101, 202–204, 203
NCEE. See National Center on Education and the Economy

Nearing, Scott, 39, 40
The Negro History Bulletin, 104–105, 107
Neitzsche, Friedrich, 141–142
New American Schools Development
    Corporation, 273, 276, 280
New Right, 4, 14, 248–252, 256, 262*n*7
Nixon, Richard, 248
Noble, Douglas D., 267–281, 330
Noffke, Susan E., 12, 101–113

Oakes, Jeannie, 194
Objectives. *See* Goals and objectives
O'Hannian, Susan, 182
Oleneck, Michael R., 107

Pagano, Jo Anne, 15, 380–395
Paideia Group, 196*n*11
Papert, Seymour, 272, 274
PEA. *See* Progressive Education Associa-
    tion
Pedagogy: critical, 112; culturally rele-
    vant, 13, 201–221; emancipatory, 112;
    questions of, 110
Planning. *See also* Curriculum; concep-
    tual questions in, 80, 89–91, 94;
    critical perspective, 92–96; curricu-
    lum, 79–96, 137, 324; deliberation in,
    84–85, 137; descriptive question in,
    80, 87–89, 94; elements of, 79, 80;
    emancipatory approach, 92–93; em-
    pathic understanding in, 143; institu-
    tional level, 90; instructional, 90, 91,
    91*tab*; linear view, 82, 84, 89; means-
    end reasoning process in, 82; objec-
    tive, 82; organizing elements of, 81;
    politics of, 101–113; procedural
    question in, 80, 83–87, 94; rationality
    in, 89–90; role of experts in, 89, 92;
    societal level, 90; steps in, 80;
    teacher-pupil, 119–125; technical
    production perspective, 80–91; Tyler
    Rationale, 79, 80, 81, 83, 87, 89, 90,
    92
Policy: analysis, 112; direction, 24; edu-
    cational, 25, 268, 275, 276; social, 24,
    25; state, 112

Political: action, 93, 181; apathy, 179,
    180; decisionmaking, 181; develop-
    ment, 104; efficacy, 181; equality,
    194; institutions, 5; isolation, 185;
    movements, 34–53; participation,
    186; power, 5; repression, 104; under-
    classes, 188; values, 59
Politics, 6; of content selection, 13; in
    curriculum, 3–15; of identity, 382;
    local, 181; national, 181; of organiza-
    tion, 12, 101–113; participation in,
    181; of planning, 12, 101–113; of
    schooling, 15; of technology, 315–317
Polkinghorne, Donald E., 140, 141
Popham, James, 81
Posner, George J., 12, 79–96, 81
Poverty, 37, 48
Power: cultural, 173*n*9; differential, 14;
    discrepancies of, 31; disparities of,
    254; distribution of, 144, 153; eco-
    nomic, 5, 173*n*9; and knowledge, 13;
    personal, 191; political, 5; in text
    publishing, 164
Progressive Education, 105
Progressive Education Association, 30,
    31, 258
Public Education Information Network,
    187
Publishing, textbook, 13; censorship in,
    167; and class structure, 163; as com-
    merce, 163–170; competition in, 164;
    decisionmaking in, 170–172; division
    of labor in, 165; and gender, 165;
    influences on, 163; internal factors,
    164; profitability of, 167–168; relative
    autonomy in, 170–172; structural
    conditions, 160–163; technology of,
    172

Race: cultural reproduction of, 159;
    differences in computer use,
    328–329; dynamics of, 158, 159;
    inequities, 5, 7, 48, 253; social condi-
    tions of, 30
RAND Corporation, 273
Rand School of Social Science, 35

Raskin, Marcus, 7
Rationality, 89–90; curriculum, 95; in planning, 96
Ratteray, Joan D., 107
REACH. *See* Respecting Ethnic and Cultural Heritage
Reagan, Ronald, 248, 251
Reality: classroom, 65; cultural-economic, 256; curriculum, 12, 58–76; economic, 317–322; generative themes in, 93; knowledge of, 285; and narrative, 140; negotiating with, 140; physical, 285; shared, 142; social, 253, 285, 350; views of, 93
Reform, 382; center-periphery, 363; child-centered, 62; curriculum, 6, 23, 24, 26, 28, 34–53, 59, 103, 105, 183, 187, 188, 360, 363; economic, 35; education, 274, 275, 276; impact of, 31–32; racial, 103; social, 35, 201; top-down, 182
Relationships: curriculum/evaluation, 15; curriculum/social justice, 137; dialectical, 209; in effective curriculum, 89; of exploitation, 157; to knowledge, 12; knowledge/learner, 12, 102, 106, 109, 110, 112; knowledge/power, 13; patriarchal, 165; school/community, 42; schools/justice, 104; social, 45; structural, 142; teacher/student, 92, 217; technology and employment, 14
Republican Party, 42, 247, 248–252, 262*n*7, 382
Research: action, 107; military, 270–275, 336*n*64; by "others," 206–207
Resnick, Lauren, 272
Respecting Ethnic and Cultural Heritage, 111
Ricoeur, Paul, 140, 143
Rodriguez, Richard, 146
Roosevelt, Theodore, 42
Rorty, Richard, 143, 392
Rose, Mike, 146
Rousseau, Jean-Jacques, 180
Rugg, Harold, 8, 30, 31

Sacks, Oliver, 390–391
Sartre, Jean-Paul, 145
Saturn School, 277
Schank, Roger, 272, 274, 279
School(s): as agents of socialization, 59, 70*n*11; boards, 34; "break-the-mold," 273; budgets, 10; centralized control of, 10; community relationships, 42; control of, 59, 185; corporate agendas, 275–281; cost savings in, 4; critical inquiry in, 66–68; current situations in, 58–76; democracy in, 8, 117–132; discourse of, 260; efficiency in, 4; expansion of, 35; for-profit, 277, 279; free spaces in, 191–192; functions of, 60, 60*tab*; funding crises, 53, 326; knowledge, 52; as laboratory sites for technology, 274; one-track systems in, 188; organization of, 187; practices in, 8; private, 277, 326; and production of learning, 81, 173*n*5; segregation in, 103, 347; self-evaluation in, 358–377; social functions of, 22, 178; weekend, 55*n*31
Schwab, Joseph, 6, 9, 84, 85, 86, 89, 92
Scientific management movement, 27
Sculley, John, 273, 276, 281
Segregation, 103, 347
Self: access to, 393; achievement of, 138–140; actualization, 146; autonomy, 142; awareness, 111; conceptions, 215–216; construction, 140–142, 143; criticism, 51; definition, 140–141, 153; description of, 140; determination, 146; direction, 106; discipline, 192, 249; evaluation, 15; expression, 51; governance, 178, 179, 181, 185; growth, 141; idea of another, 142; identity, 138, 145; interpretation, 392, 393; knowledge, 350; motivation, 250; movement from, 144; narrative, 140; and nothingness, 140–141; notions of, 13, 137–154; preservation, 23, 25; realization, 76; reconstruction, 146; search for, 118;

Self (*continued*): sense of, 139, 148; shaping, 144; understanding, 138, 142
Shavelson, Richard, 272
Shedd, Kendrick, 42, 43, 44, 46, 50
Shulman, Lee, 201
Simons, Helen, 15, 358–377
Sirotnik, Kenneth A., 12, 58–76
Sizer, Ted, 269
Small, Albion, 30
Smith, Adam, 250–251
Snow, Richard, 272
Social: action, 257; activism, 35, 47, 56*n40*; adjustment, 351; alternatives, 192–193; awareness, 44; bonds, 252; change, 22, 25, 26–27, 30, 39, 52, 104; class, 27, 52; commitment, 147; control, 26, 35, 59; cooperation, 39; crises, 253; criticism, 47; development, 104; disorder, 250; efficiency, 26–27, 29, 32, 59, 104; equity, 47–48, 201; existences, 142; ferment, 35; goals and objectives, 74; good, 193, 250, 251; homogenization, 347; imagination, 148, 153; inequalities, 7, 30, 203, 213–214, 253, 326; institutions, 22, 25, 30, 196*n10*, 252, 253, 257; interaction, 171, 216; intolerance, 107; isolation, 212; justice, 68, 104, 112, 137, 138, 149, 150, 191, 201, 251, 258, 381; laissez faire, 24; literacy, 330–331; meaning, 118; morality, 39; oppression, 104; order, 7, 59, 177, 178, 180, 252; organization, 177; pathology, 249; pluralism, 347; policy, 24, 25; predestination, 27; pressures, 14; privilege, 144; problems, 44, 48, 52, 246, 249, 251, 268; progress, 246; psychology, 86; reality, 253, 285, 350; reconstructionism, 30–31, 70*n11*, 104; reform, 35, 201; relations, 45, 215, 216–218, 220; reproduction, 59; responsibility, 39, 68, 145, 190; stability, 177, 178; stratification, 59, 347; studies, 31, 44; systems, 44; traditions, 24; welfare, 30
Social Democratic Party, 37
Socialism, 12, 34–53
Socialist Teachers Bureau, 36
Society for Curriculum Study, 108
Spencer, Herbert, 23, 24, 25, 28
State: departments of education, 6, 358; intervention, 24, 25, 34, 253; policy, 112; welfare, 262*n7*, 382
Steinmetz, Charles P., 40
Stenhouse, Lawrence, 364
Stories. *See* Narratives
Streibel, Michael J., 14, 284–308
Student: interactions with teachers, 12; performance, 13
Students: achievement, 65, 211; African American, 13, 201–221; behavior, 252; classroom time, 61, 62, 63, 64; culture of, 217, 220; decisionmaking by, 187, 191–192; effect of computers on, 314–333; empathic understanding of, 143; empowerment of, 15; home/community environment of, 202–204; initiative of, 29; interactions with teachers, 62, 63, 71*n19*, 117–132; participation, 118, 119; successful, 201–221; validation of, 260
A Study of Schooling (Sirotnik), 60–64, 71*n26*
Sumner, William Graham, 24, 25
Sunday School movement, 12, 40–51, 55*n30*
Sussman, Esther F., 43
Systems: command-and-control, 271; computer-based, 270; design, 273; economy, 293; efficiency, 293; instructional, 90, 293; integrated learning, 274; "intelligent tutoring," 279; management, 6; one-track, 188; participatory, 180; political, 179–182; production, 82; reliability, 293; slogan, 9; social, 44; symbol, 285, 286; tutoring, 270

Taba, Hilda, 79, 83, 84, 88, 91, 92
Taylor, Charles, 141, 392
Taylor, Frederick Winslow, 27

Teachers: assessment of, 208; autonomy of, 108, 245; classroom time, 61, 62, 63, 64; computer training for, 323; conceptions of, 108; contempt for, 243; defining roles of, 102; depowering of, 323; development of, 364; effect of computers on, 314–333; as emotional components of learning, 232–233; empowerment of, 15; as facilitators, 106; interactions with students, 12, 62, 63, 117–132; replacement by computers, 279; role in drill-and-practice programs, 291; role of, 110, 112

Teaching: automated, 271; control of, 184, 322; culturally relevant, 202–204, 212–214; and curriculum, 230–243; depersonalization of, 14; deskilling of, 14; effective, 9; ethical conceptions of, 13; and gender, 230–243; impact of, 246; indoctrinative, 250; interaction with students, 71n19; machines, 270, 271; narratives of, 13, 137–154; sociology of, 215; standardized techniques, 6; status of, 215; strategies, 69n1; and technology, 314–333; trivialization of, 232

Technology, 14; as autonomous process, 315; corporate agendas, 275–281; credential factor in, 327; development, 274; in education, 267–281, 284–308; and education policy, 275, 276; effects on labor market, 316; employment needs, 14, 317–322; ethical issues, 316, 317; expansion of, 279; expenditures, 268; funding for, 274; growth of, 315; implementation, 268; influence of, 11; legitimacy of, 14; merchandising of, 269; military legacy, 270–275, 336n64; myths of, 317–322; politics of, 315–317; pressures to use, 14; and program sacrifice, 325–326; of publishing, 172; restructuring in, 278; social role,

330–331; and teaching, 314–333; and unemployment, 326

Teitelbaum, Kenneth N., 12, 34–53

Testing: achievement, 65, 81, 211, 348; criterion-referenced, 270; intelligence, 270; national, 276, 358; on-line, 295; standardized, 6, 183, 211, 270, 348

Textbooks, 13; adoption policies, 168–170; commerce of, 157–172; culture of, 157–172; managed, 167; marketing, 160; as merchandise, 160, 163–170; relative autonomy of, 170–172; standardization, 185

Theories: alternative, 12; of change, 363–365; cognitivist, 270; cultural deficit, 204, 224n23; of culturally relevant pedagogy, 201–221; culture-epochs, 28; curriculum, 3, 6, 22–25; 118; default, 205; deficiencies of, 85–86; of democracy, 179; development of, 112; evaluation, 360–365; evoluutionary, 22–25; grounded, 205; learning, 83–84, 270; participatory, 181, 196n10; Piagetian, 85, 86; planning, 79–96; protectionist, 181

Thomas, Elizabeth, 38, 39

Thought: critical, 65, 111, 185; democratic, 248; reflective, 65; technical, 330–331

Title IV funding, 111

"Toyota Problem," 184

Tracking, 194, 329

Training: automated, 271; basic skills, 66, 73; computer, 323; computer-based, 271, 272; devices, 271; efficiency in, 27; embeeded, 272; inservice, 111

Twentieth Century Fund, 183, 196n11

Tyler, Ralph W., 79, 80, 81, 82, 83, 88, 89, 91, 92, 95

Unemploment, 48; acceptance of, 37, 321; rates of, 314; and technology, 326

Urbanization, 35

Utilitarianism, 344, 346

Values: common, 65; conflicting, 65; creating, 145; cultural, 254; curricular, 3–15; democratic, 193–194, 257, 383; ethical, 383; ideological, 59; moral, 248; of New Right, 14; political, 59; of subcultures, 107; traditional, 249–250, 252, 256
Villegas, Ana Maria, 204
Vocationalism, 270, 276

Walker, Decker, 79, 87, 88, 89, 92, 138
Walling, William English, 39
Ward, Lester Frank, 24, 25, 30
Watt, Ian, 163
Webbing, 189

Weilbacher, Gary, 12, 117–132
Whiting, Helen, 101, 105, 106
Whittle, Chris, 277
Will, George, 180
Willard, Emma, 234
Williams, Raymond, 8, 157, 163
Willinsky, John, 144
Willis, George, 15, 339–357
Wittrock, M.C., 272
Wood, George H., 13, 177–195
Woodson, Carter G., 103, 105
Wright, Robert, 383
Wynne, Edward, 250

Young Socialists' Magazine, 43